SWIMMING PRETTY

SWIMMING PRETTY

THE UNTOLD STORY OF WOMEN IN WATER

Vicki Valosik

Liveright Publishing Corporation

A Division of W. W. Norton & Company
Independent Publishers Since 1923

For information about permission to reproduce selections from this book, write to
Permissions, Liveright Publishing Corporation, a division of
W. W. Norton & Company, Inc., 500 Fifth Avenue, New York, NY 10110

For information about special discounts for bulk purchases, please contact
W. W. Norton Special Sales at specialsales@wwnorton.com or 800-233-4830

Manufacturing by Lakeside Book Company
Book design by Beth Steidle
Production manager: Anna Oler

ISBN 978-1-324-09304-6

Liveright Publishing Corporation
500 Fifth Avenue, New York, N.Y. 10110
www.wwnorton.com

W. W. Norton & Company Ltd.
15 Carlisle Street, London W1D 3BS

1 2 3 4 5 6 7 8 9 0

To my mom, Gerry, whose love and
support make everything possible

Contents

SWIMMING
PRETTY

PROLOGUE

"I don't want fast. I want pretty."

These were the words theater impresario Billy Rose told one of the fastest women swimmers in America after watching her sprint across the Ambassador Hotel pool at breakneck speed. Esther Williams, a national freestyle champion, had been recruited to audition for the starring role in the San Francisco production of Billy Rose's Aquacade, a glitzy waterfront extravaganza featuring a cast of five hundred swimmers, divers, dancers, and musicians. As Williams stood by the pool, dripping wet and towering a full 9 inches over Rose, she countered: "Mr. Rose, if you're not strong enough to swim fast, you're probably not strong enough to swim 'pretty.'"[1]

This exchange between Rose, whose shows traded in female bodies in motion, and teenaged Williams, whose Olympic hopes had just been dashed with the cancellation of the 1940 Summer Games, was emblematic of the paradoxes faced by women swimmers of the time. Their livelihoods, which often hinged on a revolving door between the worlds of entertainment and competitive sport, were both propelled and constrained by tensions between beauty and strength, aesthetics and athleticism. Williams never got her chance to compete for the Olympic gold, but after performing as "Aquabelle Number One" in Rose's show, she became the star of her own film genre, the MGM Aquamusical—splashy, midcentury movies featuring swimming themes, dazzling synchronized water ballets, and brilliant Technicolor. These hit films launched Williams to the pinnacle of Hollywood fame and, by glamorizing the water, inspired a generation of women swimmers and helped propel the popularity of the newly minted sport of synchronized swimming. Although she is the most well known today, Williams was actually just one in a long line of female aquatic performers dating to the nineteenth century whose "pretty swimming" proved pathbreaking and influenced not only the development of "synchro" but also the very genesis of women's swimming in America.

In the Victorian era, which was marked by a newfound interest in physical culture, as well as an explosion of mass entertainments, the worlds of sport and spectacle were constantly overlapping—and swimming was no exception. These overlaps created unique career opportunities for the rare woman who had both expert swimming skills and a flair for the stage, such as the British "natationist" (from the Latin *natare*—"to swim") Agnes Beckwith and American "Lurline the Water Queen." These women were practitioners of a form of aquatics known as "scientific" or "ornamental" swimming, which focused not on speed or distance but on a repertoire of movements—such as the "porpoise," the "propeller," and swimming with hands and feet bound—that developed and demonstrated physical mastery in the water. Although these moves dated to the sixteenth century, they had only been practiced by men until Beckwith, Lurline, and the other natationists and water queens they inspired began performing them at royal aquariums and in water tanks rolled onto music hall and variety theater stages on both sides of the Atlantic. Their graceful performances not only wowed packed audiences who had never seen women display such physical dexterity, especially in the water, but also helped break down the many barriers that had long kept members of their sex from learning to swim.

In the early twentieth century, Annette Kellerman picked up where they left off, becoming one of the most famous women in America for her vaudeville acts that combined "fancy swimming" (as the growing repertoire of ornamental aquatic moves was coming to be known) with dancing and diving, as well as her daring feats on the silver screen as cinema's first aquatic stuntwoman. As a swimming superstar, Kellerman used her platform to encourage other women to swim and to push for sensible swimwear for them to do it in. Her advocacy helped usher out corsets and heavy woolen bathing costumes, while her success as a performer gave rise to an entire industry of "diving girls" who swam and dove—sometimes from 100-foot ladders—with traveling carnivals that pitched their big tops at towns and whistle stops across America.

These generations of women swimmers traded on a combination of athletic skills, daring, looks, and entrepreneurial pluck to make their unconventional livings, some reaching international fame and fortune at a time when few women had the chance to attain economic independence. Many, like Esther Williams, started out as athletes competing in races or setting endurance records but found greater opportunity, and sometimes greater social acceptance, in the world of show business, where beauty and strength intersected and women could present their physical power with poise.

The styles of performative swimming these women popularized soon made their way into American Red Cross lifesaving programs where water pageants featuring bearded Neptunes and mermaid ballets demonstrated the beauty and value of swimming, and into physical education programs where instructors set ornamental stunts to music and put their swimmers in pretty patterns. Before long, this group swimming to music had a new name and big ambitions, and "synchronized swimming" quickly became one of the most popular and spectacular forms of entertainment of the midcentury. It was also one of the few athletic activities for generations of female students. From early on, its practitioners had their eyes on the Olympics, but it would prove to be a long and uphill—though ultimately successful—battle for this "women's sport" to be seen as a serious athletic pursuit and to gain acceptance into the highest echelons of sport.

Synchronized swimming—renamed "artistic swimming" in 2017—has since become an increasingly technical and tremendously athletic sport. It requires strength, flexibility, and endurance, all delivered with absolute precision and uniformity of movement while upside down in the deep end of the pool. Yet it has long been an easy target for sports purists because of the sparkly costumes, gelled hair, and smiles worn by its athletes, and because they don't see the hard work going on under the surface to create the artistry above it. As often as not, mentions of synchronized swimming bring to mind pop culture parodies of the sport or aquamusical-inspired images of grinning women floating effortlessly in pretty patterns. As *Sports Illustrated* put it in 1999, synchronized swimming is "overlooked when it's not misunderstood," and is portrayed as "always Esther Williams and sometimes Austin Powers."[2]

I had similar misconceptions before I tried synchronized swimming for the first time through a class at my local pool—more than a dozen years ago now. I was in my early thirties and knew virtually nothing about the sport, vaguely expecting flowered swim caps to be involved, but thought it sounded like a good way to merge my twin loves of being in the water and dancing. The "class" turned out to be more of a longstanding weekly meet-up of a group of women who had done water ballet or competed in the past, and the "students" were all several decades my senior, a few even old enough to be my grandmother. But once they slipped into the water, they were all as graceful as mermaids and generously set about teaching me, the beginner, the foundational body positions and propulsion techniques of synchronized swimming.

Even though I was only learning the rudimentary basics, it was so much harder than I imagined. I had never tried to maneuver my body into such unlikely positions in the water, and each new skill seemed preposterously difficult at first. I recall going home one week and telling my husband incredulously that these synchro ladies expected me to float on my stomach and then, slowly bending at the waist, push my head and torso down to create a 90-degree angle to my legs, which were somehow to remain stationary on the surface. But that position, the "pike," was only the beginning because next came raising a leg into the air until it reached vertical alignment with the body, which required wildly flailing the arms (in a move called "sculling") to keep from sinking. But despite the difficulty (my husband called it "water torture" when I made him try some of the techniques), I loved the challenge of learning to work *with*, instead of against, the water, and I found even the smallest victory—whether over gravity, buoyancy, or my own self-doubt—exhilarating.

At the end of the fourteen-week class, one of the women, a retired opera singer who was a member of the Washington, DC–area masters synchronized swimming team (masters sports offer competitive leagues for adults) invited me to join her at a team practice. I was hesitant. Now that I knew how hard it was, I feared I wouldn't be good enough. I had never thought of myself as an athlete. Plus, I'd have to perform in a bathing suit! But once the idea had been planted, I couldn't let go of it and decided to go and see what real synchronized swimming on a team was all about. At the practice, I was greeted by a group of energetic, latex-capped women aged twenty-four to seventy-two. I joined them in the deep end of the pool and, at their urging, demonstrated what I had learned—a basic scull, a back lay-out, a splashy, sinking attempt at raising a pointed "ballet leg" toward the ceiling—as they graciously offered pointers and encouragement. I knew from that first practice that I had found my people: these women of all ages and professions who find delight and camaraderie in the water but would rather dance in it than swim laps. So when they invited me to come back, I did.

They needed a fourth person to create a second entry for the championships a few months away, so they began teaching me their *Nutcracker* routine, and before I knew it, I was officially on the team and training for my first synchronized swimming competition. Swimming in a group routine is light-years harder than practicing techniques alone, as the movements are not only done faster but are also combined into long, inverted sequences called "hybrids" and come in unrelenting, rapid succession while the team is scurrying all over the pool—and in my case frantically trying to keep up and stay in pattern. At times, I thought the routine would defeat me, if not with its dizzying upside-down spins then surely with the dangerously long stretches between gasps of air. But as the weeks and months went on, my body became stronger and my lung capacity grew to meet the new demands. Soon, I was keeping up—even if my form was lacking and my "verticals" dangled a foot or two lower in the water than everyone else's.

But then, only a couple of weeks before the competition, my teammates announced it was time to do a "goggleless swim through." Seeing my perplexed expression, they explained that we wouldn't be wearing goggles at the meet so it was time to get used to swimming the routine without them. I hadn't so much as opened my eyes underwater without goggles since grade school, when I began wearing corrective contact lenses, but I reluctantly took them off and cued up on deck with my teammates. "Music's on!" someone called out. We heard the first strains of Tchaikovsky's "Candy Canes" and dove in. But without my goggles, everything was a blur under the water—made much worse by my extreme nearsightedness. I scrambled to find my place in the pattern, but I couldn't tell who was who. After a spinning hybrid, I surfaced facing the wrong way and nearly kicked my teammate in the face. Somehow, not having that protective shield between my eyes and the water made me suddenly and acutely aware that I could not breathe, as if an expanse of blue haze was closing in and suffocating me. Panic set in, and I started coming up early before finishing the hybrids to cheat and snag an extra breath. Not even a minute into the routine I was so discombobulated I had to swim to the sidelines as my teammates kept going without me.

When the routine ended and they asked me what happened, I was simultaneously sheepish and indignant. "This is ridiculous . . . I can't see!" I said. "I need my goggles!"

"Nobody wears goggles," my teammates chimed in unison. "They ruin the look," offered one. "You can't make eye contact with the judges while wearing goggles," said another. "It just *isn't done*."

I was perplexed. Weren't goggles considered essential for aquatic athletes? After all that practice, I couldn't believe we would deliberately handicap ourselves by refusing basic equipment that would enable us to compete at our best—simply because it didn't "look good." Ultimately, my teammates had mercy on me and conceded to let me wear goggles at my first meet on the condition that I promise to practice without them over the following year to be ready to swim goggleless at the next annual competition. I gladly agreed, but their strong feelings about goggles and aesthetics had gotten me questioning: Are we athletes first or are we performers? Is what we are doing a sport or is it entertainment?

Turns out, as I learned from researching this book, this question is older than synchronized swimming. Women swimmers have navigated tensions between athletics and performance, sport and spectacle, for generations—long before they ever began swimming in synch.

Swimming Pretty traces over a century of aquatic performance, from the tank shows of variety theater to the development of synchronized swimming and its 1984 elevation to Olympic status. Although this is a story about women—and one that largely takes place in America, where synchronized swimming as we think of it today came into existence—we must begin across the pond and with men: the gentlemen swimmers of the Renaissance and Enlightenment eras who treated swimming as a science and discovered new ways to maneuver the human body in water; "swimming professors" of the 1800s took it from there, using "scientific swimming" to demonstrate their mastery over the aquatic element. Women, in the early days, were lucky if they got to watch. But once the "fair sex" got their toes wet and started doing fancy moves of their own, it was clear they had found their element—one in which they could be both graceful and strong—and one in which they soon had men beat.

These women, and the generations who came after them, "swam pretty," but they were more than just bathing beauties, and their impact extended far beyond the water. Using their skills not only to entertain but also to educate and inspire, they dropped national drowning rates and emboldened the swells of women who learned to swim in the first half of the twentieth century; they modeled a new kind of female strength that bolstered the rallying cries for women's suffrage; they parted the waves for other women athletes and not only helped swimming become the first major competitive sport for women in America but also innovated an altogether new and beautiful collaborative aquatic sport—one that prioritized skill, versatility, and form over speed. And every step of the way, these swimming women defied society's rigid expectations of what was proper and possible for their sex.

But the tensions Esther Williams articulated between "swimming fast" and "swimming pretty," sport versus spectacle, have never fully gone away—as was demonstrated by reactions to the sport's name change in 2017. The international swimming federation, FINA (now World Aquatics), announced in July of that year that effective immediately, synchronized swimming would be called "artistic swimming." Many in the synchro community felt that the change would undo all their hard work to be taken seriously and that the term "artistic" would detract from the perceived athleticism of their sport. An online petition titled "Our sport is called 'SYNCHRONIZED SWIMMING!'" launched shortly after the decision received eleven thousand signatures and thousands of public comments, including one that said: "'Artistic Swimming' sounds like something society ladies did with their bosom friends at garden parties or after tea in the early twentieth century. Synchronized swimming is a REAL sport for REAL athletes." But despite the outcry, the change became permanent, eventually being adopted by the sport's national federations all over the world, and the name "artistic swimming" made its Olympic debut at the Summer Games in Tokyo in 2021.[*]

I kept up my end of the bargain with my teammates and faithfully practiced without goggles, and although it still gives me anxiety, I haven't worn them at our annual competition in over a decade. I now see it as just another part of the mental and physical challenge—another example of the unseen physicality it takes to make a sport aesthetic. And after researching this book, I have a greater appreciation for the fact that swimming can be—and is—both strong and pretty. There is, after all, beauty in the collaboration and camaraderie of synchronized swimming. And there is certainly art to be found not only in the dynamic ways the human body can move in the water but also in the ways that our collective movements add up to something bigger and more dazzling than anything we could create alone. I am grateful to the generations of women who laid the foundation for this dynamic sport and, in the process, helped make the ability to swim a given for the majority of American women today. Collectively, their stories reveal how women—both as individuals and together—found joy and power in the water and provide another angle through which to understand the diversity of paths to women's liberation in the first half of the twentieth century.

---

* Synchronized—now "artistic"—swimming and its precursors have been called a variety of names over the years (scientific/ornamental/fancy swimming, water ballet, etc.). Throughout the book, I will refer to these forms of aquatics and their various components (stunts, figures, elements, and so on) by whatever names were used at the time.

CHAPTER 1

SCIENCE

Expert Swimmers can do whatever they
please in the water; they can walk there, stand
still upright, or lye still, or sit down.[1]

−EVERARD DIGBY, 1587

It was a fine early summer afternoon in England, and the port at Chelsea was just slipping out of sight when Benjamin Franklin—at the urging of his fellow passengers—kicked off his buckled shoes and tossed aside his heavy jacket. John Wygate, a fellow printer whom Franklin had taught to swim, had been regaling the gentlemen aboard the ferry with stories of Franklin's fishlike agility in the water and the peculiar aquatic tricks he could perform. They had spent the morning viewing taxidermied crocodiles and rattlesnakes at Don Saltero's curiosities shop and weren't ready for the day's amusements to end, even as they headed back to Blackfriars. Franklin likely put on a good show of modesty, demurring at first to the group's excited requests for a demonstration, but was no doubt secretly pleased as he undressed for his dip in the Thames—he loved both an audience and any excuse to get in the water. With his short breeches, knee socks, and frilly-collared shirt folded safely away, leaving only his birthday suit, nineteen-year-old Franklin leapt off the edge of the boat. Some of the men's hearts may have quickened at the thought of their own heavy, landlubber bodies plunging into the dark water; overboard was not a place most people in the eighteenth century went voluntarily. Despite the great amount of time spent on ships and ferries, swimming was a rare skill among men. Among women, it was unheard of—even suspect.

Franklin, however, was in his element—and it showed as he floated effortlessly on his back, bobbed like a spinning top with his knees held tightly to his chest, and dove under and above the surface like a porpoise. This future statesman and political philosopher, known in London as the "Water American," was a proud practitioner of what would later be called "scientific swimming."[2] He could float on his back and raise a leg straight in the air, mastlike—much as a modern-day synchronized (or artistic) swimmer would do. He could make a circle on the surface, his head remaining still in the center like the point on a compass as his legs rotated around it. He could swim on his back, arms free to ferry dry clothes or declarations and treaties high above the water. He could even swim on his belly with his wrists tied behind his back.

Franklin performed his aquatic feats that day in 1726 "both upon and under the water" all the way to Blackfriars, a distance of about three miles, and recalled that they "surpris'd and pleas'd those to whom they were novelties."[3] Franklin, who had harbored a love of swimming since his boyhood when he taught himself to swim in the Mill Pond near his family home in Boston, wrote in his autobiography that he learned these particular tricks from a book by a Frenchman named Melchisédech Thévenot: "I had from a child been ever delighted with this exercise, had studied and practis'd all Thévenot's motions and positions, added some of my own, aiming at the graceful and easy as well as the useful."[4]

Although he credits Thévenot for his sleek aquatic moves, they actually originated with an Englishman and Cambridge theologian named Everard Digby, who, in 1587, authored England's first swimming manual of the modern era. Digby's book, *De Arte Natandi* (The Art of Swimming), contained descriptions and woodblock illustrations of a variety of useful and aesthetic, as well as downright odd, stunts one could do in the water, such as the "ringing the bells" turn, "carrying the left leg in the right hand," keeping "one foot at liberty," "the leap of the goat," and even paring one's toenails with a knife while floating. In providing instructions for these aquatic "refinements," Digby hoped to revive swimming—a once revered skill that had all but died out during Europe's Dark Ages—and elevate it from a crude, mechanical function of the hands and feet to an artful science. He promised readers that through frequent practice of the precepts laid out in his little tract, they "may attain to the habit of Swimming perfectly."[5]

Digby's *De Arte Natandi* was translated within a few years from its original Latin into English by a man named Middleton, but it wouldn't reach a wide audience until Thévenot translated the text to French in 1696, adding a lengthy introduction and improved illustrations. Thévenot's translation, which was published as *L'Art de Nager* and makes only a passing mention in the introduction of Digby—referring

An illustration from Digby's De Arte Natandi *of "playing about the water with one foot," a move synchronized swimmers would recognize as the "sailboat."*

to him as "an English Man wherof I have here made some use"—was then translated into German, Spanish, Italian, and again to English. As Thévenot was a scientist well-known among Enlightenment-era thinkers, it was the version with his name splashed across the cover that Franklin and others would discover—while Digby would be largely forgotten.

And although Digby wouldn't live to see it, his book, helped along by the Renaissance-inspired embrace of classical ideas, would indeed help spur the aquatic revival he dreamed of. His repertoire of movements—and the techniques he used to achieve them—would be studied and practiced by science-minded gentlemen swimmers like Franklin, later expanded and performed by aquatic artists of vaudeville stages, and, eventually, codified and elevated by female athletes into the competitive sport of synchronized swimming—which was christened as an Olympic event almost exactly four centuries after Digby's book was first published.

AQUAPHILES TO AQUAPHOBES

As a passionate and skilled swimmer born on the cusp of the modern era, Digby was a century or two ahead of his time—or, one could say—a millennium behind. In ancient Greece, swimming was considered a skill as fundamental as reading, with Plato using the phrase "unlettered and unable to swim" as shorthand for an uneducated person. The Romans were even more famous for their celebration of all things aquatic. On any given day, men and boys in the Roman capital could be found splashing in the sea or the Tiber River; women swam too but mostly in private bathhouses. Every town across the Roman world, no matter how small, had to have at least one thermae, public heated baths that served both hygienic and hedonistic purposes, with wine flowing and orgies stretching through the night as well-to-do Romans soaked and socialized. In many towns, larger baths, or natatoria, were purpose built for the more serious pursuit of swimming.

Even when they weren't in the water, the Romans surrounded themselves with it, beautifying their urban centers with ornate fountains and waterscapes fed by complex aqueduct systems. On holidays, inland residents flocked to coastal resort towns like Antium, Baiae, and Naples to soak in the ocean vistas. Romans found tranquility in the sights, sounds, and smells of the sea—after all, Venus, the goddess of love and beauty, was formed from the froth of its waves. Just as Poseidon had ruled the seas for the Greeks, Neptune commanded Rome's waters, winds, and storms, while lakes, rivers, and springs were populated with lesser deities.

Emperors, the mortals at the helm of the mighty Roman empire, demonstrated their power through water as well, particularly through their ability to engineer this precious resource for use in lavish—and often gruesome—spectacles. Among the grisliest were *naumachia*, waterborne gladiator games of mortal combat in which slaves and prisoners were set aboard small ships and forced to fight one another to the death in naval battles staged in lakes and flooded amphitheaters. When the Flavian Amphitheater, now known as the Colosseum, was completed, Emperor Titus celebrated in 80 CE by filling its basin with water and hosting naumachia and other aquatic entertainments, including an enactment of Leander's mythological swim to his lover, Hero. In another act, described by historian Kathleen Coleman as "an ancient equivalent of synchronized swimming," a large group of women dove, cavorted, and created shapes in the water. Playing the role of water nymphs, or Nereids, the women likely swam nude, their bodies illuminated by torchlight as they formed the outlines of a star, trident, and ship.[6] Similar but smaller aquatic productions called "Thetis-mimes" were popular across the Empire. Orchestra basins of amphitheaters, such as the Theatre of Dionysus in Athens, were waterproofed and filled to create pools where women would swim and pantomime mythological stories.[7]

However, as Christian beliefs and practices began taking hold, there was an intentional renunciation of the pagan practices of Rome. Early church fathers like John Chrysostom, Archbishop of Constantinople during the fourth century, sought to discredit the Thetis-mime shows, maligning the performers as prostitutes, and warning parishioners that going to see them would lead directly to "shipwreck of the soul."[8] Thermae and pools were viewed as playgrounds for sinners and wastrels, glaring symbols of Roman indulgence and excess, while water increasingly came to be associated with pleasures of the flesh— the very pleasures Christians were supposed to deny themselves in this life if they hoped to achieve paradise in the next. Even before the collapse of the Western Roman Empire in 476 CE, many of its pagan practices were banned, and over the years its theaters, pools, and aqueducts were either destroyed or left to fall into disrepair.

As invading tribes took over former Roman territories, they brought vastly different views of the water. Whereas Greco-Roman mythology populated the earth's waters with divine characters, the seas and rivers of northern cultures were teeming with monsters rather than gods. Nordic fishermen and sailors were at the mercy of Kraken, a colossal, ship-sinking cephalopod; Jörmungandr, a venomous sea serpent; and Nikr, a seafaring horse that appeared tame, only to lure human prey to their watery deaths. To these newcomers, beachy shorelines were not arenas for reflection or frolic, but represented the edge of safety and the very end of the known world, beyond which lay a "witch's brew" of dangers.[9]

By Europe's Middle Ages, Rome's aquatic paradise was a distant memory. Churchgoers were reminded that God had used water to destroy the earth, while the few Bible verses that mention swimming were interpreted as signs of man's helplessness and drowning as a metaphor for sin.[10] Superstition, rather than science, dictated their relationship with the natural world—so much so that even the simple act of floating could be taken as a sign of witchcraft. Eventually, getting wet, other than for baptism, was to be avoided, as water was blamed for weakening the body and spreading disease and plagues. Instead of controlling water and harnessing it for their enjoyment and social utility, as their ancestors had done, humans came to fear it, associating it not with health and pleasure but with death, condemnation, and the terrifying unknown.

SWIMMING'S SCIENTIFIC REVOLUTION

Water's bad rap held for roughly a millennium, until the start of the early modern era—precisely when the lonely aquaphile Everard Digby came swimming along. With the Gutenberg printing press having reached England, Digby, a Cambridge student, saw an opportunity to help his countrymen reclaim their aquatic skills and set about writing his manual. His decision to write in Latin, the language of serious texts, may have been in part to compensate for what he knew to be a poor choice of subject matter. After all, swimming had come to be held in so "litle esteme"—to use the words of his fellow Englishman Sir Thomas Elyot—that it had been banned by Cambridge authorities.[11] Digby also made a point—lest his aquatic maneuvers be considered frivolous—to detail their many practical uses. His "bells turn," for example, could be used if a swimmer needs to change directions to avoid boats, floating timber, rocks, or "a thousand other accidents."[12] Knowing how to swim on one's belly with arms clasped behind the back would be useful to those unfortunate enough to find themselves fleeing captivity with their hands bound.[13] Digby's technique for holding a leg aloft in the air was his Swiss Army knife of swimming skills—one that could be used to disengage a lower extremity from weeds, massage away a cramp, pull on boots, or even ferry a parcel across a river by tying it to a big toe, all while floating comfortably on one's back. Although experts—both then and now—can make this floating leg extension look easy, Digby cautioned that it is harder than it appears. In addition to keeping the lower leg "employed," wrote Digby, it is the "office of the hands to keep up the body" by "moving them to and fro, like Oars." He was describing a form of propulsion called "sculling," which involves moving the hands in a figure-eight motion and remains a key skill for synchronized swimmers.

Despite his focus on usefulness, Digby, who believed that "expert swimmers can do whatever they please in the water," did include a few tricks that appear to serve no purpose other than showing off—like his "beating the water" move, in which the swimmer would raise both legs into the air then bring them down with a dramatic splash.[14] Digby never once mentioned speed—swimming would not develop into a competitive sport in England for nearly three hundred more years. His focus, instead, after Europe's centuries-long hiatus from the water, was rediscovering and sharing what the body could do in it.

An illustration from Thévenot's translation, L'Art de Nager, demonstrating how to "boot oneself" in the water.

And Digby wasn't the only one looking at the water with fresh eyes. The Renaissance had sparked an era of science and exploration, as well as renewed interest in classical antiquity. The embrace by Renaissance thinkers of Greco-Roman languages and ideas lent these bygone cultures new legitimacy across Europe and prompted a revival of many of their practices, including those centered around water. Long-neglected Roman baths were rebuilt in towns like Bath and Buxton, and naumachia made a comeback when Grand Duke Ferdinando hosted a mock naval battle to commemorate his wedding in 1589. Soon, the landed aristocracy of England likewise began hosting naumachia on the lakes of their estates.

As European explorers circled the globe, they were often surprised to discover that during their thousand-year hiatus from the water, much of the rest of the world had gone on swimmingly. "The capsizing of the frail canoe of the natives of Otaheite [Tahiti] is regarded by them as a subject of merriment," observed the British Captain Stevens. "They immediately swim about sportively in the water, right their slender vessel, and skull away as if no danger or accident had occurred to them."[15] In Japan, swimming had become both a martial and performance art, with the most talented practitioners writing calligraphy, manipulating fans, or dispatching weapons while swimming, sometimes in heavy armor. Africans and Native Americans were also frequently mentioned as being faster and stronger swimmers than Europeans, and several incidents were documented of enslaved men aboard wrecked ships saving their enslavers.

Thévenot, the translator of Digby's book, was also a founding member of the French Academy and publisher of one of the earliest collections of travel writings, and thus served as an important bridge between Digby's work and Renaissance ideas. In his introduction to his translation, Thévenot included discussions of swimming in antiquity and its contemporary practice in other parts of the world, lamenting that such skills had been lost in Europe. He also explained the physics of swimming and suggested that it was a useful skill worth pursuing by those of the "most elevated conditions of life," such as explorers and young aristocratic men embarking on their educational "Grand Tours" of Europe. Although Thévenot ironically never learned to swim himself, his positioning as a respected scholar lent an air of authority to Digby's aquatic moves and added to the appeal of his book to later Enlightenment thinkers like Benjamin Franklin.

The fact that swimming was thought to be learned through study further bolstered its suitability as a pursuit for men of refinement, and by the seventeenth century, it was—according to the etiquette manual *The Compleat Gentleman*—a requisite skill for every "Noble and Gentleman."[16] Tutors offered lessons, usually tying pupils to a rope dangling from the end of a pole, while books offered "parlour practice" ideas for the gentleman who wanted to acquire the basics from the privacy of his home or preferred to learn from nature's "best professor"—the frog. Simply put a frog in a punchbowl filled with water, lie belly-side down on a bench, and mimic the frog's moves.[17]

How gentlemen learned to swim in 1845.

But for Benjamin Franklin, an observational scientist who harbored a lifelong fascination with water, there was no better way to learn than to just get in and experiment. In fact, he advised a nonswimming friend that the best way to overcome his fear was to use his own body to test out the concept of buoyancy. Wade into a river or lake, instructed Franklin in his letter, toss an egg a few feet ahead, then try to dive in to retrieve it. "You will find," he wrote, "it is not so easy a thing to sink as you imagined."[18] Franklin's method for developing what he called "experimental confidence" is revealing of his scientific approach to the water, whether in a lab or in a pond. As a boy, he invented a pair of swimming paddles from painters' palettes and likely became the first windsurfer, using a kite to pull his floating body across a pond "with the greatest pleasure imaginable."[19] Later, many of Franklin's discoveries as a physicist were related to water as well, such as the effect of atmospheric pressure on its boiling point, the calming effect of oil on its surface, and the relationship between water depth and resistance.

It's not surprising then that Franklin, as both an aquaphile and a scientist, would be drawn to Digby's aquatic maneuvers, which deconstruct swimming and floating to their essential components and enable the swimmer to experiment and feel the effects of even the slightest variations.[20] For example, when holding a leg aloft, even a tiny shift in the angle of the hands as they scull could mean the difference between traveling headfirst versus feetfirst in the water—or sinking like a rock. "Scientific swimming," as the form of aquatics based on Digby's moves came to be called in the 1800s, enabled Franklin to participate in the ultimate water experiment—one in which he used his own body to better understand the natural laws governing what, to him, was nature's most interesting element.

In an era not known for its stringent copyright protections, Franklin's correspondence on swimming, along with pages and pages of text copied verbatim from Digby's book (by way of the English translation of Thévenot's French version), were published in the short tract *The Art of Swimming, Made Safe, Easy, Pleasant and Healthful,* with Dr. Benjamin Franklin listed as the author. Franklin was no plagiarist, however, as the booklet was compiled in 1819, almost thirty years after his death, and his name attached to sell copies.[21] But as a result of the widely distributed tract, Franklin is often erroneously credited as the originator of many of Digby's moves—just as he erroneously credited Thévenot—and has even, somewhat jokingly, been dubbed the "Founding Father of Synchronized Swimming."

Despite this string of mis-accreditations, the outcome was that, thanks to Digby's and Thévenot's books, swimming was being discussed by prominent men of science like Franklin and losing many of the stigmas that had been long attached to it. And that, according to an argument put forth in *Early American Literature*, may have even put the final nail in the coffin of the horrific and centuries-old practice of swimming witch trials.[22] Instructional pamphlets on how to "swim" an accused witch circulated across England in the 1600s, with one advising to strip the accused woman down to her smock, bind her arms across her chest, and toss her in a river: "If she swimme, you may build upon it, that she is a Witch."[23] If the "lucky" woman sank, she was presumed innocent and pulled from the water, though

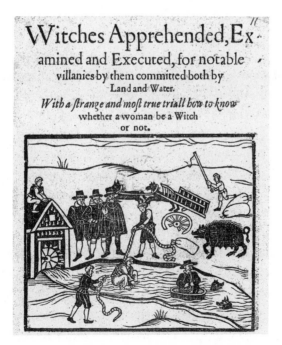

The "swimming trial" of accused witch Mary Sutton in 1613.

not always before she drowned. The practice—which was based on the idea that water, the holy instrument of baptism, refused to receive those in league with the devil—had seen a resurgence in the seventeenth century, but debates over its virtue began to take on a more scientific tone in Franklin's lifetime, demonstrating an increased understanding of the natural laws governing humans in water. Philosopher Francis Hutcheson explained in his 1722 "Historical Essay Concerning Witchcraft" that "bodies of all creatures are near to an equal poise with the water," and that any number of factors impact whether one sinks or floats.[24] Add woolen petticoats, he writes, and it's anyone's guess whether "half of the old Women in the Nation might swim."[25] Franklin showed what he thought of the subject using humor; in his satirical essay "A Witch Trial at Mount Holly," a frustrated mob goes to such lengths to sink their buoyant "witches" that in the end one of the accused is so "surpriz'd at his own Swimming" that he begins to question his own innocence.[26]

By the 1700s, water-based transportation had become an everyday part of life for people of all social classes, and so too had accidents, fires, and drownings. Franklin believed the ability to swim would relieve the masses of the "slavish terrors" they felt on even a common ferry ride and called for making swimming a mandatory part of education—for boys, that is.[27] Despite all his fervor for swimming, Franklin did not openly advocate for women or girls to learn. It was simply assumed that they did not swim. Franklin's wife, Deborah Read, never joined him on his many trips between Europe and the colonies, citing her fear of the long sea voyage.[28] Like virtually all women of the era, she would have been completely helpless if she fell overboard. As one woman wrote the following century, things not having much improved for her sex by then, "When an accident happens, even a dozen yards from land, women can do nothing but cling, in helpless groups of five or six, to some brave man who risks his life to save them; and the result is, all sink in one miserable heap."[29]

What would ultimately help swimming trickle down to the masses—and eventually to women—was the growing popularity of mineral-water bathing, the only acceptable water activity for women on either side of the Atlantic.

Mineral spas became fashionable destinations in the 1600 and 1700s for the wealthy seeking the water's medicinal properties, their popularity further fueled by the rediscovery of ancient Pompeii, the glory of its water gardens and baths preserved. Mineral-water bathing even spread to the American colonies, where British trends followed a few decades behind, with George and Martha Washington known to be regular visitors to Berkeley Springs, in what is now West Virginia. In 1752, a London physician, Richard Russel, took note of the tremendous popularity of the inland baths, looked around at the endless expanses of saltwater surrounding his island nation, and saw pound signs. He moved to the seaside village of Brighton and published *A Dissertation on the Use of Sea-Water in the Diseases of the Glands, Particularly the Scurvy, Jaundice, King's Evil, Leprosy, and the Glandular Consumption*, which lauded the miraculous power of the salty brine to cure any imaginable ailment—whether by drinking it or dunking in it. His text was devoured by water-therapy devotees eager for a change of scenery and inspired a proliferation of coastal resorts and sea-bathing infirmaries. The good doctor, and now oceanfront property owner, sat back and watched his sleepy town, and others like it along England's coasts, turn into cosmopolitan spa getaways for fashionable Londoners—men and women alike.

However, for the latter, these forays to the seaside were fraught with challenges to maintaining feminine decorum, and as they would long into the future, the solutions imposed on women prioritized modesty over both their enjoyment and safety in the water. Women bathers wore long, shapeless gowns to conceal their figures, but they tended to billow up dangerously around the arms and neck in the waves. As a fix, the wearers often attached strings to the front and back, tying them between the ankles, or, in the case of Martha Washington, sewed weights into the hems to hold them down. Another problem was the tendency of fabric to become clingy and transparent when wet. Eighteenth-century ladies couldn't very well traipse back to their lodgings in such a state, so resort owners came up with an inventive solution: the bathing machine, a horse-drawn shed on wheels where bathers could change clothes as they were carted down to the water. Some were equipped with awnings to provide additional privacy during the bath. A waiting attendant, usually a matronly woman, would help them out, dunk them unceremoniously in the saltwater medicine, and send them back the way they came.

Even though the beaches were gender segregated—with male violators charged 5 shillings, or sometimes a bottle of wine—the procession of bathing machines during the women's hour always attracted a "gang of idlers," many of whom likely thought the view was worth the penalty.[30] Others kept the required distance, ogling female bathers through telescopes and opera glasses—a pastime young men sportingly called "naiad hunting." Women confined themselves to a tiny, sequestered spot of sea, put up with the indignities of dank, rickety bathing machines, and struggled in ridiculous costumes that made even the simple acts of moving and floating in the water impossible. Even so, that wasn't enough for one London newspaper, which blamed the "gross indelicacy" of the Peeping Toms on the women themselves, writing that they "do not confine their water frolics to the bath under the awning, but boldly, wander away, and so expose themselves to the vulgar throng."[31] Men, on the other hand, splashed about in the surf just as God made them—naked and carefree as seabirds. Unburdened

Women using the bathing machines at Brighton Beach in the early 1800s.

by social and physical constraints, male bathers could venture into deeper water and gain confidence as they practiced their swimming skills. In short, bathing was for women and swimming was for men.

Nonetheless, the lure of the seaside holiday continued to grow, fueled by the cultural tastemakers of the era and greater ease of travel. Romantic Era artists and writers looked to nature for inspiration in an industrializing world and regularly incorporated water, swimming, and the sea into their writing—and in turn, romanticized the seaside holiday for the upwardly mobile. Lord Byron, who made swimming part of his manly image, famously enacted the mythological swim of Leander across the Hellespont (now Dardanelles) and wrote about plunging into torrents, exulting in his own strength as he rode the "swift whirl of the new breaking wave" in his poem "Manfred." Others, like novelist Charlotte Brontë, described the spiritual awe or near transcendence the ocean inspires. "The idea of seeing the sea—of being near it," she wrote, "fills and satisfies my mind."[32]

Nautical themes made their way into British theater as well, most spectacularly through "aqua dramas"—plays that incorporated actual water into the plot and set design. One of the earliest was at Sadler's Wells Theatre, which in 1804 presented *The Siege of Gibraltar*. It was advertised as a grand aquatic spectacle featuring "real Ships and Gun Vessels . . . with a real representation of the Humanity of the English in saving their Enemies' drowning Sailors from destruction."[33] Water was pumped into the theater from a nearby river to fill a 90-foot-long cistern under a stage that could be removed for the aquatic scenes. The "real" miniature ships, as well as Neptune's chariots and other vessels used in future aqua dramas, were operated by water boys, who were fortified for the long nights half-submerged in unheated water with a glass of brandy.[34]

By the nineteenth century, steamship and rail travel, increased wages, and greater leisure time put a trip to the actual seaside within reach of much of the British population—and they headed there in droves. Captivated by details of the delicate ecosystems published by naturalists like Philip Gosse and Charles Kingsley, and further driven by the Victorian love of collecting and cataloging, many plucked souvenirs from the shorelines to create home aquaria. Purveyors of public entertainments seized on the trend, building grand royal aquariums and "crystal palaces" to bring monsters of the deep to the masses. Tales of peril on the high seas, from Captain Ahab's epic battle with Moby Dick to the twenty-thousand-league adventures of Captain Nemo, further fueled their "hydromania"—a term coined by a writer of the era. As historian Charles Sprawson wrote, "anything to do with water seemed to exert extraordinary fascination" for the Victorians. Or put more poetically, they had a "love affair with 'moistness.'"[35] It seems only natural then that this mass mania for all things aquatic soon extended to swimming—both as a recreation and as a wildly popular form of entertainment.

SWIMMING PROFESSORS AND MISTRESSES

While a smattering of private pools were built in England starting in the early 1800s, most swimming was done in oceans, rivers, or lakes— albeit only by a stalwart, male minority. But that began to change late in the first half of the century alongside a growing public health movement to provide hygienic places for the cramped urban working-class masses to bathe. It was codified into national law with the Bath and Washhouses Act of 1846, and hundreds of public baths were built in a matter of a few years in communities across England. Some of the larger facilities doubled as "swimming baths," offering places to learn and practice natation and giving rise to a cottage industry of aquatic professionals known as swimming professors. These self-styled "professors" were working-class men who served as superintendents at the baths and offered swimming instruction to male patrons. Women, however, would have to continue waiting for their chance to learn, as most swimming baths were open to men only, while women were relegated to smaller facilities strictly for bathing.

Although there had been a dearth of swimming books following Digby's, with increased interest in swimming in the nineteenth century came an explosion of publishing on the topic in England. A Mr. Frost, swimming professor and surveyor of chimneys, set off the trend in 1816 with his book *Scientific Swimming; Being A Series of Practical Instructions, On an Original and Progressive Plan, By Which The Art of Swimming May Be Readily Attained, With Every Advantage of Power in the Water.* As swimming was not yet thought of as a sport, early writers like Frost were "in doubt whether to call it a science, an amusement, or an art," wrote Ralph Thomas in his 1904 bibliography of swimming literature.[36] Other texts included Dr. James Bennet's *Art of Swimming Exemplified by Diagrams, From Which Both Sexes May Learn to Swim and Float on Water,* one of the few to mention women, and *The Science of Swimming as Taught and Practiced in Civilized and Savage Nations,* written by "An Experienced Swimmer."

Few of the strokes we think of as standard today had yet been developed, so swimming instruction typically focused on three major types of natation: "front" or "chest" swimming—what we now call the breaststroke—was the most commonly practiced, as it was graceful, kept the head above water (as it was practiced then), and most closely resembled the actions of the original professor—the frog; "side swimming" was considered the most powerful stroke for going against a tide, while "swimming on the back" was little more than kicking while floating. That left plenty of room in these books for discussions of maneuvers that built directly on Digby's repertoire; these moves were often included under the label of "scientific swimming," but were sometimes interchangeably called "ornamental," "trick," or "fancy" swimming.

But unlike Digby, these nineteenth-century swimming authors no longer felt compelled to provide justification for including these seemingly superficial stunts. Scientific swimming was simply viewed as a natural progression of skills. Mastering a wide repertoire of movements

Captain Andrews demonstrates scientific swimming stunts,
including (left to right) the "spinning top," "washing tub," and
swimming on the back without the use of the arms.

and propulsions was thought to develop confidence and poise in the water—which, in the era before organized sport, were the primary reasons for learning to swim in the first place. Sergeant John Leahy, a swimming teacher at Eton College, explained in 1875, "The various positions and attitudes into which the limbs have to shape themselves in ornamental swimming all help to give confidence because they are new and strange."[37] Scientific swimming required learning new ways of being in the water, as the movements did not use standard arm strokes or kicks and instead relied on sculling. Some used no propulsion at all, and instead required strong floating skills. One list of scientific stunts in a boys' magazine article on "manly exercises" included several of Digby's moves, plus "floating on the surface of the water, and whilst in that position, representing Grecian statues."[38] Another stunt, motionless swimming, was precisely what it sounds like, and one young man reportedly floated for ten minutes without moving so much as a pinky at a demonstration.

Competitions were held at least as early as 1843, when the British Swimming Society awarded a "prize in fancy swimming"; a dozen years later, eight hundred people gathered to watch candidates vie for the Leander Medal for Scientific Swimming at the Albion Baths in London, where competition for fame in this "higher branch of *arte natandi*" was said to be fierce. Following the competition, Professor George Poulton issued a public challenge, wagering the massive sum of £100 that he could beat any man in the country in a "trick-for-trick" match.[39]

For working-class swimming professors, who cobbled together a living through a combination of competing for cash prizes, giving exhibitions at swimming galas, and teaching their craft, scientific swimming provided the ultimate way to demonstrate their aquatic prowess and mastery in the water—and thus attract students. As a result, they were constantly expanding their inventory of moves. Professor Poulton's "fine specimens of scientific swimming" were said to include moves called "The Crucifix" and the "Dying Gladiator," while a one-legged ornamental swimmer, Professor Charley Moore, was known for floating with his leg encircling his head, a feat that always commanded "deafening and prolonged applause."[40] The bibliographer Ralph Thomas wrote that the growing difficulty of these feats demonstrated how rapidly swimming was advancing and pointed out that

A swimmer demonstrating the "porpoise," which was similar to a surface dive.

even among Digby's original moves that were still being practiced, like the porpoise, the execution had become "far neater."[41]

As sporting events, swimming galas were seen as venues for men to develop and demonstrate their masculinity—so much so that one newspaper called women "decidedly out of place" at these events.[42] Moreover, they were usually held outside of working hours, either too early or too late for a respectable woman to be out, especially in the presence of the "rough" men and crude language of the sporting world. But Professor Frederick Beckwith, superintendent of Lambeth Baths, one of London's largest natatoriums, realized he could expand the audience at his galas if he made them more family friendly and began calling them "aquatic entertainments." Articles noted the care he took in arranging the details so that "the fair sex might be represented amongst the spectators," like hanging baskets of flowers from the ceiling and adding live music to the proceedings.[43] Increasingly, the words "Ladies specially invited" began appearing on advertisements, and as one writer noted, usually implied that "something more graceful than the ordinary racing" would be on the program.[44]

This "something more" often included performances of scientific swimming by Professor Beckwith's children. As early as 1855, his six-year-old daughter Jessie and her four-year-old brother "Master Willie" were astonishing spectators with their graceful feats. As Beckwith's family grew, he added more "water babies," including his younger daughter Agnes, prompting other professors to do the same. While the professors' sons would often participate in races and challenges at the galas, competitions were off-limits to the daughters, who instead performed their graceful feats during intermissions and at the conclusions of shows. Even though they were limited to a small part of the overall event, the daughters—or "faire artistes"—were hugely popular. *London Society* noted of Beckwith's entertainments that although "thousands go there to see the sights go on," little Jessie could single-handedly draw more spectators than the rest of the show's "whole array of talent."[45] These events helped to further stimulate interest in swimming. *The Era* wrote that most of the audience at Beckwith's galas could not swim, but hopefully "the sight of persons moving easily and comfortably in the water" would inspire them to want to learn.[46]

This was especially true for female audience members, who were inspired to see the gracefulness and dexterity of their swimming sisters and the new kind of physicality for women that they modeled. The era's strict separation of public and private spheres had long relegated women to the safety of home, leaving men to brave the world outside, while the ideals of passive and delicate femininity had so discouraged women from doing any physical activity that frailty had become the hallmark of modern womanhood (at least for middle- and upper-class women . . . those from the working class could not afford the "luxury" of inactivity). And if a woman wasn't frail from inactivity, corsets and couture took care of that. The smartly dressed woman, wrote Lady Greville, "walks about like a trussed fowl, with mincing gait, balancing herself on high-heeled, pointed boots, her centre of gravity displaced, and her waist looking like it must snap at the least shock."[47] Miss S. R. Powers, a reformer and swimming advocate, wrote that her generation of women had become so sedentary that they had stopped expending even the mere "forty-mouse power" of which they were capable. But Powers believed, as she argued in her 1859 pamphlet "Why do not women swim?" that swimming was precisely the thing that could help her sex restore "that physical vigour, those firm muscles and strong nerves . . . that have gone out of fashion for them."[48]

Swimming was also coming to be seen as a matter of safety for women, just as it had been recognized—a century earlier—as such for men. Harriet Martineau, one of the earliest sociologists, declared in 1859, "English women have four limbs, and live in an island, and make voyages . . . in short, run the universal risks in regard to water; and, therefore they have a claim to be taught to swim."[49] That was precisely the argument that enabled a group of women to secure London's first swimming bath for ladies a year earlier when they had convinced male city council members that since womankind is "equally liable . . . to watery perils," they should have the same access to the means of acquiring the skills of self-preservation as men.[50] Their new bath, the St. Marylebone Bath for Women, featured elegant scrollwork, "lofty sky-lit rooms," and heated water that cascaded from a lion's mouth onto a giant seashell then into the forty-foot-long pool. The atmosphere and quality of swimming baths had improved considerably and had begun attracting middle-class customers who had been put off by associations the earlier baths had held with hygienic reform efforts targeting the urban poor.[51]

But even as more baths opened to women, a problem remained. Who was to teach the growing numbers of women who wanted to learn? Lessons between male teachers and female students were impractical due to gender segregation at bathing places and largely viewed as inappropriate. Professors who dared to teach women opened themselves up to a host of problems, as illustrated by what happened

Victorian women were eager to learn to swim, as demonstrated by postcards like this from the turn of the century.

to a Professor Pearce at the Ramsgate beach. He was teaching a female student to float when a water ripple turned up the student's bathing dress. Pearce quickly pulled it back down, and even though she was wearing pantaloons underneath—the women's bathing costume having evolved by this point to skirt and bloomer sets—witnesses claimed to have been scandalized by the incident and the professor was called for a court summons.

To one frustrated mother, eager for her daughters to gain swimming skills, the solution was obvious. She wrote in a letter to the editor of *English Woman's Journal*:

> Writers in the present day urge us to have our daughters taught swimming. I have always wished that mine should learn that accomplishment, both for health and safety's sake; but when at home we have no swimming-bath within reach, and when we go to the sea-side, where the great pond invites them to swim, there is no one to teach them how. I cannot send them to the gentleman's bathing place to learn, nor bring a gentleman with them to the ladies' place. Now, I ask why should not some strong-bodied steady-minded young women be trained at the swimming-baths, to serve hereafter as *swimming mistresses*?[52]

With a clear need for women's instruction, the wives, daughters, and sisters of the swimming professors—many of whom had been brought into the aquatic profession by their male relatives—were just the swimming mistresses to meet the demand. At Lambeth Baths, Professor Beckwith began offering weekly women's hours, with his wife and teenaged daughter Agnes giving lessons, and other female relatives of swimming professors began doing the same at baths across the country. However, unlike their fathers and brothers, women instructors were not referred to as "professors," as that was a title reserved strictly for men. Siblings Harry and Emily Parker were listed in the 1881 census as a professor and a teacher of swimming, respectively, even though one article noted that Miss Parker "may be said to be a professor of swimming, for she has been engaged for some time past with her mother in teaching the art to ladies."[53] On the rare occasion that a woman was acknowledged for doing the work, it was still never used as a title in front of her name, as women were not supposed to presume to claim such high levels of expertise. But even if they were not called professors, the influence of these women swimmers was growing, and they would soon be pushing and testing the limits of what humans could do in the water right alongside men—and it was a fourteen-year-old girl who would lead the charge.

THE SPORT OF SWIMMING

On September 2, 1875, several thousand people gathered on the banks of the River Thames to see history being made. It had been announced that Agnes Beckwith—a "mere child" at fourteen—would swim from London to Greenwich, a distance of five miles.[54] Whether or not she could complete such a swim had been widely discussed in newspapers. But the professor's daughter seemed to have little doubt, and at 4:55 that afternoon, Agnes, wearing a rose-pink swimming dress made of llama wool and trimmed with braids and white lace, set out on a brisk side stroke.[55]

Interest in distance swimming was at a fever pitch in England. Only months earlier, Captain Paul Boynton had "swum" across the English Channel wearing an inflatable suit. It was considered a remarkable feat, until that August, when Captain Matthew Webb set out to swim from Dover to Calais without any such aids—just man versus water—and succeeded. Webb's accomplishment was beyond what anyone at the time had believed to be humanly possible and sparked a mania for endurance swims, with everyone racing to set new records. Even the *New York Times* took note of the great "spirit of emulation" that Captain Webb's daring inspired among his countrymen and the reporter wrote with bemusement, "to read the British papers, it would almost seem that a large number of the people of that country just now are engaged either in jumping off bridges and performing swimming feats, or in contemplating them."[56]

But nothing like this had been done by a woman until Agnes set out on her swim the following month. As she made her way down the Thames, eager onlookers cheered and waved from bridges and buildings, and she returned her appreciation by blowing kisses to the crowds. When Agnes reached Greenwich after one hour and seven minutes, the papers reported that she was greeted with the "wildest enthusiasm," and a band aboard the steamer that had accompanied her the entire way played "See the Conquering Hero Comes." Not the least bit tired, Agnes took a large hula hoop–style ring handed to her from someone aboard the steamer, and deftly maneuvered the prop, swimming in and out of the loop for about 50 yards. Then she demonstrated a few scientific swimming feats for the crowd, just as Franklin had done in the same river a century earlier.[57]

The feat, staged with the help of her father, Professor Beckwith, shrewdly capitalized on the mania for long-distance swimming and propelled the start of Agnes's celebrity. But such attention always brings competition, and the same month Emily Parker, also from a swimming family, swam from London Bridge to Blackwall, two miles longer than Agnes's swim. Not wanting her achievements eclipsed, Agnes doubled her distance two months later, swimming from Chelsea to Greenwich Pier, then doubled it again, reaching 20 miles on the Thames, which would stand as the women's long-distance record for three decades.

Agnes told reporters she undertook her feats to encourage others of her sex to learn to swim. And she did. At a gala following her third swim, Professor Beckwith announced that the ladies' swimming class at Lambeth Baths—taught twice weekly by the "Heroine of the Thames"—had grown from five to fifty students.[58] One hundred years later, Sports Illustrated marked Agnes's swim to Greenwich as the start of spectator sports for women, and even newspapers at the time could sense the significance of her accomplishments and were abuzz with discussions of what they would mean for the fair sex.[59] The London Journal declared that in "these days of women's rights man can no more claim the water as his exclusive domain than he can the land."[60] The Penny Illustrated predicted that no English girl would "remain ignorant of swimming . . . now that those little mermaids, Agnes Beckwith and Alice [Emily] Parker, have set the lasses so courageous an example."[61] Before long, Agnes had her sights set on trying to cross the English Channel, telling a reporter that she hoped to find a sponsor to support her attempt so that she could prove that "what man can do, may also be done by a woman."[62]

But some thought these public spectacles had gone too far, and the tone of the media turned critical. Women's swimming was all fine and good—so long as it was done in moderation and out of public view. *The Graphic* expressed admiration at the skills of Agnes and Emily but added, "We hardly like young ladies indulging in this public exhibition of their natatory abilities."[63] The *Sporting Gazette* professed to support swimming becoming a part of every girl's education but added that there was "something decidedly revolting in the sight of a woman making a public exhibition of herself as an athlete before a roaring mob."[64] The *Penny Illustrated* wrote, "Miss Agnes, now you have given such ample proofs that you are a duck of a girl, stick to your proper vocation—that of teaching your sex to swim."[65]

The growing world of sport was apparently not a place for women. But soon it wouldn't be a place for the male professors either. Sports in England were becoming increasingly organized, with governing bodies and standardized rules. At the same time, there was a movement building among "gentlemen athletes" toward an amateur ethos in sports, which espoused the idea that athletic competitions should not be engaged in for cash pots and silver cups, but for nonmonetary, "higher" ideals like camaraderie and personal betterment. But unlike these recreational sportsmen who could afford the leisure time and expense to play just for the "spirit of the game," working-class athletes like the swimming professors relied on whatever income they could generate through their physical skills—whether performing, teaching, or winning the occasional cash prize—to put bread on the table.[66] Deemed "professionals," the swimming professors were increasingly disqualified from competitions, and when the Amateur Swimming Association (ASA) was formed in 1886, their exclusion was formalized.

The ASA not only banned any athlete who had ever been paid for an activity related to the water—even working as a bathhouse attendant—from its competitions, but also became the self-appointed gatekeeper for swimming instruction, putting itself in charge of deciding who was worthy of obtaining its new teaching certification. This was clearly aimed at the professors, with one amateur proponent writing condescendingly, "why 'Professor' I have never been able to understand" and applauding the ASA for its efforts to eradicate their "slovenly styles of swimming."[67] Although women had never been a part of most swimming competitions, the ASA formalized their exclusion as well, disallowing them from competing in any ASA event. As working-class professors were pushed out of teaching and competitive opportunities, that left just the income from organizing galas and giving demonstrations—hardly enough to support a family on. As a result, the professors and other professional swimmers, plus their wives and daughters, would turn increasingly to commercial entertainments to make a living.

In a way, the shift was a win for women swimmers. The world of sport had relegated them to the half-time shows at swimming galas, pushed them out of endurance swimming, and excluded them completely from races and competitions. But in the world of show business—where talent determines who gets to play—women swimmers would soon become the main event, while their popularity as queens of the crystal tank would inspire others as far away as America to emulate and join them. As individual performers and athletes, many would achieve international acclaim, while collectively they would push against restrictive ideas about their sex and open news spheres of opportunity for women. Together these women would write the next chapter of swimming.

CHAPTER 2

STAGE

People talk of the grace of skirt dancing, of the agility of lawn-tennis, of the gyrations of the practiced skater, but surely the true poetry of motion is exemplified in the movements of the ornamental swimmer.

—HEARTH AND HOME, 1891

Eighteen-year-old Agnes Beckwith was dressed in a smart black bathing leotard accentuated by blue silk stockings. Pearls dotted her neckline and hair, giving the entire ensemble a nautical flare. It was around a quarter to four on a May afternoon in 1880, and five years had passed since Agnes had made history swimming 5, 10, then 20 miles on the Thames. Now she was embarking on a different kind of endurance feat: a thirty-hour swim in the Westminster Royal Aquarium's whale tank. She stood next to the wall of gleaming water as her father, the famous Professor Beckwith, introduced her to the crowd—some eight hundred strong—that had gathered to watch. Until ten o'clock the following evening, Agnes would remain in the tank's deep water, forgoing sleep and taking her meals of beef broth, minced meat, and coffee on a floating tray. She would be allowed only a single hour of respite, if needed, and the Aquarium's elegant grand hall would remain open throughout the night so that patrons could come and go during Agnes's swim.

After the professor concluded his welcome and the applause subsided, Agnes stepped forward and invited any lady present to inspect her costume and confirm there were no compressed oxygen or flotation devices concealed under her clothes. Several takers followed Agnes to her dressing area, and after a few moments, the satisfied "jury of matrons" nodded their approval to the audience. A pianist struck up a jaunty tune, and Agnes slipped a sailor's costume on over her bathing dress and climbed the steps to the top of the tank. Just as the hour chimed, she dove into the water, which was 6 feet deep at its shallowest and had been steam heated to a comfortable 80 degrees. Agnes surfaced and smiled at the audience, then made a show of unbuttoning the sailor jacket, where she "discovered" a flask tucked in the pocket. Much to the amusement of the crowd, she took a long swig. Next came a demonstration of

*Poster announcing Agnes Beckwith's performance
at the Royal Aquarium in Westminster.*

undressing in the water, an important skill in case of falling overboard from a ship. Once unburdened of the midshipman's outfit,
Agnes swam across the tank on her stomach, then on her back. She
waltzed in the water to the piano tunes, then set out on a sprint,
prompting friends to caution her to take it easy. After all, she had
a long night and day ahead of her. But Agnes completed her thirty
hours "without any sign of distress," having passed the time giving demonstrations of ornamental swimming, chatting with spectators, and reading the newspaper while gliding around the tank.[1] In
fact, it wasn't long before Agnes was at it again, more than tripling
the duration of her swim-a-thon to become the "Champion of the
100-hour swim."

THE TANK ACT

Since making her debut as an endurance swimmer on the Thames at the age of fourteen, Agnes had become one of a small but growing number of professional women swimmers—often called "natationists" from the Latin *natare* (to swim)—who were taking their ornamental swimming skills beyond the baths and sports venues and into the world of commercial entertainment. By the last quarter of the nineteenth century, rises in leisure time and wages, along with greater ease of travel, had created an insatiable demand for entertainment among the working and middle classes on both sides of the Atlantic. It was the era of the music hall and variety theater, and acts centered around physical feats, like body builders and gymnasts, were popular thanks to a growing interest in physical culture and the muscular Christianity movement. Meanwhile the Victorian mania for water and the popularity of swimming galas in England had created a unique niche for aquatic entertainers like Beckwith.

Swimming baths and aquariums such as the one at Westminster were a natural fit for these swimming acts. Initially envisioned as temples to science and culture, the elegant aquariums of the Victorian era featured glass-domed ceilings and grand halls with tree-lined promenades, fountains, and walls of water teeming with exotic fish. However, they were costly to build and expensive to maintain, and proprietors were soon trying to boost ticket sales by adding more "down market" entertainments like hypnotists, human cannonballs, tightrope walkers—and ornamental swimmers. Agnes Beckwith gave daily performances, as well as ladies' swimming lessons at the Westminster Royal Aquarium, showing the "fair sex how to master the water, and swim and dive and float as dexterously as a Mermaid." Her popular lessons were even patronized by the Princess of Wales, who would take her daughters to learn from England's best female swimmer.[2]

At commercial entertainment venues where water wasn't a natural part of the environment, such as music halls and pleasure gardens, swimmers brought their own—performing in small portable tanks that could be filled and then rolled onto stages. Typically around six feet long and four to five feet wide and deep, these tanks were made of plate glass sides held together by iron or steel frames. Before the start

An illustration of the Beckwith Frogs performing at Cremorne Gardens in 1869.

of the act, they would be surrounded by scenery or foliage to suggest a mermaid's lair or the haunt of an ancient water sprite. The tank's glass sides provided audiences with an eye-level view, as if they were underwater with the swimmers, but at the same time, their small size limited the amount of actual swimming that could be done in them. Ornamental swimming became the primary focus since many of the stunts could be performed stationary. Performers supplemented their acts with a variety of entertaining underwater parlor tricks, like eating and drinking while submerged and retrieving gold coins from the tank floor with their mouths.

Versions of the "tank act" had been around since the 1860s, when a man using the stage name Natator, or the "human frog," entertained audiences at London's Cremorne Gardens. Naturalist Francis T. Buckland in his book *Curiosities of Natural History* documented Natator's performance, which included sitting "tailor fashion" on his tank floor while blinking and grinning at the audience through the plate glass, eating a sponge cake, and drinking a "halfpenny worth of milk." After smoking a lit pipe underwater, and turning up to twenty-four somersaults in a row, Natator's grand finale was a subaqueous song and dance number to "Froggy Would a Wooing Go." Audiences were convinced he could hear the piano onstage because the bubbles rising from his mouth kept beat with the music.[3] Professor Beckwith, two years later, toyed with a similar idea, performing at Cremorne with his then teenaged son Willie and an assistant as the "Beckwith Frogs." However, these acts didn't really take off until a decade or two later, when the swimming professors and their families were pushed out of competitions and teaching and toward more commercial opportunities. By that point, women had become part of the family swimming acts, and it quickly became apparent that the biggest crowd pleasers were not the underwater pipe-smokers, natators, or frog-men, but rather their "mermaid" sisters.

A review of a tank performance by Agnes and her younger sister Nellie at Canterbury Theatre noted that the audience was fixed on the pair's every move. Agnes drank a bottle of milk, wrote on a slate, and picked up shells, but it was the cleverness of her underwater swimming maneuvers that prompted a reviewer to exclaim that she must have had gymnastic training.[4] Brother-sister duos were popular as well, with one of the most well known being Professor James Finney and his sister Marie—the latter of whom made a name for herself as the first woman to dive from London Bridge. The Finneys performed individual ornamental stunts and a variety of tandem maneuvers like gliding over and under each other using only their arms, which they held close to their sides like fins, for propulsion and their crossed legs to steer their direction. Reviewers wrote they surely had learned this move by watching fish. One of their biggest crowd pleasers was an underwater game of Euchre the Finneys played using a set of oversized porcelain playing cards they had custom made for their act.[5] Swimming alongside brothers or under the chaperonage of a swimming professor, whether a father or family friend, gave the performances of these early female natationists "social sanctioning," and advertisements for female performers always made these connections clear.[6] One typical show announcement stated: "Miss Beckwith, as is well known, comes from a swimming family of the highest order, both for duration and ornamental feats of natation."[7]

The portability of the tanks made swimming acts widely popular among proprietors of a wide range of entertainment venues. At seaside towns, where commercial amusements were concentrated to meet the seasonal swells in demand, they could even be set up inside kiosks on promenades and piers. Charles Dodgson, better known by his pen name, Lewis Carroll, under which he authored *Alice in Wonderland*, was an avid connoisseur of female tank shows, particularly during his holidays at the coast. He recorded in his diary four different trips to see the "marvelous underwater performances" of Miss Louey Webb, who performed under the aegis of Professor Reddish on the West Pier in Brighton. Dodgson wrote: "She did some sewing, writing on a slate, etc. under water: sometimes being under nearly a minute . . . Miss Webb is 18, and, as she is beautifully formed, the exhibition is worth seeing if only as a picture."[8] An avid people-watcher with a known proclivity for young girls, Dodgson noted in his journals at least seven additional visits he paid to similar swimming shows over the years. These included those of the various Beckwith daughters and of "Lurline the Water Queen," a Bostonian who was making waves on both sides of the pond.

Although these acts originated in England, which was far ahead of America in terms of swimming skills and interest, transatlantic travel was becoming faster and more comfortable. This enabled performers to move between the entertainment circuits of England, America, and the European continent. As early as the late 1860s, a few of Britain's enterprising male swimmers took their tank acts abroad, performing as "man-fish" in American circuses and helping aquatic entertainments catch on in the United States. In 1883, Agnes and Willie Beckwith traveled to the States for the first time to perform at several New York venues, including the Natatorium on East 45th Street, where they were able to do more actual swimming than they could in their six-foot tank.

A reporter for the *New York Times* noted that Willie stayed underwater an impressively long time during his eating and drinking act but spent much of the article on Agnes's performance, which he found to be more interesting. In addition to her usual hoop swimming, underwater undressing, and various propulsions, she imitated a propeller, "walked in the water" with her hands above her head, "waltzed in the aqueous fluid," and demonstrated stunts called "the Christian martyr" and "the prayer." The latter, joked the reporter, would be useful if caught in a steamboat collision "as it gives one an opportunity to pray for help while he or she paddles shoreward."⁹ (Incidentally, the same move would be included in the first synchronized swimming manual as "the mermaid's prayer.") It seems that Agnes's ornamental swimming had widespread ripples, as a newspaper reported shortly after that she had introduced "a fancy movement in the water to waltz music" that was being practiced by a group of high-society ladies at a private natatorium nearly halfway across the country in Chicago.¹⁰

VERITABLE MERMAIDS

Performing physical feats in public, especially while wearing form-fitting attire, was not generally seen as a respectable career for women in the Victorian era. Nevertheless, the natationists enjoyed widespread public approval—and increasingly for reasons that had less to do with their family connections and more to do with their actual swimming. Even though scientific swimming had only a few years earlier been strictly a masculine pursuit, it was increasingly being described in terms suggesting gracefulness and beauty—attributes seen as more fitting for women than speed, strength, or endurance. In an article about Agnes Beckwith, *Hearth and Home* magazine wrote, "People talk of the grace of skirt dancing . . . but surely the true poetry of motion is exemplified in the movements of the ornamental swimmer."¹¹ This style of swimming took great skill, but the natationists performed their ornamental feats with such mastery they made it look easy. Reviewers often noted that a performer wore "an expression of perfect content" or that she looked refreshed after an exhibition, as though she could have continued for hours.¹² This view of ornamental swimming as an activity that was not only graceful and feminine but also a physically moderate activity made it more widely acceptable than other forms of athletic performance for women. Endurance walking, for example, was a popular spectator sport, and its female practitioners (called pedestriennes) would walk around tracks as audiences watched and placed wagers. Although these women came from similar working-class backgrounds, the performances of the pedestriennes, who demonstrated more overt physical exertion as they trudged around in long heavy skirts for hours at a time, were thought of by genteel Victorians as "grotesque," while natationists, who twirled around glistening tanks in leotards, silk tights, and pearls, offered a "more acceptable and reassuring vision of femininity" and were thus embraced.[13]

Certainly, the natationists' costumes were part of the appeal for some audience members who enjoyed seeing young, well-conditioned women in form-fitting attire. Descriptions of Agnes Beckwith's "flesh tights" and "decollete bodice" hint at the sexual allure and titillation these shows offered. Similar costumes on other stage performers could cast the wearers in a negative light, but for the natationists it was understood that they could not perform their feats in the heavy, cumbersome dress and bloomer ensembles women were supposed to wear elsewhere in public waters. Moreover, the language used to describe these swimmers may have given them some leeway in their dress. Historians of the stage have noted that when scantily clad performers were associated with the allegorical or symbolic trappings of exoticism, divinity, or heroism, they were elevated to a higher moral plane that made their revealing dress acceptable, much as the nude in classical art—which served as an ideal representation of beauty—was elevated above mere nakedness.[14] As natationists were often referred to as nymphs, naiads, undines, and "veritable mermaids," this gave them an otherworldly patina that set them apart from the requirements of mortal women.[15]

The connections that the early natationists established between femininity, performance, and swimming would not only create a decades-long demand for female swimming entertainers but also enabled women to reclaim their rightful place in the water as they inspired more and more women to learn to swim. It wasn't just their graceful moves that were inspiring, but their bold and daring feats in the water as well. When Agnes Beckwith swam with her hands and feet bound with ropes at one show, a newspaper reported, "there is not a woman in the vast house who breathes, so great is the suspense."[16] The natationists' shows helped educate the larger public about swimming. Their shows, even at commercial venues, often included demonstrations of different strokes and lifesaving techniques while a narrator would explain their movements. Agnes would show audiences how to save a drowning person by "rescuing" her brother Willie, often getting laughs by dunking him along the way or pulling her victim by the ears.[17] One man credited having seen Agnes's demonstration with enabling him to save the life of a woman who had thrown herself into a river. Several of the natation-ists had themselves saved lives—including Agnes, who plunged, fully dressed, into the water at Margate to save a drowning woman. "What a daring thing for a woman to do!" exclaimed a magazine, pointing out the drag that her long skirts would have caused in the water.[18]

When 640 people died in the wrecking of the steamship *Princess Alice* in 1878, Agnes was held up as a model in newspaper articles encouraging readers to become "versed in swimming." *The Graphic* added that readers need not be able to swim heroic distances like Captain Webb or become a skilled "show-swimmer" like Agnes Beckwith in order to improve their chances in the water, as "much more humble achievements would have sufficed to save scores of lives."[19] Similar calls for women in the United States to learn to swim wouldn't come until the next century, following America's own horrific steamship tragedy.

By 1887, Agnes and Willie Beckwith had become so well known that they were recruited, reportedly at huge expense, by America's greatest showman, Phineas T. Barnum, to perform as "Aphrodite and Leander of the Waves." Before seven thousand spectators gathered for P. T. Barnum's Greatest Show on Earth at Madison Square Garden, Agnes strolled onto an elevated platform wearing a long, golden robe. As a hush came over the crowd, she handed her robe to a waiting attendant, revealing her neck-to-foot white stockinette costume and what one writer described as the most "graceful muscular develop-ment" any daughter of Eve ever attained.[20] Once in the water, the program stated, she "darts, dives, flashes and disappears like a truant mermaid, and with hands and feet tied, floats like a swan."[21]

By this point, the Beckwith name had become so well known that enterprising swimming entertainers tried to appropriate it—particularly in America, where there was less chance of the falsehood being discovered. Shortly after Agnes performed with P. T. Barnum, ads began appearing across the United States for swimming perfor-mances by a Clara Beckwith and a Cora Beckwith, neither of whom was an actual Beckwith—nor even British for that matter.[22] The for-mer, born Clara Sabean, was from Nova Scotia, where she spent her childhood splashing in the local river when she wasn't begging or help-ing her family sell foraged mushrooms. Clara adopted Beckwith as her stage name, and began using it in real life as well, even publishing a

Clara "Beckwith" performing her tank act, as illustrated in her 1893 book Learn How to Swim: Pointers about Swimming and Aquatics.

short memoir in which she claimed to have been born in Lambeth, England—likely confusing the name of Lambeth Baths in London, where Professor Beckwith taught, with the name of his hometown. As for Cora "Beckwith," she was actually a McFarland from Maine, though ads for her shows called her the daughter of a famous professor of swimming in England.[23]

Likely, the Beckwith impersonators were looking for ways to set themselves apart in an increasingly crowded field, as female swimmers were becoming popular entertainers in America as well. Women natationists in England emerged from Britain's thriving and respected swimming communities, eventually making their own way independent of a family name. But in America, where there was not yet a culture of swimming, aquatic artists were born purely from the hardscrabble world of show business—and they were forming their own unique brand of entertainments.

LURLINE AND THE AMERICAN WATER QUEENS

Back in 1875, when Agnes Beckwith was just fourteen and preparing for her first history-making swim of the Thames, a young woman from

Boston named Sallie Swift was preparing for a similarly transformative aquatic debut—one that would make her America's first woman swimmer of the stage. Swift had for several years been performing with Madame Rentz's traveling burlesque show, but on November 8, 1875, she would slip into her crystal tank at Tony Pastor's new family-friendly Olympic Theater, transformed from a "female Hercules" who picked a banjo and juggled wooden clubs in front of rowdy male audiences into "Lurline the Water Queen," who would glide and dart through shimmering water before fashionable audiences.

Swift's personal metamorphosis was both indicative of, and enabled by, larger transformations happening in American society and its burgeoning entertainment industry. During the Civil War, concert saloons had popped up wherever soldiers with a few dollars to burn were stationed, creating a market for cheap entertainment that targeted male audiences and appealed to popular rather than refined tastes. The demand for entertainment—further fueled by rapid industrialization, mass immigration, and urban growth—continued after the war. These changes gave rise to a proliferation of traveling performance groups like Madame Rentz's, formed in 1870, a year after

*Portrait of Sallie Swift in swimming
costume for her Lurline act.*

America's first transcontinental railroad was completed. The Rentz show combined minstrelsy and female acts like Swift's with large burlesque and cancan dance numbers, which were all the rage in New York, and sold the package to men in rural towns across the country as big-city entertainment.

These types of "variety" shows—so called because they were comprised of a variety of unrelated acts—were extremely popular among certain groups of men, but polite audiences and patrons of the "legitimate" theater considered them vulgar and their working-class audiences unsophisticated. And as variety theaters offering these styles of entertainment maintained earlier associations with seedy concert saloons and male drunkenness, they were not a place any gentleman would take his wife or daughter. A review of Madame Rentz's show described men of all ages pouring into a Savannah, Georgia, playhouse until even standing room was at a premium. Throughout the show, which, the reviewer noted, was not designed to "elevate the taste or improve the morals," the men stamped their feet and hooted at every "extra display of comely limbs."[24]

But Sallie Swift, who night after night "brought down the house with her wonderful exhibitions of strength and grace," was destined for greater things. In addition to possessing talent and showmanship beyond her station, she was described as a "modest and comely" young woman with a body "cast in a mould that Venus de Medici might have been proud of."[25] Plus, Swift had a skill even more rare among women than juggling or playing the banjo: she knew how to swim.

Swift's big break would come via Tony Pastor, a showman who got his start as a child performer at P. T. Barnum's American Museum, worked his way up the ranks to theater management, and was now one of a handful of men in variety who were trying to clean up the industry. As the manager of a theater in New York's notoriously rough Bowery district, Pastor had looked out at the audience one night and was suddenly struck by the glaringly obvious—there were no women![26] He and every other variety theater manager were missing out on half of the potential ticket-buying public. Pastor believed that if he could make variety theater respectable, he would not only bring in the women but with them a higher-status clientele willing to pay more for quality entertainment.[27] Pastor banned obscene language from his theater, offered giveaways of hats and fabric to entice lady patrons and early matinees so that they could come on their own or bring their children, and began advertising his Opera House as "The Great Family Resort of the City."[28]

In rebranding popular entertainment as "safe" for women and middle-class audiences, Pastor knew he had to be careful not to lose the male crowd. But a new all-female entertainment troupe, Lydia Thompson's British Blondes, that was taking New York by storm had shown that it could be done—and how. Like other burlesque shows, Thompson's displayed plenty of "leg," but it did so through clever and saucy satire that poked fun at Victorian conservatism. Women of the middle and upper classes flocked to see these transgressive members of their own sex perform at New York's top theaters, while their husbands happily tagged along to enjoy the view, if not the humor. To Pastor and other theater managers looking to expand to the middle class, the popularity of Thompson's show demonstrated that these audiences didn't mind a bit of raciness, so long as it was presented in a chic, rather than tawdry, way—a balancing act that became the hallmark of America's most successful showmen for years to come.[29]

Pastor, who had a male swimmer on his roster, could see what a perfect fit a women's swimming act would be in this new paradigm— one that would combine elements of female agency and athleticism with titillating costumes. Harry Gurr, an expat British swimming champion known as the "pocket Hercules" for his diminutive but muscular stature, had come to America in the 1860s with the Hanlon Brothers Circus. Gurr was said to be able to do anything he wanted in the water except sleep and was hired away in short order by Tony Pastor to perform a "man-fish" act in a glass tank, which he'd been doing with Pastor's traveling troupe ever since. With Pastor seeking to debut the first such act featuring a woman, Gurr recruited the beautiful juggling banjoist Sallie Swift, who was said to have had "a partiality for natation from her babyhood," and set about teaching her the tank trade.[30]

In October 1875, an ad in the *New York Clipper* announced a "new wonder" coming soon to the Olympic Theatre on Broadway: "Lurline The Water Queen, The Only Female Aquatic Performer Or Lady Fish In The World."[31] It was a clever stage name, not only because of the lilting rhyme but also because "Lurline" was the name of a siren of the Rhine River in German folklore. Sharing her tank, noted the announcement, would be the "amphibious wonder, Watson the Man-Fish," though his full name was not given. Their act was billed as appropriate for ladies and children.

When the aquatic duo stepped onto the stage at the Olympic a few weeks later, Swift removed her robe and climbed the ladder fixed to one end of the tank. Considered tall at 5'7", she appeared every bit the queen of the water in her flesh-colored tights and leotard covered in silver spangles that shimmered like an armor of fish scales.[32] The clear water was illuminated by a light in the tank so that even her smallest movement could be observed and appreciated. Swift turned somer-saults and contorted her body, like a true mermaid, into captivating poses, all the while smiling and looking straight into the audience with wide-open eyes and her dark hair floating loosely around her face. She was joined by Watson for an underwater picnic of apples and cakes, followed by a relaxing post-dinner smoke. As a finale, they fixed a chair to the tank floor and swam deftly over and under each other, weaving in and out of the chair's rungs with the "utmost precision."[33] Their show was proclaimed an "unqualified success," with the *New York Dispatch* noting, "In our lengthy experience we have witnessed nothing to equal the feats performed under-water by Lurline and Wat-son."[34] By spring, they were touring with Tony Pastor's traveling troupe and performing at upscale variety theaters across the country, from Brooklyn's Academy of Music and the Howard Athenaeum in Boston to the Metropolitan Theatre in Sacramento—and many in between.

Reviewers marveled at Lurline's endurance, grace, and "utmost self-possession" in the foreign element. One wrote, "Should Old Nep-tune himself come among us, he could display no more grace and ease under the water than Lurline the Water Queen."[35] While Watson was no doubt very good at his job, what caught everyone's attention was clearly the novelty of a woman performing these difficult feats, with one newspaper declaring: "Standing room only at the Olympic, and *the attraction is Lurline*."[36] There were other man-fish acts, after all, but Lurline was "the only woman fish." Within a few weeks, "LURLINE THE WATER QUEEN" had become the all-caps headliner, with Watson listed as her assistant—when he was mentioned at all.[37]

Appearing alongside a male stage partner gave female variety per-formers more respectability, but in return they usually had to take a back seat and let the man control the content of their act and take the larger share of the profits. Yet in the case of Swift and Watson, ads announcing their opening show boasted that she had been engaged at the considerable expense of $100 for each of her eight weekly perfor-mances, while there was no mention of how much Watson was being paid.[38] Perhaps unsurprisingly, in October 1876, less than a year after their debut, the *New York Clipper* announced Lurline had separated from her partner Watson.[39] Much like the natationists who got their entry and respectability from men but then quickly outgrew them, Swift would be just fine on her own.

Swift was appearing as Lurline for packed audiences all over the country, her popularity seemingly based not so much on what she did in the tank but on *how* she did it—as an "artiste." For her apple trick, she would peel the fruit with "amusing deliberation," then offer a piece to one of the passing goldfish who swam with her in the tank. She would write phrases on a slate while underwater, then turn and show them to the audience. For her chair finale, always an audience favorite, Swift wound through the chair rails, with, in the words of one newspaper, "astonishing ease . . . refreshing indifference, agility and *sang froid*."[40]

Swift could also hold her breath for what seemed like super-human amounts of time, with an ad for her show with Tony Pas-tor proclaiming, "Three Minutes And Four Seconds Under Water. Lurline The Water Queen."[41] Her shows always included a demon-stration of her "power of prolonged immersion," but even this part of her act incorporated a strong sense of dramatic flair: she would spend a few minutes breathing deeply, then sink to the bottom of the tank and, with eyes closed, remain perfectly motionless.[42] Outside the tank, a gong clanged every thirty seconds she was submerged. The following account written by an audience mem-ber demonstrates the building suspense, particularly after the two-minute gong had sounded:

Ten, fifteen, twenty seconds, ticked slowly away—I never knew them so slow in passing—and still no movement. Her face had lost its colour, for all the vessels were filled with dark venous blood, the muscles had become rigid, and the constrained expression of her features was painful to behold; still she remained unmoved. I felt an arrest of my own respiration, and my heart bumped audibly—to myself, at least—against my ribs; when, after the hands had passed the half minute, the eyes opened, the teeth became visible, and Lurline rose slowly to the surface after 2 minutes and 40 seconds submersion.[43]

Another review summed it up: "This phenomenal lady has actually confounded the public by her unprecedented performance."[44] With skills that very few swimmers could match today, Swift's aquatic abilities would have been astounding to audiences in 1870s America, where swimming for both sexes, but especially women, was practically non-existent. Unlike in England, with its plentiful swimming baths, many of which had begun to open to female patrons, American women had very few places to bathe, let alone swim. England's century-long passion for sea-bathing had long since trickled down to its masses, but in the United States, visits to the seaside did not begin to gain widespread popularity until after the Civil War. Chas Weightman, a friend of Gurr's who had also immigrated from England with a man-fish act, wrote in reference to the US that "swimming baths for ladies are not yet among the institutions of our free, happy and refined country." As a result, the swimming skills of American ladies were far behind those of their continental cousins.[45] There were a few floating baths in eastern cities as early as the 1860s, and although they were primarily intended as bathing places for the urban poor, a few offered swimming lessons or the opportunity to practice. Boston, Swift's hometown, was among the earliest cities to offer floating baths, which may have been where she developed her swimming skills prior to learning the nuances of the tank, as later articles would claim that Swift had spent her childhood lolling about underwater at Boston's beaches.[46]

Despite the dearth of female swimmers, Swift's show had proven so successful that theater managers were determined to find—or make—their own water queens. Only a month after her debut as Lurline at the Olympic, the *Brooklyn Daily Eagle* announced that the theater was offering a reward of $5,000, an astronomical sum at the time, to "any lady who can accomplish Lurline's feats under water."[47] The Great New York Aquarium—built in 1876 in the grand style and with the same unrealized, high-minded goals as England's Victorian aquariums—even opened its tanks as a training ground for young women interested in developing an underwater act. Within a year of the aquarium's opening, they were offering a show featuring Captain Quigly, who would don a deep-sea diving suit and perform underwater carpentry tasks, and Miss Vivienne Lubin, a "very comely 'water nymph,'" who ate, drank, and pretended to sleep.[48] Although Vivienne only stayed at the New York Aquarium about three weeks, moving on to become "Vivienne Lubin the Water Queen" with a traveling circus, the aquarium offered similar shows for several years, often referring to the unnamed female performers simply as the "water queen."

Swift may have sensed the encroaching competition—as she posted a notice in the *New York Clipper* claiming to have copyrighted, at threat of prosecution, the titles "Lurline, the Water Queen, At Home in the Water, and Woman Fish."[49] Perhaps she wanted to remain a big

Advertisement for the grand opening of the Great New York Aquarium.

fish in a small pond, or maybe she was simply ready for her next adventure, but in July 1877, Swift joined the international circuit of traveling performers, setting sail for Spain, where she was to appear at theaters in Madrid and Barcelona. Spanish papers called her act "an entirely new spectacle" and noted that she was showered with applause and repeatedly called back onstage for an encore.⁵⁰ Invitations poured in from cities across Europe, and Swift's two-month engagement stretched into a decade abroad. Her fame grew along with her mileage, with one newspaper writing that Lurline—as she was referred to in European papers rather than by her real name—had "created the greatest sensation in most of the cities of America and the Continent . . . Paris, Madrid, Lisbon, Vienna, Berlin, Hungary, and St. Petersburg."⁵¹

With success came improved stage equipment, including a tank that stretched an impressive 14 feet long by 5 feet wide and was filled with a steady supply of colorful fish. The tank was brilliantly illuminated—by oxyhydrogen lights at first and then with incandescent electric lamps by the early 1880s—and the play of the light on the water, combined with the movement of the fish, was described as "magical" and "poetic." Her success and elegant appointments also drew more select audiences to her shows. In Portugal, Swift spent several months in Oporto, where members of the royal family were regular patrons of her show and even invited Swift to pay a visit at the palace.

While Lurline was in Germany, newspapers announced that, for a full year, her portrait had been one of the top-selling photographs in

Broadside of Lurline the Water Queen in her tank at the Circo Price in Portugal.

Berlin—a sign of her growing fame.[52] Portraiture was popular in the Victorian era, and the likenesses of well-known figures and performers could be purchased as cabinet cards, small inexpensive photographs mounted on cardstock. Studios would announce in the newspapers when anyone well known was coming in for a sitting, such as an announcement in the *Chicago Tribune* just a year after Swift launched her aquatic act that "Lurline the Water Queen" was one of several celebrities photographed recently at Gentiles, the Italian photography studio on State Street.[53] When Swift was in Paris in the early 1880s, she took a session at the prestigious Nadar studio, which photographed all the notable stage personalities who passed through the city and was known for its use of artistic trompe l'oeil backgrounds—of fish and sea vegetation in the case of Lurline—to depict the performers in action.

While these images serve as good measures of Swift's popularity, perhaps the best endorsement for her athletic talents and skill as a performer came from the positive reviews she received in England, where she made her British debut as Lurline at the Oxford Musical Hall on Boxing Day 1882. Even as a stranger to a country with such a strong swimming community, Swift received "marked approval from very critical and experienced audiences," wrote "Aquarius," the pen name used by sports journalist Robert Watson. After having seen Lurline's show in its entirety, Aquarius concluded that "no better under-water performance has ever been seen in England."[54]

British audiences were so abuzz at the durations of time Swift spent underwater that Hunter Barron, the Honorable Secretary of the Swimming Association of Great Britain, showed up at the Oxford with his stopwatch to make an official recording. He reported, with astonishment, that Swift remained underwater holding her breath for 2 minutes, 51¼ seconds, the longest for any woman and second only to Professor Peter Johnson, who was said to have exceeded 4 minutes. Additionally, Barron timed each of Swift's underwater segments, reporting that she remained submerged for 1 minute and 12 seconds to peel and eat an apple and spent similar lengths of time underwater on her other tricks.[55] Barron was so intrigued by Swift's abilities that he invited her to his office to breathe into a Lowne's spirometer. He found Swift's lung capacity to be 200 cubic inches, nearly double the average for a young, uncorseted woman.[56] Even so, he wrote that Swift's capacity was probably even higher on a good day since she was suffering from a cough and her chest expansion was impeded by a heavy fur coat when he made his measurements. Barron concluded his report by assuring readers that not only was Lurline's performance "remarkable for its elegance and interest," but it was also "thoroughly genuine."[57]

DIME MUSEUM QUEENS

In Swift's long absence, an entire cottage industry of water queens developed across America, though they performed not in elegant theaters for royalty, as Swift was doing in Europe, but as novelty acts at dime museums, which became popular after the launch of P. T. Barnum's American Museum featuring "live exhibits" like the conjoined twins Chang and Eng. Dime museums offered hodgepodge collections of oddities and relics plus curio hall "freak shows" and performances by "lowbrow" entertainers like contortionists, magicians, sword swallowers, and bearded ladies. By the 1880s, most dime museums had a steady stream of water queens passing through, like "Josephine the Water Queen," and "Evaleen the Water Queen," who was said to provide "a pleasing change from the long array of human monstrosities who have disported about the curio hall" at the Wonderland Museum in Hartford. At Middleton's Dime Museum in Cincinnati, Evaleen's show attracted enormous crowds, with one newspaper reporting: "When she leaps into the tank, sinks gracefully beneath the surface, reclines upon the bottom . . . murmurs of delight and admiration are heard on all sides."[58]

Although most performers adopted "water queen" as part of their stage name, Cora (McFarland) Beckwith preferred to go simply by her adopted one. Her show at the Palace Museum in Minneapolis included a "score of water nymphs" who gave an "altogether charming exhibition of the science of natation" and performed a comic sketch in which they pretended to save Cora from drowning.[59] Perhaps for the Clarke Street Dime Museum in Chicago, where Cora performed at the same time as Harry Houdini, her ornamental swimming act, which did not involve eating sponge cakes or smoking underwater, wasn't seen as eccentric or "freakish" enough for the curio hall, because ads show that it was rebranded as Cora Beckwith with her "funny school of fat girl bathers."[60]

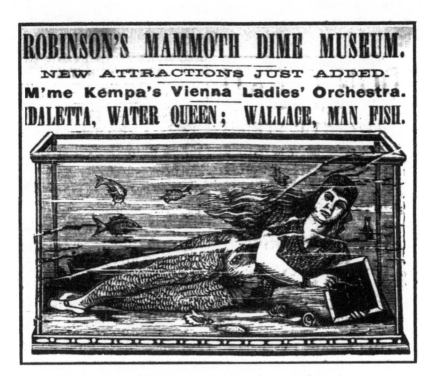

Newspaper ad for a water queen show at Robinson's Mammoth Dime Museum in New Orleans.

The life of a dime museum water queen was far from glamorous. In an 1881 article titled "The Water Queen's Story," an unnamed museum performer, likely La Selle the Water Queen, shed light on some of the unique workplace challenges and hazards that came with the job.[61] Interestingly, one of the biggest dangers was the threat of drowning in plain sight. Because of the popularity of Lurline's breath-holding act, demonstrations of prolonged immersion became a requisite part of any water queen show, despite the danger and extreme discomfort they posed to performers. The water queen described how, after about a minute and a half submerged, one's head feels "swelled to busting," followed by a roaring in the ears and blurred vision. One time, she reportedly held her breath so long a pleasant drowsiness settled over her and the idea of death by drowning became suddenly "delightful." This phenomenon, now known as shallow-water drowning, or hypoxic blackout, can be fatal and has been experienced by many aquatic performers, including Esther Williams and even present-day elite synchronized swimmers. Even so, a review of one of La Selle's shows noted with disappointment that she remained submerged "only" two minutes and change.[62]

The tanks themselves could pose hazards. While much was made of the beautiful electric illumination of Lurline's tank, many of the dime museum tanks were still using gas combustion lighting, with one performer describing the jets of gas blasting above the surface of the water as "tongues of flame" threatening to singe her hair every time she emerged for a breath.[63] Additionally, with the tanks being made of plate glass, they sometimes shattered with performers inside, as happened to Chas Weightman when a spooked horse kicked his tank during his man-fish act. His tank burst almost instantly, spitting Weightman out across the shards.[64]

Yet despite the hazards, audiences were sometimes reluctant to believe that the performers were really underwater. The world of dime museums was, after all, full of hucksters and fakers, and trick tanks with water running between double glass panes had been used on occasion for the display of "living mermaids." Moreover, for audiences with limited swimming experience, the skills required for the water queens' feats were impossible to imagine. One performer said that she did her act with her hair loose and flowing, instead of in a braid, so that it would float around her face and show the "skeptical public" that she really was submerged.[65] Perhaps this need to prove the "realness" of the water was why Swift had introduced darting fish into her tank.

Performing in a dime museum was exhausting work, with curio hall performers having to repeat their acts between twelve and twenty times over the course of the day and late into the night. For water queens like Evaleen, whose tank of sparkling water at a museum in Cincinnati was said to be "constantly surrounded by curious, expectant people," days were spent in perpetual dampness.[66] And the pay among museum performers varied wildly: "Freaks," who offered something rare and brought in the most customers, could make up to $200 per week, while the best-paid performers of physical acts made $25 to $35 a week—significantly more than the $12 to $15 salary of a skilled workman—but it often ran much lower.[67] Swift, on the other hand, had been so well remunerated for her Lurline act that newspapers reported upon her return to America in 1886—by which point she had performed as far away as Japan, Australia, and India—that she was worth $50,000, a tremendous fortune for anyone at the time, but especially for a woman.[68]

But even though Swift had reached huge fame abroad, it seems that in her decades-long absence, American audiences had moved on, or maybe she had helped popularize the water queen idea so much that the market was saturated. In 1886, an announcement was posted in the papers that Lurline the Water Queen would be opening at Tony Pastor's theater, but there are no further mentions of Lurline in the entertainment pages.[69] Six years later, Swift was suddenly in the news again—this time not for her act but for a sensational, headline-grabbing public altercation with Eugene Sandow, the father of modern bodybuilding. According to newspaper accounts, Swift met Sandow in Europe when he was a lowly circus performer and loaned him money to start a strongman act, which eventually propelled him to international fame. Years later, when Swift asked him to repay the money, Sandow claimed not only that he already had, but that it was Swift's "lover" who loaned it to him in the first place. Taking the mention of a lover as slander to her good name, Swift showed up—wielding a horsewhip—outside of a casino in New York where Sandow was performing.[70] When he brushed her aside, Swift struck the huge man, threatening to expose him as a cheat. Headlines like "Lurline the Water Queen Horsewhips Sandow the Magnificent" were splashed across newspapers, with some painting Lurline as an opportunist or calling her a "dime museum freak."[71] The world wasn't necessarily a kind place to has-been water queens. Swift again dropped out of the public eye until April 1898, when the headline "Death of a Water Queen" was printed in newspapers around the world. One read:

> "Lurline, the water queen," who has just died in London was the sensation of three continents ten years ago, at which time she had $50,000, every cent of which was made on the exhibition stage. Lurline was a Boston girl, and her real name was Sallie Swift.[72]

Articles noted that Swift had once performed before crowned heads of state and had been the "idol of theatre-goers of three continents," but added that she had lost her fortune in her final years and died penniless in a "dingy Bloomsbury lodging." Some conjectured that her untimely death at age forty-five was due to addiction to morphine or drink, while others blamed her reduced circumstances on unscrupulous associates.[73] Another more kindly suggested that the loss of Swift's fortune was due to the "generosity which had always been her characteristic when she was prosperous."[74]

Although her name has long been forgotten, Sallie Swift was a trailblazer who demonstrated female athleticism in the water long before the idea of a woman swimmer had even crossed the minds of most Americans. Unlike the British natationists, she was not part of a swimming community and didn't enjoy the safety of family respectability, yet she still managed to navigate her own way against the current and create a life for herself beyond the confines of her era. In doing so, she made her mark in the world and on her generation, and created a path for others to follow.

TROUPES OF FAIRE ARTISTES

By the last decade of the nineteenth century, audiences were hungry for more sensational aquatic entertainments put on by ever larger groups of swimmers, and the venues that hosted such shows evolved accordingly. In these new, more spectacular aquatic productions, the stars of the water were not just individual women but entire troupes of female natationists.

In Blackpool, the Coney Island of England, where investors were pouring money into luxurious, purpose-built amusement complexes, a replica of the Eiffel Tower opened just off the main promenade in the spring of 1894. The new Blackpool Tower was the tallest man-made structure in the British Empire, reaching 518 feet, and although that was only about half the height of the original, it featured something the Parisian tower did not: the Blackpool Tower Aquatic Circus. The circus structure, which sat in the basement between the tower's four legs, featured a center ring that could be hydraulically lowered and filled with water—42,000 gallons, which would gush up through perforated floorboards in less than a minute—so that equestrian circus acts could be followed immediately by a grand aquatic spectacle under the same roof.[75] The water would flow beyond the original bounds of the circus ring, filling the area beneath the spectators' seats; this enabled the swimming cast—who would enter the water out of sight of the audience—to make a surprise entrance by swimming underwater and suddenly surfacing in the center. The first part of the show included performances of ornamental swimming by the famous Professor Johnson and his daughters, and James and Marie Finney—the latter of whom also performed a dive from a height of 60 feet into the tank. Following an intermission, several of the Finney women, along with other female swimmers, put on "the most magnificent Water Pantomime" called "Undine, or The Water Fairies Ballet."[76] Marie and the Johnson sisters were so integral to the success of the circus's first season that they were presented with diamond brooches and gold bracelets.[77]

The Blackpool Tower Aquatic Circus was modeled directly after the Nouveau Cirque, which had been built in Paris a few years earlier by the creator of the famed Moulin Rouge cabaret, Joseph Oller. The idea was so novel and successful that soon similar circuses were being built across Europe and England, and even all the way in Chicago,

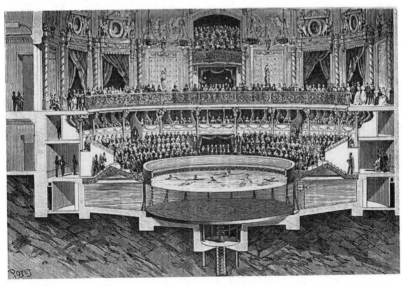

*A rendering of the cross section of the Nouveau
Cirque's water basin by Louis Poyet.*

where the showman Frank Hall built his English Circus and German Water Carnival using similar flooding technology and hired one of the Beckwith impersonators, Cora, as a performer.[78]

In 1893, Captain Paul Boynton, the one who had floated across the English Channel in his inflatable suit, excavated an arena to create a 400-foot-long oval lake to host the World's Water Show at Earl's Court. It was a true water extravaganza, including boat rides through grotto caves and the world's first water ride, a 275-foot chute that shot flat-bottomed boats halfway across the lake at the "speed of an express train," drenching its passengers (Boynton would improve upon and export his invention as the Shoot the Chutes ride to amusement parks at Coney Island and elsewhere in America).[79] The water, which was illuminated with a dozen huge electric lights "equal to 120,000 candle power," was filled with every kind of aquatic performer imaginable: water walkers who strolled on the surface in pneumatic shoes, people floating in rubber suits like Boynton had worn on the English Channel, water bicyclists, canoe racers, and even a mock naval battle between ships. But the star performer in Boynton's show was Agnes Beckwith, who appeared as "Queen of the Waves" supported by an entire cast of English and American female swimmers. Agnes had by this point been headlining her own troupe of "faire artistes"—who were said to be "the acme of refinement, grace, and talent"—and had reached such a level of celebrity that the weight of her name alone was enough to attract large audiences, even as she and her troupe performed in ever larger and higher-profile events.[80] In fact, many of the top women natationists were now traveling in their own troupes, independent of male family members.

Much credit was given by the media to these female troupes for raising interest in women's swimming; *The Era* wrote in 1899 that Agnes Beckwith's swimmers had popularized the art of swimming through their "graceful and very expert" performances, inspiring many to study natation.[81] Moreover, through their unconventional careers, these performers were expanding the public sphere—and even the idea of having an expertise to offer—to more women. "Everybody knows that Miss Beckwith, acting the sometimes thankless role of pioneer, is largely responsible for the present vogue of swimming among her sex," wrote the *London Daily News* in 1903. "Before her time the idea of the lady expert was laughed to scorn, but since Miss Beckwith started upon her career public opinion has changed."[82]

Not only had these aquatic role models helped swimming become an acceptable activity for their sex, but they had also demonstrated levels of physical strength and skill that challenged what Victorian society and the medical community held to be true about women's physical capabilities. A long article in Chicago's *Inter Ocean* newspaper in 1883 on trends in swimming noted, "Perhaps in no way is man's endurance, and woman's too, better exhibited than in their power to remain entirely underwater." As examples, the article lists the records of water queens Lurline and La Salle: 2 minutes and 51 seconds at the Oxford Music Hall for the former, and 3 minutes and 46 seconds at Continental Hall in Paterson, New Jersey, for the latter. Agnes Beckwith, "the champion female swimmer of the world," was included in the list of "big swimmers," with details of her exploits on the Thames and in the Royal Aquarium. The uninitiated, wrote the author, would be astonished to hear what "the accomplished swimmer, the variety artist of the wave" can do.[83]

Women of the nineteenth century had few, if any, arenas where they could exhibit their strength and physical ability without social repercussions—let alone demonstrate abilities that rivaled men's—but the water was fast on its way to becoming that place. Even with the scant few records we have of the actual words of professional female swimmers of the era, there is evidence that this was important to them. Agnes Beckwith on multiple occasions cited her goal in her endurance swims as showing that women could do whatever men—the "so-called 'Lords of Creation'"—could do.[84] In discussing her skills in the tank, one water queen said in an interview, "I can do anything under water that a man can do, eat and drink, and one thing he can't do—I can sew."[85]

But of course, the idea of women demonstrating physical equality with men was met by many with apprehension. "Fragile woman, so often considered as a mere plaything for man," noted the *Inter Ocean* writer, "has more than once both astonished man and humiliated him by her exploits of endurance in the water." Even though the writer discussed these swimmers' accomplishments, his choice of the word "humiliated" seems telling of a sneaking discomfort at this newfound strength. When mentioning Lurline's breath-holding record, he called it "a very difficult feat for a woman considering her incapacity to keep her mouth shut above water."[86] The conflicted writer concluded his thoughts on women swimmers as follows: "For a fragile vessel, she has performed feats on the frisky wave more marvelous even than those accomplished by her male rival, and has done them far more gracefully." Although woman cannot rival man on land, he wrote, "she excels him in her grace of movement in the water, and becomes in its embrace as fair a nymph indeed as ever floated in the mythic waters of Greek mythology."[87]

Despite the growing anxieties over the ways women were changing, for the most part, the water would become and remain a safe place for them to gain and demonstrate their physical abilities. Professional swimmers of the stage had indeed challenged dominant ideas about women's capabilities, ruffling some gills in the process. But at the same time, their strength and skill, which enabled them to make their difficult feats beautiful to watch, transformed them into something other than women: they were mermaids, nymphs, queens of the water. They made swimming "pretty," and in the process they created a link in the public imagination between aquatics and femininity that would continue for generations.

CHAPTER 3

STARDOM

Those who contend that woman is too weak physically to contend with man at the voting booth . . . should go to the Lyric Theater to see Annette Kellerman in *A Daughter of the Gods*. Either she is a super-woman or women are surely entitled to rank with men in physical endurance.

—*JOURNAL OF COMMERCE,* 1918

"It's going to be a perfectly awfully informal lecture," Annette Kellerman told the thirteen hundred women who had piled into Broadway's Colonial Theatre in November 1909. Kellerman had launched a vaudeville swimming and diving act a few months earlier, and her figure had quickly become the admiration and envy of women across the country who flocked to her public talks eager to hear her secrets to beauty, health, and happiness. Her methods were so simple and commonsense, she assured the audience, that they were within reach of every "society lady or shop girl."[1] *Simply eat more fish and vegetables*, she preached, *wear sensible clothes, and most of all, get out and swim!* After all, the ocean was a better beautifier, asserted Kellerman, than "any serum produced in any million dollar laboratory, or all the beauty specialists on Fifth Avenue."[2]

Kellerman, born in 1886 in Sydney, Australia, had barely begun her stage career but was already well on her way to becoming one of the most famous women in America. Through her illustrious stage and film career, she would build a reputation as a fearless aquatic stuntwoman, a bold swimwear maverick, and a danseuse of the water who is often credited as the mother of synchronized swimming. And as the Victorian era was drawing to a close, Kellerman was precisely the type of role model that American women had been aching for. The "ideal" nineteenth-century woman had been passive, retiring, and modest, avoiding physical activity or exposure to the elements, and doctors had long warned that exercising feminine minds and bodies would sap them of the vital energy they needed for their higher reproductive callings. But all that was rapidly changing by the turn of the century, and women were taking jobs, going to college, even beginning to agitate for the vote. As this "New Woman" hiked her heavy skirts and entered squarely into more and more "male" spaces—with some even daring to bifurcate those long skirts in order to spin around town on bicycles—everyone had an opinion on how all of this would impact women of the future. One article predicted that "woman, grown big mentally, is apt to grow big physically" and develop the "physical accompaniments of a decisive manner" like a wide mouth, square jawline, and big feet.[3] But Kellerman, the beautiful Diving Venus, promised a uniquely aesthetic strength that would upend conceptions of female frailty and challenge the puritanical ideas she believed had, for far too long, held women back.

And one of the first steps, she would tell her audience, is to get rid of those danged corsets—the most ridiculous of all the evils that fashion had perpetrated against women. *You can't be brave when you can't breathe!* she would declare.[4] Women had been sold the idea that they needed corsets not only to narrow their waists but also for "support." *Pooh!* said Kellerman. *Just do some sit-ups instead!* Why should a woman be "laced up in steel," she asked, when it is so much more natural and beautiful to be "laced up by the tissues of her own well-knit muscles"?[5]

If the crowd at the Colonial Theatre that November looked at her askance, they couldn't be blamed. After all, a reporter in attendance wrote that she looked like she had been poured into her dress by "the most expert of corsetieres." But Kellerman assured them, "the only bones about me, girls, are the ones that nature gave me." Then to prove it, she pulled off her dress and was left standing on the stage in a tight stockinette bodysuit—her own unique creation for swimming. As the audience giggled and whispered in surprise, she took it a step further, grabbing hold of her swimsuit and ripping it right down the side of her waist. "See!" she exclaimed, "there's nothing underneath but me!" And with that, the curtain behind her was opened, revealing a large tank of water and a diving board which Kellerman promptly climbed onto and began her swimming exhibition, reminding the crowd that this was precisely how she attained her splendid physique. "Many a woman went away vowing to learn to swim," wrote the reporter after Kellerman's performance, "if she had to break ice to do it."[6]

THE MAKING OF A MERMAID

Even though Annette Kellerman would become the most famous and daring swimmer of her day, her first foray into the water had not come naturally—or even willingly for that matter. Unlike the natationists who learned the family trade of swimming as soon as they could walk, Kellerman was raised in a musical family by parents who ran a classical conservatory out of their home. Swimming was not a priority in the Kellermans' bourgeois world of ballet and music lessons, and Annette might have never learned if not for a doctor's orders. Born with "soft bones"—a disease later known as rickets—she had to wear painful braces on her legs as a child. One of the many physicians her father, Frederick Kellerman, consulted suggested that swimming might build up her strength. But when he told Annette he was taking her to the baths to learn, she begged him not to make her go, writing later that she had been "terrified at the thought of swimming" and couldn't bear for anyone to see her underformed legs.[7] But despite her objections, Mr. Kellerman took Annette, along with her sister and brothers, to Cavill's Baths in Sydney to learn from the best, the famous British swimming professor Frederick Cavill, who had relocated his family to Australia. It took Annette three times as many lessons as her siblings, but swimming proved to be the medicine she needed and her condition improved. "Only a cripple can understand the intense joy that I experienced," wrote Kellerman, "when little by little I found that my legs were growing stronger."[8]

Struck with the "mermaid fever," Kellerman learned all she could, from racing strokes to ornamental swimming stunts, and even diving. By her early teenage years, she was entering—and winning—races and distance swims, working up to ten miles in the Yarra River, and even received a job offer to give exhibitions alongside the fishes in the Melbourne Aquarium's 60-foot tank. Although her mother didn't see professional swimming as a respectable path for her daughter, money was tight since the Kellermans had had to close their conservatory due to a national recession, and Annette took the job. Her exhibitions were so well received that she was soon dreaming of bigger ponds. In May 1905, Annette and her father boarded a ship bound for London, where there were more lucrative opportunities for professional swimmers. With only £40 between them, they planned to send for the rest of the family when they met with success abroad.[9]

But once in England—an island of swimmers—the Kellermans realized they were small fish; plus, they had no connections to the world of show business. With their funds dwindling, Annette needed to make a name for herself—and fast. They posted announcements that in late June eighteen-year-old Annette would swim from Putney to Blackwell—a distance 6 miles longer than Agnes Beckwith's 20-mile swim, which still held as the women's record after thirty years. In that time, however, the Thames had become far more polluted with industrial waste and sewage. "I shall never forget that swim through the flotsam and jetsam of London," recalled Kellerman of her record-breaking swim, "dodging tugs and swallowing what seemed like pints of oil from the greasy surface of the river."[10] Their plan worked, though, and soon after her swim Kellerman scored what was likely the first corporate endorsement deal for a female athlete.

The *Daily Mirror*, which had become England's first pictorial newspaper to make the switch from illustrations to photographs, offered to sponsor Kellerman if she would join an upcoming competition to try to cross the English Channel, a feat that had not been repeated by any swimmer since Captain Webb's crossing in 1875. Kellerman, the only woman in the race, would receive a weekly allowance during her eight weeks of training, plus a lump sum based on her performance in the competition. But just as importantly, the *Daily Mirror* would feature regular pictures and write-ups of her progress, promising Kellerman "the greatest campaign ever launched about a young girl."[11]

Arriving for her training on the Dover coast with only a halfpenny remaining between them, Kellerman and her father secured housing through their wits and lived on bread and milk until their first allowance came through. They didn't have money for newspapers, so, as Kellerman recalled, they peeked over the shoulders of strangers "to see what the sporting man was saying about us." Training for a serious swim could not be done in the traditional women's bathing costume, which Kellerman called "unfit for use except on dry land," so she opted for a man's short racing suit instead.[12] The day of the competition, Kellerman—alongside six male swimmers—staked out her spot on the Dover shore, pasted automobile goggles to her face, and slathered porpoise oil on her body to keep warm. She'd have to stay in the water at least three hours to receive the base payment from the *Daily Mirror*. No one succeeded in making the crossing that day, but Kellerman got farther than any of the men, earning £30 and making a name for herself as the first woman to seriously attempt the crossing. Kellerman continued doing attention-grabbing feats, hopping over to Europe to compete in races in the Danube and Seine rivers. For the latter, she was again the only woman in the race and placed third out of seventeen competitors, so thrilling Parisians that they tossed flowers to her into the water.[13]

With her fame growing, nineteen-year-old Kellerman received a fortuitous invitation to give a swimming demonstration at the exclusive Bath Club in London before royal guests, including the Duke and Duchess of Connaught. She planned to perform in her man's racing suit, but when the bath's manager caught wind of it, he strongly advised against exposing her thighs to such a noble audience.[14] Since Annette didn't have money for a proper costume like those worn by professional lady swimmers, she sewed a pair of inexpensive black stockings to her racing suit, creating a long, sleeveless bodysuit that hugged her curves like a glove and gave her limbs full freedom of

Annette Kellerman in her famous one-piece swimsuit.

movement.[15] This "one-piece"—so called because it was made of a single garment as compared to women's multi-piece, complicated sea bathing ensembles—would not only become Kellerman's signature look but would, in the coming decades, revolutionize women's swimwear. Newspapers as far away as America took note, with one writing in 1906 that Kellerman shunned "corsets and shoes and stockings and a cumbersome skirt and neck chains and bangle bracelets and padlock charms when she goes into the water," opting instead for a simple suit of her own creation that weighed only 2 ounces.[16]

Within a year and half of her arrival in England, Kellerman had reached the major leagues and was performing at London's biggest venues alongside the country's top female swimmers, including Marie Finney. The two were cast together, with Kellerman taking the lead role, in an aquatic spectacle called "The Treasure Ship of the Fairy Seas," which was part of the London Hippodrome's 1906 Christmas special. Their act was staged in what was said to be the largest tank ever used in a theater and featured a set designed to look like a coral cave with divers working on a treasure ship. Kellerman wore a costume of actual fish skin. Billed as "champion lady swimmers of the world," Kellerman and Finney, according to reviews, made "delightful mermaids and their ornamental swimming was something to envy and remember."[17] "Envy" might have been the operative word because Lizzie Johnson, one of Professor Johnson's daughters, wrote to the *Evening News* asking to know when, exactly, Miss Kellerman had won the title of "lady champion." Johnson pointed out that she herself had never been beaten by another woman and challenged the Australian interloper to a competition of ornamental, speed, or endurance swimming at any sea, lake, or bath of Kellerman's choosing. In a diplomatic, and perhaps slightly condescending response, Kellerman expressed "high appreciation" of Miss Johnson and, after rattling off a lengthy list of her own records, noted that she was perfectly content to let the public make up its own mind regarding who merited the champion title. As for the challenge, she received so many, Kellerman told the paper, that she regretfully could not possibly meet them all. "You see I am booked up to the end of the year," explained Kellerman. After that, the article added, she was headed to America for what she hoped would be a long stay.[18]

Kellerman was true to her word, and the following spring, she and her father boarded the *Celtic*, a steamship bound for New York City.[19] America was waiting for her, with a New England paper's headline declaring: "Famous Swimmer Coming." The newspaper pointed out that the name Miss Annette Kellerman was well known to followers of aquatic sports, who would no doubt welcome the news of her expected arrival in the country.[20] She would be giving demonstrations in New York, reported the article, before heading west to begin an engagement in Chicago at one of America's premier amusement parks.

On May 11, 1907, more than seventy-five thousand thrill seekers passed with anticipation under a large banner hanging over Chicago's 63rd Street that proclaimed, "Abandon Care All Ye Who Enter Here." It was opening day of White City amusement park's third season, and despite the unseasonably cold weather and a freak flurry of snow, eager crowds filed through the gates. They were there to soar, dip, and zoom on mechanized rides like the Whiz, the Chutes, and Devil's Gorge, and to be dazzled by the Great Babcock, who rode his motorbike at purported speeds of 150 miles per hour through a loop of death. They would gawk at the cobra dancers, the circus of "educated fleas," and the village of "native Igorrotes." And new on the docket this year, visitors could admire the "Australian mermaid," Annette Kellerman, who was hailed as the greatest woman swimmer in the world.[21]

For 10¢, fairgoers could enter Kellerman's open-top enclosure and watch her perform—in her signature one-piece swimsuit—demonstrations of ornamental stunts like the porpoise and sixteen different dives from a platform into her 14-foot tank. Kellerman could jackknife, spiral, twist, and tumble in the air, and then cut the water as clean as a knife, prompting the *Chicago Tribune* to write that she came nearer to being "the reincarnated daughter of Neptune than any woman who ever dove from a springboard."[22] At the same time, her "Australian splosh," a somersault dive ending in an intentionally splashy cannonball, always got a laugh from the audience. Soon Kellerman was giving fifty-five shows a week and papers were calling her act one of the principal attractions at White City.

In a theme that would continue her entire career, newspapers credited Kellerman's success to both her skill and her appearance, in near equal measure. *The Billboard* complimented her "magnificent physique and graceful accomplishments," while the *Chicago Tribune* described Kellerman as a flawless swimmer "who is at her best in her bathing suit."[23] Within a few weeks of her debut, Riverview, one of Chicago's rival amusement parks, started a competing diving act featuring local swimmer Lottie Mayer, though her reviews were not as favorable. Mayer did not bound up to the springboard with the same "verve and dash" that made Kellerman such a treat to watch, wrote one. Plus, she waited too long before diving, "as if dreading each leap." To add insult to injury, the article noted that "nature has cheated Lottie a little in the curve department." Mayer's was just the first of many copycat acts that would pop up, though as the article predicted, Kellerman would remain the "champion of the tank."[24]

Americans at the turn of the century were "going out" as never before, and White City and Riverview were just two of the dozens of amusement parks that had proliferated—along with vaudeville theaters, carnivals, and other commercial amusements—as part of the boom in popular entertainments. The expansion of electricity in urban areas made for well-lit streets, and nowhere was brighter than glowing amusement park midways and dazzling vaudeville marquees; White City even boasted to be "the most brilliantly lighted spot on the face of the globe."[25] These new illuminated public leisure spaces gave young men and women greater freedom to mingle with one another. In fact, during her summer engagement at White City, Kellerman met a young promoter named James Sullivan, who would become her manager—and later her husband. Comfortable that he was leaving his daughter in good hands, Frederick Kellerman, whose health was failing, left the US to return to his wife abroad.

The following season, Kellerman accepted an engagement at Wonderland, an even bigger amusement park located at Boston's Revere Beach that included Pawnee Bill among its featured performers. Kellerman's act proved to be just as successful in Boston, though her swimsuit attracted more attention in conservative New England than it had in the Windy City. The *Boston Post* even published a limerick about her choice of attire. It began:

> No more the Gibson bathing girl
> Shall grace the Newport summer whirl.
> Annette declares her garment's wrong,
> At both ends too extremely long . . .[26]

Kellerman even claimed, several years later, that her swimwear got her arrested during her time in Massachusetts. According to the now ubiquitous story, Kellerman had gone down to Revere Beach for a swim in her one-piece, but before she got the chance, she was hauled off by a police officer for indecent exposure. "Me, arrested!" she told a newspaper in 1953 as she recounted the events, adding that it had been quite a shock for her father, "for I was his innocent protected little girl."[27] Kellerman then—as the story goes—pleaded her case in court, arguing that it was impossible to do any serious training in the standard women's bathing costume. A sympathetic judge supposedly agreed and allowed Kellerman to wear her suit, so long as she promised to cover herself with a cloak until she got in the water—a small but significant victory for women's swimming.

The arrest story—which was later dramatized in the Esther Williams biopic about Kellerman's life, *Million Dollar Mermaid*—has become as much a part of Kellerman's legend as the one-piece swimming suit itself. It has been repeated, as fact, in books, magazines, scholarly journals, major American newspapers, documentaries, and in Kellerman's own authorized biography. Yet the story seems to have originated with Kellerman herself and historians have found no primary evidence—state documents, police files, court records, or newspaper reports—to corroborate her account, with a few suggesting the arrest never happened.[28] But whether or not these specific events occurred, there is truth at the heart of the story: the policing of women's bathing attire was real, as were requirements that those who wished to swim do so in clothing that was not only heavy and cumbersome but also unsafe—and it was Kellerman's crusading that would help to change that.

SPLASHING INTO VAUDEVILLE

Kellerman may or may not have had a run-in with the law during her time in Boston, but she did catch the attention of another Bostonian who had just as much power to propel her to national attention: a man named Benjamin Franklin (B. F.) Keith, who sat atop America's biggest entertainment empire. By the turn of the twentieth century, variety theater had been replaced by vaudeville, a grander, more polished form of popular entertainment. While vaudeville productions shared similarities with their variety precursors, including the way shows were built around an eclectic mix of individual acts, at the industry level, the two were very different. Variety theaters had been managed locally, with acts booked directly between venues and performers, whereas vaudeville was centrally managed, with a handful of massive theater conglomerates determining which acts would appear where. The most powerful of these was led by B. F. Keith and his business partner, Edward Albee. The Keith Circuit, as it was generally known, was also sometimes dubbed the Sunday School Circuit because of Keith and Albee's efforts—building on what Tony Pastor started—to provide clean entertainment appealing to a higher level of clientele. They famously posted rules for their performers that included "Don't say 'slob' or 'son-of-a-gun' or 'Holy Gee' on this stage unless you want to be cancelled peremptorily," and adopted the French term "vaudeville," which sounded more cosmopolitan than "variety" and didn't carry the same association with rowdy concert saloons.[29]

But for all their moralizing, Keith and Albee—like all vaudeville managers—looked for any thinly veiled excuse to put women onstage in scanty clothing. When they heard about the Australian Diving Venus performing in her one-piece swimsuit at Wonderland, Keith personally made a trip to check out her act. Duly impressed, he offered Annette Kellerman a substantial weekly salary of $300 to perform twice a day in his vaudeville theaters.[30] It was the opportunity that Kellerman, eager to leave behind the grind of amusement parks, had been waiting for.

Kellerman made her vaudeville debut in November 1908 at Keith's Fifth Avenue Theater in Manhattan, where a large tank was erected onstage for her fifteen-minute act. Diving was not yet a developed sport or art form in the United States, especially for women, and audiences found her act—and her costume—fresh and novel. A reviewer for *Variety* noted that her "exuberant spirit" made her fondness for the water apparent and seeing her dive and dart through it in her snug black bodysuit brought to mind a "handsome seal in the elegant physique of a woman." The writer concluded with, "Miss Kellerman is a great big vaudeville card," and predicted immense fame in her future.[31]

In vaudeville, an act's place within the show's sequence was telling of its popularity, as the biggest names were saved until the end. Soon after Kellerman's debut, a paper reported that there was an "unmistakable movement to the doors" following her act, indicating that Kellerman was clearly the one people were coming to see.[32] A week later, she was moved to the coveted finale slot; even then, as the concluding act of a long show, audiences still called her back for an encore. Kellerman was soon headlining at New York's biggest vaudeville houses on the Keith Circuit, including the Alhambra and the Colonial Theatre. At the latter, Kellerman's name, emblazoned outside in electric lights, drew huge crowds. A reviewer wrote that saving Kellerman to the end of the night gave all the other performers a shot at the full audience, "for no one leaves until the swimmer appears."[33] Six months later, her salary had increased fivefold to $1,500 a week, and within a year, newspapers reported that she was the highest-paid performer in vaudeville.[34] The following year, the Vitagraph Company made a short motion picture of Kellerman's swimming and diving act that was projected at vaudeville and theater houses across the country, further spreading her fame.

Even as she commanded a massive salary, Kellerman couldn't forget the lean years in England and, driven by a fear of ending up in poverty again, was always developing new skills and looking for ways to set herself apart. In lieu of a bathing cap, she would perform with a scarf tied around her head with an attractive low side knot. When asked about her look, she responded simply that she believed in being original: "Every little bit helps when you've a name to make for yourself."[35] Moreover, Kellerman wasn't content to be "just" a swimmer and desperately wanted to avoid being lumped in with dime museum entertainment, saying, "People ask if I can eat a banana at the bottom of a tank, but I don't want to be a freak."[36] Since childhood, she had dreamed of being a dramatic actor, and after just a few weeks on the Keith Circuit, she began experimenting with adding simple story lines to her swimming act. For her sketch "On the Beach at Boulogne," Kellerman would appear onstage in an airy summer dress, then enter a bathing machine, which was set up next to her tank.[37] She would emerge moments later, attired in the typical skirted bathing costume, surprised to find a cameraman waiting for her. A whimsical chase would ensue as Kellerman skittered across the stage, deftly evading the paparazzi while simultaneously performing a toe dance and throwing and catching the diablo—a juggling prop she learned to use in France.

Finally, she would dive into the tank, evading her pursuer for good. In the water, she would remove the old-fashioned suit and emerge wearing her signature one-piece, which signaled the start of the aquatic portion of her set. Over the years, she would add tightrope walking, daring high dives, classical pointe ballet, singing, physical culture lectures, and even a cross-dressing impersonation of a monocled English Johnny to her act, prompting the *Los Angeles Times* to declare in 1921 that Kellerman had become the most versatile woman on the stage.[38]

For female vaudeville performers like Kellerman there was often tension between their own desires to maintain social respectability through the performance of higher arts and pressure from theater managers to satisfy audiences with more suggestive entertainment. At one point, Edward Albee, who was considered the publicity brains of the Keith Circuit, arranged large mirrors all around Kellerman's glass tank to give audiences the best possible view of her sleek silhouette. When a theater manager questioned him, Albee responded matter-of-factly, "Don't you know that what we are selling here is backsides, and that a hundred backsides are better than one?"[39] Although few reviewers were as blunt as Albee, the constant comments and discussion of Kellerman's body show that he wasn't off the mark. In describing her dives, they noted the "tightening of young muscles," her "pulsing with the exertion," and the way her "lithe body" bent like a willow bough as she curved through the air.[40] And of course, few failed to mention the silhouette made by her black tights that fit like a "second epidermis," so snugly that a well-worn dime couldn't find a place to hide between the suit and her skin.[41]

Yet despite the defensiveness she exhibited regarding the artfulness of her act, the physical display of her body was one area where Kellerman never felt the need to make apologies. She saw the body—especially one that was active and healthy—as something to celebrate, not hide away. And many reviewers followed suit, with one writing, "There is a fine, wholesome, out-of-doors flavor of youthful health and spirit about her," and another likening her to a "sprite born of the seafoam—the very embodiment of youth and vigor and health and beauty and grace."[42]

Kellerman served as a reassuring example that the emerging "New Woman" of the twentieth century could be physically active without losing her femininity or sexual allure. Writers constantly noted with surprise that Kellerman was strong without being masculine—two

A headline from Ladies' Home Journal *in 1912 reflects the era's social anxieties around women's growing physical activity.*

characteristics presumed to go together. "Her strong shoulders are capable of buffeting the waves; her supple arms and splendid chest give her the same appearance of power and proportion that one notices in the athlete," wrote one of Kellerman's admirers, "and yet she is not muscular, but delicately built, with slender ankles and tapering wrists."[43]

With greater numbers of young women engaged in recreational athletics and school physical education programs for the first time, the *Ladies' Home Journal* dedicated a full article to widespread concerns that athletics were "making girls bold, masculine, and overassertive" and "robbing her of that charm and elusiveness that has so long characterized the female sex."[44] A newspaper in 1909 declared that America's young women were turning into a "race of amazons," citing as evidence the opinions of "noted authorities"—men from professions as varied as art, education, and clothing manufacturing. Gone, these men said wistfully, were a woman's soft curves, symmetrical proportions, the "graceful, sloping shoulders" of their great-grandmothers. In their place were flat chests, "hard, uncompromising lines," "hips devoid of any flesh," and the knotty muscles of a pugilist. A dressmaker shared his woeful tale of corsets rendered ineffective: "Ten years ago, you could mold a woman's figure. Not today. Her shoulders are broad and you can't narrow them. Her waist is large and you can't compress it." A painter too mourned the good old days when a model's main objective was preserving herself for the artist's brush, whereas now she thoughtlessly "risks facial beauty by playing outdoor games or basketball."[45]

While most discussions cited similar anecdotal "evidence" of women's masculinization, there was one man who claimed to have the data to address the question scientifically—and his Exhibit A was none other than Annette Kellerman herself.

THE PERFECT NEW WOMAN

Back in 1908, when Kellerman was performing at Wonderland Amusement Park in Boston, she received a visit from Dudley Sargent, a medical doctor and Harvard professor, as well as founder of the Sargent School for Physical Training. He told Kellerman about a study he was conducting with ten thousand women to determine the perfect female proportions. Sargent was a proponent of anthropometry, the use of systematic measurements to make inferences about human physiology (and often to make spurious claims about racial differentiation and white supremacy). He had previously declared Eugene Sandow, the strongman who was horsewhipped by Lurline the Water Queen, to be the ideal male specimen. Now, in his quest for the perfect woman—as measured against the classical Greek ideal epitomized in the Venus de Milo— Sargent had, for two decades, been collecting detailed data on female students at Wellesley, Radcliffe, Smith, Vassar, and other colleges. He had heard about the beautiful Diving Venus performing across town, and after seeing Kellerman's physique for himself, asked if she would participate in his study. "Why not?" Kellerman replied with a laugh.

In Sargent's office at Harvard, Kellerman stood in her one-piece swimsuit as the professor ran his tape measure down and around every inch of her body, scribbling numbers on a little notecard, growing more excited by the minute. He measured the girths of her waist, neck, wrists, ankles, calves, and thighs; her height standing and sitting; and even the depth of her insteps. Sargent was particularly impressed by the young swimmer's lung capacity, which he measured by having her blow into a balloon. Once he finished, Sargent gave Kellerman a Navajo rug to wrap around her body and led her onto the stage of a Harvard lecture hall. Before two hundred startled students, he removed the rug and declared Kellerman to be the most perfectly developed woman he had ever encountered—the "female form divine."[46]

In 1910, the *New York Times* published a full-page spread on Sargent's findings, with a headline declaring, "Modern Woman Getting Nearer the Perfect Figure."[47] Sargent reported that, while it was true that the average middle-class white woman had larger feet, a thicker waist, and narrower hips than a generation earlier, he believed these to be the positive results of improved diets, greater physical activity, and less constricting clothing—rather than signs of her growing masculinity. "The American woman of to-day is becoming more like the Greek ideal of the beautiful," he declared. As evidence, Kellerman was pictured in her one-piece suit, alongside the caption: "Annette Kellermann [*sic*], who, according to Sargent, Is Nearest to a Perfectly Proportioned Woman of the 10,000 Examined." The article provided such detailed data on Kellerman's measurements—thirty-five data points in all, including the circumference of her chest at the ninth rib, with lungs expanded as well as emptied—that a sculptor could have easily created a statue in her exact likeness.[48]

Someone hoping to make it in show business couldn't have asked for better advertising material than being declared the "Perfect Woman." Nor could swimming have benefited from a better publicity campaign, as both Sargent and Kellerman credited her perfect physique to her activities in the water. Sargent wrote that for women hoping to achieve Kellerman's "beautiful side lines and artistic proportions," there is no better exercise than swimming.[49] Kellerman, who extolled the beautifying virtues of swimming at every possible opportunity, claimed that it would "make the thin woman fat and the fat woman thin," and give the body "smoothness" by covering muscle tissue with a pleasing layer of fat.[50]

Following Sargent's study, publicity materials for Kellerman's shows and appearances frequently listed her measurements alongside those of Venus de Milo. Although Kellerman benefited from the comparison, she never took it too seriously, joking that she had better ankles than the Greek goddess. Nor did she subscribe to the "silly notion" that Venus represented some sort of feminine ideal: "She is only a graven image of one man's ideas of feminine beauty and the fact that that man died two thousand years ago does not make her perfect," wrote Kellerman.[51] But more importantly, the frozen tranquility of Greek statues did not inspire the version of modern womanhood Kellerman espoused. "The charm of Greek women lay in their expression of repose, of calm," she wrote, "but the body of today is more aggressive, it is slender, its beauty lies in a shape that expresses motion, that can *do* things."[52]

Kellerman was a zealous advocate of physical activity for women. In addition to her hugely popular lectures, in which she encouraged women to break out of their sedentary habits, she wrote newspaper and magazine articles with exercise tips, authored two books—one on swimming and another on health and beauty—and launched a mail-correspondence physical culture course. She never missed a chance to rail against the "prudish and Puritanical ideas" that had impeded women's natural development, writing in her 1918 book *Physical Beauty: How to Keep It*, that young women had been not only corseted and gowned to the point of absurdity but also "imbued with the idea that it is most unlady-like to be possessed of legs or to know how to use them."[53] She argued that "if more girls would swim and dance and care for athletics instead of rushing into matrimony as the only joy in the world, there'd be fewer divorces."[54] At the same time, Kellerman understood that the reason her athleticism was appreciated and admired was because it was thought to contribute to, rather than detract from, her beauty and charm. "No matter how much of an athlete a girl may be, she should never forget that she is a woman," she told one of her audiences.[55] For Kellerman, swimming provided a perfect middle ground; it was the one sport in which a woman could be "absolutely 'feminine' and yet be efficient."[56]

In 1918, Kellerman also published *How to Swim*, one of the very first female-authored books on the subject. Although she didn't write it explicitly for members of her own sex, throughout the book Kellerman addressed concerns that were unique to women, such as finding places to swim where they wouldn't be embarrassed or harassed, and suggested techniques they could practice at home to gain confidence and shorten their learning curve once they were in the water. *How to Swim* includes chapters for advanced and professional swimmers as well, covering the best strokes for speed and endurance and a wide range of ornamental stunts. But in a significant shift from prior books on swimming, all of the illustrations throughout feature *women* as the experts demonstrating the stunts, strokes, and dives. The only male depicted in the book is a cartoon man who appears in the lifesaving chapter, but rather than being the hero, he plays the role of the drowning victim.

If swimming was the thing Kellerman loved best, women's bathing attire was the thing she most loved to hate—and a topic to which she devoted considerable space in her writings. Nature had endowed woman with advantages for swimming, such as greater buoyancy, resistance to cold, and endurance, argued Kellerman, yet "Dame Society has bequeathed her serious handicaps." And the most serious was the "regulation" bathing costume, which was made of 7 to 10 yards of fabric and loose, flowy layers that would become like weights when saturated and tangle with one's legs in the water—that is if they didn't float up over the face and suffocate the wearer first.[57] Adeline Trapp, a swimmer and early adopter of Kellerman's simpler swimming costume, described later in life the beach ensemble of her youth, which

Kellerman demonstrates how to break a wrist hold when saving a drowning victim's life in How to Swim.

included, in *flannel*, "a pair of bloomers that ended in ruffles below the knee, usually a big sailor collar, and a voluminous skirt . . . Then there were stockings, bathing shoes of some kind, sleeves which came below the elbow, also ending in ruffles, and a bathing cap that looked like a boudoir cap, or else a straw hat tied under the chin."[58] And underneath all of this, fashion magazines like *Harper's Bazar* encouraged the use of bathing corsets "unless a woman is very slender."[59]

To Kellerman these bathing costumes were the very thing that kept women from swimming. In America, she observed, "the majority of boys and youth can swim, but the same remark hardly applies to their sisters or sweethearts."[60] She pointed out that at seaside resorts, few women and girls ventured beyond the lifelines and even in shallow water "hold on to the ropes as if they were afraid to let go of them, which indeed they are." Kellerman added for good measure that she'd like to find the "idiotic male prudes" responsible for these costumes, dress them in similar ones, send them overboard, and see how well they do.[61] She encouraged women to ditch their "lead chains" in favor of lightweight, skirtless garments of close-fitting tights—like the ones she wore.

Sure enough, within a few years of her arrival in America, reports of women wearing "one-piece" suits were popping up. A 1909 article noted that society ladies at the "exclusive natatoriums" of major East Coast cities had adopted tights and fitted suits like Kellerman's.[62] Soon knitting mills were producing "Kellerman suits" in a variety of colors and selling them in department stores. At Gimbels, where they sold for $3.75 in 1911, an ad for several kinds of bathing suits noted that "the Annette Kellerman" was the most ideal for actual swimming.[63] Even so, few women—other than small pockets of serious swimmers like Adeline Trapp—dared to wear them on public beaches, so they were primarily worn at pools and baths, which were segregated by gender in the early twentieth century.

Kellerman's meteoric rise to fame had naturally spurred imitators, and by the early 1910s, a circuit of professional women swimmers and divers were appearing on vaudeville stages, and at carnivals and on film screens—all in Kellerman suits. Many even copied her signature bandana side knot. "I was being copied all over the country," she later wrote. "I realized my vogue was taking a decided slump, that the diving Venus proposition was rapidly becoming passé."[64] Moreover, with the growth of the silent film industry, vaudeville was no longer at the avant-garde of the entertainment world. Kellerman, who understood that it is easier to get to the top than to stay there, decided it was time for her next reinvention.

THE MOVING PICTURE MERMAID

The 1910s were an exciting time in the nascent film industry. In the early years, production had been limited to making short moving-picture reels to be projected onto portable screens at vaudeville theaters, like the Vitagraph production of Kellerman's dives, but studios were increasingly moving to feature-length films that played at

A movie poster for Kellerman's 1914 film Neptune's Daughter *demonstrating some of her on-screen feats.*

purpose-built cinemas. Kellerman saw this emerging world of "movies" as the perfect way to combine her aquatic skills with her acting ambitions, so she commissioned a screenwriter to plot out a fantasy marine adventure story. After shopping it around, she convinced Universal to make it into a movie titled *Neptune's Daughter*, with her playing the lead role—a mermaid named "Annette," who sets out to avenge the death of her sister. In the process, she transforms into a mortal, chases down evildoers, survives being hurled over a 60-foot cliff with her hands and feet bound, falls in love with the king, and heroically saves his life when a coup is launched against him.

The movie was filmed on the Bermuda coast, but since submarine videography was still in its infancy—the first film using a submerged camera would come out the same year as *Neptune's Daughter*—the underwater scenes were shot through the glass wall of a 16-foot square tank that was erected on the beach and filled with marine life. The day of the underwater filming, tourists gathered on the beach to watch, holding their breath as Kellerman and director Herbert Brenon, playing the role of her enemy, slipped into the tank. There had been murmurs over whether the glass, which had been specially ground to prevent blurring in the video, could hold back the tank's 18 tons of water.[65] When nothing happened, everyone relaxed, the cameramen turned their cranks, and the underwater fight scene began. But then suddenly there was a loud boom, like a cannon shot. The glass had cracked, and within a split second a deluge of water ripped through the narrow opening, carrying Kellerman and Brenon through the shards and spitting them out, along with an octopus and a baby shark, 20 feet from the tank. The actors both sustained deep cuts but survived, while the incident only further built public anticipation for the film.

When *Neptune's Daughter* came out in the spring of 1914, it played to capacity audiences for weeks at theaters across the country—with a movie house in Chicago showing it four times a day to accommodate demand—and broke all ticket records in San Francisco.[66] It was hailed as a "pictorial triumph" and a trendsetter in motion pictures.[67] The *Chicago Tribune* wrote that Kellerman exhibited "the aquatic prowess for which she is renowned—untrammeled by the confining walls of a vaudeville natatorium."[68] Another paper wrote that in addition to demonstrating her remarkable swimming skills, she proved "that she is a splendid actress, a graceful dancer, an expert swordswoman and a mistress of a hundred other arts."[69] But if audiences were impressed by *Neptune's Daughter*, they were nothing short of astounded two years later by Kellerman's daring performance in her second—and widely considered best—film, *A Daughter of the Gods*.

Produced by William Fox with the first ever million-dollar film budget, *A Daughter of the Gods* was unprecedented in its magnitude and extravagance. The three-and-a-half-hour epic spectacle was shot in Jamaica on 223,000 feet of film and featured 21,218 actors and extras—including 300 dancing girls and 200 mermaids, all of whom were costumed in expensive lamé, tulle, silk, sequins, and pearls. The sets required 2 million feet of lumber to build, plus thousands of barrels of plaster and concrete. An entire Moorish city was erected just to be burned to the ground in a single scene.[70]

But even in a film that grand, Kellerman herself remained the main attraction, as she swam through a pool of crocodiles, dove from a 100-foot tower, and deftly maneuvered her bound body through a series of dangerous waterways. The *San Francisco Chronicle* reported that the intrepid actress swam "down rapids, through caverns, under floodgates, out into the open sea and thence back to be dashed, piniored against the rocks"—all with her hands tied behind her back.[71] Although Kellerman appeared to do the impossible, the writer assured readers that there was no trick of the camera and that her "fortitude and daring" were every bit as real as they appeared. Kellerman was indeed brave, but she wasn't stupid or reckless, joking in an interview that she made sure the crocodiles had been fed triple rations for dinner before she got in the water with them.[72] For her high dive from the 100-foot tower, the base of which was surrounded by protruding jagged rocks, Kellerman told the film crew she would do it only once, so they better get the footage they needed. With seven cameras trained on her, Kellerman took the strongest headlong leap she could and missed the rocks by only three feet.[73]

In addition to pushing the physical limits, Kellerman—who is typically considered the first woman to appear nude in a film—also pushed the boundaries of acceptable dress. She most famously appeared in nothing but a long wig with strategically placed strands of hair for a scene in *A Daughter of the Gods*, but in some of her other films she wore full-body, flesh-colored tights that gave the illusion of nudity, prompting a reviewer

*Kellerman, who is considered the first woman to appear nude in
a film, poses for a scene in* A Daughter of the Gods *(1916).*

to comment on her "flitting white and nymphlike among the trees."[74]
Naturally, seeing Kellerman nearly nude was as big of a draw for some as
her acting or her aquatic daring. After the opening of *Neptune's Daughter*, a West Virginia housewife made headlines for gashing her husband's
head with a potato masher, saying in her own defense: "That scoundrel
went to see that Annette Kellerman movie three times in three days, and
he'd tell me every night what a pretty form she had."[75]

But Kellerman, who found nudity to be artistic, was certainly not
a passive object of the "male gaze," a term coined in 1975 by feminist
film theorist Laura Mulvey. In classic films, argued Mulvey, the typical female character served as a passive sexual object to be gazed at
and to motivate the actions of the hero; she did not exist outside of the
feelings she inspired in the male character, whose response to those
feelings—whether desire, anger, jealousy, or fear—moved the story forward. Mulvey's widely applied theory is useful for understanding how
different Kellerman's films were. Motivated by their own desires and
agendas, her heroines were the ones whose actions drove the narratives.
Moreover, her characters solved their own problems, whether going to

battle to save lovers or jumping from cliffs to escape sexual enslavement. In one of her later films, *What Women Love*, Kellerman dove from atop a schooner's mast to evade a villain fast on her heels. The two wrestle on the ocean floor until Kellerman delivers a knockout kick in the gut, then swims to the surface and into the arms of her waiting sweetheart—whose assistance she clearly did not need.[76] One reviewer warned that Kellerman can fight underwater, "so if you ever have trouble with her don't choose the Atlantic Ocean as a battle ground."[77]

Not only did Kellerman's films project a greatly expanded vision of female physical and mental capability—but they did so at a critical time for American women. The rally for women's suffrage was building when *A Daughter of the Gods* was released in 1916, and several reviewers couldn't help but draw connections between the athletic prowess Kellerman demonstrated and calls for women's political equality. The *Journal of Commerce* wrote, "Those who contend that woman is too

Kellerman makes a spectacular dive from a 100-foot tower for her grand epic A Daughter of the Gods.

weak physically to contend with man at the voting booth . . . should go to the Lyric Theater to see Annette Kellerman in *A Daughter of the Gods*. Either she is a super-woman or women are surely entitled to rank with men in physical endurance."[78] Another newspaper wrote:

> After seeing her you may feel like defying any ten-foot man in the audience to declare that the sex of which she is the perfect and ideal example hasn't the courage to fight or the ability to vote or do anything else they choose to do. If votes were measured by physical or mental courage, Miss Kellermann would demand a million of them.[79]

While the medium of film enabled Kellerman to soar to new heights, it didn't hold the same energy and excitement for her as the live stage, and she wrote that the screen was "a poor substitute to any one who has been on the other side of the footlights."[80] Throughout her film career, during which she made five feature motion pictures, Kellerman continued performing onstage, moving back and forth between the movies and vaudeville, her fame in one further fueling her popularity in the other. Sadly, only her final film, *Venus of the South Seas*, has survived in full. The rest remain only as partial copies or are considered lost films.

MOTHER OF SYNCHRONIZED SWIMMING

In addition to becoming film's first aquatic stuntwoman, Kellerman, who has often been called the mother of synchronized swimming, introduced many moviegoers to ornamental swimming. A review published in *The Moving Picture World* noted that after diving from a cliff in her film *What Women Love*, Kellerman "was seen to turn and leap and squirm and do 'cart-wheels' and spin on her toes, then on her head" in the water. It predicted that girls at local beaches would be imitating her "stunts." Moreover, Kellerman directed what is almost certainly filmdom's first episode of swimmers performing in mass synchronization. In a little-known "mermaid ballet" scene in *A Daughter of the Gods*, one hundred women encased in shimmery tails performed perfectly matched rhythmic swimming strokes in the water. The trade journal *Motography*, which dedicated an entire article to the scene, wrote that Kellerman, "the greatest artist of her kind in all the world," dared not trust the training of the mermaids-to-be to an assistant and spent weeks working with them herself to make the scene perfect.[81]

For the scene, Kellerman hired the best women swimmers from all over the country, but once they got to work, she was surprised to discover how few of them could keep on swimming once their legs were bound up in mermaid tails and put out of commission. Kellerman, who—like any ornamental swimmer—was right at home swimming sans this or sans that, considered being able to travel through the water without the use of one's legs a basic skill for anyone who claimed to be an expert. So to make her mermaids seaworthy, she set about teaching them to make their arm strokes more powerful and efficient, and reported proudly that after three months the majority could swim at least a quarter of a mile using only their arms.[82] Next, the mermaids spent hours learning how to execute their new powerful strokes in unison. "There must be no chaotic movement in the water scenes to distract attention," wrote *Motography*. "There had to be perfect synchronization—poetry applied to motion."[83] Matching one hundred swimmers, who were practicing in natural bodies of water and in all kinds of weather, required weeks of training, but Australia's *Daily Standard* reported that the mermaids stuck at it, even as they were "dashed again and again against jagged rocky ledges."[84]

Their work paid off, and reviewers praised their "perfection and synchronization of stroke."[85] When the head of the studio, William Fox, watched the footage, he personally cabled a note to Kellerman telling her it was the most beautiful work in a motion picture he had ever seen. "Your genius has in the mermaid scenes made it possible for our picture to exceed the Russian ballet artistes for grace and rhythm," he wrote.[86] Kellerman was clearly proud of the scene and the work that went into making it, and wrote a chapter titled "Mermaids to Order" about the experience for her book *How to Swim*.

For theater audiences, the mermaid ballet would have been made even more striking by the live orchestral accompaniment. There was a new trend in silent films to commission "synchronized musical scores," which were written to match not only the moods and themes of a film but to accentuate the precise actions being performed by the actors. *A Daughter of the Gods* featured one of the earliest and best examples of these scores, with one reviewer writing that it was "synchronized with every incident in the picture . . . with unusual timeliness."[87] Another wrote that the music and action were so perfectly matched that in a scene where Kellerman throws down a strand of pearls in anger, her gesture "falls in exactly with instrumental crash and beat of the drum."[88] Although the articles about the score do not expressly mention the mermaid ballet scene, given the music's perfect and precise timing to the action *and* the mermaids' rhythm and synchronization, it is quite likely that the swimmers' movements were synchronized not only with one another but also with the music—one of the key aspects that would later distinguish synchronized swimming from other forms of water ballet.

Although training one-hundred women swimmers to move in perfect unison was no easy feat, the bigger reason Kellerman remains associated with synchronized swimming—and was eventually honored by the International Swimming Hall of Fame as a "forerunner" to the sport—was because of her own gracefulness and skill in the water. Kellerman was a lifelong student of ballet, which enabled her to expand on and elevate the stunts of the scientific swimmers and natationists of a generation earlier and apply a heightened level of artistry to everything she did in the water. George Browne, an educator and

Kellerman demonstrates the "submarine," which would later be called the "ballet leg," in How to Swim.

an international skating judge, wrote in 1917 that although Keller-man's movies offered drama and excitement, to him, the real "fine art" was to be found simply in watching Kellerman swimming alone in her glass tank.[89] Since Browne had an interest in kinesiology, Kellerman granted him a private audience so that he could study her movements underwater, an experience he wrote about in his article "The Psychology of Grace." Some of the ornamental swimming stunts she performed for him included the "rolling log," the "horizontal coil," and the "reversed pendulum." The last was a very difficult feat that involved suspending oneself vertically in the water—head down, feet up—then slowly swinging the entire body, which must be kept straight, so that the head reaches nearly to the surface on one side, then swings back down and up the other side, like the pendulum of a grandfather clock.

Browne wrote that Kellerman looked back on her days as an endurance and speed swimmer with gratitude for how much she had evolved and that she was "making her swimming less athletic and more artistic every year."[90] Kellerman shared a similar sentiment, saying later, "I never forgot that I was a dancing diver, not an athletic diver—and oh, there's a difference! It's one of the reasons I have lasted as long as I have."[91] What they meant was not that her swimming or diving were becoming less physically difficult or athletic, but rather that her skill enabled her to use an "economy of effort" on the physicality and focus instead on the gracefulness of her movements. Browne even referred to Kellerman as an "artistic swimmer," presaging what practitioners of synchronized swimming would be called more than a century later.

Kellerman serves as an interesting bridge between the scientific swimmers who preceded her and the synchronized swimmers who would follow. In *How to Swim*, she included a lengthy section on "fancy swimming," with some stunts dating back to Digby, like the leg aloft or the porpoise, which Kellerman wrote is one of the most difficult to do correctly. The former is called the "submarine" in Kellerman's book and features the added twist of allowing the body to sink or rise through the use of sculling while leaving only a bit of the periscope (leg) sticking out. But under Kellerman's watch, these movements became more elegant. The submarine, for example, is illustrated with a cartoon version of Kellerman extending a perfectly straight leg with pointed toes, whereas the previous illustrations of male swimmers usually had flexed feet and slightly bent knees—which would be considered poor form indeed by later synchronized swimmers. She also included stunts that would become enshrined in the first synchronized swimming handbook a couple of decades later, such as the "over and under," in which two swimmers reverse positions by gliding in opposite directions above and beneath each other, and which is known to present-day artistic swimmers as the "plank."

Kellerman was aware of the rich (and male) scientific swimming traditions she was building on, not only sharing some of Benjamin Franklin's swimming tips but also providing a list of stunts from Thévenot's book (though like Franklin, she seems unaware that Digby was the originator). Anyone who can do Thévenot's tricks, wrote Kellerman, "would have been the idol of small boys who lived one hundred and fifty years ago."[92] But she was also aware of the evolution, writing that the difference between Thévenot's "old-time book of hints" and her book "may be taken as a measure of our progress in aquatic sports."[93]

For Kellerman, one of the greatest acknowledgments that she was indeed an artist of the water came in late 1916 when she was invited to take the place of her idol, prima ballerina Anna Pavlova, on the country's largest stage at the New York Hippodrome. Built in 1905, the Hippodrome took up an entire city block and featured an opulent grand lobby with marble elephant heads dotting the crown molding like gargoyles and plush velvet seats for fifty-five hundred patrons. But its most impressive feature by far was its massive stage that could accommodate six hundred performers at a time and featured state-of-the-art technology for producing aquatic spectacles that made those at Sadler's Wells and Blackpool Tower Circus look like puddle splashing by comparison. The 60-foot stage apron, which curved out into the orchestra, could be lowered to create a tank 14 feet deep that was filled from spillways under the stage wings. It was equipped with pumps that could handle 150,000 gallons of water per minute to generate ocean waves, rainstorms, or gushing waterfalls.[94] Only a year after its opening, the Hippodrome's tank had already become legendary as stage managers used its underwater air chambers to mystify audiences and make aquatic nymphs appear and disappear from its watery depths.

In keeping up with entertainment trends, the Hippodrome later moved to revue-style shows featuring three major acts, each with its own famous headliner and large supporting cast. Pavlova's "Sleeping Beauty" ballet extravaganza was the highlight of "The Big Show" at the Hippodrome in 1916, so when Pavlova decided to take her entourage on tour, the Hippodrome needed to replace her with someone of equal drawing power for the following season. Kellerman, whose million-dollar film *A Daughter of the Gods* was thrilling audiences just two blocks down at the Lyric Theatre on Broadway, was a natural choice. The *New York Times* announced in December that for the Hippodrome's upcoming season the "danseuse who sails through the air" would be replaced by one who "sails through the water."[95]

Even though the Hippodrome was equipped with the ideal stage for an aquatic spectacle, its sunken pool was frozen solid, being used for another act that featured an ice-skating ballet. Since they couldn't melt the ice for Kellerman's "Enchanted Waterfall" scene, the

The New York Hippodrome, where Kellerman performed her enchanted waterfall act at "The Big Show" of 1917.

managers had a removable stage floor built above it and brought in four eight-foot-high glass-fronted tanks that each held 11,000 gallons of water and weighed a combined twelve tons.[96] The stage was designed to resemble grotto pools surrounded by rocky cliffs and cascading waterfalls, while the illuminated tanks became "glass-sided lakes" full of colorful marine flora.[97] The *New York Times* called it "a veritable Niagara in cloth, canvas and electric lights." The cast included wood nymphs, alligators, crocodiles, and frogs inhabiting the amphibious zones, winged fairies swooping through the air, and two hundred nymphs and mermaids who dove, cavorted, and swam in the glass tanks. The Queen of the Mermaids was Kellerman herself, "glistening in her suit of silver scales." When "The Big Show" opened, the *New York Times* was effusive, exclaiming it was the illustrious Kellerman "with such frills" as audiences had never seen before.[98]

For the *Times* reviewer, the highlight of the show was Kellerman's dive from the highest rafters above the Hippodrome stage. "On the high crags above appears the wonderful Kellerman," he exclaimed. "From a dizzy height again and again she dives. This is the heart of the matter."[99] But many in the audience were equally impressed with what she did at the finish of each dive. After cutting gracefully through the water, wrote another reviewer, Kellerman remained under the surface, "whirling somersaults forward and backward, her lithe body arching back almost into a complete hoop, then sway[ing] to and fro in most fascinating undulations and oscillations—all underwater."[100] Newspapers noted that the glass-front tanks—the largest ever used onstage—made Kellerman's "spectacular under-the-sea exhibition possible for the first time" and called her act the most enjoyed part of the entire evening's "colossal bill of novelties."[101] Kellerman had, for so many years, avoided becoming just another "tank act" by centering her vaudeville performances around diving and her expanding repertoire of terrestrial skills that she expressed surprise at learning how much the public was enjoying "the novelty of seeing her under the water for the first time." A month into the show, she announced that she was changing her act to focus on the underwater portions and would remain submerged for most of the show—fourteen minutes total—surfacing only to demonstrate her dives.[102]

A reviewer once said after watching Kellerman perform: "In the telling it sounds like very thin entertainment. In the doing, it fills the eye with flashes of exquisite motion, convinces you that there really were mermaids after all. It is an art in the making."[103] If Kellerman needed confirmation that she had become more than "just a swimmer," this was it.

But perhaps even more important to Kellerman was the fact that through her career and advocacy, she had become a role model for other women. In 1920, a female essayist wrote, "We women used to think it was 'cute' to be timid . . . the men told us they liked us that way, and we believed them." But increasingly, she continued, they were realizing the joy that comes from "fear overcome and thrown aside." The writer encouraged women to stop being shy "half-swimmers" and move beyond the "safe and shallow spots" to experience the elation that comes from trusting the water to hold them, with nothing underfoot. She cited Kellerman as a model in this and wrote that thinking of the way she had overcome her physical disabilities to become an "intrepid athlete" makes one feel "very proud of the sex."[104]

As the world's first swimming superstar, Kellerman used her platform to encourage other women to swim, and they did—in droves. And she introduced sensible swimwear that would make it possible. Moreover, she created an association between swimming and artistry that would pave the way for a new type of performative, yet athletic, swimming that would draw generations of women to the water long into the future. But she wasn't alone in her efforts. Alongside her rise to fame, other role models were emerging and droves of women were learning to swim, not only for health and fulfillment, but for their own safety—and to save the lives of others. Their work would be made more impactful because of Kellerman's advocacy and because of the beauty she brought to the water.

CHAPTER 4

SAFETY

Educate gently while entertaining hugely.

—COMMODORE LONGFELLOW

Clara Stuer was in high spirits as she stepped aboard the *General Slocum* on the morning of June 15, 1904. Filing in behind her from Manhattan's Third Street Pier, fellow members of St. Mark's German Lutheran church, their families, and friends were abuzz with anticipation. It was "the season of Sunday school excursions," as one newspaper put it, and the good folks at St. Mark's had picked a gorgeous day for their seventeenth annual picnic. They were headed to a park on Long Island's North Shore, but the two-hour trip up the East River on the *General Slocum*, one of New York's finest excursion steamers, promised to be half the fun. It would have been hard to say who looked more festive that day—the *Slocum*, festooned with pennants and flags from stem to stern, or its passengers, all dressed in their Sunday finest: women elegant in wide-brimmed hats and long dresses, girls with fluttering ribbons in their hair, and boys in knickerbockers and button-up boots. As they walked up the gangplank that Wednesday morning, many waved goodbyes to husbands and fathers who had come to see them off; most of St. Mark's parishioners were working-class German immigrant families of the Lower East Side, and few male members could afford to take a vacation, even for a day.

After waiting for a handful of stragglers, the *General Slocum* left port around 9:45 a.m. Clara and another young woman, her friend Millie Mannheimer, who had brought her niece and nephew, found seats together on the upper deck where they could watch the bustle and stress of the city fade into a serene skyline. There were, of course, no safety announcements about the location of life jackets (which were tied tightly to the high ceilings and disintegrated from disuse) or lifeboats (which had been firmly wired to the ship to keep them from rattling). Instead, as the *General Slocum* made its way up the Manhattan shoreline, a German band struck up a lively tune and children were invited to come to the main deck for soda and ice cream.

Shortly into the voyage, as the ship passed 86th Street and was entering Hell Gate, a narrow strait known for its treacherous cross currents, Millie's niece Lillie, who had been quietly taking in all the activities on the ship, suddenly said: "I think the boat is on fire, auntie! See all the smoke."[1] Millie shushed the child, telling her that such talk could create a panic. But Lillie was right, and moments later, a loud boom ripped through the ship like a cannon shot. Within an instant, Clara recalled, "the entire bow of the boat was one sheet of flames. The people rushed pell mell over one another, and in the rush I lost track of my friends."[2] Hundreds of passengers fled to the stern of the boat away from the flames, trampling children and the elderly in the panic and confusion. Those already in the rear were pinned against the railing, which quickly gave way under the pressure, sending a surge of bodies overboard. The horrific scene was described by witnesses on shore as a human waterfall cascading over the stern. Yet inexplicably the ship pressed onward, fresh wind fueling the flames.

The ravenous fire, which investigations determined started in the lamp room, devoured the ship's wood—seasoned from years of salt, sun, and countless coats of linseed oil and turpentine—and spread rapidly to all three decks, leaving hundreds of passengers with nowhere to turn except the water. As one historian wrote, those aboard the *Slocum* would have considered water "only slightly less terrifying than fire," having been "too busy and too poor" to learn to swim.[3] Panicked mothers, some holding on to three or four children, were forced to choose between hurling themselves into the swirling current or being burned alive.

Clara, unable to find Millie or the children amid the frantic mob, jumped over the rail and hoisted herself down onto the lower deck. "I began to throw off my clothing so that I would have a better chance in the water," she recalled later that evening in an interview.[4] It was a wise move; the yardage of heavy fabric required for women's dresses would have made swimming to safety difficult even for an expert swimmer. But just as Clara was steeling herself to lunge into the black water, a voice called out to her, and she turned to find an approaching tug that pulled up close enough for her and several others to jump safely aboard.

Fishermen and boaters who had hurried to the *Slocum*'s rescue pulled whoever they could from the water onto their small vessels, but many passengers who jumped or fell overboard never resurfaced. Some were dragged under by the ship's giant paddle wheels or the death grips of the drowning. Those who had managed to pull a life-jacket down from the ceiling learned too late that the cork they were made of had rotted and the preservers were as useless as sacks of dirt.[5]

Five minutes after the fire started—an eternity to the passengers fighting for their lives—the captain, who was later brought to trial for his poor handling of the event, finally ran the *General Slocum* aground on some rocks near North Brother Island, between Rikers Island and the Bronx. North Brother Island was home to a quarantine hospital (Typhoid Mary would be among its patients a few years later), and doctors, nurses, and orderlies who had rushed to the riverbank immediately began pulling victims from the shallow water—alive, dead, and dying. One nurse, Florence Denning, who was a strong swimmer according to newspaper reports, raced into deeper water to help save

One of many front-page articles detailing the horrors of the General Slocum *disaster.*

the drowning.[6] A fifteen-year-old patient, Mary McCann, who was recovering from scarlet fever, swam out repeatedly and saved a total of nine children before fainting from exhaustion.[7] Some of the boys and young men aboard were able to save not only themselves but others as well. Lillie, the girl who spotted the smoke, survived, having been pulled onto a rescue boat, but her brother and aunt, like the majority of the passengers, were not so fortunate.[8]

Roughly 75 percent of the passengers aboard the *General Slocum*—or 1,021 people—lost their lives that day. The official report of the United States Commission of Investigation of the disaster found that in "all but a few cases," those who survived did so not through their own swimming skills, but with outside assistance. The report estimated that if not for the boaters who came to the aid of passengers like Clara and Lillie, there likely would have been no more than seventy survivors in total. The commission wrote, "This indicates the almost complete helplessness of an excursion party of this particular composition, even when most of the passengers were brought to a place within at least 200 feet of the shore."[9] And by "particular composition," it was referring to the fact that of the roughly 1,360 passengers on board, only between 50 and 150 were grown men, while the rest were women and children.[10]

A NATIONAL CRISIS

Drowning rates were abysmally high in early twentieth-century America, with as many as ten thousand adults and children meeting watery graves each year.[11] Beaches and swimming holes were unguarded, and those who wished to bathe, wade, or swim did so at their own peril. Monday morning newspapers, especially in the summer months, would recount the weekend's tragic loss of life to the water, sometimes with multiple drowning articles in a single issue.

The situation was particularly dire for women. Florence Denning and Mary McCann, who both ran into the water to save passengers from the *Slocum*, were rare exceptions, and the vast majority of women couldn't swim. Many lacked even the most basic knowledge of how to maneuver their bodies in water. The *Chicago Tribune* reported that dozens aboard the *Slocum* drowned in water so shallow that they could have stood up and waded out safely if they'd only known how.[12] While this may seem inconceivable to anyone with even the most rudimentary swimming skills, George Corsan, who established the first swimming program at the Young Men's Christian Association (YMCA), wrote, "It is quite true that a woman is in danger of drowning in water a yard deep if she has not had five minutes' instruction in how to get her feet on the bottom." Corsan explained that because a woman's legs are buoyant, getting them underneath her body takes effort—albeit slight effort that quickly becomes routine—and should be the first thing women should learn in the water.[13] And yet, most American women and girls of the era never had even five minutes of instruction.

Annette Kellerman and others rightfully blamed women's bathing costumes for hindering their progress in the water, but this was only part of the problem. Women had limited access to safe and sanitary places to swim and even scarcer access to swimming instruction—especially working-class women. By the turn of the century, many cities were equipped with public baths—often floating structures built on natural bodies of water—but they were typically only open during the warmer months and were considered public health utilities, not venues for swimming or recreation. In fact, in 1904, the year of the *Slocum* disaster, New York City had not allotted any funds in its budget for swimming instructors at the bathhouses.[14]

The few indoor pools that existed at the time were typically private and gender segregated, with limited hours for women, which usually fell in the middle of the workday, putting their use out of reach for most. An article on an indoor natatorium in Chicago noted that the tank was mostly frequented by the wives and daughters of doctors and businessmen, but if it were open to women in the evenings or Sundays, working girls would come in large numbers.[15] The difficulties facing working women were further discussed by Rhode Island's children in a 1906 essay contest asking them to reflect on why girls didn't learn to swim. "These girls do not feel like learning to swim after working all day, and would not think of learning to swim on Sunday," wrote one twelve-year-old in her winning essay. "As a result, they do not learn to swim."[16] In addition to pointing out the lack of places to swim, other young essayists cited problems with the options that did exist: dirty water, the prohibitive cost of the bathhouses, crowded beaches, and rowdy boys who intimidated girls trying to learn.

Victorian mores that cloistered girls indoors and constantly framed women as weak were also part of the problem. Little boys, who were typically given free rein to play with friends in oceans, lakes, or whatever urban rivers or canals passed through their cities, learned informally, developing swimming skills through trial and error. If they didn't have swimming trunks, they simply bathed and swam in the nude. One writer noted that "a boy jumps into unknown depths, trusting to his strength of muscle and sinew to pull him through," whereas a woman harbors a "consciousness of weakness that makes her shrink."[17] Moreover, swimming was seen by many as a "vulgar" activity for girls. Adeline Trapp, who was born in 1896 and later became a leader in women's swimming, recalled the tongue-lashing a neighbor gave her father for teaching her to swim, calling it a "violation of all propriety" for a girl to do "exercises that will teach her legs to become unacquainted with each other."[18]

But despite the many challenges women faced, the *General Slocum* tragedy proved to be a national wake-up call. Within days, mothers, educators, and concerned citizens were being quoted in newspapers decrying the situation for girls, calling for greater swimming education, and exhorting women to learn and fathers to teach their daughters. The *New-York Daily Tribune* declared, "One of the lessons which the *General Slocum* horror should bring home to every woman and girl in New York City is the desirability of knowing how to swim."[19] And many were indeed resolved to learn. A week and a half after the accident, the custodian of New York's East Side floating bath reported that the number of girls coming to the baths to learn to swim had already doubled and that volunteers had stepped up to teach them. A Brooklyn newspaper headline announced, "Women and Children Eager to Be Swimmers— Swarm to public baths with Slocum Disaster Uppermost in their minds."[20] Private baths saw similar trends, and swimming instructors across the metropolis were said to be doing a "rattling business."[21]

And it wasn't just in New York: the impact of the *General Slocum* tragedy reverberated across the country, with reporters paying increased attention to local drownings and encouraging readers to learn to swim. One of these was a young marine journalist from

Rhode Island, Wilbert E. Longfellow, who had grown despondent over the numerous drownings he had to report on, especially since many of them seemed tragically preventable with either a bit more water safety knowledge on the part of the bather or better supervision at beaches. Following the *Slocum* disaster, Longfellow, who was in his early twenties, decided to "do something about waterfront drownings instead of writing about them" and joined the Rhode Island branch of the US Volunteer Life Saving Corps (VLSC).[22]

Founded in 1890 in New York, with a few branches across New England, the VLSC was the first lifesaving organization dedicated to protecting the American public—as opposed to sailors and seamen, the domain of earlier organizations—from drowning, which it did by organizing volunteer patrols of popular swimming areas and offering swimming lessons at the public baths. Its good work came to national attention when it was discovered that at least four of the child survivors of the *Slocum* had been taught to swim by VLSC lifesavers.[23]

Joining the VLSC would turn out to be Longfellow's first step toward becoming one of swimming's most influential leaders and colorful figures. However, Longfellow wasn't a strong swimmer in the beginning and had, in fact, already been rescued twice from near drownings, the second time by a stout woman who hauled him from the water so matter-of-factly it was as if she was plucking wet laundry out of a washer tub. After that experience, reported a newspaper, the young reporter "drew a deep breath and resolved to learn to swim."[24] As a volunteer with the VLSC, he met immigrants from England and Scotland who had been affiliated back home with the Royal Life Saving Society. They brought with them more advanced lifesaving techniques and a new method of artificial respiration devised by a Scottish anatomist named Edward Sharpey-Schafer. The technique involved pressing on a prone person's lower back and was far more effective—and more civilized—than the techniques commonly in use in the United States like socking victims in the face if they resisted help, then rolling them over a barrel to force chest compressions. "Lots of perfectly good barrels have been ruined by rolling drowned people on them," wrote Longfellow in his typical dry wit. "And it didn't do the poor victims any good either."[25] Longfellow worked with his Royal Life Saving Society colleagues to simplify their technique, which eventually became known as the prone-pressure method, and began teaching it to other lifesavers, as well as policemen, who were often the first responders to drowning accidents.[26]

Longfellow quickly became a respected leader within the Rhode Island branch of the VLSC and, in 1905, was appointed state superintendent and awarded the title of commodore. He successfully lobbied the Rhode Island State House for funds to purchase lifesaving equipment and to stage lifesaving demonstrations, accomplishing so much with the initial stipend of $200, the legislators gave him $1,200 and $2,000 the following two years, during which he developed crews across Rhode Island and reduced the state's drowning rate by half.[27]

But in 1907, Commodore Longfellow's work nearly came to a grinding halt when he was diagnosed with tuberculosis of the spine. Doctors sealed him up in a plaster cast from armpits to hips and ordered complete bed rest. Despite dire predictions that he had only months to live, Longfellow—a man on a mission—didn't give up. He managed to continue his work with the VLSC through bedside conferences, letters, and phone calls, then decided to disregard the bed rest orders altogether, self-prescribing a regiment of fresh air, sunshine, and light swimming exercises (after upgrading to a cast with hinges so he could move his arms and legs). Within two years, he had made a full recovery and in 1910 was recruited to the VLSC headquarters in New York and installed as the organization's general superintendent.

Under Longfellow, the goals of the VLSC expanded beyond guarding beaches to stimulating public interest in swimming. One of the ways they did this was by hosting water carnivals featuring games, races, lifesaving demonstrations, and exhibitions of scientific swimming stunts. Most likely, Longfellow and his VLSC colleagues learned these stunts from their British and Canadian counterparts from the Royal Life Saving Society. Since the late 1800s, the Society had required would-be lifesavers to demonstrate proficiency in scientific swimming stunts, such as "swimming by means of the propeller" and "somersaulting," in order to pass the lifesaving exam. Its handbooks for lifesavers included instructions for these and other scientific maneuvers, stating: "The practice of feats serve the purpose of teaching him how great is really man's command of the water, and the best methods of making most use of it."[28] Longfellow himself passed the

Royal Life Saving Society Test, earning both a diploma and a bronze medal from the organization. One typical VLSC carnival in New York included demonstrations of "twin swimming," a "combination forward march" in the water, an umbrella race, swimming with hands and feet tied, and an exhibition of fancy swimming, diving, and floating by Miss Adeline Trapp, who became one of the VLSC's earliest female members. Longfellow had recruited Trapp to the VLSC after learning of a heroic rescue she made at the age of fourteen, saving a young boy from drowning at Nassau Beach.[29]

From the beginning, Longfellow made a point to include female VLSC lifesavers at exhibitions and carnivals, believing that women and girls in the audience would be inspired to see members of their own sex who were healthy, well-poised, and "perfectly able to take care of themselves in the briny deep."[30] But this was several years before Annette Kellerman's stockinette one-piece was widely available, and it was difficult for women to demonstrate their true capabilities in the water when burdened by the shackles of their bathing costumes—a fact that was not lost on VLSC leaders. One report issued by the organization called it a "wonderment" that girls were able to swim at all given the volume of clothing they were expected to wear; VLSC leader Commodore Raynor said he'd much prefer to trust a woman over a male lifesaver but would "hate to be at the mercy of one of these

Women wringing out their bathing costumes, circa 1905.

heavily skirted ones."[31] Longfellow himself once weighed a wet bloomer suit someone left outside a bathing machine and was shocked to discover it weighed 30 pounds.[32]

The VLSC had, in the past, taken a humorous approach to the issue and held races in which some male competitors were handicapped by having to wear women's bathing dresses. But in 1909, Longfellow had a radical idea: Instead of handicapping the men, why not show the public what the fair sex was capable of if given the same freedom in the water as their male counterparts. The VLSC was planning a nine-mile race from Yorkville to Clason Point that passed through Hell Gate, the dangerous sluiceway where so many aboard the *General Slocum* had lost their lives five years earlier. He asked Adeline Trapp—who was as outspoken about women's swimwear as Annette Kellerman—if she could swim the course wearing a man's suit. She was game, recalling later that all those years of dragging around that extra yardage in the water had stirred up a "terrific rebellion" inside her.[33] Longfellow had to procure a suit from England since American men's suits consisted of separate trunks and tops (which could slip up in the water and show one's chest). Freed of the strictures of the bloomer costume, Trapp was successful, becoming the first woman to swim through Hell Gate. The newspapers marveled that a "frail" girl not even 5 feet tall had "outdistanced and outswam fifteen sturdy men contestants."[34] However, not everyone was pleased. Trapp had just secured a position as a New York schoolteacher, and the Department of Education sent her a letter warning her to never wear a bathing suit that showed any part of her body in public again.[35]

A LIFESAVING LEAGUE OF THEIR OWN

A decade into the twentieth century, the situation for women's swimming remained dire, and Trapp and others at the VLSC began to feel that there needed to be an organization dedicated specifically to teaching women swimming and lifesaving skills. In 1911, they formed the National Women's Lifesaving League (NWLL), the first women's lifesaving organization in the country, with VLSC secretary Katherine Mehrtens as its president and Trapp as one of its instructors. In an interview shortly after its founding, Mehrtens said she was "dumb-founded" when she first got into lifesaving work and learned how few women could swim. "If all girls could swim as most boys do a Slocum disaster would be impossible," she added.[36]

The NWLL began by offering free swimming lessons at the public baths but soon had to move to a private pool in Brooklyn since the baths' twenty-minute time limits were too short to accomplish much of any-thing. They kept membership fees as low as possible—$1 initiation fee and 50¢ annual dues—and applications poured in. Within two years, the NWLL had one thousand female members from nearly every trade and profession, including stenographers, schoolteachers, shop workers, nurses, actresses, and artists. Beginners learned how to take care of themselves in the water, while advanced swimmers learned how to save others and mastered a variety of skills, including diving, breaking strangleholds, and towing a struggling or incapacitated victim back to shore; and to earn a lifesaving badge, they had to do it all in street clothes.[37] At the time, women did not work as lifeguards, so the NWLL's motto was one of pre-paredness. "Our work is to help save life whenever we can, wherever we are," said Mehrtens. And many did make rescues, prompting the *New York Tribune* to write, "Until this time it has been chiefly man's privilege to save woman from drowning. Now the tables are to be turned."[38] The nearly full-page article on the League continued: "If you, being a man, get out of your depth at one of the metropolitan beaches next summer, your cry for help may be answered, not by a burly guard, but by a willowy crea-ture in a straight princess dress over a one-piece bathing suit."[39]

Another goal of the NWLL was to encourage rational swim-wear for women. In a 1913 article Trapp wrote with swimming tips for women, she encouraged them to ignore the fashion police and wear simple Kellerman one-piece suits, which by this point were being mass-produced in knitting mills. If they—or their neighbors at the beach—weren't comfortable with the form-fitting style, they could wear a light slip over the suit but should remove it in the water. She encouraged wearing caps to keep long hair under control, but not the frilly kind that flop down over one's eyes, reporting, "all the members of our association have cut the ruffles off these most becoming caps!"[40]

There was a clear ethos of making every NWLL member a "real" swimmer—the kind of girl, as Mehrtens put it, who doesn't sit under her parasol and simper but runs into the water "without fear of getting her nose sunburned and the marcel wave out of her hair."[41] Like the VLSC, the League gave public demonstrations and hosted regular swimming competitions for its members. One in 1914 at Manhattan Beach included a race using the trudgen stroke, lifesaving carries, a canoeing demonstration, and a number of "fancy," or ornamental, swimming moves, including the "rolling log," "cartwheel," and "backward revolutions," and fifteen different dives.[42] At another event, organizers set loose a pair of ducks past the breakers and the swimmers raced to be the first to wrangle a waterfowl to shore.[43]

As the League attracted and trained ever stronger swimmers, the events grew more serious, with members setting new speed and endurance records and competing against members of other women's swimming groups and clubs that were emerging. There was no national governing body for women's swimming—or any women's sport for that matter—so these events were ad hoc, but they were important because they provided some of the earliest competitive swimming opportunities for women. Some of the League's leaders, particularly Athletic Branch Chair Charlotte Epstein—known as "Eppie" to friends and colleagues—fostered

A swimming race sponsored by the National Women's Lifesaving League at Sheepshead Bay, Brooklyn, in 1914.

greater ambitions and would soon help women's swimming grow into a formally recognized and organized competitive sport.[44]

For many women, swimming was liberating—both because of the less-restrictive clothing it allowed them to wear and because of the feeling of independence that comes with being able to take care of oneself in the water. An article in 1913 stated that a "feminine movement" was afoot in the water. Women at the beaches, it continued, were "shaking off the shackles" of conventionality and grasping at "a newly-offered freedom to lead healthy, happy, vigorous lives."[45] Many of the NWLL members were vocal advocates for women's suffrage and saw a connection between their physical and political emancipation. On July 18, 1915, the League staged a race to save an anti-suffrage "dummy" from drowning. The stuffed effigy wore a long white dress, silk gloves, a red sash with the words "Anti-Suffrage" printed in black letters, and a dour expression on her hand-drawn face. The *New York Times* reported, "The water women are all good suffragists, and when it was proposed that . . . they save an unfortunate Anti-Suffragist, they all agreed with enthusiasm."[46] In front of a large crowd, the dummy was thrown into the water, and the valiant League members raced out to save their political adversary. The "honor" went to Rita Greenfield, though she admitted she would have preferred to drown the dummy.[47] The *Times* concluded that Miss Anti-Suffrage, "an old-fashioned woman who does not believe it is ladylike to swim," would have certainly perished if not for the progressive lifesavers.[48]

League members weren't the only ones making the connection between swimming and suffrage. An editorial titled "Modern Woman Is Making Rapid Progress in the Water as Well as on Land" linked women's physical accomplishments as swimmers to the inevitable political gains coming their way. "The woman of today is broader of shoulder, deeper of chest, stronger of will than she was in the old days . . . more muscular," it said. "Should she get the suffrage, as I believe she will eventually, that . . . will push her still further ahead."[49]

WATERPROOFING AMERICA

Just as leaders of the NWLL were seeking to expand their organization's scope and mission, Commodore Longfellow was trying to do the same over at the VLSC. As superintendent of the largest lifesaving organization in America, he had established swimming programs all over New York and worked with civic and governmental groups to establish their own. When the *Titanic* sank in 1912, Longfellow served on the Relief Committee and called out shipping tycoons for insisting their vessels were unsinkable rather than improving safety measures and making sure their crews knew how to swim.[50] He used the opportunity to propose building a municipal pool to be used to teach ship staff and deck crew, as well as the general public, how to swim.[51] Longfellow believed that constructing more indoor swimming pools that offered year-round instruction would help prepare the public for the summer months when the "real" swimming took place outdoors.

Longfellow regularly received requests for help from organizations all over the country and felt a growing urgency to expand the work of the VLSC to other regions. But when he appealed to the VLSC's governing board in the spring of 1913 to support a nationwide program to "waterproof America," they declined, citing budget restrictions and the work still to be done about the four-hundred-plus drownings in New York each year.[52] So Longfellow—never one to be deterred from his mission—resigned and set out on a one-man national tour to spread the gospel of lifesaving. He spent most of the year traveling by train and boat, giving lectures and demonstrations anywhere that would have him: summer camps, recreation conferences, the sporting goods sections of department stores, colleges, and clubhouses of both the YMCA and the Young Women's Christian Association (YWCA). He made the inclusion of women, as well as Black children, a priority in his work. The invitation to his "moving picture lecture" at the Bridgewater, New Jersey, YMCA printed in local newspapers announced that "colored boys and young men of the city" were especially invited, and it was for their benefit that the event was being held.[53] At a recreation convention in Richmond, Virginia, Longfellow chose "Swimming for Girls and Women" as the topic for his session, advocating for cities to build pools especially for women and citing records of New York's female lifesavers as examples of women's aquatic capabilities.[54]

During Longfellow's year of freelance crusading, leaders from the YMCA and the newly formed Boy Scouts of America approached him about launching a nationwide lifesaving and water safety program.

Both groups—plus their sister organizations, the Girl Scouts, Camp-fire Girls, and YWCA—offered activities that put youth in contact with water and would benefit from such programming, but neither had the capacity or expertise to spearhead it. Longfellow, who had not only become the nation's foremost authority on water safety but also wrote the chapter on water safety for the first *Boy Scouts Handbook*, was clearly the person for the job. And the American Red Cross, with its charter to prevent the recurrence of disasters and to care for the victims of disaster, seemed like the most logical organization to take on the project. Clearly, the nearly ten thousand drownings in America each year constituted a disaster, not just to the individual victims but to the nation as a whole. The organization's leaders agreed, and in 1914 the American Red Cross Life Saving Corps was launched with a starting budget of $5,000 and Longfellow as its national field representative.[55]

A great coiner of phrases, Longfellow gave the American Red Cross program the motto "every American a swimmer, and every swimmer a lifesaver." This slogan signaled an important shift toward thinking about water safety in terms of prevention rather than rescue—not only training lifeguards but also providing the public with the skills to take initiative for their own safety.[56] The Red Cross Water Safety Service established two levels of swimming: "beginner" and "swimmer." Those rising to swimmer had mastered the correct form of fundamental strokes, could safeguard themselves in the water, and were eligible to pursue further training and Red Cross lifeguard certification if they so desired.[57] Longfellow chartered the first Red Cross Life Saving Corps at the Baltimore YMCA, he himself taking the very first lifesaving test and becoming Red Cross Lifesaver #1. It was an insignia he would wear proudly as millions would follow and receive lifeguard certification in the coming decades. After establishing the first Red Cross Life Saving Corps in Baltimore, he moved on to Washington and Philadelphia, and within three years had chartered sixty-one corps across the country. In each town, Longfellow would work with the strongest swimmers to get them certified as lifeguards, instructors, and examiners so that they could continue to train more guards and build their local corps after his departure, thus greatly magnifying his impact.

At first, the Red Cross would not agree to make the lifeguard certification program open to women, its leaders citing doubt that women could perform the duties—and also fearing that male swimmers wouldn't take the program seriously if women were admitted. But having visited hundreds of summer camps, Longfellow had seen how "unprotected and deficient in swimming" those for girls were and knew there was a growing need for female lifesavers.[58] He also fervently believed that lifesavers did not have to be big, burly men, and that proper technique relied on skill and experience far more than brute strength.[59] Longfellow, who weighed around 250 pounds, often demonstrated this point by pulling small children from the audience and having them tow him across the pool by his hair.

Wanting to prove that women were capable, Longfellow established the World's Life-Saving Alliance for Women, an independent, but parallel, organization that mirrored the lifeguard training and certification process of the Red Cross. He hoped that through the Alliance he could build up a cadre of qualified female lifeguards who would eventually be accepted into the Red Cross Life Saving Corps.[60] Whenever he traveled for his Red Cross duties, he would meet with swimming instructors at YWCA chapters and women's colleges to promote the Alliance, administer its lifesaving test, and train female examiners. The first World's Life Saving Alliance lifesaving certificate was awarded to a woman in Maryland in 1914, the same year the Red Cross Life Saving Corps began issuing certificates to men.[61]

Since women were shut out of the membership of the nation's premier water safety program at the Red Cross, the Alliance offered an important alternative to those wishing to earn formal certification in lifeguarding, whether for volunteer or paid work. For example, at Ocean Park, California, where the volunteer lifesaving corps was one of the first in the country to accept female guards, the male members decided in 1916 to test for the Red Cross lifesaving certificate, so the female guards trained for and took the Alliance test.[62] If not for the latter option, the women, who had already had to work extra hard to prove themselves (having been laughed at when they first proposed joining), would have had no way to earn official recognition of their skills—likely jeopardizing their status within the crew.[63]

When the SS *Eastland* steamer capsized in Chicago that same

*A female lifesaver with the American Red Cross demonstrates
the prone-pressure method of resuscitation.*

year, killing 812 people, Longfellow made a rushed trip to the Windy
City, using the heightened public interest in water safety to establish
multiple lifesaving programs in the Midwest, including at the University of Chicago. This marked the beginning of lifesaving programs
in American higher education that would soon spread to colleges and
universities throughout the nation—and would be instrumental in
Longfellow's work using performance to promote swimming.[64] As
more schools and colleges built pools, many began requiring students
to pass a swimming test in order to graduate.

By the time the United States entered the First World War in April
1917, the Red Cross lifesaving program had footholds in every pocket
of the country. Longfellow moved his work to naval stations and army
camps, teaching "scores of thousands of fighting men" to swim, while
women swimmers prepared to fill in for male lifeguards called away to
the front. A paper noted that hundreds of Los Angeles society women
were training for the World's Life Saving Alliance test, as they were
"determined to do their bit in this war."[65] In Belleville, Illinois, another
paper reported that since all the high school boys who usually served
as guards at the local lake had joined the army, a woman guard had

been hired for the first time.[66] Seeing women in the lifeguard chair was so novel that some beach patrons simply couldn't behave themselves, as demonstrated at the Jersey Shore when Ruth MacNeely, who had previously been awarded a medal for saving the lives of two classmates, became the first female guard there. "She had not been on duty long before there came cries for help from the ocean," reported a newspaper. Miss MacNeely immediately swam out to help the man and tow him to shore, finding "he was not badly off and revived at once."[67] The scene repeated itself several more times that day until it became apparent to the manager that the men just wanted to be rescued by the young woman. If any man was caught out of his depth after that, he was on his own because the beach manger ordered MacNeely to assist only women and children. In many cases, women not only filled the vacated spots of male lifeguards but did the job better. A pool manager from St. Louis said he found the female guards to be "conscientious," while the "fellows are always watching the pretty girls and letting the plain ones and the men get along the best they can."[68]

By the time the war was over, women had more than proven their capabilities as guards, and in May 1920, the Red Cross announced

Commodore Longfellow with a Red Cross YMCA Lifesaving Corps as part of Learn to Swim Week, 1923.

that it would begin accepting women into its lifesaving corps, officially making them part of the organization's national efforts to
reduce drowning.[69] In an article about the decision, the *Red Cross Bulletin* pointed out that the world had moved beyond "the romantic
stage where dependence in time of accident rests on the help of some
male hero."[70] Moreover, it added, with the rising popularity of boating
and water pastimes among women, a male hero may not always be
at hand in case of an emergency. Longfellow celebrated the decision
by writing a three-page article for the *Ladies' Home Journal* detailing some of the heroics of women who had saved lives at pools, rivers, and beaches across the country, often putting themselves in great
danger in the process. "It is plain to see," wrote Longfellow, "that
women have the daring as well as the ability to brave the perils of the
deep and to be real life-savers."[71] Having established corps of qualified
male *and female* lifeguards all over the country, Longfellow would
soon expand his work to include what would become his most unique
aquatic contribution—and one that would earn him the nickname
"the Shakespeare of Swimming."

WATER PAGEANTS WITH A PURPOSE

Longfellow's ultimate goal was to make everyone a swimmer, and
that would require vastly different teaching methods from those of
the past. Students at the turn of the century often learned to swim
by wearing harnesses suspended from a pool's overhead pulley system
that supported them as they moved through the water. It was a slight
improvement over the antiquated pole-and-rope method but still
greatly limited the number of students who could learn at once. But
new pedagogies were circulating, often with a focus on group teaching
and confidence building. George Corsan, a member of the Canadian
Royal Life Saving Society, had innovated the first mass swimming
lessons at the Detroit YMCA in 1906, moving away from the standard
breaststroke—which is difficult for beginners to coordinate—in favor
of the crawl stroke, which he could teach to large groups of children
on land before having them try it in the water. Corsan, whose methods became the backbone of the first YMCA swimming program, also

advocated for the use of "stunts"—the term increasingly being used in place of scientific or ornamental swimming—and included pages of detailed descriptions in his 1914 book *At Home in the Water*. Another educator, B. Dean Brink of the American Swimming Association, devised a widely adopted method of helping non-swimmers overcome their fear of the water by focusing on mental images they could imitate, such as a "sleeping turtle" floating on the surface.[72]

For Longfellow, whose (many) often-quoted mottos included "Educate gently while entertaining hugely," the best way to waterproof America was to make swimming fun—so he opted for a mix of the mass teaching and playacting approaches, adding his own unique twist. At swimming holes and pools, Longfellow would gather his students around him in a semicircle in waist-deep water and, starting with the Brink method, have them imitate his movements, such as that of a "hungry duck" sticking its face in the water. But Longfellow, who was possessed of a great imagination, quickly moved beyond imitating animals. He would weave tales of epic swims, near drownings caused by ignorance or horseplay, and daring rescues conducted by trained lifeguards, making his students part of the stories by having them act out the scenes. The impromptu storytelling sessions were so well received, both by the students and the crowds of spectators they inevitably attracted, that Longfellow started putting advance planning into them, creating special stories to incorporate the local histories and celebrations of the places he was visiting.

It didn't take long for the Commodore to start dreaming of the greater impact his stories could have with a bit of costuming, music, and dramatic flair, so around 1920, he began setting his aquatic stories to paper, writing scripts for what he called "water pageants": plays that used the water—whether pool, lake, or sea—as their stage. With his scripts he tried to provide opportunities for swimming students and lifesavers to demonstrate their skills while also incorporating messages about the importance of swimming—"pageants with a purpose," as he would sometimes say. "We take people from the sands or banks of the pool and . . . teach the secrets of the sea," wrote Longfellow. "How much more effective those secrets are when they are dramatized and dressed in colored lights and fabrics and presented to musical accompaniment beneath a summer moon!"[73]

*Commodore Longfellow dressed as Neptune
for a Red Cross water pageant.*

One of Longfellow's earliest and most popular pageants, "Showing Father Neptune," was written at the invitation of Washington University in St. Louis for the opening dedication of the university's new pool in 1921. At the start of the play, a bugler announces the arrival of Neptune, king of the sea, who then dramatically emerges from the water, having slipped in unseen behind a screen. Regal with his long white beard and trident, Neptune looks around quizzically at the pool and demands to know the purpose of this strange body of water. The performers explain that the pool will be used to promote four noble purposes: health, safety, sport, and fun, with each of these purposes then becoming a separate episode in the play. In the Washington University production, "Health" was demonstrated by swimmers from the YMCA and YWCA, who performed swimming strokes in marching formation; for "Safety," Red Cross lifesavers demonstrated rescue and resuscitation techniques; "Sport" included relays and diving exhibitions—including one by Betty Grimes, a diver on America's first women's Olympic aquatics team; and for the "Fun" episode, there were comic diving, swimming clowns, and pajama races between married alums.[74] Longfellow himself played Neptune, his favorite role and one for which he was perfectly suited. "With his height and bulk and booming voice," wrote a friend at the Red Cross, "he needed only a flowing robe, a wig and long gray beard, a gilded cardboard crown and the symbolic trident to perfectly personify the mythological god of the sea."[75] At the end of the pageant, Neptune, who has attentively watched the demonstrations, expresses his approval of the pool and its noble purposes and officially dedicates it as part of his aquatic domain. Twenty-five hundred people saw the pageant at Washington University in its first two nights.

With growing interest in swimming and greater societal focus on community leisure and recreation, the 1920s saw an explosion in municipal swimming pool construction. Longfellow advocated for dedicating every new pool with a water pageant, believing that they were the perfect way to bring a community together and build excitement around the new facility. By 1924, "Showing Father Neptune" had been performed at the dedication ceremonies of at least seventy-five swimming pools, including an all-female adaptation—"Showing Neptune's Daughter"—developed by the Girl Scouts.[76] A production of the pageant at Hygeia Pool in Atlantic City, which featured a cast of two hundred performers and music by the Fire Department Band, attracted an audience of three thousand. When Salem, Massachusetts, produced the pageant at the dedication of an 8-acre saltwater pool cordoned off of Salem Harbor, the production drew more than ten thousand spectators. It was such a success that the town began producing an annual water pageant that grew to include auditions, a team of dance, drama, and swimming coaches, and speaking parts performed by trained radio announcers.[77] One year, in a clever publicity stunt, they sent an "invitation" out to sea for Neptune, requesting to know whether he would attend, and then had local fishermen haul in his RSVP. (It was a yes!)

The Red Cross was a highly influential organization among youth recreation and education leaders in the early twentieth century, and with its support behind the water pageant idea, their use quickly caught on and others began writing their own scripts. These were shared through the Red Cross, which distributed mimeographed materials and pamphlets through its field reps, recreation conferences, and education journals. Not only did the Red Cross serve as a clearinghouse for information on this growing canon of scripts but it also offered five- and ten-week courses in water pageantry production through its National Aquatic Schools. By the mid-1920s, pageants were being performed just about anywhere young people and water came together.

Part of the popular appeal of pageants was their adaptability to incorporate swimmers of all ages and levels, as well as different types of aquatic activities. A typical pageant at the YWCA titled "Along the River Bank" featured small children dressed as frogs and trout, intermediate swimmers as fireflies with tiny flashlights glowing under their caps, and teenage girls dressed as river sprites.[78] In colleges, they were often performed by students in swimming classes, along with the school's Red Cross Life Saving Corps. At the University of Chicago in 1927, physical educator and lifesaving instructor Katharine Curtis, who would become a key figure in the development of synchronized swimming, staged a Christmas water pageant that was said to be a "positive mirth provoker" and featured twenty-three different sketches with "innumerable and fascinating stunts" and female swimmers in reindeer antlers pulling a cutout of Santa and his sleigh through the water.[79] Pageants sometimes took the shape of short sketches within larger water shows, some of which—by today's standards—played fast and loose with student safety. At the University of Missouri's "Mermaid's Water Revue" in 1927, Captain Kidd and a gang of pirates led female swimmers to the diving board, bound their hands and feet, and forced them to walk the plank. But instead of perishing, the women surprised the pirates by untying the ropes underwater and emerging free of their tethers. Later in the show, a male student performed a "fire dive," by having his kerosene-drenched clothes lit on fire just before he dove from the balcony in a ball of flames.[80]

The 1920s and 30s saw not only a "pool-building spree" in the United States but also the racial segregation of America's swimming places—turning the water into a highly contested area, even as people were headed there in ever larger numbers. Historian Jeff Wiltse has noted that as gender segregation at pools eased, it gave way to racial segregation instead, as fears grew over Black men and white women swimming together.[81] Like other segregated spaces and public utilities of the Jim Crow era, with its supposed separate-but-equal policies, Black children and adults were banned from many of the best swimming facilities in the country, while the pools that were open to Black residents were fewer, and typically older and smaller. But despite the unequal access, Black youth leaders were, of course, equally eager to promote swimming and water safety, and water pageants were often held at city, camp, and college pools serving primarily Black communities.

The Harlem YWCA at 137th Street, originally founded as the "Colored Women's Branch," held water pageants as early as 1928 when "The Frog Prince" was performed by swimming students and the lifesaving corps as part of the organization's spring carnival.[82] At Banneker Pool, one of two pools built by the Works Progress Administration that were open to Black residents of Washington, DC, an annual water pageant was held starting in the mid-1930s. An announcement for one of its productions noted that King Neptune would be played by a lifeguard and that the pool would feature "a stage with all the lighting effects and costuming befitting such an occasion."[83] In Durham, North Carolina, Hillside Park swimming pool, which was designated for Black residents, also began hosting water pageants in the mid-1930s for its swimming students. For several years, separate announcements ran on the same newspaper pages for the "Water Pageant"—meaning white—at Duke Park Pool and the "Negro Water Pageant" at Hillside.[84] A Richmond, Virginia, newspaper made similar announcements about the pageants happening at the racially segregated summer camps.[85]

The first full book on pageantry, *Water Pageants, Games and Stunts*, was published in 1933. Written by Olive McCormick, national water safety advisor for the Girl Scouts, with a foreword by Longfellow, it covered all the steps of producing a water pageant, from writing the script to publicizing the show, and everything in between, like music, casting, lighting, and set design. McCormick's book, which came out at the height of the Great Depression, includes instructions for wardrobing turtles, gnomes, water lilies, satyrs, and even human totem poles using inexpensive materials like cheesecloth, rope, muslin, wire, and cardboard waterproofed with paraffin. The illusion of

DUCK

WATER LILLY

FIN

DRAGON FLY

SPIRAL...

FIN.

Headdresses like these from Olive McCormick's book were an important part of costuming for water pageants, as they could be seen even when the swimmers were in the water.

a mermaid's tail, she suggested, could be created by painting the legs with a combination of aluminum powder and banana oil.

As the title of McCormick's book indicates, swimming "stunts"—the repertoire of which was continuing to grow—were often incorporated into water pageants. Other components of "water ballet," or what would become known as synchronized swimming, such as group formations and swimming to music, were also very much a part of these events. In Longfellow's pageant "Neptune's Cure for Piracy," a troupe of water nymphs helps a canoe full of pirates overcome their fear of swimming by showing them how beautiful an art it can be, as they swirl in and out of circles and formations illuminated by lanterns dangling from the ends of bamboo poles the nymphs carry as they swim. They then coax the pirates from their canoe and teach them to do the crawl stroke and a series of water stunts and somersaults. By the end of the play, the pirates have become swimming aficionados and they perform, along with their nymph teachers, a series of "porpoise swims" and floating patterns.[86] Many of the early leaders in synchronized swimming, including Katharine Curtis in Chicago, were Red Cross lifesaving instructors, and as these new forms of stunt and group swimming evolved, pageants became a natural way to develop and showcase those skills.

Longfellow himself later wrote blueprints for a pageant called "Swimming in Peace and War: A Water Ballet" in which he referred to synchronized swimming as the "newest phase of aquatic dramatics."[87] He believed performative swimming of all kinds held greater potential for building public interest in aquatics than speed events, reporting in the *Red Cross Courier* in 1937 that he received constant calls for pageant material. "Everywhere I travel," he wrote, "I find an increasing demand for varied programs. 'Give us something besides races and diving competitions; give us something different.'"[88] The popularity of pageants was supported that same year in a survey of 140 high schools, colleges, universities, and camps, which found that 36 percent used water pageants in their programs, while well over half of those that did not reported that they would like to but didn't have proper swimming facilities. And of the educators and recreation directors who responded, 101 agreed that water pageants are a valuable part of educational programs.[89] Longfellow never stopped believing in the power of performance as a teaching tool. During the Second World War, he even used water pageants as a way to both entertain and educate armed service members about swimming survival techniques that could mean the difference between life and death in an amphibious war.

By the time Longfellow retired in 1947, just a few months before his death at the age of 66, the country had seen a huge upsurge in interest in swimming, with 80 million Americans participating in some sort of aquatic activity. At the same time, the national drowning rate had decreased by half: from 10.4 per 100,000 in 1914, the year the American Red Cross launched its water safety program, to 5.2 in 1947.[90] Under Longfellow's leadership, the American Red Cross had trained and qualified 100,000 water safety instructors and had issued 4.5 million certificates for swimming and lifesaving courses. "To the men, women, and children of America who do their hobby-lobbying in the water," wrote one of the Commodore's colleagues, "the name 'Longfellow' is as significant as the same surname is to lovers of verse."[91]

But his impact on waterproofing America, and particularly its women, extends far beyond what the statistics show, as much of his work took on a life of its own. Women lifesavers of the VLSC, the World's Life-Saving Alliance for Women, the National Women's Lifesaving League, and the Red Cross, each of which Longfellow had actively supported, would go on to become leaders in every developing field of aquatics. In addition to lifesaving, they were instrumental in developing women's swimming as a competitive sport and enabling women to realize their potential as athletes; some even helped establish and coach America's first Olympic team of female swimmers and divers. Others would go a different route, developing these early forms of pageantry and performative swimming into new aquatic artforms that would permeate a variety of popular entertainment genres, and eventually become its own unique branch of athletics. And Longfellow loved to see it. He wrote:

> The art of swimming is increasing very rapidly, and human beings are attaining a great mastery over the comparatively unfamiliar element of water. But for the great majority of those who need to learn more, let us not neglect to keep swimming a great game, full of fun and color and glamorous experiences.[92]

And with the foundation laid by Longfellow, and the many swimmers in his orbit, it would.

CHAPTER 5

SIDESHOW

Because huge audiences love to see beauty in danger and escaping unharmed, there has developed a great body of girls whose duty it is to take great leaps and dives and all kinds of consequent chances with their lives.

−ILLUSTRATED WORLD, 1923

Strolling the midway of the Rice and Dore Water Carnival was a true assault on the senses. Mechanical tunes wafted from the brightly painted merry-go-round, competing with the oompahs of three brass bands stationed at different points on the fairgrounds, all of which was periodically pierced by shrieks and squeals of laughter from children and adults alike who were taking a ride on the "Trip to Mars." As the fairgoers strolled, some stopped to buy bags of roasted peanuts or cups of red lemonade, and spielers called out in booming voices to "step right up" and see their attractions.

The Rice and Dore Water Carnival was the biggest and most unique traveling amusement of 1914, and its managers had chosen Portland, Oregon, to open the season. On April 4, a special diving event kicked things off, with thousands gathered along the Willamette River to witness three high divers plunge from the city's bridges into the water below. Shortly after, at 3:00 in the afternoon, a gong clanged, the gates opened, and crowds poured into the fairgrounds on Oregon Street. Ads for the Rice and Dore Water Carnival had promised visitors "freaks and curiosities of all kinds," and the midway did not disappoint. There was the wondrous Prince Napoleon, who stood tall at only 26 inches, the one-legged motordome racer, a haunted roulette wheel, and "Old Abe," a 32-foot python. There were sideshows within sideshows—a 10-in-1 and even a "20-in-1"—where for the cost of a single ticket, fairgoers could revel in novel and exotic sights as diverse as a double-bodied baby, geisha dancing girls, the "world's fattest woman and her coterie of midgets," glass blowers, a camel parade, and more.[1] As daylight turned to dusk, two thousand electric lights made the scene even more festive. It was, in the words of one newspaper, "a gilded display of wonders of carnivaldom."[2]

But despite the sheer number and diversity of these sideshow attractions lining the midway, they were all just hors d'oeuvres leading to the main event: the circus big top. Under it, visitors would be treated to the world's largest and finest water circus—the aquatic show that gave the Rice and Dore Water Carnival its name. The idea of a water circus was new to most of the Portland crowd, and a newspaper advised readers not to expect the usual "ring full of sawdust" when they entered the tent, but instead "a miniature lake, brilliantly illuminated."[3] Indeed, the circus "ring" was actually a round tank holding 75,000 gallons of water, around which were stationed ladders, springboards, acrobatic apparatus, and risers of seats for two thousand spectators.

The water circus had everything a land circus offered—comedy, beauty, and thrilling physical feats—but with its spectacular stunts performed by aerial and aquatic experts "*over, on top* and *beneath* the water.*"[4]* For the over the water portion, a troupe of ten women performed all kinds of acrobatics from the springboard, while high divers, including the fearless Inez Fanjoy representing the fair sex, plunged from heights as high as 100 feet. There were fire divers, sack-escape divers, and even diving horses and ponies. As for performers whose acts took place on top of the water, there were logrollers who demonstrated fancy footwork on floating timbers, water walkers who sported boat shoes that let them stroll confidently across the surface, and a group of lady ornamental swimmers who were said to give a graceful exhibition of fancy swimming equal to that of Annette Kellerman.[5] And all the while these feats on and above the water were dazzling the audience, an intriguing mystery was taking place beneath its surface.

A few minutes into the show, once the crowd was good and warmed up, a figure dressed as Father Neptune, complete with white beard and trident, would suddenly appear, having inexplicably emerged from under the water. A hush would fall over the audience, and in a booming voice, Neptune would greet the land dwellers. He had come from his watery kingdom, he explained, to bid his mermaid daughters home. Twelve women in scaly costumes would appear on stage and reluctantly agree to return to the depths with Neptune. Bidding the audience farewell, the mermaids would descend unseen steps under the water until they had completely disappeared out of sight, leaving the surface just as calm as if they'd never been there. The audience would look around inquisitively, murmuring, *Where did they go?*

How long could they hold their breath? The master of ceremonies would feign unease but eventually, seeing the surface unstirred, declare that the show must go on.

A half hour would pass, the mermaids nearly forgotten in the excitement and chaos of ponies plunging through the air and clowns splashing into the water as they tripped over their giant shoes. Then, without warning, Neptune would resurface and—as reported by one reviewer—"at last, the tension is relieved . . . and a genuine sigh of relief escapes the audience on beholding the happy mermaids appear, one at a time, on the water's surface . . . none the worse for their long absence in 'the deep blue sea.'"[6] Addressing the crowd again, Neptune would report that his mermaid daughters had regaled him with such splendid tales of life in the sun and amongst the flowers that he had decided to return to terra firma for good. The announcer would smile and nod, while the audience remained just as puzzled. *Where had these swimmers been? How had Rice and Dore achieved such a feat?*

THE CIRCUS'S WATERY EVOLUTION

Bill Rice and Harry Dore ran the largest and most famous water circus of their day. Although they were not the first—and would hardly be the last—to add aquatic performance to American circuses or to present an underwater disappearing act, they *were* the first to combine the two, devise a way to make it portable, and take it all over the country. Swimming had made its way into the American circus as early as the 1860s, when a few traveling shows, such as the Hanlon Brothers, featured man fish and water queen acts in small glass tanks like those popular at dime museums. P. T. Barnum had showcased Agnes and Willie Beckwith's scientific swimming in his 1887 Madison Square Garden show, and Frank Hall's brick and mortar English Circus and German Water Carnival in Chicago, modeled after the Blackpool Tower Aquatic Circus, had featured aquatic acts like the fancy swimming of Cora (McFarland) Beckwith. But these were all stationary shows, and it wasn't until 1895 when Barnum and Bailey squeezed a swimming pool under its iconic big top that the full water

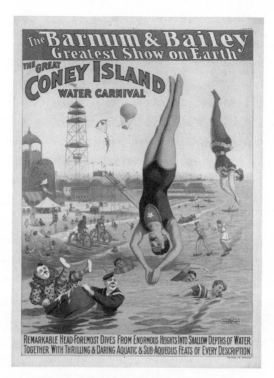

*A poster from Barnum and Bailey's water carnival,
featuring high divers, fancy swimmers, water
walkers, and other aquatic performers.*

show became part of the uniquely American traveling circus and carnival tradition.

P. T. Barnum and James Bailey, two of the biggest names in the outdoor show business, who had joined forces in the late 1880s, ran what was by far the largest circus enterprise in the country at the time. In addition to their famous three-ring circus, the show boasted a hippodrome track for equestrian acts, two stages, and seats for fourteen thousand people—all under a single gargantuan canvas. It took sixty-nine double-size train cars to haul their mountains of paraphernalia, hundreds of employees and performers, and a menagerie that included twenty-four elephants, more than the number of pachyderms owned by all other American circuses combined.[7] But in 1895, Barnum and Bailey's Greatest Show on Earth got even greater when they added a fourth circus ring—one filled with water. It required an advance crew to dig a 42-foot-wide hole (to match the diameters of the other three rings) and line it with a massive, specially designed rubber insert before the entourage arrived in each new town.[8]

Barnum and Bailey's Water Carnival included, among various aquatic acts, a farcical pantomime in which a bride, groom, policeman, and full German band all end up in the water. But the highlight was a plunge made by diver Louis Golden from a height of 85 feet, an act that was said to be worth the cost of admission alone.[9] The high dive was something entirely new and remarkable in 1895 and was greatly anticipated by audiences across the country. Its natural element of danger made it well suited to the circus, and soon, smaller outfits began adding their own miniature water carnivals, with male high divers. It wouldn't have occurred to American showmen of the late nineteenth century to put a woman at the top of the ladder, as the requisite athleticism, skill, and steely nerves were considered masculine traits.

But interest in aquatic amusements saw its biggest leap starting about a decade later when the New York Hippodrome, where Annette Kellerman would later perform, began using underwater technologies in new and inventive ways. In 1906, the Hippodrome debuted "Neptune's Daughter," which took a page out of Britain's earlier aqua dramas and added a mysterious twist—one that would serve as inspiration for the Rice and Dore Water Carnival. In the story, characters such as the mermaid queen Sirene would emerge from underwater, appear to stand on its surface, deliver dialogue, and then submerge again as easily as if they were walking on and off stage. At the end, an entire cast of mermaids would appear, seated in a ship with Neptune that would rise to the surface and then sink again as both the cast of villagers and the audience stared on in slack-jawed amazement. The *New York Times* wrote at the end of the season, "No spectacular invention or innovation of recent years has aroused such popular interest or awakened such widespread curiosity as the mermaid scene in 'Neptune's Daughter' at the Hippodrome."[10]

How did it work? As the *Times* reported, the cast simply hung out underwater in diving bells, breathing air that was pumped in and trapped in the bells' domes.[11] The writer called the bells "mermaid apartments," and wrote that together they looked like an underwater village of huts on stilts. Each apartment was equipped with an underwater phone to relay signals when it was time for a character to appear; on the cue, the actor would swim out and stand on top of her diving bell to perform her part, then swim back the way she came. There was also a man stationed at each apartment to pull the mermaid to safety if she got disoriented or tangled underwater. The grand finale required more breath-holding, as Neptune's ship was not under a diving bell but mounted on a hydraulic lift. Its passengers had to swim from their bells, hold their breath while they found their spots, and wait for the ship to rise to the surface. In a 1909 production, the Hippodrome made an entire army of forty-eight men and forty-eight women disappear underwater, using a long, inverted trough-shaped diving bell.[12]

The Hippodrome show revolutionized the ways that water could be used to entertain and awe. And although the theater's full system of technology was patented and kept under lock and key, the basic concept of using trapped air for underwater respiration has been understood for thousands of years—Aristotle wrote about it in 360 BCE—so once the Hippodrome unleashed its dramatic possibilities, the idea was there for the taking by anyone, including carnival managers like Rice, Dore, and others who were in the business of making spectacle portable and delivering it to the masses.[13]

The first to latch on to the idea of an aquatic vanishing act was showman Frank Hatch, who in 1911 launched the Hatch Water Circus and Allied Shows. It promised to provide audiences with "an exact repetition of the famous New York Hippodrome with all of its aquatic and spectacular features," including a mermaid ballet in which a troupe of lady swimmers disappeared from sight.[14] But launching a show like that was fraught with challenges, and with it being only six years after the *General Slocum* disaster, one of the most vexing was finding enough women swimmers. *Variety* reported ahead of the opening of the Hatch circus that the poor recruiter tasked with finding performers was "in the throes of despair." For three weeks, reported the article, he'd been haunting Long Island's beaches asking nearly every woman he encountered if she could swim. So far, he'd found only one—a woman who gave swimming lessons at Coney Island whom he immediately hired and christened "Dolphine, the Water Queen"—but the show needed more. "If male swimmers were needed, he could get a million," wrote *Variety*, "but the woman thing has him 'buffaloed.'"[15]

But it was the tank itself that posed the biggest challenge. Even though Hatch's production was meant to be a traveling show, advance arrangements had to be made at each venue to excavate a 100-foot-long hole and line it with concrete—basically creating a large in-ground pool (for comparison, the typical community pool today is 75 feet long) in every town they visited. As the one responsible for these arrangements, Hatch's booking agent—Bill Rice—would have been well aware of the expense and impracticality involved.[16] Perhaps for these reasons, the following year, the Hatch Water Circus underwent a quiet reorganization, and what emerged was the Rice and Dore Water Carnival, managed by Rice and his associate Harry Dore. (Hatch would remain in the carnival business, specializing in motordrome walls of death instead of disappearing mermaids.)

The new partners tweaked and experimented with ways to make do with smaller tanks, downsizing from one that held 200,000 gallons in their 1912 season to 75,000 gallons the following year.[17] By 1914, Rice and Dore had worked out and patented a tank that was large enough to accommodate seventy-five performers and was equipped with basic technology to produce a Hippodrome-style disappearing mermaid ballet. Yet it was portable enough that it could be set up and removed quickly, enabling them to play in a different town every week. Using a tunnel-shaped diving bell leading from the steps to a hidden backstage exit, the mermaids would disappear underwater, emerge unseen behind a wall or screen, then change clothes and rejoin the show, giving the illusion that they were an entirely new set of performers as they dove and demonstrated ornamental swimming stunts. When it was time for them to reappear, they would don their mermaid suits, retrace their steps through the tunnel, and reemerge with Neptune from his watery kingdom. The *Great Falls Tribune* of Montana wrote that the Hippodrome's "Neptune's Daughter" "was never conceived to be possible as a traveling exhibition until the inventive genius of Rice and Dore overcame all obstacles, so this immense mystifying entertainment could be presented to all America." This alone, said the article, made their show a record-breaker and significant in the annals of amusement history.[18]

By contracting with dozens of midway concessionaires to supplement their show, Rice and Dore turned their enterprise into a full-blown traveling carnival, though the water circus remained the feature event. After opening in Portland, they continued to Saskatchewan, Great Falls, Birmingham, and Yazoo City, Mississippi, with papers across the country calling the water circus a "masterpiece of stage craft" and exclaiming, "Something new at last!" Large turnouts were reported everywhere they went, with one paper noting that the concessions' spielers were all smiles thanks to the "money crowd."[19] In Louisville, Kentucky, the water circus was so popular performers had to go without dinner on closing night in order to accommodate the massive crowds with an extra evening show.[20]

THE RISE OF THE DIVING GIRL

When Annette Kellerman launched her popular diving act at White City in 1907, showmen of the outdoor amusement industry immediately saw dollar signs. There was clear commercial potential for shows that put young athletic female bodies on display yet remained—because of the physical skills being demonstrated—in the realm of respectability. Soon similar "diving girl" acts were appearing as part of large water circuses like Rice and Dore's and as smaller individual sideshow concessions. As early as 1911, the same year Frank Hatch launched his water circus, *The Billboard* announced that another showman, Harry Six, was running three diving girl troupes at fairgrounds in New York State, Vermont, and Canada.[21] A Connecticut newspaper reported shortly after that the Danbury Fair was replacing its diving horse concession with a diving girl act. It joked that horses already had to worry about being replaced by automobiles, and now even the ones with diving skills couldn't count on steady work.[22]

Even though the supply of women with swimming and diving skills was scant in the early years, as Hatch had learned when trying to staff his troupe of disappearing mermaids, it didn't stay that way for long. Before Kellerman paved the way, making her graceful plunges on stages across America, the idea of becoming a career diver would have been unimaginable for most women, but Kellerman's crusading, along with the work of lifesaving groups, had prompted public interest not only in swimming but also in diving, and the opportunity to leverage aquatic skills into a paying job held great appeal for many young women. The *Los Angeles*

Evening Express noted in 1911 that "Swimming as a vocation for women is engaging the interest of girls of the beach district and promises to develop opportunities worth considering."[23] In fact, Bill Rice hired high diver Inez Fanjoy for his water circus after spotting her practicing her dives off the pier at Venice Beach near LA.[24] Interest in women's diving was greatly furthered when a platform diving competition, along with one in freestyle swimming, were added as Olympic events for women at the 1912 games in Stockholm (though the male gatekeepers of American sport refused to send any women to compete in the events).

Women who wanted to be part of a diving girl act needed a broad range of aquatic skills, including scientific swimming stunts, which were performed between dives to help fill out a show, and fancy dives. Although diving would later become its own aquatic discipline distinct from swimming, there was less emphasis at that time on specialization in sports. Diving skills, as well as familiarity with lifesaving techniques and the ability to do a few ornamental stunts were all just part of the skill set of a well-rounded aquaticist. Lifesaving organizations, which were teaching women to swim by the hundreds, treated diving as an essential skill since it provided the fastest form of water entry, and seconds count when trying to make it to someone at risk of drowning. A water carnival organized by Adeline Trapp in 1914 under the auspices of the National Women's Lifesaving League featured not only demonstrations of lifesaving carries and swimming stunts but also an exhibition of fifteen different fancy dives, including front and back jackknifes and the "apache," "falling statue," and "roly poly rocker" dives.[25]

As part of the turn-of-the-century interest in gymnastics, many pools featured equipment like pommel horses, trapeze bars, and rings suspended above the water that facilitated learning advanced acrobatic dives. A swimming teacher at a Chicago natatorium told a reporter that her female students—just regular girls—would swing from the rings, then leap through the air to the trapeze and even climb to the rafters and dive from 35 feet. On the springboard, she said, they could turn backward and forward somersaults "equal to any circus performer."[26] Kellerman's book *How to Swim* included multiple pages on acrobatic and trapeze diving. She wrote that many people fantasize about flying through the air under a circus big top. "But what the acrobat does professionally at the risk of his neck," wrote Kellerman, "you can do as an amateur over a swimming pool with no risk at all."[27] With such abundant opportunities to gain aquatic skills, and plenty of jobs to be had, by the early 1910s, thousands of diving girls attired in Kellerman suits of every length and color were circuiting the country, plunging, somersaulting, and jackknifing into small water tanks erected on carnival and fair midways, at amusement parks, and on vaudeville stages in every pocket of America.

Diving girl shows often hosted diving competitions that were open to female competitors from the general public as a way to draw crowds to their shows and to recruit new performers. When Maude Gray, a young woman living in San Francisco, heard that a diving girl act from New York was in town and holding a contest on the show's closing night, she grabbed her "little short red suit" and secured a spot in the competition. She had learned to swim at San Francisco's Lurline Baths just a few years prior, determined to do so after nearly drowning in a canoeing accident. At the baths, Gray and a friend began working with an instructor to practice the trapeze and springboards, spending all of their free time perfecting their form. Gray's hours of practice paid off, as she not only won the contest but received a job offer that same night from the show manager. The troupe was leaving for their next gig the following week, but the other performers would train her and get her ready, he promised. Maude wired the news to her parents and, with their blessing, was soon on a train to Sacramento to start her new life as a diving girl.[28]

Another young woman, Lucile Anderson, who would become one of the most successful aquatic performers in the carnival world, also got her big break at a diving competition. In 1912, newspapers announced an upcoming contest at the Empress Theater to find the best female diver in her hometown, Salt Lake City, Utah. The competition was hosted by a decorated lifeguard named John Conroy, who was looking to start a show called Conroy's Six Diving Nymphs. As a young woman who excelled in swimming and diving and had been raised by parents who were vaudeville comic performers, twenty-year-old Anderson would have known the opportunities that could come with winning such a competition. Newspapers reported that the contestants performed a number of difficult feats but none that topped Lucile's impressive trapeze dive. Dangling upside down from a swinging bar, she was pulled 15 feet into the air before letting go and plunging headfirst into the tank below.[29] Soon after, Anderson received a letter from Conroy. "Will you have your Mama take your measurements and send [them] to me with your weight and height, chest, bust, waist, hips, upper thigh, midway between knee and hip, knee, calf, ankle, upper arm, fore arm?" he asked Lucile.[30]

Shortly after, Anderson made her performance debut in Conroy's show. It opened with a somewhat vainglorious display of Conroy's life-saving medals and awards arranged on a pedestal and Conroy himself flexing his rippling muscles in front of a red velvet curtain. Ads noted that he was assisted by a bevy of diving girls whose poses showed "to what perfection the human body can be developed by proper care and healthful exercises."[31] The second act featured diving and swimming feats by the female performers in a tank backed by a large mirror so the audience could see their movements. This format may not have been to Anderson's liking because she left after a few months and moved to Los Angeles, where she joined the Ocean Park Life Saving Corps and began swimming and competing with women from the Los Angeles Athletic Club, supporting herself by working as a stenographer.[32] Incidentally, one of her teammates was Aileen Allen, who would compete

Lucile Anderson (left) and other cast members of her water circus in 1919.

on America's first women's Olympic aquatic team and later coach an unknown but promising young swimmer named Esther Williams.

Like Anderson, many diving girls got into their profession because of an interest in swimming competitively. Women's swimming had not yet, in the early 1910s, become a formalized sport, so it was not subject to the strict amateur rules banning professionals from competitions. Some performers regularly entered challenges or staged endurance feats to build a name for themselves, or, like Anderson, volunteered their swimming skills as lifesavers. Lottie Mayer—the one who got her start performing in a show at Riverview Amusement Park meant to rival Kellerman's at White City—once swam 26 miles in the Mississippi River from Alton, Illinois, to St. Louis, Missouri, setting a new record time before making it promptly to the Majestic Theater for her afternoon matinee appearance as the "Diving Queen."[33]

BEAUTIFUL BALLYHOO

Although some diving girl shows were performed in vaudeville theaters or as acts within larger water circuses like Rice and Dore's, it was primarily on the midways of carnivals and fairs where they really thrived. These acts typically used aboveground tanks about 12 feet wide that were surrounded by riser-style elevated seating and hidden from view of the midway by a large wooden or metal "front"—a façade painted with images of mermaids, diving girls, and silhouettes of young women in fitted suits. Sometimes the fronts included a small platform where the performers would make a teaser appearance—called a "ballyhoo" in the carnival world—before the start of shows to draw an audience. The Harry Six Diving Girls show was said to have one of the most elegant setups, featuring a canopy that was "better lighted than many permanent theaters" and talkers (the men who served as the masters of ceremonies) who were "resplendent in full evening dress, with high silk hats." A publicist who traveled ahead of the show used contests and other clever devices so effectively that their slogan, "Oh, You Beautiful Diving Girls," was said to be heard all over town well in advance of the carnival's arrival.[34]

While the water tanks were hidden behind a show's front, the high-dive ladders—which soared from 40 to 110 feet into the air—were not. High dives were often referred to as "free acts" because anyone on the midway could see the diver leap and descend through the air without paying. To get a good look at the landing, however, or to see the rest of the show, they had to buy a ticket. The high-dive free acts served as advertising for the entire carnival, especially at night when the ladders were illuminated with electric lights like a beacon. But once a performer scaled such a highly visible ladder, there was no going back, as Maude Gray learned. Following her first show engagement, which had taken her all the way from Sacramento to New York with numerous stops in between, Gray got a job performing three shows a day at a diving concession at White City, where Kellerman had gotten her start. A 25-foot high-dive board above the tank wasn't being used, and although it was higher than any board Gray had plunged from, she had always "delighted in doing dangerous things," according to her memoir, and decided to give it a try one night after the show. Armed with little more advice than "don't hesitate," she climbed the ladder. The tank looked smaller from the board than she expected, but as concessions were closing, there was a stream of fairgoers headed down the midway toward the park exit. "The crowd began to stop when I was spotted on the high platform," wrote Gray. "Well, I knew I could not 'chicken out' so, in my bright purple tights, I spread my arms and off I went. It was a perfect dive and I was so proud of myself!"[35]

By the middle of the decade, diving girls shows had become so synonymous with the carnival atmosphere that no outdoor amusement could afford to be without one. In a description of the Elks' "Razzle Dazzle" carnival in New Orleans, *The Billboard* wrote, "It was a carnival pure and simple, from the barker with the 'hot-dogs' to the diving girls."[36] One could even buy inflatable toy diving girls—plump little ladies in black tank suits with arms spread as if in mid-flight—at 90¢ a dozen from a rubber novelties company.

The classified pages of trade papers for the "show business" like *The Billboard* and *New York Clipper* demonstrate the huge demand. Diving girls were wanted by agents, carnival managers, concessionaires, and stage producers. They were wanted in all caps: "AL. T. HOLSTEIN WANTS DIVING GIRLS." "WANTED IMMEDIATELY

--- DIVING GIRLS." A New York agent declared "DIVING GIRLS WANTED AT ALL TIMES . . . Salary $10 and tights."[37] Ads promised good working conditions and bookings at major fairs. Mills and Rudloff's Big Water and Diving Girls Show boasted that they had leased a 60-foot Pullman sleeping car for their 1912 season, while others promised steam heated dressing rooms and water tanks.[38] One ad stated simply, "You know you are treated right with this show."[39] With both shows and performers constantly on the move, hiring was often done sight unseen, based on written communications or personal recommendations, so inquiries about a performer's measurements or requests like "Send photo in tights with first letter" were common.

Diving girls occupied an interesting middle ground between the worlds of showgirls, sportswomen, and sideshow attractions. Their work clearly required athletic training and skill, but the physical appearance of these young women in form-fitting attire was a big part of the appeal, just as it was for Kellerman and had been for the previous generations of female swimming performers like Agnes Beckwith, Sallie Swift, and the host of natationists and water queens they inspired. The British magazine *The Sketch* noted in 1912 that Kellerman's vaudeville act had been so enormously successful that "it was imitated everywhere, until people said that all that was wanted was 'a shape and a bathing-dress' for a woman to do a diving act."[40] Show reviews constantly commented on the physical appearance of the "perfectly formed performers" like Inez Wood (Lucile Anderson's sister who was also a performer) and her "bevy of diving feminine divinities" who made a "picturesque scene of female loveliness."[41] A review of Conroy's Diving Nymphs waxed poetic on the beauty of their wet and lustrous "fleshlines."[42] As a rhyme in a 1912 newspaper put it:

We've sat and watched the diving girl
When she has come to bat;
While it may be she wore a smile
We never noticed that.[43]

Almost as soon as carnival owners started profiting from diving girls (and their swimsuited bodies), motion-picture men got in on the action, with one writing in a movie trade magazine, "I don't have to tell any show man how the diving girls have always been one of the best ballyhoos for a carnival company."[44] In 1911, Mack Sennett produced a short film called *The Diving Girl*, which featured comic actress Mabel Normand, who was known to be a strong swimmer, performing dives from a pier at Coney Island in a Kellerman suit. Sennett, who would soon become famous for his Keystone Cops slapstick comedies, began hiring carnival diving girls, including Lucile Anderson, for bit parts in his early films and making their images a key part of the film's promotion. One trade magazine advised that for movies featuring diving girls, theater managers need not worry about ad copy but could simply "let the pictures do the talking." Sometimes, promoters sent traveling "choruses" of six to eight diving girls to make public appearances in towns where the films were showing. But as *Motion Picture News* pointed out, it didn't matter if the girls were actually in the films since audiences wouldn't know the difference anyway. Just dig up "a fairly good swimmer," the magazine advised, make up a few anecdotes, put her in a bathing suit, then "give her the spotlight—how about red?"[45]

Of course, some people, especially church ministers, it seems, took offense at these young women revealing their "shapes." When the Golden West Aquatic Maids performed at the 1914 California State Fair in Sacramento, Maude Gray, who was traveling with the show, was picked as the featured acrobatic diver. "I was given a pretty red, Annette Kellerman 1-piece bathing suit," she wrote, "and was thrilled with my part in the show."[46] Newspapers gave the Aquatic Maids stellar reviews, but Reverend Langford of First Baptist Church denounced their act, calling it a "mad endeavor to make money by pandering to the prurient curiosity of certain elements." He warned that the show would destroy the modesty of both the spectators and the performers, though it appears that the good reverend's Sunday sermonizing did not have the intended effect. Crowds at the following week's show were "almost too big to handle," thanks to the free advertising.[47]

MAINTAINING RESPECTABILITY

For female performers who worked for carnivals, circuses, and fairs, the challenge of maintaining respectability was not just about costuming but about the industry itself, which sometimes had a seedy reputation. In the hierarchy of diving girl gigs, brick and mortar trumped circus tents and vaudeville stages were more respectable than carnival side-shows, as the latter were associated with freaks, carnies, shills, pick-pockets, and cooch shows. In the classifieds, carnival outfits solicited diving girls alongside every type of sideshow attraction imaginable— from ballyhoo barkers and talkers, to palm readers, calliope players, glass blowers, tattooed men, "midgets," "real Hawaiians," and dog and pony shows. Organizers of the Mineola Fair posted: "Freaks and Side Show People and Diving Girls wanted." Sometimes female divers were solicited alongside other "leg show" performers, with one asking for "Posing Girls, Diving Girls, Oriental Girls."[48]

Diving girl shows were presented at every imaginable level of polish, from Harry Six's resplendent silk-hatted talkers to divers at second-rate carnivals performing in a hodgepodge assortment of bathing suits they supplied themselves. One young man, H. E. Wilkinson, who worked a short gig as a ticket collector at a diving-girl concession,

A scene from the 1928 silent film The Spieler *depicting a typical carnival diving girl show of the 1910s.*

painted a rather unglamorous image of the show in his memoir *Memories of an Iowa Farm Boy.* The show happened to be headed by Cora "Beckwith," who had co-opted the Beckwith name for her dime museum act in the 1890s and had since become the matron of a diving girl sideshow concession. Wilkinson arrived just as the ballyhoo was about to begin, and the spieler—or "bullet-head," as Wilkinson calls him—was giving the performers inside the tent the signal to get ready.

> Presently the "bally" appeared, consisting of a stoutish woman well past middle age, and a half dozen assorted girls, none of them very shapely. All of them were wearing rather dirty bathrobes which they proceeded to shed in what I presume they hoped was a tantalizing manner, to reveal bathing suits in not much better condition than were the bathrobes. As they lined up at the front of the platform before the tent they went into a somewhat listless dance, and broke into a chorus of a song which seemed to revolve mainly around something that happened "Down among'st the sugar" . . . Bullet-head clanged loudly on a gong as the song ended and started rasping out his exhortation to the crowd, which by then was quite sizable, to "step right up boys—see Cora Beckwith and the Diving Girls—and the Diving Girls—see them swim—see them splash—see them dive— the show starts in just a moment!"[49]

The spieler's shouting had to compete with the loud voice of the neighboring concession's barker, who called out to passing crowds to come and see "Robertuh! Robertuh! She eats MUD! She eats MUD! You'll never believe it till you see it!"[50] Even with shills working the crowd and pretending to buy tickets while the diving girls danced, their ballyhoo oftentimes didn't rustle up enough customers, wrote Wilkinson, and they'd have to repeat the entire performance two or three times before enough seats were filled to start the show.

Carnival managers and circus showmen going back to the days of P. T. Barnum, who touted his Greatest Show on Earth as "the mighty moral magnet," used a variety of approaches to dispel the rough reputation of their industry. The physical work of performers necessitated close-fitting clothing that wouldn't drag or snag during a performance, which for women meant costumes that in any other context would be considered flagrantly immodest. So to justify their dress, circus talkers would emphasize the danger and athleticism in the women's acts, pointing out that they couldn't very well swing from trapezes or stand on the backs of galloping horses while tangled up in long dresses. They also regaled audiences with information on the women's husbands and children—sometimes fictionalizing connections to European circus lineages—to show that they came from respected backgrounds and had natural feminine urges toward domesticity.[51] Female performers had to follow curfews and strict rules about their dress and behavior outside of the big top.

Although the strictures of the Victorian era were easing by the heyday of the diving show, many of the same concerns and double standards still existed in the outdoor show business. Diving girls, who were usually young and unmarried, traveled with female chaperones and "room mothers." Producers of diving girl shows who were interested in maintaining a clean reputation—which was needed to score a spot with the better carnivals and state fairs—showcased (or exaggerated) their performers' achievements within the worlds of swimming and diving, and focused on the educational value of watching professionals demonstrate their craft. The Rice and Dore Water Carnival, which was considered one of the cleanest, featured—according to reviews—performers of "high class character," including Inez Fanjoy, who was "well entitled to the honor of champion woman diver of the world."[52] Its "diving girls of renown" were said to demonstrate their techniques "for the edification of the public."[53] Another review noted that the management protected its "record for cleanliness, always offering bright, entertaining, and costly attractions, for nothing of an immoral nature has even been tolerated."[54]

This reputation for providing family-friendly entertainment enabled Bill Rice to secure an engagement at the Panama–Pacific International Exposition, which was anticipated to be the most prestigious amusement event of 1915. A 600-acre world's fair on the San Francisco waterfront, the Expo was launched to celebrate the completion of the Panama Canal, one of the most ambitious engineering projects ever undertaken. It was also meant to signal to the world that San Francisco, which had spent a decade rebuilding following the devastating earthquake and fires of 1906, had finally rebounded. The First World War had broken out in Europe the year before the Expo, but America was still safely removed from the fighting and eager not only to glory in its own achievements but also to have some fun. No expense was spared in constructing the palm-shaded boulevards, fairyland lagoons and waterways, or the grand exhibition halls featuring demonstrations of the latest technologies and inventions and hosting representatives from countries all over the world.[55]

Within this sprawling wonderland was a mile-long stretch of professional sideshow concessions and amusements collectively called the Joy Zone, which was said to have more "tingle and ginger" than any other midway ever built.[56] Among its dozens of attractions were the 14-acre Toyland with an entrance guarded by 90-foot toy soldiers, a cyclorama that showed a moving panorama of the Battle of Gettysburg, an "Indian village," a working motion picture studio, and a baby incubator flanked by a lagoon of live storks. Nestled between a miniature replica of the Grand Canyon and a '49 camp depicting a bustling mining town

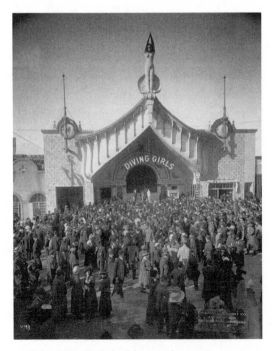

*The Diving Girls building at the 1915 Panama–
Pacific International Exposition.*

was a tall building with an inward sloping gable roof—and at the peak was mounted a giant statue of a woman with arms raised, preparing to dive. Underneath her hung an arc of electric letters spelling out "Diving Girls." For 10¢, fairgoers could enter and watch the Neptune's Daughters Diving Show, which was produced by Bill Rice and included among its performers both Maude Gray and Lucile Anderson. Gray recalled in her memoir how exhilarated she felt to secure a job at the show, writing, "It seems like I stepped out of the country road dust into City gold dust!"[37] Not only was working at a world's fair more exciting and prestigious than at carnivals, but with the Expo running February to December, it provided nearly a year of steady work with a single employer—no small thing for women who lived gig to gig.

Bill Rice modeled the show at the Expo after his traveling water circus, combining swimming, diving, and other aquatic feats with his famous underwater disappearing act—only it was bigger and better. For the Expo, his setup featured a floor that could be raised and lowered to carry a boat for Neptune and his mermaids to the surface, much like the original show at the New York Hippodrome. *The Billboard* wrote that the water could "appear to be as solid as rock" one minute, with dancers moving on its surface, and "free as air" the next with "clowns and animals playing about in its depths."[38] The *San Francisco Examiner* called the show "one of the best spectacles on the Zone," praising it as "amusing, instructive and interesting." It noted that the performers put on "a charming and skillful programme of swimming and fancy diving" that included all the swim strokes and dives "known to professional swimmers."[39]

Thanks to its educational and wholesome framing, the Neptune's Daughter show was one of the few "girl" shows that made it past the censors. Reformers from groups such as the Exposition's Women's Board and the YWCA didn't hold a very high opinion of the Joy Zone, calling it a "frivolous locality where all the dime excitements are sequestered." They saw some of the more titillating shows as exploitative to the young girls they employed—many of whom had traveled alone from all over the West to find work—and had several shows censored or shut down. Yet the YWCA's representative at the Expo said that she found the swimming and diving girls "quite pleasing" and, despite their form-fitting suits, expressed concern only regarding the health of the performers. There was a large warm-water tank outside of the concession's building—a grander version of the ballyhoo platforms at side shows—where the girls would do a few stunts to attract ticket buyers. But running from the warm water through the frigid night air left them with "hideous chills," she wrote. "Two of them could scarcely speak and coughed miserably."[60] Worse, the water didn't seem to ever be changed, and there was a rash of burst eardrums among the diving girls due to being under the water so much—claims that were substantiated by newspapers. One reported that the diving girls were frequent users of the Expo's emergency hospital, including two visitors just the previous evening suffering from an abscess in the eardrum and a fractured knee.[61] Miss Bobbie Dean, the high diver, was reported by *Variety* to be covered in black and blue where her body repeatedly struck the water doing twenty-six shows in a single day.[62] And—as the YWCA representative pointed out—they did all this for $12 a week.

RISKY BUSINESS

As carnival concessionaires sought to offer greater novelty, aquatic performers had to be willing to take on ever greater risks. After leaving the Expo, Gray was offered a position in the Water Lions and Diving Nymphs show, in which she would share a tank with one other woman and several sea lions. At first Gray was frightened of the animals but quickly grew fond of them, though she wrote in her memoir that she always maintained a healthy respect for their size and strength. For the act, Gray and the other swimmer would pretend to teach the animals to dive, blow kisses, and do different water stunts, and the sea lions in turn would perfectly imitate their actions. Audiences were charmed, and papers commented that it was difficult to say who was more at home in the water—the "human mermaids" or the "sea monsters."[63] For the most part, the two species got along swimmingly, except for one time at a Denver amusement park when what was meant to be a playful lifesaving demonstration turned scary. The idea was for Maude to pretend to drown so that Curly, the sea lion, could "save" her by swimming out with a rope and towing her back to shore. But as Curly was headed to the pretend victim, he got spooked by camera flashes and ran berserk. "With mouth wide open and a loud bark, he came toward me," wrote Gray. "I was scared; it was not easy to run through about three feet of water!" Ultimately it was Curly who got the biggest fright and hid under some boards until he could be coaxed back into his crate.[64]

Meanwhile, Lucile Anderson had taken on new aquatic challenges after the Expo. Still working with Bill Rice, she became the star of his new carnival concession, Rice's Submarine Girls. The show featured a variety of underwater gadgets, cleverly tapping into the public's sudden interest in marine technology following the start of the First World War. In a large glass tank, Anderson would don the Divinhood, a new diving helmet that gave wearers greater mobility than prior deep sea diving suits. The metal hood, which was open on the bottom, worked a bit like a diving bell in that it trapped air pumped in through a hose leading to the surface of the water. According to ads for the show, the US Navy had adopted the hood for submarine warfare and ship repair work, but Anderson used it primarily to eat, drink, read, and recline underwater in her tank of metal and glass.[65] Another new technology the show introduced was the underwater wireless telephone through which Anderson conducted a full interview with a journalist and would answer audience questions.

But the most sensational part of the act was the "Great Chest Escape," in which Anderson dramatically cut her way out of a sunken wooden chest. A write-up of the show in Sioux City, Iowa, reported that members of the audience were called upon to inspect the chest, lock Anderson inside with nothing but a seaman's knife, and then throw the chest into the tank. The reporter wrote that it took Anderson three full minutes to cut her way out, adding, "it is claimed that death would overtake her in another half minute." The paper called it "the most sensational act ever presented underwater."[66] In New Jersey, Anderson's escape was hailed as "a wonderful demonstration of human endurance and venture."[67]

The daring acts of performers like Anderson in turn upped the stakes for others, and nowhere was this truer than in the area of high diving. Just as Lurline's demonstration of "prolonged immersion" in the nineteenth century made audiences at every dime museum demand to see similar breath-holding stunts, prompting performers to push the limits of safety as they tried to stay underwater for increasingly longer

Advertisement poster for Bill Rice's Submarine Diving Girls show.

lengths of time, the high dive became a requisite part of the diving girl act—and as the ladders got higher, the tanks got smaller. Lottie Mayer later in life estimated that she dove from well over fifty bridges in her day, in the "battle for publicity."[68] *Illustrated World* wrote, "Because huge audiences love to see beauty in danger and escaping unharmed, there has developed a great body of girls whose duty it is to take great leaps and dives and all kinds of consequent chances with their lives."[69] And it wasn't exaggerating about taking chances with their safety or lives. In 1913, newspapers reported that a performer with the Six Diving Belles—a show Anderson later traveled with—died when she "was hurled from the springboard she was testing" just before the start of their act. The tank was still behind the stage curtain, with a comedian out front working the audience, when she fell. Incredibly, the show went on with the five remaining diving belles, who had to perform in the same tank where their coworker had just had a fatal accident.[70] But despite the dangers, conquering the high dive was essential for any diving girl who wanted to make it to the big leagues or run her own show—and the biggest of the big leagues was the high dive from the rafters of the New York Hippodrome.

Following Kellerman's spectacular dives at the Hippodrome in 1917, the theater began making high dives a regular feature of all its shows. Every night young women plunged from the Hippodrome's 125-foot proscenium into a tank twelve feet in diameter and filled with six feet of water. The job paid in the hundreds per week, an irresistible salary for someone working their way up the sideshow-to-vaudeville ladder, despite the extreme danger. The *Boston Post*, in an article about Margaret Stanton, a hometown diving gal who had made it to New York's biggest stage, pointed out that Boston's building codes allowed no structures higher than 125 feet—the same height from which Stanton dove—and challenged readers to imagine themselves diving from the top of one of Boston's twelve-story buildings. "No wonder the very thought of such a plunge appalls you," wrote the *Post*. "It takes courage, extraordinary courage."[71]

Another Hippodrome diving girl, Helen Carr, made over 300 successful dives, but on her 304th, she emerged from the water completely blind—her retinas torn beyond repair. Diving into shallow water requires special techniques, including curving the body backward so as not to strike the bottom. However, that makes it impossible for the diver to lower her head and allow the crown to take the blow, putting it on the face instead. The *San Francisco Examiner* calculated that Carr struck the water of the tiny pool at a speed of 80 feet per second—nearly 55 miles per hour—and reported that doctors blamed her sudden blindness on the repeated impact to her face.[72] Even at lesser heights, hitting the water the wrong way could be just as dangerous. "Doc" Carver, a former sharpshooter and partner of Buffalo Bill in his Wild West Show, was running separate diving girl and diving horse shows at an amusement park in Oakland when he got the idea to combine the two. He posted a notice in 1913 offering $100 for any girl willing to sit bareback on one of his horses and ride it off a 40-foot tower into a tank below.[73] There was no shortage of takers and he eventually moved the act to Atlantic City's Steel Pier, where one of the riders, Sonora Webster (who later married Doc's son, who was twenty years her senior, after he took over the business) was blinded when her horse lost its balance and they both hit the water wrong.

Webster continued performing as a blind rider for eleven more years, and her life story was made into the Disney movie *Wild Hearts Can't Be Broken.*

There is precious little room for error with high diving, and performers reported numerous close calls they'd had, whether due to a shift in the wind, a spectator rocking the ladder, or a leaky tank making the water level a foot shallower than expected. Once a runaway bull caused panicked fairgoers to surge all around Lucile Anderson's tiny tank while she was on the high dive ladder.[74] Even humidity had to be accounted for. Inez Fanjoy told a reporter when performing in Montana what a difference she could feel from the state's "rarefied atmosphere." "Oh, you feel so light and fairy like, as you drop through the air here," said Fanjoy, "while at sea level the humidity is so great that the air seems to hold you back." She said that normally she never touched the bottom of the tank when landing her 75-foot dive, but in Montana, she nearly always did.[75]

Diving girls were ranked at the top of the stunt world and were called upon to perform all kinds of feats on film, such as diving from cliffs and canoeing or swimming through rapids. *Picture-Play Magazine* wrote that of the "dare-devil girls" doing stunts onscreen, expert equestriennes, swimmers, and divers were the most sought after and were among the highest paid, commanding $10 or more a day, according to the skill level required.[76] *Illustrated World* reported that some were paid as high as $25, as diving was considered "the biggest risk in the stunt game."[77]

By 1917, Lucile Anderson had built enough name recognition to launch her own company, posting an announcement in *The Billboard* that April—the same month the United States entered the war raging in Europe—that the "Lucile Anderson Company" was now accepting bookings.[78] As the headline act of "Lucile Anderson's Water Frolics," she dove from an eighty-foot ladder into a four-foot tank—"a most thrilling bit of entertainment," in the words of a New York newspaper.[79] Her traveling concession joined different carnivals over the years, including the World at Home Shows, which *The Billboard* estimated traveled with fifty-two cars plus the engine, making it the longest carnival train in America.[80]

Women like Anderson were striking out on their own, including in the world of business, more than ever before, while the ongoing war was further unsettling traditional gender norms as American women proved capable of doing a host of things previously thought possible only for men. By 1920, Lottie Mayer was running her own highly successful disappearing act, having devised and patented a tank that could accommodate the requisite air chambers yet was small enough to fit on vaudeville stages. Her performers would dive underwater, then almost instantaneously reemerge wearing new costumes. Audiences loved this so much that the costume change became the key aspect of her show, and she eventually got the underwater wardrobe switch down to eighteen seconds.[81] Mayer and Anderson, as owners of their own concessions, remained in the business far longer than most, with Mayer still running her show at state fairs in the 1950s and Anderson performing her high dive into her forties and taking her show all over the United States, as well as to Europe, the West Indies, and South America. When Mayer later reflected on her career, she credited the success of her show to the "ever rising interest in swimming" and the fact that women had begun to "do more than merely dip their toes into the water."[82]

And indeed they had. Women were swimming farther and faster, performing ever-more-daring aquatic feats, and plunging from increasingly spectacular heights. The famous suffragist Carrie Chapman Catt believed that woman's political freedom would come "hand in hand with her bodily strength" and that before they could achieve equal rights, they must demonstrate an equal level of physical health with men.[83] Swimmers and divers—and particularly those of the carnival and stunt world—were certainly doing that. Diving girl Janet Ford was said to be "absolutely without nerves, doing things that a man would not attempt."[84] The Albuquerque *Evening Herald* wrote, "Inez Fanjoy the fearless will laugh at destruction and present her thrilling sky dive twice daily for the public's approval."[85]

As momentum for women's suffrage grew, Josephine DeMott, who performed acrobatics bareback on speeding horses in the Barnum and Bailey Circus, believed that female performers of the carnival and circus world who roamed the country doing "daring deeds of a kind unknown to the people outside" could be great messengers for the cause.[86] A similar sentiment was echoed by Elizabeth Cook of the

Women's Political Union, who declared, "There is no class of women who show better that they have a right to vote than the circus women, who twice a day prove that they have the courage and endurance of men."[87] DeMott launched the 800-member Suffragette Ladies of the Barnum & Bailey Circus and began leading suffrage rallies riding on her horse Comet. She described in her memoir the pride she felt using her physical skills in support of the movement, making Comet rear up dramatically on his hind legs while she "waved a suffrage banner with a firm hand and a high arm."[88]

Although the majority of women in the circus and carnival worlds did not use their physical skills to promote suffrage in ways as visible as DeMott on her white horse, collectively, they played an equally significant role. Through their performances that demonstrated physical talent, innovation, strength, and daring, they modeled a new type of womanhood that challenged outdated ideas about women's capabilities and proper stations in life. As *The Billboard* wrote, the female performers of the Rice and Dore Water Carnival demonstrated every kind of dive imaginable and "none of them did any knitting on the way down."[89]

CHAPTER 6

SPORT

Masculine holders of championships in athletics,
look to your laurels! Sundry members of the so-called
weaker sex, having obtained the vote and many other
things upon which they had set their dear, fluttering
little hearts, are now out for far bigger game.

–LITERARY DIGEST, 1923

As the massive ocean liner *Berengaria* coasted into New York harbor on August 27, 1926, Gertrude Ederle watched from the deck. This was the final stretch of her journey home from Europe, and the celebratory atmosphere was almost more than she could take in. Boats of all sizes circled her ship—from fishing vessels to fireboats spraying their water hoses and blaring their horns, to New York's official welcoming tug carrying her beaming parents, her former Olympic teammates, and city dignitaries—everyone eager to greet their hometown hero. "Trudy," as she was often called by friends and newspapermen alike, had just made history as the first woman to swim the English Channel. She had also completed the grueling swim in a record time of fourteen and a half hours, beating all five men who had made the crossing before her, the fastest of whom she beat by over two hours. Now, as this smiling twenty-year-old in a powder blue serge coat and new cloche hat was escorted from the cruise liner to the VIP ferry to the waiting motorcade, it seemed that all of New York was there to congratulate her.

The city's official greeter, Grover Whalen, "Mr. New York" himself, rode with Ederle and her father through the throngs of cheering crowds, their car bookended by police escorts. As the motorcade slowly made its way up Broadway, the skies rained with paper confetti thrown from Manhattan's skyscrapers, creating the look of a festive snowstorm on that late summer afternoon. The parade eventually reached City Hall, where Mayor Jimmy Walker waited to place a medal around Ederle's neck. After they smiled for the flashing cameras, the parade continued all the way to Ederle's German immigrant neighborhood, where she was feted by thousands more and crowned "Queen of the Waves." Crowds that day were estimated at two million, making it the largest ticker-tape parade New York had ever thrown for anyone—especially for an athlete, and most especially of all, for a woman.

Ederle's swim came at the height of the "Golden Age of Sport"—an era when sports became big business and the country's top athletes were celebrated as national heroes. The war was over, the economy was booming, and Americans were using their greater disposable income and leisure time to attend games and matches, propelling professional baseball and boxing, college football, and even women's competitive swimming and diving into massive spectator events. And with the expansion of radio and the creation of dedicated sports pages, people were consuming athletics in new ways as well.[1] Wire transmission enabled photographs to be disseminated across the country within hours, helping make sports stars like Babe Ruth and Jack Dempsey more famous than the top actors of the day. And now a mere girl ranked among them.

But Ederle's achievement carried a significance far beyond the sports hubbub of the decade. As the *Literary Digest* put it, a "bob-haired nineteen-year-old daughter of the Jazz Age" had given the world an "unanswerable refutation of the masculinist dogma that woman is, in the sense of physical power and efficiency, inferior to man."[2] Sports writers and editors busied themselves predicting the impact Ederle's accomplishment would have on the budding field of women's

Gertrude Ederle on her way to becoming the first woman to swim across the English Channel.

athletics. "Athletic sports will be made more popular, and new champions will appear," declared the *Washington Post*. "The development of physical grace, strength and health will be most useful to the race. The American girl is all right!"[3]

AMERICA'S NEW GIRL ATHLETE

The 1920s marked a new era of "free, vigorous, outdoor girlhood," and swimmers were leading the pack.[4] Physical education, which had become mandatory in the public schools of nearly every state and was offered by most colleges, had played a huge role in helping girls and women become more active.[5] In the late 1800s, physical education programs focused on improving individual bodies, using rhythmic work and light calisthenics for women and strength training and gymnastics for men. At the start of the twentieth century, however, the emphasis for the latter shifted to team games and organized sports, which were thought to prepare young men for the competition they would face in a modern, capitalist society. Although many didn't see these same skills as necessary for women, female physical educators begged to differ, arguing that women were engaging in the public sphere more than ever and therefore also needed the character traits and skills that sports fostered. "Women are taking places in the industrial, commercial, and intellectual world today as integers, no longer as fractions," wrote an educator at Bryn Mawr in an article advocating for girls basketball programs. "[She needs] the same equipment for seizing an opportunity, using it well, and passing it on, that the man requires."[6]

Outside of colleges, young women of all social classes were playing sports through recreation clubs, church groups, and industrial sports leagues organized by employers. Many companies in the 1920s offered robust sports programs with remarkably high participation among both male and female employees. In 1923, the Chicago branch of Western Electric alone saw more than 500 female employees participate in the company's bowling program, 120 in horse riding, and 100 in rifle shooting competitions.[7]

Even with the growth of athletic options in schools and industry, however, women's entry into *official* sportdom did not come without a fight. In the United States, the Amateur Athletic Union (AAU), founded in 1888, was the ruling sports body for all amateur, competitive sports—which, at the time, were exclusively for men. The AAU had the power to legitimize a sport by sanctioning its competitions and holding national championships, and even deciding which sports and which athletes went to the Olympics. Organizations like the National Women's Lifesaving League (NWLL), which from their earliest days held swimming competitions for their members, knew that AAU acceptance was the key to helping women's swimming grow as a competitive sport—but the AAU was not interested in admitting women to its boys' club. And the biggest obstacle came directly from the top: AAU president James Sullivan. A former advertising agent for the Spalding sports equipment company, Sullivan had become the most powerful man in American sports, even serving, through his position at the AAU, as default head of the US Olympic Committee.

Sullivan dismissed repeated requests from female leaders to admit women's swimming to the AAU—even after swimming and diving were added to the Olympic program for women at the 1912 games in Stockholm. Ida Schnall, considered the best all-around woman athlete of her time (and who once served as an understudy for Kellerman and later became the star diver of her own movie), longed to compete in the diving events and took her appeals all the way to the mayor of New York. Met with sarcasm and the suggestion that she direct her concerns to the king of Sweden, Schnall wrote the following to the *New York Times*:

> James E. Sullivan is again objecting to girls competing with the boys in a swimming contest. He is always objecting and never doing anything to help the cause along for a girls' AAU. He has objected to my competing in diving at the Olympic games in Sweden because I am a girl. . . . He objects to so many things that it gives me cause to think he is very narrow minded and that we are in the last century.[8]

At this, Sullivan only dug in his heels. Not only was the United States not among the eight countries who sent women athletes to the 1912 Olympics, but the US Olympic Committee even went on record as being "opposed to women taking part in any event in which they could not wear long skirts."[9] England and Australia, with their strong swimming traditions, won the two women's swimming events, and Sweden, an early leader in gymnastics, won the single diving event. The women's wins were not counted toward their countries' total scores, but in 1914 the International Olympic Committee (IOC) voted to change that and to include women's event scores in the final tallies moving forward. With more countries planning to send women swimmers to the next Olympiad, officials at the AAU could see that the US was at risk of falling behind in international rankings because of their leader's antiquated views.[10] At the same time, Charlotte Epstein, NWLL athletic branch chair, had been making allies at the AAU behind the scenes, shrewdly learning AAU rules better than most of its officials and making herself an indispensable member of several AAU committees.

When Sullivan died unexpectedly in September 1914 during an emergency surgery, the biggest barrier standing between women and the world of sport was suddenly gone. Two months after Sullivan's death, the AAU voted to admit women's swimming, making it the first women's athletic field to be given official amateur sport status in the United States. But their dress remained a concern to AAU officials, who didn't like the shorter racing suits women wore at NWLL competitions. Deciding it was now the AAU's right to "dictate the costumes the mermaids shall wear," they promptly ruled that female competitors must be covered in dark suits from neck to toe, and on top of that, they had to wear bathrobes until they got in the water.[11] Even so, the *New York Times* proclaimed that AAU acceptance was a "brilliant victory for the fair natators."[12] Not only would it open the door for national swimming championships, a necessary precursor to the Olympics, but it would also pave the way for other women's sports to follow. The following year, the AAU sanctioned its first ever women's event—a fancy diving contest as part of the Sportsmen Show at Madison Square Garden—with the medals given out by none other than Annette Kellerman.[13]

With official sports recognition and the opportunity to compete in championships, women's swimming took off and clubs offering serious training began forming across the country. The most famous was the Women's Swimming Association (WSA) of New York, which was founded in 1917 by Charlotte Epstein and other National Women's Lifesaving League leaders. Meeting in humble rented pools in lower Manhattan, the WSA would become a hub of women's swimming excellence and the home of future swimming stars. Divers were coached by Adeline Trapp, the one Commodore Longfellow recruited to swim Hell Gate, and the swimmers by former water polo player Louis de B. Handley, who was known as a true gentleman and famously wore a suit and tie with elegant spats over his dress shoes to the steamy pool. Both volunteered without pay.[14]

Handley had a keen interest in speed swimming and began experimenting with ways to make the Australian crawl, a common racing stroke, faster: increasing the number of kicks per breath from three to six, modifying the arm movements, and eliminating the scissor-kick side rotation for breathing, having swimmers instead turn their heads just enough to get a gulp of air.[15] The new and faster American crawl was said to have a "machine-like precision," and as Handley began teaching it to all WSA swimmers, the club quickly rose to the top of their field. The stroke would also enable the first several American women's Olympic teams to dominate the sport, and would later be used by Gertrude Ederle, who joined the WSA at the age of twelve, to defeat the English Channel in record time.[16]

The 1916 Olympics had been canceled because of the First World War, but the 1920 Olympiad in Antwerp, Belgium, was looming on the horizon, and a number of serious female competitors honing their skills in clubs across the US were eager to partake.[17] As WSA swimmer and diver Aileen Riggin later reflected, "It was only natural that the Olympic Games should be one of the many goals toward which the erstwhile weaker sex was striving."[18] At first, the US Olympic Committee remained opposed to sending women, said Riggin, as they wanted the games to remain as they had been in ancient Greece—for men only—but Epstein marched down to their office, told the men they were being "silly," and pointed out that plenty of other countries would be sending women. "That sort of turned the tide," said Riggin.[19] The committee finally agreed and a women's aquatics team was assembled, with the selection based on AAU championships—though the Committee had the final say. Six of the fourteen-member team came from the New York WSA and the rest from a handful of states and the territory of Hawaii. The two youngest, WSA divers Aileen Riggin and Helen Wainwright, were only fourteen, while the oldest, Aileen Allen, one of the original Ocean Park lifesavers, was mother to a fifteen-year-old daughter.[20]

On July 26, 1920, the fourteen women swimmers and divers—wearing matching navy blazers, white flannel skirts, and straw hats—joined more than 250 male athletes and boarded the Navy transport ship *Princess Matoika*, headed to Antwerp. (Incidentally, among the male swimmers was Norman Ross, who would win three golds and, in the following decade, coin the name of a future Olympic sport: "synchronized swimming.") These aquatic athletes made up America's first real women's Olympic team, as only a few individual women had competed in prior Olympiads: a single female golfer in 1900 and a handful of archers in 1904. The only other American woman athlete

Olympic diving champion Aileen Riggin performs at an aquatic carnival in New Rochelle, New York, 1922.

headed to Antwerp in 1920 was a figure skater (there were not separate summer and winter games at that time, and the skating events took place at an indoor rink). Having a full team of women competitors representing the country at the Olympics signaled a massive stepping stone for America's female athletes. As one historian wrote, their arrival at the highest level of sports had been an "arduous journey fraught with angst and argument and all the animus" male sports leaders could muster—but they made it.[21] And the significance of the moment was not lost on these young women. Diver Betty Grimes wrote shortly afterward, "I think we were all impressed with the fact that we must not only represent the American swimmers, but the American women," while her teammate Thelma Payne said that any victory she might have "belongs to her whole sex."[22]

Grimes used her time aboard the *Princess Matoika* to interview her female teammates for a newspaper article titled "We're Going to Win the Swimming Events," which gives a rare window into the motivations and feelings of these women athletes.[23] WSA swimmer Ethelda Bleibtrey told Grimes about her scientific approach to training, explaining that she "diagrammed on paper mathematically the correct crawl stroke," then practiced it slowly and methodically, perfecting her form. For races, she simply put "more steam" into it—an approach that would soon win her two Olympic gold medals. Others discussed how they kept their heads in the game during races. Irene Guest, for example, would start out at a fast pace and then settle into her rhythm by singing hymns to herself, or occasionally the popular song "My Love's Like a Red, Red Rose." Diver Thelma Payne told Grimes that she "attributes her success entirely to feminism," explaining that the first time she tried to do a one-and-a-half backward somersault dive, she almost chickened out on the springboard. But then she "thought of that haughty creature, man," and decided if he could do it, so could she.

During the thirteen-day trip, everyone stayed in shape however they could: track athletes ran circles around the deck, javelin throwers tied ropes to their javelins, hurling them into the sea and then reeling them back, and swimmers strapped themselves into a small canvas tank with a harness that enabled them to swim stationary sprints. Practice was likely a welcome distraction from the terrible food, uncomfortable lodgings, rat infestation, and stench of formaldehyde on the ship—which was still potent from the *Princess Matoika*'s recent trip to bring home the bodies of eighteen hundred American soldiers.

Remnants of war still lingered in Antwerp, too, and the city did not have the funds or manpower to build a pool, so the aquatic events took place in a canal. The water was so cold that some swimmers were carried out nearly unconscious, and so dark that divers couldn't tell up from down once submerged. Aileen Riggin, the smallest member of the Olympic team at 4'7" and 65 pounds, recalled thinking, "the water is black and nobody could find me if I really got stuck down there."[24] But on the day of the opening ceremony, the sun came out and everyone was in good spirits. Doves were released into the air as a symbol of peace, and the new Olympic flag, with its five iconic rings representing the coming together of the continents, was raised for the first time.

But when the American women received the knee-length, elbow-length regulation cotton swimsuits they were expected to compete in, they couldn't believe their eyes. Dry, the suits were as baggy and shapeless as sacks, yet when they got wet, they became transparent and "fit a bit too well," said Riggin. Once they'd all had a big laugh over the ridiculous suits, the team revolted and refused to wear them, opting instead for their own practice suits they brought from home—short, wool Jantzen suits for the divers and black silk racing suits for the swimmers.[25] They weren't about to be international laughingstocks at their Olympic debut.

The American women completely dominated the aquatic arena, winning all the medals in the three swim events—the 100- and 300-meter freestyle and the relay (male swimmers had seven events, including a 1500-meter freestyle event, but the IOC had deemed the 300-meter sufficiently strenuous for women). The WSA's Ethelda Bleibtrey was the star of the swimming show, earning gold in both individual events and leading the team to victory in the freestyle relay. One paper wrote, "Hitherto women had been content to copy men, but Ms. Bleibtrey swam with the easy, rhythmical grace characteristic of her sex."[26] The American crawl had not yet reached other countries, and the US women not only finished the relay a full half minute ahead of Great Britain, which took second place, but also set a new world record. There were two diving events for women: fancy and platform, though the Americans only competed in the former. Fancy diving had practically been invented in America and advanced by a generation of diving girls, and when the contestants from other countries saw the American girls practice their flips, twists, and jackknifes, they withdrew from the competition, leaving America to sweep the event, with Aileen Riggin taking the gold.[27] The medals were given out by the king of Belgium himself, Albert I, and his sons. The 1920 Olympics marked the shift of swimming dominance from England to the US, as the American women would continue to reign at the Olympics throughout the decade and into the 1930s.

With their astounding success, the members of the first US women's Olympic team became overnight media darlings, their pictures splashed across newspapers, magazines, and newsreels. Men's sports had multiple domains for showcasing talent and producing national sports heroes, but the 1920 Olympics provided the first such platform for women, making these champions America's first highly visible female athletes.[28] These young women not only captured the public imagination but also paved the way for others to follow, with the US Olympic Committee heartily supporting the participation of women swimmers and divers in the 1924 Olympics and sending a team that included Gertrude Ederle and again dominated women's aquatics.

The 1920s women's team arrived home not only with Olympic medals but with new political rights. The 19th Amendment granting American women the suffrage was ratified on August 18, only four days after the opening ceremony in Antwerp. Women's physical liberation had truly come hand in hand with their political emancipation, just as many had predicted it would, and some even ranked the two as equally significant. *Woman Citizenship*, the official magazine for the League of Women Voters, wrote, "Nothing in the world more strikingly marks the great gap between the girl of today and her grandmother than that girl's place in the world of sport. Neither her vote, nor her skimpy dress, nor her plainness of speech, is more expressive."[29] Women weren't just playing sports and voting, though. They were pleading cases before the Supreme Court, practicing medicine in every state, designing buildings in the nation's great cities, registering patents, and making scientific discoveries, and they comprised 12 percent of the country's newspaper force.[30] Women's progress was suddenly undeniable—and everywhere.

And swimmers were the symbol not just of the new girl athlete, but of this modern, emancipated woman.

Then in 1922, the unthinkable happened. A nineteen-year-old student at Northwestern University named Sybil Bauer (who would join the 1924 women's Olympic team), swam the 400-yard backstroke in six minutes, twenty-four seconds—which was four seconds faster than the fastest man. With Gertrude Ederle's Channel crossing still four years away, it was the first time in recorded history that a woman beat a man's athletic record. "The tradition of the girl athlete is not yet established," wrote *The Nation*, and yet already she can "outclass all the women in her field and all the men as well."[31] Some took Bauer's feat as a sign that women, now awakened after "centuries of inactivity," were catching up.[32] Alarm bells started ringing. A writer for *Literary Digest* warned in 1923, "Masculine holders of championships in athletics, look to your laurels! Sundry members of the so-called weaker sex, having obtained the vote and many other things upon which they had set their dear, fluttering little hearts, are now out for far bigger game."[33]

And indeed, they were. Not only did women swimmers want to have the same events at the Olympic games as men, but Sybil Bauer even wanted to compete against them. Athletes of other sports, like track and field and basketball, were pushing for AAU acceptance and had their eyes on the Olympics as well. For these athletes, Bauer's achievement was just the beginning. Women were "crowding to the front in sports" and laying claim to the records and laurels that had previously been the purview of men, wrote Ethelda Bleibtrey. She predicted that soon "the world's sports crowns will fall, one by one, before the 'weaker sex.'"[34] *Woman Citizenship* asserted: "The world of sport will eventually prove whether or not the weakness of the weaker sex may not have been a trifle exaggerated."[35] And if women were no longer the weaker sex, what did that say about men?

BUT WOMEN IN SPORTS SHOULD LOOK BEAUTIFUL!

Things had gotten out of hand, as far as many gatekeepers of male sport were concerned. To them, athletic competitions were bastions of masculinity, where men could prove their manliness and virility. The modern world, with its white-collar jobs and mechanized assembly lines, had minimized the importance of physical strength and created fears over declining distinctions between the sexes. With fewer outlets for men to demonstrate their physical superiority over women, the playing field of sports had taken on greater symbolic significance.[36] In fact, providing an arena for such displays of "manliness" had been a big part of the impetus behind the revival of the ancient Olympic spectacles in 1896. As Pierre de Coubertin, the father of the modern Olympics, put it, the ideal at the heart of the Olympics was "the solemn and periodic exaltation of male athleticism" with "female applause as reward."[37]

To de Coubertin and many others in the world of sport, this stronghold of male competition was no place for women—and in fact went against their very natures. An article by a physician and physical educator named Luther Gulick argued in 1906 that early man's survival depended on his ability "to run, to throw, to strike"—the same skills at the core of modern sports—whereas woman's survival depended on her industry in the home and skills as a mother. Therefore, he concluded, "athletics do not test womanliness as they test manliness."[38] As Frederick Rand Rogers of the New York State Education Department put it, men are mobile like animals, whereas women are more "plant-like" and rooted to the home. Rogers argued that athletic competition would foster "domineering impulses," "belligerent attitudes," "combative natures," and the "will to power"—traits that were undesirable and even ruinous to women.[39]

As if all that wasn't bad enough, women who engaged in sports made ugly spectacles of themselves, argued these men. It had long been considered grossly unladylike for a woman to exert herself physically in public. Even going back to the biking craze of the late 1800s, women were cautioned to guard against "bicycle face"—a wild and "widely expectant expression," with drawn lips, and flushed faces marred by deep lines around the mouth and dark shadows under the eyes.[40] Victorian repulsion at female exertion had not gone away, and as women participated in increasingly physical sports, the criticisms grew harsher, with language expressing outright disgust.

Samuel E. Bilik, referred to as a "foremost authority in physical education," wrote that athletic training makes women "not only unattractive, but *actually ugly*."[41] To Bilik there was "nothing more disgusting than the sight of a wide-hipped, stubby-limbed, she-athlete, wallowing awkwardly all over the running track." Track and field sports (accepted as women's events by the AAU in 1922 and the Olympics in 1928), were thought by many to be too physically intensive for women and raised particularly strong ire in critics like Bilik. Moreover, there were classist and racist associations with these sports since they were relatively inexpensive to participate in and popular among women in working-class industrial leagues and at Black-serving colleges and institutions. One man described women crossing the finish line with faces "twisted and contorted and pitted with the gray lines of exhaustion."[42]

The litany of offenses committed by other female athletes was plenty long. They included, according to doctors, educators, and sportswriters, "moustaches of perspiration," "protruding neck muscles," "fixed scowls," "damp and scraggly" hair, "blistered, peeling noses," and beet-red faces that "glow like incandescent lamps." Paul Gallico, a well-known sports journalist of the 20s and 30s, seemed to sum up what a lot of men felt when he wrote, "It is a lady's business to look beautiful, and there are hardly any sports in which she seems able to do it."[43] It is tempting to dismiss his statement as representing an extreme view, but given that his article, unequivocally titled "Women in Sports Should Look Beautiful," was published in *Vogue* and reprinted in the *Reader's Digest*—and that Bilik's assertion that sports make women "*actually ugly*" was quoted as fact in newspapers across the country—this was apparently not the case. Later, in his book *Farewell to Sport*, Gallico really let loose and dedicated an entire chapter to the subject of "muscle moles," a term used for women who played sports that required overt—or "masculine"—demonstrations of strength. He wrote:

Here come the golf gals in their rough, tweedy clothes, with a sturdy stride, hips and shoulders aswing. Their faces are weathered, their skin tanned and dried by the sun and wind. . . .

Next the tennis ladies. . . . Look at the shoulders on them, the forearms and the legs. Those legs! The quick stops and starts and the running do knot up the muscles and make them hard and lumpy and do something to the knees, too.

The freaks bring up the rear guard. A pitiful crew, the female boxers, wrestlers, and ball-players. . . . For the most part they have ugly bodies, hard faces, cheap minds. . . .[44]

But before poor Gallico fell into utter despair, he remembered the fair maidens of the water:

Ah, the beaty chorus of women in sport, the swimmers and divers. Those close-fitting black swim-suits! And see that high-tower diver with the yellow hair in the pure white bathing suit. Powerful shoulders they all have, those water maidens, but their muscles are long, smooth, and flat.[45]

Gallico's opposing views toward landbound "muscle moles" and aquatic "beauty choruses" was quite typical throughout the first half of the twentieth century. A male journalist covering the 1932 Olympics painted different pictures of audience reactions to women's aquatic and field events, writing that spectators "gaze tolerantly" as girls "scramble" down the cinder track, while over at the packed aquatic stadium, they "marvel at the beauty and grace and courage and ability."[46] Women picked up on this as well, with a female physical educator writing, "Men admire the good swimmer, golfer, and tennis player at the same time that they may sneer at the successful woman track star or softball player."[47] Clearly, swimming didn't cause the same hand-wringing over the future of femininity as other sports. But if swimmers were leading the pack of "new" athletic women—and in fact were the ones usurping men's athletic records—why weren't they subject to the same types of criticism and even personal attacks as other women athletes of the era?

For one, swimming was considered a gentle and aesthetic sport. It didn't involve "violent" elements like swinging bats, hitting balls, or plowing into teammates, while the cool and hygienic water hid the athletes' exertion.[48] Gallico himself found the backstroke to be "graceful and full of rhythm," and described its practitioners' faces as "wreathed and softened by the white foam they churn up in the green waters."[49]

Moreover, the long association between feminine beauty and aquatics had continued ever since Dudley Sargent declared that swimming had molded Annette Kellerman into the perfect woman, and in the ongoing furor over feminine muscles, swimming remained the exceptional sport thought to beautify rather than uglify the female body. An article on Riggin titled "Water Nymph Won Beauty by Her Swimming" claimed that she had been an "ungainly youngster" until she took up aquatics.[50] Another declared that the "glamour of the modern American mermaid is striking," and proves that "there's no surer way to feminine health and beauty than natatorial sports."[51] Even as competitive athletes, female swimmers were often referred to in the media as "fair natators," "water queens," "mermaids," and "nymphs." An article from 1923 discussed the training of American women swimmers ahead of an upcoming contest against New Zealand's best "water queens." It noted that the preparations of the "sleek water nymphs of this continent . . . to repel the fair invaders attract the eye and speak well for the health, swimming skill, and beauty of young American womanhood."[52]

For newspaper editors in the heyday of mass print media, these glamour athletes, and their swim competitions, were a goldmine—particularly for sports pages targeting male readers and looking to boost sales by publishing pictures of scantily clad women. Whereas pictures of "nightclub cuties in leotards" might get newspapers barred by the mail censors, pointed out Gallico, those of "an octet of naiads" in wet, clinging garments were seen as legitimate.[53] After all, they were athletes simply wearing the uniform of their sport. Pictures of women swimmers and divers became a mainstay in newspapers, prompting Gallico to write:

> Nothing of late years has been able to approach in sweet innocence, coupled with undeniable sex appeal, photographs of handsome young girls in revealing bathing suits lined up on the edge of a pool, waiting for the starting gun, or poised on the end of a springboard or diving tower, or caught in mid-air in full flight. It is news—sports, decent, completely privileged, in good taste and at the same time arresting and stimulating as all get out.[54]

While male swimmers were typically depicted "in action" in the water (when they were shown at all), photographers preferred full-body shots of their female counterparts posing on deck.[55] Some newspapers opted to forgo articles altogether and just run pictures of the women. A study of coverage from the 1932 Olympics found that more than half of the pictures of female athletes were printed without an accompanying article—as if their physical appearance was all the reader needed to be aware of.[56] A headline above a picture of the 1932 Olympic women divers in swimsuits asks, "Is There Immodesty in This 'Undress'?" The subheading provides the answer—"No, Only Grace, Beauty, Harmony"—but leaves the reader to wonder whether their "undress" would be considered modest if they weren't beautiful.[57]

Even when there were articles, they nearly always downplayed female swimmers' athletic achievements. A *Los Angeles Times* article covering the 1932 Olympic aquatic events opened the women's section by lamenting that the women's low-back swimsuits had been banned from competition. The author then informed the reader that there were three distinct types of diving misses on the American team: the tomboy, the baby, and the vamp. Taking the first category was "husky but symmetrical" Georgia Coleman; "the baby," Katherine Rawls, was "about as big as a minute" and couldn't weigh more than 90 pounds soaking wet. Taking the honors for the third group was the "suave" and "sylph-like" Jane Fauntz, whom the writer described as tall and bronzed—but not as the bronze medalist she was. The fact that these athletes took the Olympic trifecta of gold, silver, and bronze isn't even mentioned in the article at all and must be deduced from the summary of scores included in tiny font at the end.[58]

Even if the publicity was a double-edged sword, Gallico argued that it was precisely what enabled women's competitive swimming to grow from a niche event that took place in cloistered spaces into a large and successful spectator sport that at times drew larger crowds than a championship baseball game or a heavyweight prizefight.[59] Sometimes newspapers, particularly in towns looking to attract tourists, would sponsor swim events—whether competitions or exhibitions featuring national champions—just to generate "news" and to fill the paper's pages for days with photos of "girls, girls, girls. And what girls!"[60] The papers got their "exciting pictures," wrote Gallico, "and the girls got their necessary publicity."[61]

Swimmers may have come to represent the carefree modern girl, but the focus on their femininity and sexual appeal assured men that this new emancipated woman was not a threat, and that gender distinctions were still firmly intact—even if women were now racking up Olympic medals.[62] The 1920s experienced an explosion in advertising and corporate branding, and companies looking to create markets for their mass-produced commercial goods were increasingly turning to the use of sexualized portrayals of young women to sell products. In the dawn of this "show and sell" era, the swimmer—and all she represented—emerged as one of the most valuable marketing tools of the decade.[63]

THE JANTZEN DIVING GIRL SELLS OUT

When Jantzen Knitting Mills released its 1920 summer catalogue, the cover featured an illustration of what would become the company's iconic logo: the Jantzen diving girl—a young, carefree woman frozen in mid-flight, arms spread in a graceful swan dive. The Jantzen diving girl wore a short, red, form-fitting suit like those of the Olympic swimmers and divers, accessorized with fashionable matching socks and a knitted toboggan cap. Her hair was bobbed short, a look that came to be associated with flappers but was a style that swimmers helped popularize and was worn by two thirds of the 1920 Olympic team. "I was in salt water all day and couldn't do a thing with my hair," said swimmer Ethelda Bleibtrey. "It looked horrible on dates. So I bobbed it. It caused quite a sensation."[64] If the Jantzen diving girl further resembled members of the 1920 team, it was because she was a composite based on sketches artist Florenz Clark made while watching divers train ahead of the summer Olympics at the Multnomah Athletic Club in Portland, where the Jantzen factory was located.

Jantzen marketed its knitted suit as being for real swimming and promised the "utmost freedom of action in the water." Ads pointed out that it was worn by record-breaking athletes who "do things you believed only mermaids would attempt." To further promote their suits, Jantzen sent out ten thousand stickers of the diving-girl logo for

A 1925 advertisement featuring the famous Jantzen diving girl.

stores to display in their windows, and before long the swimsuit was being worn at women's swimming clubs across the country. Jantzen dubbed their product as "the suit that changed *bathing* to *swimming*."

But as Jantzen was taking the "real swimmer" angle in its marketing, others realized that you didn't need actual swimmers to profit from their image—thus was born the "bathing beauty." And nowhere was the bathing beauty more prevalent than in the Sunshine State, which was going through a massive land boom in the 1920s.[65] As real estate magnates like the famous Miami Beach developer Carl Fisher were turning Florida's swamps and Everglades into high-end resorts, they were constantly seeking ways to attract tourists. One day Carl's wife, Jane, went for a swim at one of Fisher's beachfront casino pools and decided to remove her stockings from underneath her swimming skirt, even though they were mandated at most beaches. A preacher in a nearby town got wind of it, condemning Miami Beach as a modern

Sodom and Gomorrah. As curious crowds poured in to see what all the fuss was about, Carl realized he had his advertising campaign: "We'll get the prettiest girls we can find and put them in the god-damnedest tightest and shortest bathing suits," he exclaimed, "have their picture taken and send them all over the goddamn country as 'The Bathing Beauties of Miami Beach!'"[66]

By the early 1920s, the bathing beauty was everywhere, the whole-some image of the swimmer having been co-opted by every indus-try looking to make a buck off of women's bodies. Just months after the American women's swim team made its historic Olympic debut in 1920, a hotel owner in Atlantic City organized a "bathing beauty revue," the first of what would grow into the Miss America Pageant. The contestants, all in bathing attire, formed a mile-long parade of "mermaids" as they made their way to the boardwalk.[67] The winner, Margaret Gorman of Washington, DC, was crowned "The Most Beautiful Bathing Girl in America."

Mack Sennett, the owner of the Keystone film company, jumped on the beauty bandwagon as well. While his films of the 1910s had fea-tured real-life "diving girls" from carnival circuits performing aquatic feats in their no-nonsense Kellerman suits, in the early twenties, he shifted instead to hiring actresses to pose, giggle, and frolic on the beach in frilly bathing attire. "Sennett's Bathing Beauties" appeared in chorus line–style groupings, forming "decorative feminine back-ground[s]" for his pie-throwing, slapstick comedies.[68] Soon Fox's Sunshine Girls and bevies of bathers hired by other competitor stu-dios were flitting across movie screens. The magazine *Motion Picture Classic* pointed out that most people imagine the bathing girl of the cinema as an aquatic creature "who eats, sleeps, talks, and dreams of—water." But in reality, it noted, "the majority of the girls can't swim."[69] Even so, Keystone's publicity materials framed the bathing beauties as champion swimmers and fictionalized their achievements as athletes.[70]

But while bathing beauties paraded on stages and screens, battles were raging on public beaches, where women who wanted to *actually swim* were held to different standards. Many beaches still required stock-ings to cover every inch of the leg, and the Kellerman one-piece suit was often banned unless a skirt was worn on top of it. Police and censors enforced whatever local rules were set, measuring women's skirts, citing offenders, and sometimes even arresting them. A newspaper quoted a woman in a one-piece telling a beach censor she simply wanted to swim with the same freedom as men instead of "floundering around in useless, draggy clothes." But all she received in response was an unsympathetic, "Then don't swim!"[71] In Atlantic City, beach ordinances banned skirtless one-piece suits and required that no skin appear between the hem of a woman's skirt and the top of her stockings, but no one seemed to mind the abundance of bare knees and skirtless suits among the Miss America contestants just yards away on the boardwalk.[72] In short, it was more acceptable for a woman to parade in these safer and more efficient swimsuits than it was for her to swim in them.[73]

Even though the double standards frustrated female swimmers, the bombardment of images of women in abbreviated swimming attire—whether real swimmers pictured at their competitions or the

A beach censor at a Washington, DC, beach measures swimsuits to make sure the hems are no higher than 6 inches above the knee.

bathing beauties of the movies, pageant stages, and Florida's marketing campaigns—did have a normalizing effect on the public that helped usher out the final dregs of the restrictive, cumbersome bathing costume. By the second half of the 1920s, restrictions were easing at beaches around the country. But as bathing, which had required concealing oneself, gave way to real swimming, which increasingly involved displaying the body, there was a new focus on "being seen"— and with that came new body anxieties and fashion hoops for women to jump through.[74] As stockings were removed, women's bare legs were showing for the first time. An ad from 1923 titled "The Stockingless Vogue" promised that with the X-Bazin French depilatory system, women could "bathe stockingless without self-consciousness."[75] Advertisements for waterproof makeup encouraged women to "look like an attractive mermaid instead of a washed out one, when you go swimming."[76] One could also buy "powder that sticks in spite of the waves" and "an eyelash pencil that remembers its duty, even under water."[77]

Whereas a woman could once go to the seashore with "just" her heavy bathing costume and cap, noted one writer, "Now she invests in the 'beach costume' and some fifteen or twenty suitable accessories": like flesh-colored rubber corsets, waterproof vanity cases, bathing bracelets, stockings and pebbled slippers to match, a parasol, walking stick, and rubberized satin beach wrap, to name just a few.[78] A fashion writer of the era credited both Mack Sennett and Annette Kellerman as the two greatest influences on shaping what the modern swimming suit had become—though their approaches couldn't have been more different. Kellerman, she wrote, "made elimination her motto," reducing the suit to its simplest form that was "built on the premise that a woman occasionally likes to get into the water as well as loll on the beach." But Sennett found her practical suit "ugly, undeveloped and unimaginative," and set about adding silks, satins, laces, feathers, furs, and jewels in his quest for picturesqueness.[79] Sennett's approach naturally won out with manufacturers who were eager to make swimwear into fashion items that could be deemed obsolete ahead of next season's model.

Kellerman's "elimination" of heavy fabrics and coverings had been in service of her swimming, and the Olympic team's shorter suits— and even their bobbed hair—were about their needs as athletes. As a result of these mavericks pushing the limits, American women had

Mack Sennett's Bathing Beauties wore swimwear but didn't do much swimming.

been able to develop and assert their skills in the water, and even prove themselves on the global arena. Yet as commercial advertisers and manufacturers co-opted their aesthetic, their image increasingly became tied to glamour. The *idea* of the swimmer and what she represented, and what she could *sell*—modernity, youth, beauty, leisure—was more important than the actual athletic skills that made her so revolutionary.

As various American industries were profiting off of female swimmers, the great irony was that under the strict rules of the AAU, athletes could not make a single dollar off their sport. If they did, they would be considered professional and stripped of their amateur status, which was what enabled them to compete in AAU or Olympic competitions. It was the same amateur ethos that had pushed the swimming professors out of competition in England. Diver Aileen Riggin, who worked as a magazine journalist, couldn't even *write* about swimming or diving—the subjects she knew best. Although being a high-profile amateur athlete was fun, it was also "terribly expensive," she recalled.[80] Not only did competitive swimmers travel for meets, but they were in huge demand to give exhibitions. The AAU supported and facilitated these events, but since the swimmers weren't allowed to accept remuneration, the AAU pocketed any profits for the organization's coffers. Although the athletes' travel expenses were paid and they were often entertained beautifully, said Riggin, they still had to cover expenses like clothes, hostess gifts, telegrams, and tips. Not surprisingly, many athletes "turned professional" after one or two Olympiads if they found a way to earn a salary by monetizing their athletic skills and expertise. But for women, there were few opportunities in the world of sport. "There were no college scholarships for women," said Riggin. "There were no women coaches. There were no professional jobs."[81] So for most, that left the world of entertainment, which was eager to receive them.

The media often treated a film or stage contract as a huge coup for female athletes, tacitly implying that these venues that celebrated female glamour rather than strength were more appropriate outlets for their skills. Following the 1928 Olympics, backstroke competitor Eleanor Holm worked for a short while as a dancer with the Ziegfeld Follies. When she left the show to train for the 1932 Olympics in Los Angeles, reporters expressed surprise, writing that Holm gave up "what most American girls would consider the greatest thrill of all—being behind the footlights in a Ziegfeld show." But to Holm, leaving a job as a showgirl for another shot at the Olympics was a no-brainer. "There is a thrill about competing for your country," said Holm. "It gets in your blood."[82] But it all ended well, according to reporters, because Holm scored not only a gold medal in Los Angeles but also—as the "prettiest Olympic contestant"—a contract from the movie moguls, signing with MGM to play Tarzan's Jane (though the papers didn't mention that she stipulated no swimming in her contract, as she had her eyes on a third Olympiad).[83]

Aileen Riggin turned professional in 1926—after winning both a silver medal in diving and a bronze in the backstroke at the Paris Olympics—to take a job as a live-in celebrity entertainer-athlete at the swanky, new Deauville Hotel and Casino on the Miami Beach waterfront. She and other divers and swimmers, including Gertrude Ederle, gave exhibitions in the sprawling swimming pool in the evenings while a band played. "Our duty was to be seen," said Riggin. "We'd greet people. We'd swim. We'd put on little exhibitions and diving."[84]

It was the golden age of sport, and Olympic champions were highly sought after as entertainers, particularly aquatic athletes.

Swimsuit pageants had been staged at Miami Beach hotels ever since Carl Fisher decided to make his town the home of the bathing beauty, but the addition of *real* divers and swimmers turned these "displays of cheesecake" into legitimate entertainment that drew both male and female audiences, prominent locals and tourists.[85] "A bathing beauty was one thing, a swimmer was something else," wrote Buck Dawson, former head of the International Swimming Hall of Fame.[86] And if she was both, with Olympic medals to boot, that was pure gold! Shows at the Deauville and other resort hotels like the Miami Biltmore grew to include stage acts, such as comedians, jazz bands, and singers, and water acts like alligator wrestling, canoe races, and even "mermaid fishing." By the second half of the 1920s, "water shows were sprouting up everywhere the Florida real estate speculators could build a pool or clear a beach," wrote Dawson. "A whole new entertainment subculture grew up around the pools of South Florida and then moved north, east and west, much as vaudeville had emanated from New York to crisscross the country."[87]

When Gertrude Ederle, who won a bronze medal at the 1924 Olympics, was in training for her attempt to cross the English Channel, she, along with Riggin and diver Helen Wainwright, was invited to give exhibitions at the New York Hippodrome's "Sports Carnival"—a show featuring sports-themed acts and other athlete celebrities, like

A water show at Florida's Hollywood Beach Casino in the early 1920s.

heavyweight champion Jack Delaney. The Hippodrome dusted off Annette Kellerman's tank for their aquatic act, "On the Shores of Old Miami," in which Ederle demonstrated the American crawl, the stroke with which she hoped to conquer the English Channel, and Riggin and Wainwright performed ornamental swimming stunts and fancy dives.[88] The small size of the tank—six feet deep and not quite wide enough to do a swan dive without hitting the sides—was a constant source of anxiety, recalled Riggin. It may have been large enough for Kellerman and carnival diving girls, but "we weren't really professionals," she said. "We were sports who happened to be on the stage."[89] After Ederle's successful Channel swim a little over a year later, she was in huge demand for appearances, so she bought Kellerman's tank from the Hippodrome and the trio of Olympians took their show on the road for a twenty-six-week tour. As national heroines they were given the red-carpet treatment, greeted at train stations by city mayors and hosted at city halls for luncheons.

THE BACKLASH IN EDUCATION

Once these swimmers and divers had broken the AAU and Olympic glass ceilings, and in such spectacular manner, interest in other competitive sports for women had exploded—and the resistance somewhat eased. In 1922, the AAU accepted women's track and field, and only a few years later, added basketball and began holding national championships for both. "We did a lot toward getting women's sports accepted in America," said Riggin. "We didn't even know this was what we were doing."[90] Industrial leagues were hosting high-stakes championships and churning out serious women athletes, and even at high schools and colleges female students were participating in interschool competitions and state tournaments.

And once again, there were the skeptics—but this time they were women. The growing intensity of competitive women's sports had sparked heated debates over the value and appropriate role of athletic competition for women and girls, particularly among female physical educators. These women looked at the AAU and Olympics, both of which had men at the helm, as promoting a model of sport that created elite cadres of specialized champion athletes and emphasized winning at all costs.[91] This model, they believed, had infiltrated men's physical education programs, which were increasingly dominated not by educators but by coaches who were commercially incentivized to win. Whereas organized sports had been touted earlier in the century as a way to prepare youth for the modern world, in practice, these female educators argued, they had benefited only a small number of the most talented students, leaving the rest behind. The goal of athletics programs should be to make "every boy and girl a finer, bigger, broader man or woman," wrote Agnes Wayman, head of physical education at Barnard College, not to "put a few on pedestals and worship them because of records in this and that sport or event."[92] These educators felt that physical education programs had failed not just young men but the entire country, as the draft for the First World War had shown that nearly 40 percent of fighting-age men were not fit for strenuous service. Instead of creating a generation of strong, healthy youth, argued Wayman, men's physical education programs had made sports stars of the few and fans of the majority.[93]

And now Wayman and others feared that women's physical education programs had begun falling into the same patterns. Moreover, they believed the pressure to win pushed young women beyond their physical limits, while the excitement of competing in front of cheering crowds could fray their fragile nerves.[94] The medical community had finally condoned *light* physical activity for women, but with athletic training becoming more intensive, concerns over reproductive harm had resurfaced in medical and educational circles. Even swimmers weren't immune. "In those days . . . it was not considered healthy for girls to overexert themselves or to swim as far as a mile," Aileen Riggin recalled. "People thought it was a great mistake, that we were ruining our health, that we would never have children, and that we would be sorry for it later on."[95]

Looking for a way to rein in women's physical education programs, a group of vocal educators approached the War Department, which had created the National Amateur Athletic Federation (NAAF) to promote standards for physical training as part of national preparedness efforts. They advocated for the creation of a women's branch at NAAF and pointed out that women had stepped up during the war, serving as active-duty military nurses and filling positions at factories and stateside offices of the armed forces, showing that their health and fitness could not be ignored. The War Department agreed, and in 1923, the Women's Division of NAAF was formed, with Lou Henry Hoover, the wife of Herbert Hoover, as its leader.

The Women's Division provided female physical educators a unified platform from which to voice their concerns and create a different model for girls' and women's athletics—one of total equality of opportunity. Its motto was, "A team for every girl and every girl on a team."[96] As part of its sixteen-point creed, the Women's Division called for the complete elimination of interschool competitions for high school and college women. They wanted to ensure that facilities and programs benefited the physical fitness of all girls equally instead of "developing the superior prowess of the few."[97] Twenty influential national organizations signed on to the platform, including the American Physical Education Association, the National Council of Parents and Teachers, the Association of Directors of Physical Education for Women in Colleges and Universities, the American Association of University Women, and the YWCA, as well as over 150 colleges and universities.[98]

With such wide endorsement of its ideals, the Women's Division ushered in an era of formalized consensus about how women's high school and collegiate athletics should be regulated and spread an anticompetitive ethos that virtually wiped out varsity sports for female students.[99] Between 1924, the year NAAF issued its creed, and the end of the decade, the number of colleges and universities sponsoring intercollegiate competitions for women dropped from 22 percent to 12 percent.[100] Varsity sports for women continued to decline precipitously, and by the late 1930s had almost disappeared.[101] In many places, they would not return until the hallmark Title IX legislation of the 1970s, which prohibited sex-based discrimination in school programs, including sports.

Colleges for African American women were an important exception to the anticompetitive ethos. A study in the late 1930s found that 75 percent of Black colleges supported intercollegiate athletics for women, whereas that figure was 17 percent at predominantly white schools.[102] While white educators were reducing competitive athletic opportunities for their students, educators at historically Black colleges were fostering a "concept of womanhood that embraced strength, self-reliance, and competitive spirit," which to many educators at these schools meant allowing girls to participate in any sport that was open to boys.[103] A majority of schools across the country had barred track and field for female students, but it continued to be offered at a few Black institutions, including Tuskegee Institute in Alabama and Tennessee Agricultural and Industrial State University.[104] Some scholars have argued that white, middle-class physical educators "defined themselves in contrast" to not just the male model of sports but also to those of working-class industrial leagues and African American universities.[105] Wealthy women had their own world of genteel sports like tennis and golf, and working-class women filled the ranks of industrial leagues, so female physical educators "staked out" the middle class for creating physical activities that promoted their "professional view of the healthy, self-controlled, feminine woman."[106] As one educator wrote, "It should be the ambition of every department of physical education to preserve and add to the desirable feminine qualities of girls and women."[107]

Yet despite the curtailment of sports for women and girls, interest in swimming among female students was at an all-time high. And ironically, this enthusiasm had been fueled by the stellar examples set by the American Olympic team and Gertrude Ederle. As Louis de B. Handley put it, the "great impetus which has been given to women's swimming" was due to the champions of the "competitive side of the sport."[108] The National Committee on Women's Athletics of the American Physical Education Association took note of the heightened enthusiasm these competitors brought to the field of aquatics and advised instructors in its 1927–1928 handbook to be "careful to use this interest in a sane way and through it to encourage all the non-swimmers in the world to become swimmers, instead of forgetting their ideals and trying to make a name for themselves by producing a few champions."[109]

Educators would do just that, capitalizing on this interest by innovating new styles of swimming—ones that focused on collaboration over competition and prioritized skill over speed. These innovations would build on the glamour and drama of aquatics established by previous generations of swimming sportswomen while providing fresh challenges for swimmers and fostering new athletic skills in the water. It was a combination that would prove to hold both unlimited creative potential and massive spectator appeal.

CHAPTER 7

SYNCHING UP

Interest in speed swimming is now at its height, but
what of the many hundreds who enjoy the water and
are not built for speed? Why not center our interest
upon grace and ease of movement in the water,
developing the esthetic values of swimming?

—KATHARINE CURTIS, 1928

K atharine Curtis's Modern Mermaids had something new for the 1934 Chicago World's Fair. Donning white bathing suits and caps, and short capes draped around their shoulders, a parade of thirty young women filed in before several thousand spectators at the Lagoon Theater, which looked out across Lake Michigan. They paused for a moment on the stage built over the water as former Olympic swimmer and master of ceremonies Norman Ross introduced them with a promise: these mermaids would synchronize their swimming to music![1] The women descended steps leading down to the lake and entered the water unseen by the audience; then, using matching arm strokes, they swam in rows of three into the lagoon. Their leader, Curtis, who remained on deck, gave the cue for the music to begin.

The Modern Mermaids performance was part of a free waterfront show at the "Century of Progress" World's Fair, celebrating the centennial anniversary of the city of Chicago. Other acts included high divers, trapeze artists, and high-wire stunters. When the show organizers decided to add underwater lights in the "lagoon" and were looking for an aquatic act to showcase them, they immediately thought of Curtis, a physical education instructor with Chicago Public Schools and chair of the women's competitive swimming events at the Fair. Turns out, Curtis had just the thing up her sleeve. For a decade, she had been at the forefront of a growing number of women educators experimenting with new forms of group swimming to music. She corralled her current and former students, supplementing their ranks through open auditions, to create a cadre of sixty swimmers for her Modern Mermaids show.[2] Although each performance featured only half that number, the show would run three times a day, so she needed a full set of alternates.

Once the swimmers reached the center of the lagoon, they broke into two groups, each surrounding a large floating black disk. Those in the center of each group grabbed hold of the disk and, as they floated on their backs, other swimmers held their feet and connected to one another, building out a large snowflake pattern.[3] As a twelve-piece band played along, the women shifted between lacy designs, gliding in and out of starfish, webs, and swirling circles. When the song ended, the audience applauded enthusiastically, but the Modern Mermaids weren't finished. They performed rhythmic routines as well, wowing the crowd as they moved in and out of sharp lines while executing matching strokes and interspersing their swimming with stunts like the porpoise and dolphin—all in perfect unison. A press release in early July wrote of the show:

> For all the world like airplanes in formation, the swimmers dive, turn, show the crawl, breast and back stroke, and finally swim from sight, all to the strains of and in time with music. . . . Every arm is raised at the same instant. On the dive, every head disappears below the surface at the same moment and, somehow, all reappear together.[4]

Originally, the swimmers, who ranged in age from seventeen to twenty-three, planned to wear Krepe-Tex rubber swimsuits—"the newest thing at the time," recalled one Modern Mermaid—provided by way of sponsorship from the US Rubber Company. But when they tested them out, thankfully at a dress rehearsal, many of the suits split wide open when they hit the water, so at the last minute they opted for plain swimsuits, which was just as well as their white color practically glowed against the dark water.[5] Their show was particularly dazzling at night, when the submerged bed of colored lights backlit their formations from below, prompting a reporter to call them "pictures and designs of living beauty in water."[6] The Modern Mermaids were originally contracted to perform for one week, but their show was so popular the Fair extended it to the end of the summer, and then again until the end of October—or whenever "ice forms in the Lagoon."[7] The *Chicago Tribune* wrote that no other show at the Fair had thrilled as many visitors as the Modern Mermaids and credited the swimmers' "skill and artistry" for keeping them on the bill all season with ever growing popularity.[8]

Everyone loved the Modern Mermaids show, but no one seemed

The Modern Mermaids at the 1934 Chicago World's Fair, including
Katharine Curtis, who appears in a black swimsuit in the back row.

to know what to call it. Newspapers variously referenced the thirty "feminine swimmers who disport daily" in the Lagoon, describing their performance as everything from "ballet stunts," to "figure swimming set to music."[9] But the prize for sticking power went to Norman Ross, who had become a radio announcer in his post-Olympics career. He called it "synchronized swimming" in his announcements during one of their performances, and the Fair's publicity team, which had been referring to their act as a "grand water ballet," quickly picked up on the term. A press release in August read: "Performing ten complicated routines in perfect unison, thirty five modern mermaids are revealing to patrons of the Lagoon Theater at the Chicago World's Fair, the highly modern art of synchronized swimming."[10]

In a letter of commendation, the Fair's general manager for events wrote, "Synchronized swimming is new even to the 'water minded' and seems almost impossible to the 'land-lubber.'" But these young women, he noted, had proven to be "experts in such group swimming."[11] Although this style of swimming was actually *not* new to the "water minded," it was the first time most of the general public had seen anything like it. Synchronized swimming (though it wouldn't be widely called by its newly minted name for some time still) was, in 1934, part of a budding branch of aquatics rapidly taking off in schools and recreation programs across the country. Katharine Curtis was not only among the vanguard of this new field but would, just a few years after the Modern Mermaids show, lay the foundation to turn group swimming to music into an organized competitive sport.

As a fifteen-year-old, Katharine Whitney (Curtis) made headlines when she became the first woman to swim across Lake Mendota in Madison, Wisconsin, in 1912, a distance of three and a half miles. She raised eyebrows for wearing a man's swimming suit for the feat but was also praised as a "youthful Annette Kellerman," a comparison that would become far more apt than the writer could have imagined at the time.[12] Two years later, Katharine enrolled at the University of Wisconsin, where she swam, skated, played basketball, baseball, and hockey, and was named best all-around female athlete

Katharine Whitney (Curtis) as a young swimmer.

on campus—though her greatest love would always be swimming.[13] She graduated with a degree in physical education in 1917 and became "sports mistress" for the all-girls Principia School in St. Louis, where she started the school's first field hockey and basketball teams.[14]

Physical education was a growing professional field for women, spurred by the great demand for trained female professionals like Curtis to lead athletic programs for both high school girls and the skyrocketing number of college women, who by 1920 made up 47.3 percent of all enrollments in higher education.[15] Universities, teaching colleges, and professional schools like the Sargent School for Physical Training were graduating thousands of women with physical education degrees who would go on to lead athletic programs for women and girls not only at educational institutions but also at YWCAs, camps, and recreation centers.

Most of these women had progressive ideas. They were the generation who had idolized Annette Kellerman growing up, pushed the boundaries in women's swimwear—donning their one-piece suits in defiance of beach censors—cheered on the first female Olympic team, and then cast their first presidential ballots only a few months later. But they were also starting their careers just as the movement against competition in women's athletics was gaining momentum and rigid ideas about acceptable athletics for girls were solidifying. A survey in 1924—the same year the Women's Division issued its platform calling for the end of varsity sports for female students—found that of fifty polled directors of physical education programs for women in leading universities and colleges, 86 percent were opposed to intercollegiate competition.[16]

The Women's Division, however, was careful to clarify that they weren't against *all* competition for female students—just the type that focused on *winning*, like "open track meets or open swimming meets, with important championships at stake."[17] They believed that deemphasizing the individualistic drive to win would enable athletic programs for girls to focus instead on fostering desirable social traits, which were, in the words of Ethel Perrin of the Detroit Board of Education, "cooperation, loyalty and good sportsmanship."[18] Or, as the Girl Scout handbook put it, team games should train girls to "efface themselves as individuals and to play as a member of the team . . . to cooperate."[19]

As a result, at the majority of colleges and high schools, boys enjoyed varsity and extramural sports while girls were limited to intramural games and "play days"—field days in which schools would come together for female students to participate in loosely organized athletic "games," with teams arbitrarily chosen in order to avoid pitting school against school. Play-day proponents believed that the emphasis on "play for play's sake" allowed every girl to gain the social and health benefit of sports, without the overexcitement of real competition, though of course not everyone agreed. "I picture the girls in a Play Day as sheep, huddled and bleating in their little Play meadow," said Ina Gittings, director of physical education for women at the University of Arizona, "whereas they should be young mustangs exultantly racing together across vast prairies."[20] Gittings argued that when students are forced to play games with no broader significance or reward for skill, it takes away all the motivation and joy that sports have to offer. Moreover, she posited, when a few star performers are able to rise to the top, it is good for the middling athlete as well, as she will be inspired by watching the skill and expertise that is demonstrated through athletic competitions.

But in the opinion of S. E. Bilik (the one who said competitive sports make women "actually ugly"), unserious and low-stakes athletics—precisely the kind offered at play days—were all that respectable female students wanted. "Left to her natural inclinations," he wrote, "the average womanly woman will readily enough 'play' at her favorite sport, but she will refuse to take it more seriously."[21] As his comments hint, female athletes who wanted more robust competitive options risked being categorized as "unwomanly." As a result, they often had to emphasize or even exaggerate their femininity in other domains outside of sports to make amends for their "transgressive behavior" on the playing field, a practice feminist scholars have called the "female apologetic." Sometimes others took the liberty of "apologizing" for them. An article about the sportswomen of Madison, Wisconsin, which included descriptions of Katharine Curtis's sports accomplishments, likened these girl athletes to the "New Woman," with a headline declaring: "She plays nearly everything the Madison boy does and at the same time is a home lover." The article predicted that soon the New Woman would:

Play at nearly every game where man now excels.
Get out in the open air and rough it.

YET
She will cook
She will play the violin and piano
She will be a lover of the home and
She will have all the refined qualities of the ideal woman.[22]

Physical educators—women who had chosen to dedicate their educations and careers to the progressive idea of providing athletic opportunities for girls and helping them become active, healthy women—dealt with many of the same stigmas as female athletes. And because of their interest in sports, the scope of their work being limited to members of their own sex, and the fact that many never married, they were particularly vulnerable to homophobic insinuations.[23] Moreover, physical educators were not entirely accepted by university colleagues from more academic disciplines, especially in the Depression years, when there was animosity against working women, who were seen as taking jobs from men. Some scholars have argued that a key way female physical educators mitigated these perils and protected themselves and their female students was by developing programs that highlighted, rather than diminished, gender differences.[24] Betty Hartman, an educator at Ohio State University, wrote that when trying to determine what athletic programs are acceptable for female students, instructors should consider their future role in society as wives and mothers and ask, "What does the average American man expect of women?"[25]

Regardless of whether Hartman, Curtis, or other physical educators agreed with the prevailing anticompetition ethos—and certainly many did not—this was the context in which they navigated their careers and tried to provide meaningful activities for their female students who were more interested in sports than ever. It is not surprising, then, that many turned their attention to swimming. Not only was interest high among students, but it remained a noncontroversial activity due to its value as a lifesaving skill and its associations with feminine hygiene and beauty. Swimming clubs for women began popping up at schools and colleges across the country, one of the earliest being the Tarpon Club, which was founded by Katharine Curtis at the University of Chicago in 1923, the year after she took a teaching position there.[26] However, unlike men's competitive swim "teams" that were part of varsity athletics, these groups were considered "honorary" clubs and fell under the jurisdiction of physical education departments or extracurricular programming. Most early women's clubs put their energy into producing water pageants or working through the Red Cross lifesaving curriculum, though a few experimented with quasi-competitive offerings for their students like intramural contests and telegraphic meets. For the latter, participating schools would hold swimming contests at their home facilities and then call in their students' times to a centralized authority who would tally the scores and announce the winners. Instructors at Barnard decided to dispense with points and winners altogether, instead rewarding participants in intramural "competitions" with gold stars next to their names on a chart for each event—such as the 100-yard freestyle, the trudgen, or the back crawl—they performed "satisfactorily."[27]

Naturally, these options were frustrating for female students who wanted real competition. Jane Fauntz, who became a diver on the 1928 and 1932 Olympic teams, competed on her Chicago high school's swim team for one year before the Illinois High School Athletic Association curtailed all interschool competition.[28] When she became a student at the University of Illinois, she competed in telegraphic meets, but found the experience lacking: "We would swim our event against the clock, and then we would telegraph our times to the other schools," said Fauntz. "So who knows who was telling the truth or who was really champion?"[29] With such limited and unsatisfying options, many instructors, including Katharine Curtis, began looking beyond races to find other ways to challenge their students in the water and keep up their interest in swimming.

STUNTS, FORMATIONS, AND MUSIC

So, what else was there to do in the water besides swim fast? Three key areas physical educators began focusing on in the 1920s were stunt swimming, group formation work, and the application of musical rhythm to the water—a trio of distinct aquatic skill sets that would ultimately come together and form the foundational building blocks of synchronized swimming.

Curtis was an enthusiastic proponent of stunt swimming, which she defined as "all swimming activities other than standard swimming strokes."[30] Although the repertoire of swimming stunts—the same genre of maneuvers previously called scientific or ornamental swimming—had greatly expanded since the days of Everard Digby, many built on the same foundational techniques he outlined and that the swimming professors and natationists had used less than a century earlier. Curtis had first been exposed to this type of swimming by Joe Steinauer, a former vaudeville acrobat and the diving coach at the University of Wisconsin, when she was a student there. Even though Curtis had set swimming records as a teen, she considered herself to be more of a graceful swimmer than one oriented toward speed and found stunt swimming to be a stimulating challenge.[31] She began working with Steinauer to apply the techniques and movements from his aerial acrobatics to the water.

When Curtis became a swimming and physical education instructor at the University of Chicago, she visited the newly built women's recreation center at Ida Noyes Hall and was delighted to discover an indoor swimming pool with an elegantly curved ceiling, skylights, and rows of windows. "When I took one look at the women's gym and pool," recalled Curtis, "I knew I'd be spending a lot of time there."[32] The following year, she established the Tarpon Club and set about teaching the stunts she had practiced with Steinauer.[33] "I stole his routines," wrote Curtis. "Whatever he did in the air, I taught my students to do in the water."[34] Curtis believed that practicing stunts enabled swimmers of all levels to develop confidence and poise in the water, and wrote that stunts provided "infinite possibilities for the development of poetry of motion with accent on ease, line, rhythm, and harmony of bodily motion rather than speed."[35]

Another early and enthusiastic stunt practitioner within women's education circles was Gertrude Titus, a physical educator from Massachusetts. Titus had learned this style of swimming around the turn of the century from a coach named Herbert Holm, with whom she swam in Boston's Brookline Club.[36] Holm competed and performed on swimming circuits that had put him in contact with professionals like Professor James Finney of England, which may have been how he learned the techniques of scientific swimming. Holm gave performances at swimming carnivals and taught stunts to his students at Brookline, including Titus. When Titus became a physical educator, she passed these stunts to her own female charges, as well as to numerous other teachers through a course she taught on swimming instruction pedagogies for several years at the Boston School of Physical Education camp.[37] One of her protégées, Gertrude Goss, would, like Curtis, become influential in the development of synchronized swimming.

Whereas Curtis and Titus used stunts to foster poise and strength, Goss found them to be a fun alternative to straight swimming, so when she graduated and began her first job in 1917 at Winthrop College in South Carolina, she incorporated them into her own swimming classes.[38] Goss would have her biggest impact, however, at Smith College, where she became the director of physical education in 1924 and remained in that position until her retirement twenty-seven years later. At Smith, an all-girls' school, the aquatic club had started as a lifesaving corps, but Goss soon had the Smith College Lifeguards "turning cartwheels, doing handstands, somersaults and 'playing like porpoises.'"[39]

As the practice of stunt swimming caught on, Curtis, perhaps seeking alternative competitive options for her students in the face of the decline of interschool races, began dreaming of holding competitions in this style of aquatics. "Interest in speed swimming is now at its height, but what of the many hundreds who enjoy the water and are not built for speed?" she wrote in her 1927 article, "A Plea for More Interest in Stunt and Fancy Swimming."[40] She asked why diving should be the only aquatic sport with a competition based on form and pointed out that stunt competitions were already happening north of the border.

Indeed, only a few years earlier in 1924, Canada had begun holding ornamental swimming competitions, and while the original scientific swimming contests in England dating back to the 1840s had been strictly for men, in Canada it was women vying for the honors. Two years later, the country held its first national championship in "The Art of Graceful and Scientific Swimming" in Montreal, using stunts from the Royal Life Saving Society handbook, the competitors

How to combine swimming strokes and stunts, including the front crawl with the porpoise and the backstroke with a dolphin, followed by a ballet leg—as illustrated in Gertrude Goss's book Stunts and Synchronized Swimming.

fittingly attired in Annette Kellerman suits.[41] It was won by Peg Shearer, who would later become a leader in the development of synchronized swimming in Canada.[42] George Corsan, who developed the YMCA swimming program, supported the idea of a women's stunt swimming competition, which he believed was a more suitable alternative to races:

> Women should not be trained for hard, strenuous swimming sprints. Contests between women's colleges and clubs should be confined largely to fancy style and grace, rather than to speed. . . . Novelty and ornamental swimming are women's specialties and they far excel men in such events; and their skill is greatly admired by the men in the audience.[43]

Although the stunt competition idea didn't catch on in US schools, stunts themselves certainly did—their spread facilitated through education and swimming conferences, and through swimming books. All of the most widely used swimming texts of the time dedicated pages, if not entire chapters, to providing detailed descriptions of various swimming stunts, including Kellerman's *How to Swim*, George Corsan's *At Home in the Water*, WSA Coach Louis de B. Handley's *Swimming for Women*, and a wide range of Red Cross swimming and pageantry materials.[44] In her 1928 book *Education Through Physical*

Education, Agnes Wayman included stunt swimming, along with stroking "for form," and non-strenuous water games, on a list of approved aquatic activities for adolescent girls (on her "condemned" list were men's-style water polo and distance swimming for speed).[45] She suggested incorporating "trick swimming" into the play-day program and included a long list of stunts such as sculling, imitating a torpedo, marching in the water, somersaults, imitating a porpoise, waltz stroking, and even "singing in the water."[46] In 1932, a survey of colleges and universities found that 73 percent used stunt swimming as part of their aquatic programs for women.[47]

The second major area of experimentation for swim clubs was formation, float, or form swimming—terms used somewhat interchangeably to refer to groups of swimmers making shapes in or on the water, a practice dating to at least the first century when swimming "Nereids" formed a trident, anchor, ship, and stars in the waters of the flooded Colosseum in Rome. A women's magazine in 1891 described Agnes

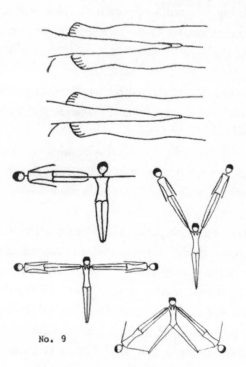

No. 9

An illustration of some of the many ways
swimmers can connect in floating patterns.

Beckwith and three other lady swimmers making floating shapes on the water at a performance at the Westminster Aquarium, writing that the swimmers "propel[ed] themselves imperceptibly in the form of a Maltese cross," then changed positions, forming an XXXX with their extended arms and legs. Finally, with "the hindermost surging up the water with her feet," the group imitated a tugboat pulling a line of barges.[48] Larger "picture float" groups had been popular in England and Germany since the early twentieth century. They featured women moving through sequences of connected floating patterns while musicians played gentle tunes in the background—much like the Modern Mermaids would later do at the Chicago World's Fair.

Louis de B. Handley endorsed "ornamental team floating" for the collaborative problem-solving skills it fostered, as it required teamwork not just to make the patterns but also to find interesting ways to connect, expand, and contract them, and to shift smoothly from one formation to the next at the signal of the leader.[49] Instructions for a floating routine that Gertrude Goss published in *Beach & Pool* magazine illustrate how this worked in practice. According to her instructions, ten to twelve swimmers dive into a pool in unison, then, using stylized arm strokes, swim into a circle. At the whistle, they stop and tread water facing one another: "Whistle—quarter turn to right. Whistle—Drop back easily on backs," wrote Goss. "Bring feet up and place one on each side of neck of girl in front."[50] Once connected, the swimmers' bodies form the outline of a circle, which they then spin like a wheel on the surface by sculling in unison. Goss's instructions continue with the circle opening into a line then breaking into various formations, and finally back into a circle. But this time their bodies form the spokes of the wheel rather than its outline, the swimmers alternating their heads and feet pointing outward, and each grabbing the ankles of her neighbor on either side. At the whistle, those with their heads pointing outward extend their arms while the feet-out group spreads their legs into V shapes, and the combination of everyone's expansions transforms the shape from a tight clump into a large, lacy snowflake.

The term "formation swimming" was also used to refer to groups of swimmers stroking or moving through the water in set formations, rather than floating in patterns on the surface. This type of formation swimming had been practiced by young men at YMCAs as early as 1915 and would

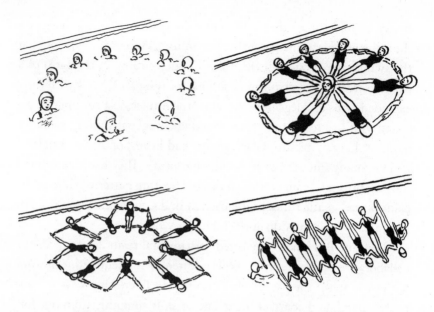

Illustrations from Goss's book showing swimmers getting into formation, creating different kinds of circles, and preparing to expand an "accordion" float.

be taught as part of aquatic military swimming drills during the Second World War.[51] The more swimmers that were involved, the more elaborate the patterns could become, even spelling out words or school initials. One instructor shared that when working out formations for her swimmers, she liked to use buttons, pushing them around in various arrangements on her kitchen table until she settled on patterns that she liked.[52]

After stunts and formations, the third area of experimentation was setting it all to music. From Natator's underwater jig to "Froggy Would a Wooing Go," to Agnes and Willie Beckwith's water waltz to string accompaniment—"in which both kept time admirably to the music of the band"—and later to Red Cross water pageants featuring brass ensembles, music had long been a part of aquatic entertainments.[53] It had also been used to motivate swimmers, including Jabez Wolffe, who had bagpipe players serenade him from accompanying boats to help him keep up his pace and morale during his many attempts (one of which was finally successful) to cross the English Channel.[54] Although the application of music to aquatics was not a new idea, until Victrolas and phonographs came along, the only options for music required live accompaniment, making it impractical for day-to-day swimming. So as these portable music devices became increasingly affordable in the 1920s, physical educators leading swim clubs seized the opportunity to bring tunes to the tank, setting up gramophones directly on their pool decks. When Curtis discovered that there was a "nickelodeon" by the pool at the University of Chicago, she was so excited she had it rigged so that it would only take special tokens, which she then hid from her colleagues. "I didn't want the other teachers hogging the machine," she later confessed.[55]

Gertrude Goss cited a host of benefits to applying music to the swimming program: "While music is being played, the beginner who is tense and rigid, becomes relaxed" she wrote. "The intermediate swimmer gains a sense of rhythm . . . and the advanced swimmer, having already relaxation and rhythm gets added enjoyment out of swimming lengths."[56] Moreover, she found that with music playing, her students would forget the time and want to keep swimming even after class ended.[57] Articles like Goss's "Swim to Music—It's Fun" and "Set Your Swimming to Music," published by the American Physical Education Association and *Camping Magazine*, respectively, helped the idea spread quickly through education and recreation circles. Shortly after the stock market crash of 1929, a newspaper reported that Skidmore College was piping in radio music through a loudspeaker directly above the pool. "Market reports and solemn speeches are tuned out, but every variety of music is tuned in," the article reported. "Every girl is urged to calm her nerves and sustain her strength by 'musical swimming.'"[58] A survey in 1932 found that 12.6 percent of colleges with women enrolled used music as part of the swimming program.[59] By 1946, another found that 76 percent of surveyed schools had swim clubs, and of those, nearly 80 percent incorporated music into their aquatic programs.[60]

In the early days of swimming to music, most instructors put on records and just let them run in the background for ambiance, but Katharine Curtis wrote that she quickly became "annoyed by the fact that the swimmers did not 'keep time' with the background music." She felt the urge to make the swimming "one" with the rhythm just as it was in dance—or as she put it, "combine swimming with swing."[61] Moreover, she thought that trying to swim to the beat might be a way to challenge her advanced students, so she began teaching them to perform their strokes in conjunction with set musical patterns. She called it "rhythmic swimming" and wrote that "it was an instant success."[62]

Before long, Curtis and others were adding stunts and formations to the musical mix, creating song-length routines. Goss suggested an organic, student-led process of turning on the music and letting the swimmers improvise. She found that "without making conscious effort . . . the swimmer makes his strokes fit the rhythm of the music."[63] Once they had worked out their own rhythms, she would encourage the swimmers to start making patterns in the water as a group, and then from there to add stunts.[64] Waltzes were typically preferred as a starting point for their consistent beat. Curtis wrote that at first, the only song her swimmers knew was "Merry Widow Waltz," but after swimming a few routines to that "old faithful," they became bored with its three-quarter-time rhythm.[65] Then on a vacation to Mexico, Curtis purchased a record for the song "La Cucaracha," featuring exciting new beats. "I brought it to my swimming class and let the girls loose to do what they could with it," she recalled.[66]

By building on and combining elements from existing forms of aquatics—stunts, formations, and swimming to music—physical educators had created something entirely new. To Curtis, what made this new form distinct from earlier styles of related swimming, like that done by floating pictures groups in England and Germany at the turn of the century or the scientific and ornamental swimmers of England and Canada, was twofold: first, combining stunts and rhythmic strokes created true "*swimming* routines" rather than floating ones; and second, the music was integral, with the movements in the water executed to the exact beat and measure of the accompaniment."[67] In short, swimmers were no longer performing stunts in isolation or gently floating while some string instruments played in the background. Instead, they were dolphining, spinning, ballet-legging, waltzing, and stroking—all in unison, all in formation—their every movement dictated by the beats blasting from the electric turntable.

MAKING IT SYNCH

A new aquatic activity had been born, and, although no one knew it yet, the basic foundation had been laid for a future Olympic sport. So who was first? Who invented this new style of group swim-dancing in the water that would soon become known as synchronized swimming? The answer is "no one"—or rather no one individual—according to Marian Stoerker, the first person to undertake a serious exploration of the origins and development of synchronized swimming in her 1956 master's thesis (written at Curtis's alma mater, the University of Wisconsin). Stoerker found that in the early 1920s, simultaneous and related developments in the combination of stunts, musical rhythm, and formations were happening across the country and "seemed to spring up in any location where there was a swimming program."[68] Although Stoerker concluded that the origination of synchronized swimming cannot be attributed to a single person, she did give great credit to Gertrude Titus, Gertrude Goss, and Katharine Curtis as being among the earliest and most influential innovators. She noted that in 1922, Gertrude Titus organized a water pageant for Rochester University students using music "for the rhythmic element to synchronize the swimmers with each other."[69] Curtis, she wrote, likely began experimenting with these same elements soon after founding the Tarpon Club in 1923. Goss introduced rhythmic swimming to the Smith College Lifeguards in 1924 and, according to Stoerker, arranged their first public performance the following year. Some articles about Goss, however, indicate that she was arranging "water ballets" as early as 1921 at Winthrop College in South Carolina, where she taught before moving to Smith. Although a handful of other early contributors were mentioned in Stoerker's thesis, Goss and Curtis would become the leaders in carrying synchronized swimming forward—and in the latter's case, all the way to a competitive sport.

Until the name "synchronized swimming" came along in 1934 (and then even for some time after that), group swimming to music was called a variety of names, most commonly water ballet or rhythmic swimming. But regardless of the labels people were using, the fact that these emerging styles fit so perfectly with the era's democratic ethos of women's physical education and ideals of feminine sport helped them spread like a tsunami. "Girls have found an excellent medium for their natural grace and beauty in rhythmic or ballet swimming," wrote one physical educator.[70] Moreover, just as nineteenth-century audiences approved of the natationists' ornamental swimming because of its apparent ease, rhythmic swimming did not offend audiences with overt displays of female exertion. "Each member of the audience relaxes and thoroughly enjoys the aesthetic appeal of the grace, rhythm, timing, and ease of the synchronized movements of these performers," wrote Curtis. "There is no strain, no exhaustion."[71] As another educator put it: "The water ballet is the coed's answer to the protest that athletics makes a girl seem masculine."[72] Moreover, it was collaborative and thought to be accessible to swimmers of all skill levels, with one instructor writing that the swimmers must "be flexible in conforming individual stroke styles to a pattern set for all group members . . . making self second in terms of that which is best for the group."[73]

In the early years, group swimming found natural expression in the existing performance genre of water pageants. In 1936, Katharine Curtis published *A Sourcebook of Water Pageantry* (revised and republished as *Rhythmic Swimming: A Source Book of Synchronized Swimming and Water Pageantry* in 1942), which illustrates how these forms were interwoven. Her book includes pageant synopses, diagrams of group formations, and instructions for dozens of stunts and dives, plus full rhythmic swimming routines written to go with specific songs and to accommodate different numbers of swimmers. Swim clubs could then pull material from the various sections in mix-and-match fashion according to their needs. For a December water show, a teacher might choose the pageant "Santa Claus' Visit to Waternymphia," finding a list of key characters, costume ideas, and even ready-made text to be read aloud at the start of the show—in this case, an aquatic adaptation of the famous holiday poem: " 'Twas a while before Christmas, and deep in the sea / The nymphs were disporting themselves merrily . . ."[74] From there, the instructor could leaf through the routines to find a waltz duet for Santa and Mrs. Claus to swim, as well as floating formations and stunts suitable for her herd of eight reindeer. If looking to add comic relief, she might have her elves perform some underwater roller-skating or clown dives.

The Smith College Lifeguards were one of the few swim clubs that bypassed the pageantry and focused exclusively on rhythmic swimming—sometimes calling it precision swimming—and opting for plain suits rather than themed costumes. A show the Smith swimmers put on at Springfield College was said to feature "a new type of rhythmic water pageantry" where "synchronization was the theme."[75] The Smith College Lifeguards greatly facilitated the spread of rhythmic swimming by performing at schools all over the northeast, including Colgate, Dartmouth, Amherst, Wellesley, Vassar, Springfield, and MIT, and became an "institution" at the annual Yale Water Carnival, which was organized by the university's famous swimming coach Robert Kiphuth, who would become an important early supporter of synchronized swimming.

But the biggest impact on the spread of these new styles of swimming came that same year in Chicago with Curtis's Modern Mermaids show at the World's Fair—not only because it resulted in a new name—synchronized swimming—to coalesce around but also because of the sheer numbers of people who saw the show. One article estimated that 4.5 million people watched the Modern Mermaids perform; thousands more saw newsreel footage at movie theaters.[76] "The popular appeal was so strong that many of the spectators were repeaters returning to see one of the mermaid's shows at every visit to the Fair," wrote Curtis. "Thus, a new and intense interest, appreciation, and understanding of this new field in water activities was created and developed in an immense lay audience."[77] As the World's Fair drew to a close, audiences were still asking to see the Modern Mermaids, so they continued to perform, moving their show to the indoor pool at the Medinah Athletic Club in Chicago for the duration of the winter.

While synchronized swimming was still novel to most of the public, at least one newspaper reporter saw a connection between the Modern Mermaids performance and a new style of swimming that had made its way to the cinema, exclaiming that the Mermaids' "beautiful and lacy designs rival those of the musical screen attractions."[78] The writer was no doubt referring to Busby Berkeley's famous film *Footlight Parade*, released the year before, which featured a water ballet scene that had propelled formation swimming to true cinematic art. Berkeley was famous for his unique choreography style that used masses of beautiful women to create mesmerizing, shifting patterns shot from birds-eye angles. Berkeley had proven himself at the box office, so when he decided he wanted to apply his sensational style to the water—at the height of the Great Depression when studios were making movies as cheaply as possible—Warner Brothers gave him a blank check. For

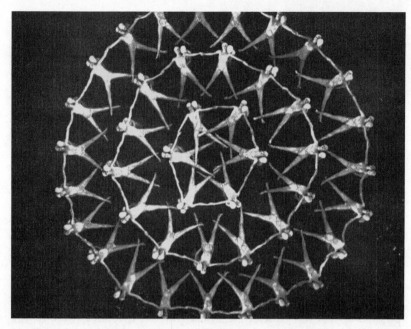

*One of the dazzling formations swimmers made in
Busby Berkeley's 1933 film* Footlight Parade.

his eleven-and-a-half-minute "By a Waterfall" scene, Berkeley had an entire soundstage converted into an 80-by-40–foot art deco pool with a waterfall pumped in at 20,000 gallons of water per minute.[79]

He hired Olympic champion diver Aileen Riggin to help with the choreography, which featured one hundred chorines moving through pinwheel and starburst formations, splitting into matching groups that curve and twist perfectly alike as if a snake were dancing in front of a mirror. He shot the swimmers from the camera's crow's nest in the rafters, illuminating them from underneath to form lacy silhouettes, and then filmed them from below through the plate-glass corridors he had installed in the bottom of the pool. "By the time he got through with that one number, there wasn't a pattern left in the kaleidoscope," wrote one reviewer, "or a Mermaid left in Hollywood's Central Casting Bureau."[80] The scene culminated with a fountain covered in swim-suited women, like tiers of a cake, towering into the air. At *Footlight Parade*'s New York premiere, the packed audience gave a standing ovation after the waterfall scene, even though the movie wasn't over. Some reportedly even threw their programs in the air.[81]

The Modern Mermaids, the Smith College Lifeguards, and *Footlight Parade* had all exposed audiences to a sleek and modern style of group swimming. As a result, swim clubs began during the late 1930s to move away from pageants and story lines—or as one instructor put it, "trite versions of King Neptune."[82] A 1937 study on the use of water pageants in educational programs reported on this trend as well, noting that the new idea in water shows was "little dialogue and much action."[83] And with instructors looking for new ways to challenge their students and showcase their growing skills, there was no shortage of ideas for water "action"—particularly those that emphasized the precision and beauty that could be achieved through swimming. One of the more intriguing innovations that emerged was shadow swimming, in which one swimmer would perform the breaststroke on the surface of the water while another would swim a few feet directly below

A synchronized swimmer at the University of Illinois models the electric lights worn by members of the Terrapin Club.

her using an inverted breaststroke, matching her movements precisely, like a shadow. This was typically done with duets, but the University of Illinois Terrapin Club at their 1939 water show "Spring Interlude" performed a triple-stacked shadow routine, titled "Garden of Moonlight," which featured "girls swimming in formations on three levels, one on the surface, another three feet below her, and the third three feet lower than the second. This unison gave the idea of two shadow reflections."[84]

But even as the pageant scripts were tossed in the waste bin and the focus shifted to the water action, a strong flair for the dramatic remained. Swim clubs experimented with a variety of effects to make swimmers' bodies stand out against the water, especially since many pools at the time didn't have underwater lights. The Smith College Lifeguards resolved this by following the swimmers with an overhead strobe light, sometimes adding a color wheel for visual interest.[85] Elsewhere swimmers in darkened pools carried or wore every kind of illumination imaginable—candles, flashlights, railroad flares, sparklers (36-inchers for a five-minute burn), and even torches made by wrapping broomstick handles with burlap and soaking them in kerosene or alcohol.[86] Another trend was illuminating swimmers' bodies with electric lights, using battery-powered strings of lights running down the swimmers' arms and legs. With the house lights switched off, they would climb down the ladder—carefully as the bulbs were glass— swim in total darkness into their starting formation, and switch on their lights in unison. For the next three and a half minutes, the typical length of a record, the audience would see not the swimmers but dozens of pinpoints of light and their shimmering reflections glide across the water, dip beneath it, come together, and split apart, making twisting, twirling formations.[87]

In the era before ready-made products, the light packs had to be made painstakingly by hand. An instructor at the University of Illinois published instructions with a supplies list that included radio pilot lamps, a dial light coloring kit (to paint the bulbs different colors), a soldering iron for the wires, rubber lamp cords to interconnect the lights, a cell battery for power, plus material for the belt to hold the battery pack and waterproof adhesive to tack down the cords.[88] When Sue Gerard, an instructor at Christian Female College of Missouri (later Columbia College) learned about using light packs from a Red Cross field agent, she enlisted the help of her electrical engineer boyfriend to make a kit for her swim club. He didn't use any switches since he didn't want the metal to rust and malfunction (and plastic materials were not yet available). Instead, the wearer had to twist the bare wires together to start the lights. He assured the swimmers that the worst that could happen was a little shock, but the night of the show, the soloist who was supposed to wear the live-wired belt chickened out. Gerard swam in her spot, performing every stroke and stunt she could think of. "It was a beautiful thing to see the lights almost disappear into deep water and then come shooting back up as I pushed from the bottom of the pool," she recalled.[89]

The use of black lights was also popular, especially when paired with luminous paints applied to costumes, caps, and props. At a community show in Cleveland, forty-eight full-length bodysuits were painted with "Conti-Glo" luminescent lacquer and donned by local youth who were said to glow underwater like "the strange fish that scientists report lurking in the ocean depths."[90] A junior college instructor in Minnesota, in

The Dolphin-Seals at the University of North Carolina, Greensboro—
pictured here performing "A Tale of the Toy"—were one of many women's
swim clubs merging pageantry with synchronized swimming.

her article titled "Black Light Your Water Ballet," described how her swim club had coated everything from costumes and mural backdrops to floating water lilies and shamrocks with phosphorescence, and even painted glowing stars on the ceiling of the poolroom. For an aquatic holiday revue, they dusted small evergreen trees with fluorescent powder and set them aboard a floating barge for swimmers to push around the pool.[91] Then for Halloween, they mounted on their heads neon orange jack-o'-lanterns made of wire-frame bases; even more remarkably, for a "Netherlands number," the girls swam with glowing windmills on their heads.[92]

It was a period during which schools and communities often exoticized different cultures for crude entertainment, and water pageants were no different, with some using racist motifs like plantation shows and depictions of Native American village settings. A survey of colleges in the Midwest reported that swimming in blackface was common in water shows, though only one of the thirty-seven polled colleges admitted to having done so. It noted a wide range of homemade concoctions swimmers applied directly to their skin—gold radiator paint, bronze powder mixed with vegetable oil, and silver glitter sprinkled over a slathering of Vaseline—sometimes used in conjunction with ultraviolet lights to achieve different effects.[93]

The use of black lights became prevalent enough to spark debate over the value of creating glow-in-the-dark swimmers, with some educators suggesting it detracted from the swimming they were trying to showcase. But another wrote in defense of neon that "the present fluorescent effects place greater emphasis on the swimmers to perfect rhythm, flexibility, and grace," and enable the audience to appreciate "the intricate skills required for good swimming."[94]

A NEW COMPETITIVE SPORT

Even though rhythmic and synchronized swimming had been able to spread, in part, because it fit so well with ideals of appropriately feminine sport, there were plenty of male students participating in school and community water pageants and learning synchronized swimming. And, of course, there was nothing inherently feminine about stunt swimming or moving as a group in the water—both of which had long been practiced by men. In fact, the same techniques used by synchronized swimmers had long been a part of Japanese martial arts—sometimes referred to as Samurai swimming—and would soon find aquatic warfare applications for American soldiers. When the Second World War broke out in Europe, it quickly became apparent that it was a very different kind of war: one that was being fought in, over, and above water. With the possibility of US involvement looming, several men—each of whom had prior experience with stunt or synchronized swimming—began developing courses and training in survival aquatics. Yale's swimming coach Robert Kiphuth developed and taught the course "War Swimming," and his students demonstrated some of its techniques at the 1939 Yale Water Carnival. Thomas Cureton, swim coach and physical education instructor at the University of Illinois, developed a course in conjunction with the US military called "Aquatic Warfare," while Commodore Longfellow, through the Red Cross, led training for soldiers in "Functional or Combat Swimming."[95]

These courses all shared an emphasis on creating "seaworthy" soldiers with extremely high levels of comfort in the water, whether upside down or right-side up, and who were equipped with aquatic skills that could increase their chances of survival if thrown into the chaotic aquatic scenarios of war. Soldiers sometimes had to swim through debris, burning oil, or torrents of bullets and needed to be able to hold their bodies high above the surface, as well as quickly duck beneath it. They may need to carry supplies and gear in the water, swim without the use of injured limbs, or tread water for hours at a time while waiting for rescue. Cureton wrote in his course manual, which he published as a book using the same title as his class, *Aquatic Warfare*, that one can prepare for such scenarios by "drilling in a great number of unusual feats of watermanship," with many of the ones he detailed aligning closely with the skills being used by synchronized swimmers.[96] For example, raising a leg in the air (a move dating back to Digby that eventually became the "ballet leg" to synchronized swimmers) could help a solider submerge quickly and quietly. In addition to the usefulness of various stunts, Cureton's manual discusses the value of formation swimming in helping military groups maintain organization, especially when "landing and embarkations have to be made quietly or in the dark."[97] If everyone has a place assigned, he pointed out, formations provide a quick way to check that every man is present, ensuring no one is left behind. Cureton advised that groups should practice shifting in the water from single-file lines to rows of three, the latter enabling swimmers to quickly get on either side of a comrade in need and provide support. Circles were best for sharing instructions with a group quickly or could be used to catch the attention of a passing airplane by having everyone make large splashing motions in unison. He even suggested techniques for what synchronized swimmers would later call "boosts" and "lifts," both of which use strong leg kicks to boost oneself or lift another person as high above the surface of the water as possible. For soldiers needing to search the horizon for land or a ship, this added bit of elevation, if only for a couple of seconds, could be critical.

By the time America entered World War II, warfare aquatics courses were being taught all over the country, primarily to men in physical education classes, but also to Girl Scout troops and YWCA groups. Kiphuth, Cureton, and Longfellow each emphasized the need for young women to learn these skills as well, as they were also headed to the front in large numbers through various military branches, the American Red Cross, the United Service Organizations (USO), and as nurses.

While it was men who found ways to apply synchronized swimming to war, it was also men who first instigated turning synchronized swimming from a collaborative activity into a competition. Katharine Curtis had, from early on, seen synchronized swimming as an activity for both male and female students—one in which they could "benefit and contribute equally and together."[98] In 1937, three years after she produced the Modern Mermaids show, Curtis founded a co-ed synchronized swimming club at Wright Junior College in Chicago, where she was teaching at the time. The following year she moved to Chicago Teachers College and started a co-ed club there as well.[99] With Curtis's two co-ed clubs both swimming in the Windy City, a friendly rivalry developed between them, and the idea of a synchro swim-off was born. The charge was led by student Frank Havlicek, who drew up the rules and a competition plan as a project for Curtis's physical education class. The theme of the term paper, Havlicek later wrote, was to "start another competitive aquatic sport for youngsters who were not fast enough to compete in swimming races."[100] Using Havlicek's rules, the competition between the two clubs was held at Chicago Teachers College in May 1939 as part of the Annual Teachers Day program.[101] The events included floating routines of up to fourteen people, large and small group routines set to music, and individual "fancy stunting," which was won by a male student.[102] Although Canada had held individual stunts competitions since the 1920s, the contest at Chicago Teachers College is considered the first true synchronized swimming competition.

The competition went so well that David Leach, chair of the Central AAU swimming committee, whom Curtis had known since her early days at the University of Chicago, encouraged her to think about making synchronized swimming a competitive AAU event. At first, she was hesitant, fearing it would leave behind the weaker swimmers, but as she thought of the competitive opportunities it could provide for those past their speed-swimming prime, she changed her mind.[103] A committee was formed to draw up rules, which included representatives from organizations in Chicago that had any experience in "'ballet' swimming"—including parks, clubs, schools, pools—as well as some of the former Modern Mermaids.[104]

Figuring out how to score the routines proved to be the most difficult part—and would remain an ongoing challenge as the sport grew increasingly technical over the following decades. One amusing idea discussed was to create panels of experts to judge their relevant categories: a military officer to judge precision, a dressmaker to score costuming, and a musician to evaluate the use of music.[105] This didn't make it past the drawing board for obvious practical reasons. Ultimately, the committee decided to follow the model used by skating and diving, assigning difficulty multiples to a recognized set of stunts. There would be three additional scoring categories: Composition (variety of movements, smoothness of transitions between stunts, and creative appeal); Style (manner in which the routine was performed—ideally with "confidence, ease, pleasure, grace, and 'oomph'"); and Accompaniment (the harmony of the moves and timing of swimmers with the music).[106] Each routine—whether a duet or "ballet event" (as the team routine was called)—would have to include at least two standard swimming strokes and two of four required stunts: the kip, dolphin, somersault, and porpoise. Beyond those requirements, routines could be comprised of any combination from a list of sixty-nine possible

AAU-approved stunts, each with its own difficulty score. For the sake of consistent execution, the committee agreed to use the descriptions of the stunts written in Curtis's 1936 *Sourcebook of Water Pageantry*.

The scoring put a heavy focus on stunts, as opposed to floating formations, for several practical reasons. As finite and recognizable units of movement, stunts were easier to assign a score value to. They also provided a way to measure a swimmer's execution against an agreed-upon ideal. Moreover, stunts were easier to synchronize with music than were the graceful and fluid floating patterns. Because of the water resistance and the added time it takes for momentum to ripple through an entire group of connected swimmers, it is difficult to transition into a new formation on a precise beat. But despite its practicality, not everyone liked the approach of prioritizing stunts over floating patterns. One coach argued that the "point-hoarders" would take the beauty out of routines and "kill the crowd appeal of synchronized swimming."[107] Whether the focus on stunts detracted from the beauty or not, the impact of the rules was that routines immediately became tighter and more synchronized.

With rules in place, the Central AAU regional chapter held an exhibition meet on March 1, 1940, at Shawnee Country Club in Wilmette, Illinois.[108] Seven local swim clubs competed, with first place going to the co-ed team from Wright Junior College, which included six women and six men, for their "Dagger Dance" routine. The meet was covered by three newsreel companies and was a complete sellout, with 350 paid ticket holders attending and 400 more turned away at the doors. One report noted that it had attracted "one of the largest and most critical water-minded audiences of recent times."[109] Although the event was a success, in order for synchronized swimming to become an official AAU sport, it would have to be voted in by AAU delegates at the national organization level.

That December at the AAU National Convention in Denver, Leach himself brought forth the proposal—but not in the way Katharine Curtis originally envisioned. The first two competitions had welcomed co-ed teams, but the AAU had strict rules that prohibited men and women from competing against one another, so the sport was proposed as two separate events—one for men and one for women. Ironically, the men's committee was more receptive, while the women's committee took more convincing, citing concerns that the meets would take too long. Both committees ultimately approved the sport, but only as one sanctioned for regional competitions. Some of the delegates who came from other branches of aquatics had never seen nor heard of synchronized swimming and requested the opportunity to see a demonstration before voting to make it a national-level sport.

Delegates who had come from the east coast were due to head home from Denver by train the following day, so Leach arranged for them to stop in Chicago and sent Curtis a telegram asking if she could arrange an exhibition. The wire reached her at midnight, but miraculously she managed to pull it together. She arrived at the Chicago Teachers College as soon as the doors opened the next morning so that she could claim a slot at the pool, and left notes on the lockers of her students asking them to participate. Someone saw the notes and got the word out, but Curtis didn't have time to brief them on the situation: that the future of the sport depended on the impression they gave the AAU officials.[110]

The train reached the Chicago station at 9:00 that cold December morning, and within an hour, the delegation was at the pool. Among the guests were Robert Kiphuth of Yale and Herbert Holm, who had so many years earlier taught Gertrude Titus his swimming stunts. Curtis later said it was "immensely gratifying" to watch the expressions of the delegates while the students swam to a Bach chorale and "Hark the Herald Angels Sing," as some were "visibly carried away by what they saw." Kiphuth raved that synchronized swimming had "opened up a marvelous new form of aesthetics," and Holm said he considered it "every bit as fascinating as diving," a high compliment coming from the head of the AAU diving committee.[111] When the AAU National Convention met again a year later in Philadelphia, the delegates voted to accept synchronized swimming as a full, national-level AAU sport.[112] But on December 7, Pearl Harbor was bombed, and suddenly America was at war. The newly minted AAU sport would have to wait several more years to hold its first national championships.

Meanwhile, Curtis—unattached (having quietly divorced years earlier), hungry for adventure, and eager to join the national effort— took a job as a Red Cross recreational director serving Allied forces stationed in Africa and Europe. Heading to the front meant leaving behind the sport she had helped create, but Curtis would, during her time abroad, not only use this new type of swimming to entertain troops—organizing what was likely Europe's first major "aquacade"—but also help spread "the gospel of synchronized swimming" in the many countries she visited.[113]

In her absence, numerous physical educators would pick up where Curtis left off, not only showing their students how to combine "swimming with swing" but also training them to teach the next generation.[114] In the coming years, the demand for synchronized swimming clubs—and instructors qualified to lead them—would grow so much that at Wellesley College physical education majors could take the course "Methods of Teaching Synchronized Swimming," while Washington University and others included synchronized swimming as units within their methodology courses on swimming instruction.[115] An instructor at a teaching college in Chicago wrote that the goal of their club was "to turn out not only good performers, but also young men and women who can teach" so that synchro could be offered at all the city's public schools.[116]

Synchronized swimming had provided a new, creative approach to aquatics. As Curtis wrote, this new field of swimming "requires endurance, not speed; versatility in the use of all strokes, not specialization in one; a keen sense of rhythm," with the practitioner's success depending not only on her strength but on her expertise in the water.[117] The appeal of synchronized swimming would prove to be as wide ranging as the skills it fostered. Already it had become an AAU competitive sport and was spreading rapidly through physical education programs. Even so, Curtis wrote in 1942: "I feel that the surface of this new field has barely been scratched. . . . The future is teeming with exciting possibilities." And she was right. Synchronized swimming would eventually reach the highest echelons of sport, the Olympics. But first, it would dazzle audiences of the stage and screen—in America and abroad—as one of the midcentury's most spectacular forms of entertainment.

CHAPTER 8

SPECTACLE

WHAT IS IT? Billy Rose's AQUACADE—the
newest thing in American entertainment—a $10
show scaled down to fit the purse of the times.
You'll tell your grandchildren about it someday.

—ADVERTISEMENT, 1937

I t was an unseasonably cold evening for early May as excited crowds, many in topcoats, filed into the ten-thousand-seat New York Marine Amphitheater built into the lakefront in Flushing Meadows Park. The line stretched several blocks through the Amusement Zone of the 1939 World's Fair, but even those in the very back could read the eight-foot-high glowing electric letters outside the theater that spelled "BILLY ROSE'S AQUACADE." As the ticket holders found their seats and turned their attention to the massive art deco stage, they were met not with the typical wall of velvet, but with a curtain made of water—a veil of mist shooting 8,000 gallons per minute 40 feet into the air and stretching across nearly the entire length of the 311-foot-wide stage. Only the two 75-foot diving towers on each end were exposed. The stage itself, which was separated from the audience by an enclosed, crescent-shaped swath of water, looked like a colorful floating island—though it was actually secured to the lakebed with two hundred steel pilings.[1]

Once the audience was seated, an "unseen hand" pulled a switch and the massive water curtain dropped, revealing—in the words of the program—"the show in all its magnificent beauty." Lined up shoulder to shoulder down the entire length of the stage were two hundred men and women in shimmering swimsuits.[2] With perfect timing, like human dominoes, the "Aquabelles" and "Aquabeaux"— everyone in Rose's show was an "aqua" something—dove headfirst into the water. They peeled into rows six swimmers deep, and with precisely matched arm strokes, each line swam into formation and made room for the next. The exquisitely straight lines broke apart effortlessly, morphing into rotating and crisscrossing patterns made of swimmers. Onstage, as many dancers strutted in plumes and heels, keeping the same lockstep rhythm as the swimmers, everyone's steps and strokes guided by the music coming from the two orchestras flanking either end of the stage. It was all so candy-colored and gloriously

1939 Program cover for Billy Rose's Aquacade in New York.

illuminated—the phosphorescent lights playing off the water lending a feel of enchantment—and the abundance and precision were welcome sights to audiences ready to move past a decade of terrible economic depression and on to a brighter future.

Billy Rose's Aquacade was an aquatic musical revue, combining all the stage elements of a Broadway show—live orchestra and vocalists, comedy acts, dancing girls—with the now-popular medium of swimming entertainment. According to the program, it featured "the glamour of diving and swimming mermaids, in water ballets of breathtaking beauty and rhythm." The show was divided into three main acts—"A Beach in Florida," "Coney Island, 1905," and "the French Riviera"—each featuring towering backdrops painted with palm trees and carnival scenes that rotated on gigantic turntables—and ending with "A Parade of States." The show tapped the talents of Broadway stage engineers, famed directors like John Murray Anderson, and a cast of more than five hundred performers bedazzled by the best costume designers New York had to offer. As one writer from the era noted, "We liked our theatrical entertainments massive and repetitious, with plenty of synchronized dances, changes of costume, and fluorescent lighting."[3] Billy Rose's Aquacade had all that—plus water.

Rose, the 4'11"-tall mastermind behind the Aquacade, had worked his way up the entertainment ranks, from songwriter to nightclub owner to Broadway producer, and had earned a reputation for creating over-the-top extravaganzas. As one journalist wrote, he had a "bigness bug" and was incapable of doing "any little thing without trying to squeeze something tremendous out of it."[4] For the Aquacade, Rose had staked a fortune on his belief that if he offered a show with the "sheen, the fun, the zest, the romance of a Ziegfeld musical" at a price the everyday man or woman could afford, "millions would throng to see it."[5] And they did. When Rose produced his first Aquacade two years earlier in Cleveland, it had been so popular it single-handedly turned the flailing Great Lakes Exhibition into a financial success. Now his bigger and better New York World's Fair production was predicted to be the most talked about attraction of the summer.

Headlining the massive cast was a star-studded lineup of Olympic champions, like divers Marshall Wayne, Pete Desjardins, and Canadian Sam Howard, who soared and jackknifed from the 75-foot diving towers with their triple gainers and double twists. "Aquaclown" Harold (Stubby) Kruger, an Olympic swimmer turned comic diver, "managed to run, bounce, and fall off five different diving boards."[6] Gertrude Ederle, who was still a household name after conquering the English Channel a decade and a half earlier, made a cameo appearance, swimming across the pool and blowing kisses to the audience. During the "Coney Island, 1905," segment, Aileen Riggin, champion of the first women's Olympic diving team, donned a full-length Kellerman suit, now a quaint relic, and performed her famous high dives.

Within this illustrious group, the biggest draws, and the ones pictured in all the advertisements, were Aquabelle Number One, Eleanor Holm, and Aquadonis Number One, Johnny Weissmuller—both Olympic champions who had leveraged their winning smiles, fabulous physiques, and athletic prowess into Hollywood fame. Weissmuller, known as the fastest swimmer alive, had won five gold medals between the 1924 and 1928 Olympics before trading his swim trunks for a loincloth to star in several of MGM's Tarzan films. Holm was a backstroke champion who competed in the 1928 Olympics at the age of fourteen and won the gold in 1932, but her real propulsion to fame had come unexpectedly aboard the SS *Manhattan* as it carried America's Olympic team to compete in the 1936 games in Berlin. Holm had stayed up one evening to have champagne with some of the distinguished passengers on board, and Avery Brundage, the head of the US Olympic Committee, found this to be improper behavior for a young woman. Claiming Holm had violated AAU rules, he booted her off the team before the ship reached Germany. "The entire civilized world was set agog," reported one writer. "Had the S.S. *Manhattan* hit an iceberg and gone down, she would have received no more newspaper space."[7] Holm was defiant, saying she did nothing wrong and reportedly telling journalists, "I could have won with a glass of champagne in one hand, a bottle in the other."[8] Holm's sentiment immediately endeared her to the American public, which was still riding the crest of Prohibition's repeal only four years earlier. Moreover, Americans had been keen to dominate the Olympiad dubbed "Hitler's Games" and were none too pleased with Brundage for eliminating the best female swimmer from the team.

Billy Rose, who had been searching for a perfect headlining act for his first Aquacade in Cleveland, marveled at the free publicity being heaped upon this young athlete—whom he would later marry—and recruited her. At each show, Holm performed a languid version of her Olympic backstroke, which was likened to a poem in the water, and a duet with Weissmuller. They swam in tandem—"as graceful as dancers"—facing each other as Holm backstroked and Weissmuller followed closely with a front crawl, a performance that, another reviewer exclaimed, "literally brings the spectators out of their chairs."[9]

The *Baltimore Sun*, however, felt Holm and Weissmuller added little to the show beyond the drawing power of their names. Instead, the writer argued, "the real stars of the show are the choruses."[10] No one thinks of athletes as artists, wrote another reviewer, but "set their athleticism to music and it becomes clear at once that it is a kind of art."[11] It seems that audiences may have come to see a handful of star athletes, but what ended up dazzling them were the scores of swimmers moving

Postcard of Eleanor Holm from Billy Rose's Aquacade.

in lockstep together, Busby Berkeley–style, in perfect precision. And it was the vision of "hundreds of arms dipping in unison in floodlit foam," wrote the *Baltimore Sun*, that would linger in the imaginations of viewers long after.[12] Some scholars have noted that the mass synchronization of ensemble choreography, whether onstage, on the screen, or in water, held great appeal in the Machine Age, "with its emphasis on clean lines and flowing patterns."[13] Rose's water chorus swam with the same streamlined aesthetic that was being touted all over the "World of Tomorrow," the title and theme of the 1939 New York World's Fair, which even included a "Futurama" ride through the utopian cities of the future.

The Aquacade ended with a star-spangled tribute to America featuring beefy Roman centurions carrying state flags and dancers strutting as they held up giant stars above their heads. The back of the stage opened to reveal "an old-time Ziegfeld staircase" that women in elegant gowns of red, white, and silvery blue, capped with Statue of Liberty–style headdresses, marched down.[14] The band played

The Billy Rose Aquacade Theater in New York.

"Yankee Doodle's Gonna Go to Town Again," which for fairgoers anxious that America would soon enter World War II would have been a patriotic salve—especially as they watched their Olympic heroes dive before a 72-foot American flag unfurled down the back of the stage.

The World of Tomorrow Fair had been launched to kick-start the US economy and to renew faith in capitalism and democracy. No exhibits about poverty or depression were permitted, especially in the Amusement Zone—though just about anything else was. The *New York Times* wrote, "visitors quickly discovered the fair's split personality. On the one hand, they were offered views of an inspiring future. On the other, they were tempted with sex."[15] One paper reported that the "frolic zone" contained five hundred girls in various stages of undress—ranging from skintight bathing suits to G-strings—with many of the exhibits involving water.[16] The Arctic Temple exhibit featured a Miss Berk, purported to be encased nude in a block of ice. The Congress of Beauty included semi-nude mermaids frolicking in a stream. Salvador Dalí's surrealist funhouse "Dream of Venus" featured his "liquid ladies," who swam in a tank of water wearing only fishnets and brassieres with cutouts for the breasts. Police cracked down on only the most brazen, such as the Cuban Village's contest to appoint a "Miss Nude 1939."

The financial value of sex appeal happened to be one of Billy

Rose's main areas of expertise, as he had run some of the most successful nightclubs and burlesque shows in New York. Raised in a tenement in Manhattan's Lower East Side, Rose had achieved success by becoming a diligent student of the public. As a songwriter, he had analyzed the top-selling tunes of the day to find the magic mix of melodies, lyrics, and tempo people liked best. Later, as a nightclub owner and Broadway producer of increasingly spectacular amusements, Rose had landed on a highly lucrative combination of "sex, sentiment, and curiosity." When he was hired to help Fort Worth create a fair that could rival the Texas Centennial Exposition planned for Dallas in 1936, Rose told the committee, "The only way to compete with $25,000,000 worth of industrial technology is with pelvic technology. We have to give them girls and more girls."[17] Two of the Fort Worth Frontier Centennial's most famous shows were "Sally Rand's Nude Ranch" and Rose's own concession, "Casa Manana," which featured topless women riding in gondolas.

Yet, for his Aquacade, Rose wanted to cast the widest possible net by providing "sexy but not shameless" entertainment, hoping to lure the "bald heads in the back row" without alienating his target demographic: white middle-class families.[18] One of his Aquacade ads, framed as a series of questions and answers about the show, asked, "Is it a girl show?" to which the ad responded, "No! Though it presents—artistically to be sure—500 of the most glamorous Aquafemmes on which the eyes have ever feasted."[19] And how better to provide a legitimate feast for the eyes than through scores and scores of beautiful swimmers?

Rose wrote in his memoir that he had the idea for the Aquacade when he went to Cleveland, asked by the city to stage a production that would revive the Great Lakes Exposition in its second season. While visiting the fairgrounds he spotted two swimmers practicing a water ballet duet to the "Blue Danube" waltz in Lake Erie's Marine Theater. It was part of a free show directed by a former diver named Floyd Zimmerman. "As I watched them, I began to multiply, and the more I multiplied, the more excited I became," wrote Rose. " 'If a water ballet looks that good with two girls,' I said . . . 'imagine what it would be like with two hundred.' "[20] He hired Zimmerman, along with Aileen Riggin, who had choreographed the spectacular water scene in Busby Berkeley's *Footlight Parade*, to orchestrate—in collaboration with stage director John Murray Anderson—the massive water ballets for his Aquacades.

When Rose put out a call for "ballet swimmers" and held auditions at Madison Square Garden, he and Anderson were mobbed by several thousand applicants. Many were dancers, and when they winnowed the crowd down to fifteen hundred and brought them to the St. George Hotel pool in Brooklyn, they discovered that at least a quarter of the aspiring Aquabelles couldn't swim a stroke.[21] Dancers had been used to fill the ice ballets in Olympic skater Sonja Henie's ice-skating extravaganza—often thought of as the frozen forerunner of Rose's Aquacades—because producers found it easier to teach dancers to skate than skaters to dance. But the same did not hold true with swimmers, especially for the specialized skills required for a water chorus.[22]

The *Baltimore Sun* wrote of the hiring criteria:

> Pretty faces were hardly considered. They don't show from the water, and there is always waterproof makeup. Those who had relied on the medals they'd won in competitive swimming were also surprised. Speed was not essential. Grace and rhythm were. With all his other requirements, Mr. Zimmerman asked for even more—an ear for music.[23]

Many who ultimately made the cut came from clubs like the Women's Swimming Association and the Brooklyn College men's varsity swim team—all "real" swimmers who decided to turn professional for the show. "And take my word for it, they need to be," wrote Eleanor Holm in an article about the Aquacade preparations. She calculated that with four shows a day, each of which required about a mile's worth of swimming, by the time the 182-day season ended, each Aquabelle and Aquabeau would swim 728 miles.[24] But even strong swimmers discovered they had to learn a whole new style.

Swimming in perfect unison with others requires diverting one's attention and effort away from the basics of swimming to focus instead on adjusting one's strength, pace, and execution to match that of the group. Moreover, even simple strokes must be relearned and drilled to ensure that every member of a water chorus performs them in precisely the same manner. Helen Starr, the chorographer for the Minneapolis Aqua Follies, one of many professional water shows that popped up shortly after Rose's Aquacades, offered practical tips on how to achieve this. In an article she wrote on coaching large, synchronized water ballets, she suggested breaking down an arm stroke into all its individual parts, with each one given its own count. For example, "on count one of the first measure the right hand makes the 'catch,'" wrote Starr. "On count two the left arm recovers to a 'V' position, on count three the left arm extends forward and the right arm executes the 'drive.'"[25]

Besides matching their strokes, the water chorus had to learn to swim in formation, which requires the ability to judge distance and adjust one's power and speed. At the Aquacades, they began by practicing in pairs, then fours, then eights, until a line of swimmers stretched across the entire pool. In her article, Starr recommended designating a leader—whoever has the best ear for music—to set the tempo and

Aquabelles and Aquabeaux swim in unison at
Billy Rose's New York Aquacade, 1939.

then putting that person on the left end of a row. In a formation with multiple rows, each is led by the swimmer on the far left, who in turn follows the swimmer directly in front of her, so that ultimately the swimmer in the upper left corner of the formation is setting the pace and tempo for the entire group. Massive groups of swimmers can be synchronized this way, she wrote, so long as every swimmer knows "whom to follow and with whom to guide his strokes."[26] As rehearsals for the Aquacades started in the winter, the swimmers met in a rented ballroom where they learned and memorized their formations, which Anderson and Zimmerman had painted on the floor, giving them a head start once they moved their practice to the water.

But of course pulling all of this together in the water still took hours and weeks of work. Harriet Wright, one of Rose's New York Aquabelles, said the show was "painstakingly planned and practiced to perfection" through a "grueling" rehearsal schedule and that swimmers were constantly sick with colds and ear infections from the hours spent in the water.[27] But those in Cleveland had had it even worse than the New York crew. At one rehearsal, a dead cow became dislodged from the underwater stage apparatus and bobbed to the surface among the swimmers as they practiced their "Blue Danube" water waltz.[28] The show was supposed to include underwater illumination, but once installed, the lights revealed so much submerged trash in Lake Erie they had to forgo the idea.

Publicity materials made much of the fact that Rose's Aquabelles were real swimmers who came from swim clubs rather than show-biz circuits. Zimmerman told a newspaper they were "just the sort of wholesome, athletic, high-school girls you'd expect to find around any pool."[29] Articles described them as being younger and more innocent than the Broadway showgirls and professional dancers who performed the non-swimming stage numbers. "Where the dancers spend their spare time taking sunbaths, the swimmers spend theirs—swimming!" quipped one reporter.[30] Rose, whose knack for publicity and ballyhoo was as keen as P. T. Barnum's, used the swimming angle to arrange creative publicity stunts in the pool. When asked how the Aquabelles had time to eat between the four daily shows, he responded, "in the water of course!" and invited reporters to bring their cameras and join them for a floating picnic. He even hosted a watery wedding for two of his swimmers, with press welcomed to attend. The swimmers themselves took pride in being part of the aquatic end of the show. Harriet Wright, who had trained for the 1936 Olympic tryouts, wrote that the Aquabelles looked down on the dancing AquaMaids as "lesser talents" who "merely stood around on the pool ledge to decorate the stage."[31]

Even though the Aquabelles were touted—and indeed saw themselves—as athletes rather than wet showgirls, Rose made sure that his wholesome, all-American swimmers still met the expectations of male showgoers. Wright described the bathing suits they had to wear as skimpy and nearly see-through, and at least one reporter agreed, writing that "the Aquafemmes lean considerably toward the Aqua*nude*."[32] As a result of both the costuming and the stylized form of swimming that mirrored the popular chorus-line dance numbers of the stage, Rose's Aquacades marked the start of a long association between showgirls and swimming. One reviewer wrote that Rose's Aquabelles swam "in rhythm to the tunes of an orchestra, their water ballet strokes rising and falling in unison like the high kicks of chorus girls."[33]

And audiences loved it. Rose's Aquacade was the most patronized show at the New York World's Fair and made $10 million in profits, more than all other fair amusements combined.[34] One reviewer called it "the biggest single piece of entertainment on earth since Barnum" and another simply wrote: "Tremendous. Gorgeous. Colossal. Magnificent."[35] Another pegged its success to the unique mix of "natation and nostalgia" with champion swimmers performing thrilling feats to backdrops reminiscent of happier times.[36] New Yorkers who'd been around long enough couldn't help but think back to the aquatic spectacles at the Hippodrome earlier in the century. A poem called "Only a Hippodrome Mother" appeared around the time of the Aquacade's opening and was written from the point of view of a disappearing mermaid who "swam in that famous old tank" but now had a daughter in the slick new Aquacade.[37]

With the world at war again, there would be no shortage of people hungry for lighthearted distractions, and Rose's mix of spectacle and nostalgia would remain a welcome respite for some time. In fact, Rose had just begun planning an even bigger show—including a scene set in "once gay" Vienna—for the second and final season of the New

York World's Fair when he got wind of plans that another showman was hatching to produce an aquacade at the Golden Gate Exhibition at San Francisco's Treasure Island, also to take place over the summer of 1940. Rose shot off a cease-and-desist letter while quickly setting plans in motion to run his own Aquacade at the Exhibition. Since the East and West Coast shows would run concurrently, Rose needed a second pair of male and female headliners. Eleanor Holm, who had recently become Mrs. Billy Rose, would stay in New York, and Weissmuller would head west to be the Aquadonis of San Francisco. To replace him, Rose brought in Buster Crabbe, another champion of the 1932 Olympics who had been snapped up by Hollywood to play heroes Flash Gordon, Tarzan, and Buck Rogers. That left Rose short just one star Aquabelle for the California show.

Scouring coverage of swimming events, Rose came across a *Life* magazine spread on the 1939 national AAU women's swimming championships in Iowa. In typical fashion, the article was titled "Pretty Girls Set Records at National Swimming Meet," and contained more pictures than text. The one of a seventeen-year-old woman named Esther Williams—shot in profile with her head tossed back and smiling in a white flowered swimsuit—was particularly striking. The caption noted that ash-blonde, green-eyed Williams had won the 100-meter title and had also been part of the Los Angeles Athletic Club (LAAC) record-breaking relay team.[38] Although it wasn't stated in the article, Williams had used the powerful overarm butterfly stroke to put her team ahead by nearly a full length of the pool.[39] The splashy butterfly was rarely taught to women as it was associated with brute strength rather than gracefulness, but Williams had learned it from male lifeguards while working as a towel girl at her local pool. Her performance at the national championships had earned her a spot on the 1940 Olympic team, but shortly afterward, the games were canceled because of the war. The same news that devastated Williams and athletes all over the country became Rose's opportunity. With no Olympics to maintain her amateur status for, he hoped he could convince Williams to "turn pro" and become the star of his Golden Gate Aquacade. He hopped on a plane to Los Angeles.

Williams, who in a few years would become one of the most recognizable women in America, was taking classes at a community college and working as a clerk at the swanky I. Magnin department store. When Rose's assistant called her at work to invite her to come to the Ambassador Hotel pool for an audition, she demurred, saying she already had a job. Her coworkers overheard the conversation and wouldn't hear of her passing on such an opportunity. They bought Williams a red swimsuit right off the rack and rushed her out the door as soon as the store closed for the evening. At the pool, Rose told her, "Do twelve of these, twelve of those, twelve of those others!" After what was enough to "ruin a mule," wrote *Collier's* magazine, Esther was still breathing as if she were reclining in a pool chair. Finally, Rose told Williams he'd seen enough of the fast stuff. Obviously she was a strong swimmer, but that's not what he cared about—Could she swim "pretty?" Williams responded with her famous line: "Mr. Rose, if you're not strong enough to swim fast, you're probably not strong enough to swim 'pretty.'"[40]

Williams got the job, but she didn't agree right away, instead contacting an agent who offered to take care of the negotiations. Once the contract was signed, she splurged and bought herself a white business suit, and two days later she was wearing it on an overnight train to San Francisco—not knowing that starring in the Aquacade was just a stepping stone for much bigger fame to come. Unlike his other headliners, Williams was unknown to the public, but Rose aimed to take care of that. He plastered images of Williams in a swimsuit all up and down California, calling her the "it and oomph girl of swimming."[41] In a page-long ad for the Aquacade titled "A Showman's Affidavit," Rose solemnly swears a list of "facts" about the Aquacade. One item read: "I swear that Esther Williams is the most beautiful girl in the history of American aquatics. (If Eleanor Holm, Mrs. Rose, reads this, I'm only kidding.)"[42]

Shortly after her arrival, Rose requested a meeting with Williams and sent a driver to pick her up from the dormitory where the female performers were staying and deliver her to his hotel room. The fifty-something showman greeted the seventeen-year-old in a silk robe with candlelight and champagne in the background. "A seduction scene, pure and simple," wrote Williams in her 1999 autobiography.[43] When she refused his advances, he angrily told her to get out. Perhaps out of spite for spurning his advances, Rose gave his "star" only one swimsuit, which she would try in vain to dry between shows by hanging it over the single bare lightbulb dangling in her dingy, damp dressing room.

Williams didn't find the atmosphere among the cast of the Aquacade much better, calling it as a "sexual carnival" where "everyone seemed to be in heat."[44] In her memoir, she described her duet with Weissmuller as a Hitchcock-inspired nightmare, writing that three times a day she had to swim fast enough to evade the "groping hands" of the fastest man on earth.[45] Perhaps worst of all, she learned that her agent had cut a deal for himself, carved right out of her salary—while Williams was getting $125 a week, he was getting $500.[46]

Although the Aquacade gave Williams a pretty awful first impression of the entertainment world, it proved to be a valuable educational experience—both in and out of the water—and one that would later enable her to return to show business on her own terms, and in her own unique style.

THE MILLION-DOLLAR IDEA

Despite being one of the best swimmers in the country, Esther Williams discovered at her first practice in the water that she still had much to learn. Whereas the water chorus was training long hours to match their strokes to the group, Williams had to learn to stand out—as a star. In order to be seen by twenty thousand eyeballs, she had to swim with her head and shoulders elevated and use big, exaggerated arm strokes. "It was not a natural swimming position," wrote Williams. "Swimming pretty took enormous stamina."[47] Moreover, it required doing exactly the opposite of what a swimmer does when she wants to go fast, precisely what Williams had spent years training to do. As the *New York Times* wrote, Williams, who had learned to swim "man-fashion" with a "husky kick" in order to win races, had to "learn to swim all over again, in graceful girl fashion."[48] However, Williams quickly discovered that her powerful kick under the surface was precisely what enabled her to hold herself high out of the water and look graceful while doing it.

Williams would use many of the techniques and stylized strokes she learned at the Aquacade to help her develop the signature brand of swimming she would later use in her films. And her style clearly

Williams and Weissmuller, Aquabelle and Aquabeau Number One,
perform a duet at the Golden Gate production of Billy Rose's Aquacade.

made an impression on the audience. Richard Reinhardt, who saw the Aquacade as a thirteen-year-old boy and later authored a book about the Golden Gate Exposition, described how he and his friends spent hours in the lakes of the Sierra trying master Williams's "synchronized windmill" in which she rolled gracefully between alternating front and backstrokes. "I have never understood how Esther Williams kept her head on, swimming around the tank that way," he wrote.[49] The show impacted another local youth, Dawn Pawson (Bean), who had grown up swimming but had never seen such large group formations of swimmers. She was fascinated by the geometric patterns and peel-off dives, saying later, "It was the group action, the beauty of all those bodies in unison. I thought, 'I want to be part of it.'"[50] After going to see the Aquacade at least six times that summer, Pawson joined a synchronized swimming club and would go on to become an international champion and an important leader in the sport.

The *Saturday Evening Post* wrote that Rose's Aquacades starring Esther Williams "gave every pretty girl in the country a yen to get in the swim," and with 15 million people having seen the Aquacades—between the shows in Cleveland, New York, and San Francisco—plus millions more on newsreel clips at movie theaters, there was some truth to that.[51] "Thousands of Americans greatly enjoyed watching the spectacle of Billy Rose's Aquacade and I am sure many went away with the desire to try their own swimming with music," wrote Gertrude Goss, director of the Smith College Lifeguards. "Some had done this before, but now, all over the country, aquacades, water pageants, swimming carnivals, etc., are in great demand."[52] For clubs that had already had a tradition of producing pageants, the Aquacades raised the bar. A town near Cleveland had been putting on an annual pageant since 1929, but it wasn't until 1937, after Rose's Aquacade had been running all summer, wrote one of the show's organizers, that performers began to make intricate designs in the water and to "stroke in rhythm to waltz music."[53]

A 1942 article in the *Journal of Health and Physical Education* noted that interest in swimming likely would have taken a slump following the cancellation of the 1940 Olympics and other sports competitions during the war if not for the coinciding popularity of Billy Rose's Aquacades, which helped keep enthusiasm high. It noted:

Swimming coaches all over the country seized this opportunity to maintain the lagging interest of their young protogees [*sic*] by converting their girls' swimming teams into ensembles of mermaids. So was born the Watercade, Water Ballet, and Pattern Swimming troupes. Schools were quick to follow the trend. Few schools today find themselves without pattern swimming classes or groups.[54]

Some of these classes were even led by former swimmers from Rose's Aquacades. One Aquabelle taught a rhythmic swimming class in Chapel Hill, requiring students to do a back flip and a surface dive and carry a weight in the water in order to qualify.[55] Another started an "aquacade" physical education class for women at a junior college in New Jersey. The class covered "all the intricate formations used in famous aquacades produced by Showman Billy Rose," plus how to "swim to musical rhythms without making a ripple, to dive on a dime, to maneuver into a perfect circle."[56]

Of course, this was the very type of swimming that Katharine

Curtis and the Modern Mermaids brought to mass audiences years earlier at the 1934 Chicago World's Fair, which could have been where Rose got his idea, rather than through his own visions of multiplying girls. As a well-known name in show business, Rose would have surely made a trip to the Chicago World's Fair, *the* event of the early 1930s. And there is evidence that he was personally familiar with the Modern Mermaids show. One of the former Modern Mermaids and a member of the Illinois Women's Athletic Club, in hearing about the New York Aquacade, sent a letter to Rose to express interest in auditioning. She wrote:

> I am twenty-five years old, 5′7¾″ in height and weigh 136 lbs. I was formally Miss Maxine Reinhard and swam with the "Modern Mermaids" at the Chicago World's Fair from June through the end of the season, and *for which act you were the announcer.* [emphasis added][57]

Although Norman Ross was the official announcer of Curtis's show, famously coining the name "synchronized swimming" during a performance, Rose certainly could have been a guest announcer at some point; there were, after all, three shows a day for the entire summer.

But regardless of whether Rose saw the Modern Mermaids, there was plenty of inspiration floating around—at schools, tourist-hungry hotels in Florida and California, at Red Cross water pageants, and in Busby Berkeley's films. Even Rose's original Aquabelle Number One, Eleanor Holm, had performed in a show called the Water Follies of 1937, led by Sam and Solly Snyder, before Rose snagged her.[58] The Snyder brothers later claimed to have laid the blueprint for the water show "a year before Billy Rose got a chunk of cash and Eleanor Holm out of producing the Aquacade."[59] *Washington Post* columnist Bob Considine traced the idea back much farther, writing that Alexander Ott, longtime water show organizer at the famous Biltmore Hotel in Coral Gables, had been experimenting with Rose's million-dollar idea since "the days when Annette Kellerman's dowdy-looking one-piece swimsuit was the subject of indignant sermons." Ott, claimed Considine, had "worked out the theory of a water ballet," which Rose, "an abler showman," built on and glamorized.[60]

While Considine considered Rose "a loud interloper and a plagiarist," many other reviewers focused on the "abler showman" aspect and credited Rose for taking existing forms and elevating them to new heights—just as P. T. Barnum had taken the traveling circus and aggrandized it to such an extent that it felt like a new form altogether and became forever associated with his name.[61] "Diving acts aren't new. Water clowns aren't new. Exploitation of swimming headliners isn't new," wrote Ruth Hopkins in the *Baltimore Sun*. "But one of Broadway's greatest producers, little Billy Rose, has brought all of these and more together, and given the collection a pattern and a name." By merging swimming entertainment with the talent, polish, and spectacle of a professional Broadway show, wrote Hopkins, Rose "put aquatics in the big money class."[62]

Other impresarios, eager to join Rose in the big money class, began producing their own water spectaculars, even before the Aquacades had closed their doors, and nearly all of them used his show as a blueprint. The Snyder brothers had blamed Rose for stealing their idea but made no secret of riding on the coattails of his success. In 1941, a year after Rose's last show, they scooped up Buster Crabbe and several former Aquabelles, launched a traveling water show, and called it Stars of Billy Rose's Aquacades. The following year, they changed the name to Snyder's Water Follies, which became one of the longest-running water shows and played all over the world. Rose's two Aquadonises became stars of their own productions—the Buster Crabbe Aqua Parade and the Johnny Weissmuller Watercade—while Floyd Zimmerman took his water choreography skills to Florida and directed the Water Revue of 1940 at the Miami Biltmore Hotel.

There was no shortage of spectators for this growing field of aquatic spectacles, as Americans had money to spend and were seeking diversion. The wartime rise in salaries had given many Americans more disposable income than they'd had since before the Depression, yet travel restrictions and widespread shortages of goods meant they didn't always have things to spend it on.[63] Many entertainment and amusement industries thrived during and after the war, and water shows, which offered a reassuring mix of patriotic and nostalgic fare, fit the folksy entertainment tastes of the midcentury particularly well. The content of Buster Crabbe's Aqua Parade was described as "fun and gee wiz stuff," and included acts like the "Gay Nineties," with bathing beauties wearing the bloomers of yesteryear, a "history of swimming" performed by the aquatic cast as Crabbe narrated to vocal accompaniment, and an "America First" finale featuring a "rocket water ballet" in the tank and an "atomic ballet" on the stage.[64]

Some shows, like the long-running Aqua Follies in Minneapolis, were produced in conjunction with larger civic celebrations. When the city hosted its first annual Aquatennial in 1940, the nine-day smorgasbord of events included daily parades, an airshow, wrestling matches, barber shop quartet performances, fishing clinics, and a water show featuring local swimmers staged in an Olympic-sized pool built on the edge of Cedar Lake. The Aquatennial became a popular annual event, and in 1943, organizers brought in professional showman Al Sheehan to take over the Aqua Follies water show and give it more "razzle dazzle."[65] Following the Rose formula, Sheehan brought in Olympic stars and national title holders, including Buster Crabbe and backstroke champion Gloria Callen, who like Williams had qualified for the 1940 Olympics but never got her chance to compete.

Every water show had to feature at least one "aquadope," comic divers who would "sleepwalk," stumble, pancake, and belly flop off the high-dive platforms—and even piggyback off one another as entire groups of water clowns plummeted to the water. Falling off a diving board might sound easy, but there was a real art to doing it safely, and the best, such as Charlie Diehl and Stubby Krueger, were former competitive diving champions. They were also always men, as women in swimsuits were supposed to be beautiful, not funny. Al Sheehan was once heard yelling at a photographer for snapping a picture of his lead water ballerina in the same frame as his water clown. "We have glamor here," he snapped, "and don't want humor identified with her!"[66]

Sheehan brought in Helen Starr, a physical educator at the University of Minnesota, to choreograph the routines swum by his water chorus, the Aquabelles (and later the Aqua Dears when he expanded his show to Seattle and Detroit). The Aquabelles ranged from twenty-eight to thirty-six members, depending on the year, which was similar in size to the Modern Mermaids show a decade prior but offered a whole new level of glamour, with one reviewer calling Sheehan's show a "lavishly-produced spectacle."[67] Besides the elaborate costumes, the Aquabelles shared the pool with swans, a fountain cascading forty feet in the air, and elaborate props like a floating Eiffel Tower for a Parisian-themed show. One year, they performed using painted tin roses as big as car tires, with a swimmer in a green bathing suit forming the stem of each floating bud.[68]

Helen Starr discussed the auditions for the Aquabelles in an interview, saying they were chosen first for swimming ability and stamina, then for good looks. A program for the Follies, however, doesn't indicate the same priorities, noting that to qualify, a girl must have "a shapely figure, a fine sense of rhythm, a supple body and a fine, impressionable mind."[69] It was not uncommon for the women's weights and measurements to be listed in show programs. Audiences at the 1948 Minneapolis Aqua Follies learned that diving champion Patricia Robinson not only had "sparkling green eyes" but also a "striking height, 5'7½" and an enviable form, featuring a well-proportioned 130 lbs."[70] With the ramped-up glamour and focus on beauty, the association Rose started between showgirls and synchronized swimming continued, with another reviewer calling Sheehan's show a "Girl-ful spectacle."[71]

The female water choruses were the bread and butter of any aquatic spectacle. Their members were given every imaginable "aqua" title, and their swimming was called everything from precision swimming to synchronized ballets, and even scientific swimming, harkening back to the professors and natationists of the nineteenth century. The Aquanymphs of Johnny Weissmuller's Watercade performed "rippling rhythms" while Buster's Aquaquettes made "ensemble floral formations" on the water while attired in headdresses made to look like tulips.[72] Elliott Murphy's Aquashow, which ran for twelve summers in the Flushing Meadows marine theater vacated by Rose's Aquacade, featured a "24-girl swimming line" called the Aquadorables, which one reviewer described as gliding "about the pool in graceful precision like so many waterproofed Rockettes."[73]

Program from the 1950 Seattle Aqua Follies produced by Al Sheehan.

Synchronized swimming was growing in popularity alongside these water shows, and the aquachoruses were increasingly staffed by women who had formal training in synchronized swimming groups—and in some cases had won championships. Jeannette McFadden (née Levinson) and her sister Minnette won the national AAU synchronized swimming duet title in 1946 and then joined Sam Snyder's Water Follies, performing as the Vinson Twins, likely making them the first synchro athletes to "turn professional." McFadden recalled that they had to adapt their synchro style to fit their new aquatic accommodations. Snyder's show was a traveling enterprise that used a portable, shallow tank that had to be erected at each venue. Snyder called his 75-by-25-foot pool the "Zeppelin Bag" because it was made of the same kind of rubberized canvas fabric as the *Hindenburg.* According to the program, it took twenty men a dozen hours of non-stop work to assemble it, fill it with 80,000 gallons of water, filter out any impurities to "afford the best view of the water ballet," then heat it to 80 degrees by blowing steam through the water. Snyder didn't want the pool to seem shallow to the audience, so the twelve-member water ballet troupe had to stay hunched down to keep their shoulders in the water. "It wasn't real, legitimate synchronized swimming," said McFadden, "but we did the best we could in four and a half feet."[74]

The sisters were also used to performing their synchronized swimming routines using music from record players, and swimming to live music at shows came with challenges for both the aquatic performers and the musicians. "With a live band, I don't care how good they are, they don't always get the tempo right every time," said McFadden. "Sometimes they play a little too fast and you're in the water and suddenly the tempo picks up and you're not hitting it. You can't get your legs up fast enough."[75] Laura Soles, who swam with Snyder's Water Follies years later, sometimes performed a water ballet solo, but since she didn't know how to count music, she relied on the conductor to keep time with her, instead of the reverse. "The director of the

Program for Sam Snyder's Water Follies.

orchestra knew that I never ended at the same time," said Soles, "so he always watched what I was doing and knew when I was coming to the end of the routine."[76] Snyder liked to travel light, so rather than take a full orchestra on the road, he would hire local bands and glee clubs to perform under the direction of the conductor he kept on staff.

Elliott Murphy's Aquashow at Flushing Meadows, on the other hand, with its location on the waterfront of America's showbiz capital, was able to attract top musical acts, including Cab Calloway and Duke Ellington and his orchestra. Musicians, and occasionally other "dry" stage acts like comedians, were the only performers to cross the color line in these nearly all-white productions. The single woman of color in the water at any of the major shows was champion diver Vicki Manalo, whose father was Filipino. Manalo turned professional after winning gold medals in platform and springboard diving at the 1948 Olympics and performed in several of the era's major water shows.

BEAUTY AS DUTY

During the Second World War, spectacular water shows weren't just for the profit of their showbiz producers, and in fact, many proved incredibly lucrative for the war effort. The Seventh War Loan GI Dinner and Aquacade, held in July 1945 at the Beverly Hills Hotel, featuring Johnny Weissmuller, Esther Williams, who was by that point a rising Hollywood starlet, the Los Angeles Athletic Club (LAAC) water ballet team, and the Tommy Dorsey Orchestra, was attended by many of Hollywood's elites. At $25,000 a ticket, the star-studded event raised $25 million in war bonds.[77] The Southern California Aquabelles, a synchronized swimming group of high school girls, was formally recognized by the US Treasury at the same event for raising an additional $26 million through their tours across California and Arizona. The Aquabelles were based out of Fort MacArthur near Los Angeles and coached by an enlistee there named Howard Ploessel, a swimmer who had qualified for the Olympics, and his wife, Velma Dunn, a silver medalist from the 1936 Olympics.

Professional shows like the Minneapolis Aqua Follies pivoted to do their part as well, with choreographer Helen Starr telling a newspaper ahead of the 1943 show, "The whole show will be patriotic in theme, completely in accord with the all-out war effort."[78] In fact, the entire Aquatennial had a "war flavor," with newsreels like "Bombing of Rome" showing clips from the warfront and parades with floats made by branches of the military. The opening performance, featuring Gloria Callen and Buster Crabbe as headliners, was used as a fundraiser, raising $17,250 in war bonds. Another Aqua Follies show shortly after included the special feature "Eleven Wounded War Heroes Tell Their Story."[79]

In addition to raising funds to support the war, swimmers, divers, and water ballerinas—many of whom had been part of competitive clubs before the war—participated in United Service Organizations (USO) and Red Cross water shows to entertain troops waiting for deployment and lift the morale of wounded soldiers back from the front. Women's competitive swimming opportunities withered during the war due to the travel restrictions affecting all sports, and also because many hotels with pools where swimming and diving teams practiced had been taken over by the military to use as hospitals. In Atlantic City alone, the War Department commandeered at least forty-seven hotels.[80] In some cases, teams dissolved when coaches enlisted in the service or were tapped to teach soldiers to swim or to train frogmen. Many competitive swimmers who didn't want to lose their amateur status by performing for pay in professional shows volunteered their talents for "water shows for the war effort." Performances were held in the pools at military bases and hospitals, as well as at the commandeered hotels. And if there was no pool available, they still made do. The Lake Shore Club, one of the earliest synchronized swimming teams, performed in the Mississippi River for military personnel in Davenport, Iowa, kicking off their show by diving in from a barge.[81]

While the Lake Shore swimmers could not see anything in the murky river water, that was not a problem in the pool at El Mirador Hotel in Palm Springs—a fact that Virginia Hunt Newman learned the hard way when she participated in a show there for wounded soldiers. Newman had forgotten her LAAC team suit, leaving her with no option but to wear the two-piece she happened to have on hand. After performing a few dives, she noticed men leaving the stands and wondered what was going on. She later found out they had gone to the pool's subterranean level to watch through the underwater windows, hoping to catch a glimpse as Newman adjusted her top underwater after each dive. "Obviously, these men weren't as sick or wounded as they would have you believe," she said. But Newman, who performed in many such shows, found the experience rewarding, saying, "It made you feel really part of the war effort."[82]

There was an attitude of "beauty as duty" during the wartime years, and as scholars of the era have noted, women in swimsuits held patriotic messaging. As such, shows sometimes featured swimsuit beauty competitions, even for female servicemembers. An "Aquacade" held in the pool at Dibble General Hospital near Palo Alto featured not only water ballet and diving performances but also a parade of Women's Army Corps members wearing swimsuits for the WAC Bathing Beauty Contest.[83] One injured solider said following a water show for veterans injured in the Bataan Death March and at Guadalcanal, "Golly, it's good to be back, it's good to see the wholesome beauty of these American girls."[84]

Aquatic spectacles and water shows had become so popular and so incorporated into the entertainment services for military personnel that they also became natural platforms for teaching wartime swimming skills. The drowning rates being reported from the battlefront were disturbingly high, and in some cases the water-related casualties were higher than those killed by enemy fire. Military leaders were looking for ways to make soldiers (and the draftable public) aware of the types of survival swimming that could mean the difference between life and death in amphibious war scenarios, and many water shows began including exhibitions of warfare aquatics. The skills demonstrated were largely based on the trainings that Commodore Longfellow, Robert Kiphuth, and Thomas Cureton had developed at the Red Cross, Yale, and the University of Illinois.

In the summer of 1942, Longfellow produced "Swimming in Wartime," a nine-act water show to demonstrate the "vital importance of swimming and particularly to a nation at war."[85] It was an elaborate production, with part of the pool staged to resemble the wreckage of a torpedoed ship, and included a demonstration of a crash rescue with male and female members of the Red Cross Water Safety Committee and swimming units of the armed forces untangling a fallen aviator from his equipment and administering medical aid, all while treading water.[86] "Swimming for offense" was demonstrated by a commando detail from the US Coast Guard Artillery, while the swimming riflemen of Fort Washington showed how a stream could be crossed wearing packs and weapons.[87] Local swimmers demonstrated a special style of breaststroke much like the one Esther Williams had to master at the Aquacade that could be used to hold the upper body high above oil-covered or debris-strewn waters. A co-ed children's group performed a "safety ballet" with musical accompaniment by the US Navy School of Music band.[88] The show was performed in at least three swimming pools in Washington, DC, including two designated for Black residents, as pools in the US capital remained segregated.

Cureton, Kiphuth, and Longfellow had all advocated for aquatic survival techniques—which were based on the same skills used by synchronized swimmers—to be taught to women as well as men. However, at water shows, when these skills were framed as techniques of war, they were demonstrated by male swimmers, while the women who had mastered similar skills performed in more appropriately "feminine" water ballets. For example, a water carnival in Corpus Christi for military personnel on Ward Island (used during the war as a radar station and training base) included a "warfare aquatics"

Swimming with one arm free to carry weaponry—a key skill in warfare aquatics—published in Watermanship *by the US War Department, 1944.*

demonstration by male recruits and a Women's Reserves (known as WAVES) group performing "aquacade swimming."[89] Fort MacArthur's Second Aquacade and Army Aquatic Show in 1944 featured a similar tactical demonstration by a team of navy aquatic experts while the Southern California Aquabelles swam a stirring "Salute to the United Nations."[90] In 1945, the Marine Corps Women's Reserve at Camp Lejeune put on the Camp Lejeune Aquacade, with a newsletter ahead of the show reporting, "The Aquacade is complete with array of feminine pulchritude in the water ballet . . . swimming in formations with motion synchronized to the musical background."[91] In addition to the all-female water ballet, there was a group of male Marine swimmers called the Mer-Marines who performed a "close-water drill."[92]

With swimming and water shows connected to the war in so many different ways, it is perhaps fitting that Germany's surrender on May 8, 1945—a date now known as VE, or Victory in Europe, Day—was celebrated at the Allied Forces Headquarters (AFHQ) in Caserta, Italy, with a massive aquatic spectacle. And it was led by none other than Katharine Curtis. Since leaving Chicago to work on the warfront with the Red Cross, Curtis had been stationed all over North Africa and western Europe, from Casablanca to Capri, and was serving at the AFHQ in Caserta when the war officially ended in Europe. Word of her background in water pageants and synchronized swimming had gotten around, and she was asked to stage an aquacade at the Caserta Palace's beautiful cascade pool to mark the occasion and provide a way for members of the Allied Forces to come together and celebrate.

Curtis enlisted the help of another Red Cross member who had worked on water ballets and put out a call for "potential Johnny Weissmuller's and Eleanor Holms."[93] But at the first practice, they discovered that none of the swimmers who signed up—which included both Brits and Americans—had ever swum to music or even seen an aquacade or synchronized swimming performance, so Curtis had to explain the basic concept from the ground up. She pulled out a "terrible old portable Victrola and some worn-out records" and tried to teach them some rhythmic strokes on dry land. "There was nothing promising about that first effort!" Curtis later wrote.[94] But she believed it could be done and pushed ahead. The swimmers only had a month, squeezing in practices during lunch hours and after work, but they pulled together an entire show's worth of routines, including a "Waltz of the Coral Nymphs," various duets, tangos, a display by twenty-four men of synchronized military maneuvers, and an all-male performance of the "Rhumba" routine from Curtis's *Rhythmic Swimming* book, with a few adaptations for the shallow water.[95]

Meanwhile, a small army of volunteers were working on the costumes and set design, using the cascade pool's nineteenth-century "Fountain of the Dolphins" as the backdrop for the stage, which featured thrones for Neptune and Aphrodite and staircases leading down to the water from the sides and center. Resources were hard to come by in war-ravaged Italy, but they managed to scrounge together fabric to outfit 259 performers, plus "jewels" and sequins to bedazzle them. There were costumes for mermaids who floated on a raft combing their golden tresses, white hooded suits topped with water lilies for the ballet swimmers, and red and white striped trunks for the men. A sixty-five-member band in military uniform provided the music.

Even though there was seating for two thousand spectators, demand for the free tickets to the AFHQ Aquacade was so great that Curtis had to add a second weekend of Saturday and Sunday performances. The morning after the first show, held on June 9, Curtis wrote in a letter home that opening night was a huge success. She particularly enjoyed seeing the "absolute wonder and unbelief" on everyone's faces that they had actually managed to pull off such a spectacle.[96] She added that "The Mighty"—US Deputy Supreme Allied Commander General McNarney and Supreme Allied Commander General Alexander—were expected to attend the following day. An estimated eight thousand members of the British and American militaries and support services in total saw the show. One audience member sent a letter of commendation to the American Red Cross headquarters in Washington, DC, that stated: "Having seen Billy Rose's Aquacade in San Francisco, I wondered just what to expect, and dared not to dream up anything like that. However, let me hasten to say that the whole natural setting had the professional shows beat . . .some of the scenes left you breathless."[97] Curtis herself wrote that when the swimmers stretched red, white, and blue streamers across the length of the pool for the grand finale and the audience rose to sing along to the anthems, "It was something worth remembering, I can tell you."[98]

Back in 1937, the year of Billy Rose's first Aquacade, Commodore Longfellow predicted that if swimming was made colorful and combined with elements of the stage, it would attract great audiences. He wrote:

> Truly the aquatic program today is limited only by the vision and imagination of those who operate it. We have swimming stadiums, seating thousands, with batteries of lights, with giant voice speaker systems needing only the guiding hand of the impresario to cash in the skill of the local swimmers, who are only too glad to have parts in big-time water drama.[99]

Even more importantly, Longfellow predicted that these types of swimming spectaculars would draw more people to the water and create new swimmers. And he was right on both fronts. Professional water shows like Billy Rose's Aquacades and Al Sheehan's Aqua Follies not only filled an entertainment niche unique to their time, but by bringing showbiz sparkle and Broadway polish to the water, they helped spur the popularity of aquatics, particularly the emerging field of synchronized swimming. Katharine Curtis had laid the foundation for the sport, but as one journalist of the era noted, "it remained for the ubiquitous Billy Rose and the New York World's Fair in 1939 to wrap up musical swimming in a flossy package and peddle it as an eye-filling (and stadium-filling spectacle)." Esther Williams and Hollywood's Technicolor cameras would take it from there.[100]

CHAPTER 9

SILVER SCREEN

It has been established that movie goers expect Fred
Astaire to dance in a movie; Bing Crosby to sing;
Roy Rogers to ride; and Esther Williams to swim.

—MODERN SCREEN, 1953

"We've come for Esther!"

Americans Paul Trejo and Art Emerson shouted their intentions as they and a gang of their fellow US Navy officers from the USS *Floyd B. Parks* stormed the wardroom of an Australian destroyer, the HMAS *Shoalhaven*. Both Allied ships were in port at Japan's Sasebo Harbor. Disguised as commandos, the Yankee raiding party had managed to slip unnoticed onto the ship, subdue the deck watch, and make it all the way to the wardroom, where their commanding officers were dining with their Australian and British counterparts. But once they burst through the officers' mess at 2300 hours that February night, their mission was unmistakable, and all hell broke loose. The *Floyd B. Parks* commanding officers were seized by the Aussies, tables were overturned, glasses and plates were shattered, and blows were delivered as everyone fought over the most sought out prize on the Western Pacific: the "Esther Williams Trophy."

It was February 18, 1950, and a decade had passed since swimming champion Esther Williams had been plucked from relative obscurity for her show-business debut as Billy Rose's Aquabelle Number One. In that time, she had become a top-grossing movie star, the world had survived one war and was on the cusp of another in Korea, and a single copy of her photograph had become the trophy at the heart of an ongoing international naval competition that, in the words of Captain Paul Trejo, was one of the "finest morale builders" for servicemen stationed in the Pacific during not just World War II but also the Korean War and long after.[1]

The tradition of the Esther Williams Trophy started in 1943 as a joke between two friends, Lindsay "Georgie" Brand and David Stevenson, officers in the Royal Australian Navy stationed together on the HMAS *Nepal*.[2] When Stevenson won the affections of a young woman whom they both fancied, he tried to ease the blow for his friend by forging an autograph on a glamour headshot of Esther Williams, which had been included in one of many packets of pinups sent to GIs around the world. Williams's photo, inscribed with the note "To my own Georgie, with all my love and a passionate kiss, Esther," hung proudly in Brand's cabin—until a fellow officer stole it. Brand stole it back, only to have it taken again and absconded to another ship to "protect Esther's honor."[3] Soon, the picture was being called the "Esther Williams Trophy" and other wardrooms were, as reported by the Royal Australian Navy, planning their own heists and hijinks "to secure the morale-boosting prize."

The battle over the trophy escalated alongside Williams's career, with submarines, cruisers, carriers, and other ships from Allied navies joining in. By the time the *Floyd B. Parks* liberated "The Esther"—as it came to be known—from the *Shoalhaven* in the months leading up to the Korean War, the trophy had its own logbook, official rules of engagement, and flag that had to be flown by any ship in possession of it. The flag featured a diving silhouette of Williams, who by that point was not only one of Hollywood's most popular actresses but also the star of her own blockbuster movie genre—the aquamusical. There were two copies of The Esther: a fighting copy, which was encased in a kapok frame to help it survive the rigors of battle at sea and had to be clearly displayed in a ship's wardroom; and the trophy copy, which was kept secured under lock and key. Rules stipulated that any ship that successfully captured the fighting copy must be presented the trophy copy within twenty-four hours. The rest of the rules were simple: Esther had to stay in the Pacific; only officers could engage in the battle for her honor (supposedly to keep things "gentlemanly"), though they could do so by any means necessary—whether by stealth, cunning, or brute force—other than firearms and clubs; Esther's "unsuccessful suitors" could be held overnight and given "haircuts."[4]

"The battles over 'ESTHER' have been the source of more scheming, skulduggery, connivance, entertainment, and diversion than any other single intra-Navy issue," wrote W. B. Hayler, another captain who went to battle for Esther. "It has also been the cause of more lost sleep, shaved heads, and sore muscles than any fraternity rushing season any college men ever participated in."[5] By the time the trophy

The Esther Williams Trophy, after it was retired with military honors.

was retired in the late 1950s, it had changed hands over 200 times and been aboard 110 submarines, destroyers, and aircraft carriers from 4 different navies.[6]

Boys wanted to date her, girls wanted to be her, fans felt they *knew* her. As one magazine wrote, "Everybody—*but everybody*—likes Esther Williams."[7] But America's favorite swimmer never imagined, or wanted, a life of fame.

When the outbreak of World War II caused the 1940 Olympics to be canceled, and teenaged Esther Williams traded fast swimming and medals for pretty swimming and showbiz, she assumed the spotlight would be temporary. For her, Billy Rose's San Francisco Aquacade had been her ten minutes of fame and a chance to make some money from her athletic talents before settling down and getting married. In fact, she said many times throughout her life that stardom was her "consolation prize" for her dashed Olympic dreams. Throughout her eight months as the star of the Aquacade, Williams had been paid frequent visits from talent and film scouts, including from Hollywood's biggest production company, Metro-Goldwyn-Mayer (MGM). They were determined to lure her to the studios, but the wild atmosphere at the Aquacades and its baked-in sexual harassment had left her wanting nothing to do with the entertainment business. "They came backstage and said: 'You're gonna be a movie star and that's *it*,'" said Williams years later in an interview. "But I didn't want *it*. If the Aquacade wasn't fun, why would the movies be?"[8] Craving instead the safety and security of a quiet life, Williams eloped with her boyfriend, medical student Leonard Kovner—entering what would turn out to be a short and unhappy marriage—and returned to her department store job at I. Magnin.

But Louis B. Mayer, the head of MGM, had different ideas for Williams and was not used to taking no for an answer. Since 1936, Mayer had been looking on as competitor studio Twentieth Century-Fox knocked out one blockbuster hit after another, all created around the dimpled, blond Norwegian three-time Olympic skating champion Sonja Henie. Movies with titles like *Wintertime, Iceland*, and *Thin Ice* featured long ice-ballet scenes with Henie at the center of dozens of beautiful skaters. With lightweight plots set in scenic winter wonderlands and mountain resorts, Henie's movies offered "an alternate universe made of powdered sugar" for anxious Americans as the country had been inching closer to the war in Europe.[9] Mayer wanted to bring audiences a similar form of escapism—one built not around snow-white fantasies, but around the California dream of golden sunshine, shimmering turquoise waters, and tanned American beauties in swimsuits. Billy Rose's Aquacades—often described as the summer version of Henie's live ice-skating shows—had demonstrated a clear market for entertainment centered around aquatic spectacle, while MGM's 1939 Technicolor hit, *The Wizard of Oz*, had shown the dazzling effects that could be achieved through the emerging world of full-spectrum color film. Mayer knew that with its massive budgets and Hollywood magic, MGM could turn the Aquacades into cinematic, musical extravaganzas to knock the skates off the competition. "Melt the ice, get a swimmer, make it pretty!" Mayer commanded his staff.[10]

Los Angeles native Esther Williams had everything the studio was looking for. Not only was she beautiful and wildly photogenic, but she was also a national champion swimmer who had qualified for the Olympics, aligning her with patriotic ideals of hard work and sacrifice. Moreover, her appeal was like that of apple pie: wholesome and generically American, with no specific regional accents or ethnic markers. MGM had previously auditioned Eleanor Holm, Olympic champion and star of the New York Aquacade, to become their swimming starlet, but according to Williams, the petite swimmer from Queens was passed over because she "talked out of the side of her mouth with an accent that rivaled Humphrey Bogart."[11]

After the Aquacade, Esther, now Mrs. Leonard Kovner, ignored repeated calls and visits to her home and workplace from MGM executives but finally conceded to a meeting with Mayer when one of the William Morris talent agency's top recruiters called to say he had personally arranged everything, including a chauffeur to take her to MGM's 178-acre campus in Culver City. When Williams arrived, she was greeted by the "MGM potentate" seated behind a crescent-shaped desk at the end of a 60-foot-long white carpet and surrounded by male executives. While the scene would have no doubt intimidated others, Williams was in a strong position—they wanted her.[12] But these movie men knew a thing or two about wooing a potential starlet, and at the end of the meeting, they took Williams on a tour of the "hall of stars," showing her the very dressing room that could be hers. She couldn't help but think back to the gimpy stool, bare dangling lightbulb, and broken mirror in her Aquacade dressing room. They finally had her attention.

But Williams reminded them, as she had many times before, that she was a swimmer, not an actress. Not to worry, they assured her; the studio would take care of that. The midcentury Hollywood studio system contracted actors as salaried employees and provided in-house acting coaches and whatever else was needed to turn their seedlings into stars. With more than five thousand people on payroll, MGM even had its own school for child actors.[13] She requested a nine-month training period before making any films, reasoning to herself that if it took nine months to incubate a baby, surely that would be enough time to make her into an actress. Mayer agreed and even offered to waive the usual screen test requirement. Williams had run out of reasons to say no.

In October 1941, a year after leaving the Aquacade, she signed on with MGM with a starting salary of $350 a week. It was a fortune for Williams, the fifth child of a sign painter and a schoolteacher who had struggled to put food on the table during the Depression.[14] For the next nine months, she poured the same discipline and work ethic that had helped her become a champion athlete into her studies at "MGM University." Her workday read like a montage from *My Fair Lady*: singing and diction lessons, drama coaching, dance classes (both ballet and ballroom), makeup and wardrobe sessions, and a dollop of finishing school lessons in poise, posture, and finesse that sometimes involved balancing books on her head. On top of all that, Williams swam every day at the Beverly Hills Hotel, having also stipulated in her contract a membership to Hollywood's swankiest pool.

Once Williams's "gestation" period was over, MGM tested her the same way they had many of their rising starlets, like Judy Garland, Lana Turner, and Donna Reed—by giving her a small part in an upcoming installment of the Andy Hardy film series. The black-and-white series starred Mickey Rooney as Andy, a teenage boy constantly lovestruck by a new girl. His rotating crushes were played by the studio's female upstarts, who would either be shown the door or given bigger roles, depending on whether test audiences liked them. For her appearance in *Andy Hardy's Double Life*, Williams wore a two-piece swimsuit. With wartime rationing of fabrics, some women's swimsuits were starting to show a bit of midriff though they still included modesty panels across the front and high waistlines to cover the navel. When Andy, lounging by a pool, gets one look at the new girl, he swoons and falls into the water and has to be rescued by Williams's character. During filming, when the director saw what a natural Williams was in the pool, he decided to add an underwater kiss between the two. In the scene, Esther twirls and lolls like a mermaid, her loose hair billowing around her face, and smiles at the camera as if inviting the viewer to join her. Despite her minor role, the testers loved Williams, confirming to MGM that they had made a good investment.

The underwater scene had been filmed in the studio's small pool, dubbed the "saucer tank," which was fine for brief water scenes, but it was far too limiting for the swimming musicals the studio had in mind for Williams. MGM was known for sparing no expense with its films, finding that investments in lavish productions were more than returned at the box office, and began work to turn an entire soundstage on the studio's back lot into a 90-by-90-foot swimming pool that was 25 feet deep and equipped with every imaginable bell and whistle. "Esther's pool," as it became known, included hydraulic lifts, a crow's nest camera platform, a crane that could move the camera both horizontally and vertically at the same time, a phone booth–sized "aquachamber" for underwater filming, an elevator for vertical traveling shots that ran from the ceiling rafters all the way down to a few feet below the water surface, and a switchboard nerve center *Life* magazine called "worthy of Army engineers."[15]

While Esther's pool was being built, the publicity department was busy running the twenty-year-old through MGM's star-making machine. They gave her more on-screen practice with a role in the black-and-white movie *A Guy Named Joe*—just one of many patriotic wartime pictures and propaganda films being churned out at the time. Pearl Harbor had been bombed only a few months after Williams signed with MGM, and with America embroiled in the war, Hollywood studios were eager to prove themselves essential to the war effort in hopes of avoiding the restrictions affecting many industries. Studios had also turned into "cheesecake mills" for the military, and expected their actresses, Williams included, to pose as pinup girls whether they wanted to or not. The *Tampa Tribune* wrote:

Ask studio fan mail department heads what their biggest mail order business is today . . . and they'll tell you it's sending cheese cake photographs to thousands of service men who write in for pictures . . . as a result, actresses who always preferred emoting to stripping have joined the parade heretofore led by dancers, swimmers and chorus cuties.[16]

For MGM, this was the perfect opportunity to get Williams's face (and figure) out there, and the studio had her posing in swimsuits for marathon photo sessions that ran from dawn to dusk.[17] Her pictures

Esther Williams on the cover of Yank, The Army Weekly, *in October 1945.*

were printed in military magazines like *Yank* and sent by the thousands to GIs in training at home and fighting abroad. One of those pictures, in a packet bound for Allied fleets in the Western Pacific, would find its way to the HMAS *Nepal*, to the cabin of Lieutenant "Georgie" Brand.

THE AQUAMUSICAL

Finally, in 1943, having built Esther her pool and established her as an upcoming starlet, MGM was ready to produce an aquatic extravaganza. In her first film, *Bathing Beauty* (initially titled *Mr. Co-ed*), Williams played a swimming teacher at an East Coast women's college and love interest of comedic actor Red Skelton. In a far-fetched attempt to woo the teacher, Skelton's character enrolls in the all-girls school where she works. Producers wasted no time getting Williams into the water, staging the opening scene around a resort swimming pool where guests lounge while listening to the music of Xavier Cugat's band. Williams strolls onto the scene wearing a white, hip-length cape draped over her swimsuit, her long legs accentuated with pink kitten heels, and makes her way around the pool as she is serenaded by a baritone from the band. When she reaches the diving board, she slips off her cape, climbs the ladder, then smiles down at the camera—her shocking hot pink swimsuit and matching hairbow practically glowing against the brilliantly blue sky—before making a perfect swan dive. It is the quintessential Esther Williams Technicolor moment.

As would be the case in most of her future films, once Williams hit the water, she was given little guidance. "Just do what you do, Esther," director George Sidney told her.[18] Williams thought back to the various exhibitions she'd been in and remembered a flippy hand movement she'd seen the diving clowns perform. She gave it a try, making the high arm strokes she'd learned at the Aquacade, adding a slight bend of the wrist on the recovery, letting her long, slender hands trail slightly, then flicking her wrist forward, as if adding an accent mark at the end of each stroke. The clowns had called it the "East River Crawl," joking that New Yorkers used the technique to flick away garbage as they swam in the city's polluted rivers, but Williams's experience with "pretty swimming" lent the same technique an elegant air and became a hallmark of her aquatic style.[19] For the two-minute water scene, she ad-libbed, rolling her body like a corkscrew through the water, porpoise diving, spinning like a tub, and windmilling, all to the tune of "Magic Is the Moonlight."

While the opening scene is intimate, with close camera framing around Williams giving the sensation of being in the water with her, the movie's finale—an Aquacade-style water ballet—is a dazzling showstopper. In fact, to direct the sequence, which featured 150 female swimmers and dancers, MGM brought in John Murray Anderson, the mastermind behind the mass synchronization numbers in Billy Rose's Aquacades. The eight-minute scene begins with the camera trained on trumpeter Harry James, then pans back to show the entire pool, flanked on each end by a full orchestra with a stage full of swirling dancers in between. Attention then turns to a long row of swimmers in iridescent pink and emerald swimsuits who dive, one by one, sideways with arms overhead, as the camera follows them down the line. As they stroke away in unison, Esther appears in front of two pink seahorses wearing a Roman toga–inspired ensemble, which she removes to reveal a white swimsuit covered in tiny, sparkling mirrors, then dives in. Underwater, she weaves and arches between the swimmers, smiling at the camera. A bird's-eye view of the scene shows a massive floating pinwheel of women, the lines of the swimmers' bodies softened by the pink flowers interspersed between them. As Esther glides, surrounded by her aquachorus, she sets off a series of waterworks and pyrotechnics. A flick of her wrist here launches a six-story geyser, a tap there ignites a flaming fountain, until the whole pool is ablaze with colorful cascades and fireworks—all supported by the pool's complex maze of underwater pipes. "Never had plumbing been put to a more glamorous use," wrote Williams.[20]

Although Williams felt the scene "defied credulity," when MGM previewed the movie to test audiences across Southern California, they were wild about the water ballet and fresh-faced Williams.[21] As for Red Skelton, the movie's original namesake, audiences were rather lukewarm over his slapstick, cross-dressing antics. Realizing they had pegged the wrong star, the studio promptly changed the film's title from *Mr. Co-ed* to *Bathing Beauty*, and made Williams the focus of its promotion. Previews for *Bathing Beauty* called her "the girl you will dream about," while *Life* magazine declared her "Hollywood's prettiest" and pictured Williams standing in front of a giant clamshell on the cover.[22]

Bathing Beauty hit theaters in July 1944, just a month after the Allied invasion of Normandy, and provided war-weary audiences with just the kind of colorful, breezy escape they sorely needed. *Showmen's Trade Review* predicted it would be "mighty acceptable entertainment to the great masses," and another noted that those unable to travel to the beach that summer would delight in the "stunning display of girls in bathing suits and swimming in waltz time."[23] The New York premiere was announced with a six-story cutout of Williams "diving" into Times Square with the words "Come on in, the show's fine!" Lines wound around the block of the Astor Theater for weeks.[24] It was the second highest internationally grossing film that year after *Gone with the Wind*.[25]

While *Bathing Beauty* had catapulted Williams to fame, industry

*A six-story Esther Williams splashes into Times Square
ahead of* Bathing Beauty's *premiere at the Astor Theater.*

insiders assumed the swimmer would be a "one-picture kid."[26] But to studio executives looking at box office returns, Williams's career was just beginning. MGM promoted her to a star dressing room, an honor reserved for their top actors and actresses, and quickly started production on her next Technicolor feature. In *Thrill of a Romance*, Williams again played a swim instructor, but this time with Van Johnson cast as her war-hero love interest. Following a meet-cute in a pool, Johnson's character admits he can't swim and gets a lesson from the beautiful instructor. This wasn't far from the truth in real life—Johnson, with whom Williams made several films, was not a strong swimmer and Williams often had to support him with a hand under his back during swimming scenes. While they were filming *Thrill of a Romance*, MGM squeezed in a short role for Williams in another movie already under production, *Ziegfeld Follies*, which was modeled after a vaudeville revue show and featured individual sketch acts by various performers. Williams's short scene depicted an underwater tank act along the lines of those performed by Lurline the Water Queen, Agnes Beckwith, or Annette Kellerman, and showed Williams performing a series of fluid, graceful movements surrounded by colorful coral.

It was these two films, both released in 1945, that cemented Williams as a star. Rather than fizzling after her *Bathing Beauty* debut, wrote *Modern Screen*, Williams had triumphed in the water again, "staging a marine ballet in *Ziegfeld Follies* such as Hollywood had never seen before," then stepping out of the pool, "learning to act and proving it in *Thrill of a Romance*."[27] Williams, however, credited the success of *Thrill of a Romance* to its being, once again, the right film at the right time. With the war coming to a close, Johnson and Williams represented all the returning soldiers and the girls they were coming home to.[28] *Time* magazine called the film "screwily wholesome" and as all-American "as a double scoop of strawberry ice cream."[29]

Williams, completely at home in the water as she performs her "marine ballet" in Ziegfeld Follies, *1945.*

Fan magazines, most of which were little more than extensions of the studios' publicity departments, catered to this girl-next-door image of Williams. When she and Kovner divorced following *Bathing Beauty*'s release, they largely looked the other way, but then eagerly covered her budding romance months later with fun-loving sergeant Ben Gage, whom she married in November 1945. The two had met at a party after he returned from his service abroad, but Gage told writers that "Esther was my particular pin-up girl long before I ever met her"—not just because she looked good in a bathing suit, he joked, but because he was an aspiring swimmer and hoped that by marrying her, he could get Williams to teach him the crawl stroke.[30] Articles abounded about their modest but tastefully furnished home and their numerous DIY projects, from bookcases built by Gage to curtains and lamps crafted by Williams.

Williams's next MGM movie, *Hoodlum Saint*, was black and white with no swimming scenes—and it was a total flop. Williams blamed the film's failure on the poor choice of romantic casting, which paired her with the considerably older William Powell and didn't jibe with her girl-next-door persona. *Life* magazine seemed to agree, writing, "The bobby-soxers at first showing screamed so loud every time they saw their Esther kissing 'that old man' that all the clinches had to be cut."[31] But to MGM executives, they had left out the most important ingredients: Technicolor water and Williams in a bathing suit—and they wouldn't make the same mistake twice.

During her eleven-year career at MGM, Williams made twenty-one movies, with *Hoodlum Saint* and *A Guy Named Joe* being the only ones with no water scenes and the only ones in black and white. For her films, MGM writers thought of every conceivable way to work in swimming scenes: her roles included the president of a swimwear company in *Neptune's Daughter*, an English Channel swimmer in *Dangerous When Wet*, and aquatic performers of all stripes, including an aquacade star, a nightclub swimmer, and an aquaclown and water skier at Florida's Cypress Gardens. In her biggest film, *Million Dollar Mermaid*, she played the ultimate aquatic star, Annette Kellerman. But if necessary, writers would stretch plots thin to get Williams in a bathing suit. When she was called on to take over for Judy Garland as the owner of a baseball team in *Take Me Out to the Ballgame*, she hoped it would be an opportunity to break out of her "'swimming star' straight jacket," but the writers reworked the story to include an incongruous swimming scene in which she lolls about in a hotel pool as three male characters watch voyeuristically from their balcony.[32]

Williams's films, which became known as "aquamusicals," mostly followed a set formula, including lots of singing and dancing, frothy love stories, beautiful costumes, and lavishly choreographed swimming sequences with tropical locales and flashy, Vegas-style performance venues as the backdrops. As the focal points of her movies, the water scenes were where MGM poured the most resources. Whether it was Esther descending from heaven on a trapeze—as she often did—a group underwater flash dance, dozens of swimmers sliding down the planks of a pink ship, or Jimmy Durante emerging from the waves on a hydraulic column playing the piano in a white suit and top hat, there was always, as one writer put it, "at least one scene that makes Niagara Falls look silly."[33] Even "simple" scenes like her swimming duet with John Bromfield in *Easy to Love*, which took place in a moonlit lagoon lined with cypress trees and beautified with swans, violinists, and a layer of twenty-five thousand gardenias and camellias floating on the water, cost up to $250,000 to produce and required about five months of rehearsals.[34]

Through all the flourishes, though, "the meat and potatoes of any Williams picture is Esther herself," wrote *Pageant*, while everything else was just extra.[35] And it was true—by 1948, Gallup polls found that Williams's name alone had the power to convince 40 percent of Americans to pull out their wallets and plunk down cash for a movie ticket. The following year, it was up to 45 percent, with only one other actress—June Allyson—ranking as highly.[36]

Although they could hardly be considered feminist by today's standards, Williams's characters resonated with female audiences in the Rosie the Riveter era when women were being called on to step up and fill the shoes of men who had left jobs to fight on the front. Williams had a muscular physique, joking in her memoir that she never needed shoulder pads because she had her own built in, and at 5'7", she was the physical equal, and often taller, than her male costars. Her visibly strong body demanded different kinds of roles than those typically assigned to actresses in midcentury Hollywood. Her characters were feminine, yet they weren't relegated to the domestic sphere. They had careers or strong personal goals that they were working to achieve, such as running a company or swimming the English Channel. Like Kellerman before her, Williams was the protagonist leading the action of her films and *men* were the supporting characters.[37] Moreover, she wasn't pinned to a particular male actor, like Ginger Rogers was with Fred Astaire. Williams was the constant, while her male costars came and went. In fact, she carried her own films so well that they became the testing ground for less experienced male actors, just as the Andy Hardy series had been for MGM's up-and-coming female stars. When asked who her favorite leading man was, Williams often answered, "the water," which she saw as her real costar.[38]

GLAMOUR UNDER THE CODE

MGM made the water glamorous and Williams glamorous in it, but it took a lot of people and a lot of innovation to get there, particularly from the studio's stylists and costume designers. The pancake makeup typically used on their actors was a disaster in the water, sliding right off Esther's face and body, leaving a murky beige film on the surface. After much experimentation, the makeup artists developed a regime that could stand up to the pool test: a thick cream-based foundation, followed by a heavy dose of powder, then "set" by the steam of a hot shower. Her hair proved even more challenging, as it had to stay put through high dives and hours of swimming and look fabulous to boot. They achieved this by coating Williams's scalp with a mix of warm Vaseline and baby oil then plaiting her hair into tiny braids that became the foundation for lush, fake braids attached with bobby pins and wound around her head like a crown or laurel wreath. The process took hours, but by the end of it, Williams was "as waterproof as a mallard."[39]

Dressing Williams for the water was another matter, and one that had to be constantly negotiated. In *This Time for Keeps*, designers made her a suit of flannel that no doubt looked great dry, but soaked up water like a woolen army blanket and became so heavy that Esther had to pull it off in the pool to keep it from dragging her to the bottom. After that, Williams started sitting in on wardrobe meetings. MGM designers were some of the best in the business and knew how to make actresses look great in whatever they were wearing, but they weren't accustomed to fashioning costumes to move with an athlete's agile body, hold their shape when waterlogged, or withstand the fading effects of chlorine. In her memoir, *Just Make Them Beautiful*, the famed MGM designer Helen Rose wrote that Williams's swimsuits were her biggest challenge because "they had to be comfortable and swimmable, yet glamorous and spectacular."[40] Rose and Williams worked together, making use of newly available materials like latex to come up with what Rose called "the first really glamorous bathing suits ever worn by swimmers." After the war, with material shortages over, fashions veering toward more feminine lines, and the California sportswear manufacturers doing booming business, the elegant and flattering, yet wearable, styles Williams wore on-screen began making their way to the masses. Cole of California even launched an Esther Williams swimwear line after Williams convinced MGM to allow her to keep the royalties (studios at the time typically controlled their stars' endorsements and kept the profits) by having Cole provide free suits for the film *Neptune's Daughter*.

Despite being the cover girl of swimming, Williams did want to get out of a swimsuit on occasion and expand beyond aquatic roles, but every time she brought it up to studio executives they took the "If it ain't broke" approach and clearly weren't interested in upending a formula that had proven to be box office gold. "I guess what MGM found was that my audience wanted that bathing suit," said Williams in an interview.[41] And of course MGM wanted it too, since the bathing suit—and the swimming Williams did in it—was precisely what made her so valuable to the studio and enabled directors to show more skin than they could otherwise get away with. Hollywood studios, from the early 1930s to the late 1960s, were subject to the Motion Picture Production Code, a set of industry standards regarding what themes and content could be depicted in movies. In the "Pre-Code" era of silent films, movies had grown increasingly risqué, especially in the early Depression years, as desperate film producers and theater chain owners—who were often one and the same—tried to lure audiences reluctant to spend their meager resources at the movies.

The Catholic Church got involved, forming the National Legion of Decency to rate movies and dictate which ones were appropriate for congregants. The film industry decided it preferred self-censorship and established a set of strict rules—including standards regarding bodily display and clothing—that all studios had to adhere to and that were enforced starting in 1934 by the Motion Picture Production Code Office headed by Joseph Breen.

In the Pre-Code era, bathing suits had been commonplace on movie screens, from Annette Kellerman's one-piece (not to mention her "nude" scenes) to Mack Sennett's Bathing Beauties to Busby Berkeley's water chorines in *Footlight Parade*. It hadn't mattered if the women wearing them did any actual swimming—and many of the actresses in these roles couldn't swim anyway. However, by the 1940s, to show a woman's legs or put her in a swimsuit, there needed to be a legitimate reason—like making a movie about a swimmer that featured *actual* swimming. That is what made Williams—a national swimming champion turned actress—so unique and prompted the *New York Times* to declare ahead of Williams's film debut, "Look, a Bathing Beauty Who Swims!"[42] A magazine article pictured Williams sitting on a pool deck, splashing her legs in the water, with the caption, "Hollywood finds starlet who can swim as well as pose by a pool."[43]

Through the medium of water, MGM could get away with racier scenes as well. In *Easy to Love*, Williams and John Bromfield swam a sensual tango in a "bed" of floating camellias and gardenias, their glistening, nearly nude bodies intertwining and slithering across each other in ways they never could have on land. *Texas Carnival*, which features Howard Keel as Williams's love interest, includes a scene of Keel dreaming of Esther as she floats gracefully around his bedroom in a white negligee. For the scene, which Williams nicknamed "Howard's wet dream," footage of her swimming was superimposed into the air.[44] Robert Wernick, in his *Life* profile on Williams shortly after the film was released, wrote, "If it had been a dancer, the Breen office would have called the whole idea unthinkable: imagine, a bed. Esther being a swimmer, everything is okay."[45]

Even though MGM did occasionally receive warnings from the Breen office about wardrobing in Williams's movies, they walked the line carefully. The studio's display of half-dressed bodies was balanced with chaste plotlines and constant reminders of Williams's legitimate off-screen swimming credentials. As a result, wrote *Pageant*, "her incessant nudism is never considered indecent," just good old "honest epidermis."[46] Williams was constantly portrayed as a unique mix of wholesomeness and sexual appeal—"a cross between Lana Turner and a seal."[47] Like Kellerman, Williams's physical allure was often linked to the health and vitality she radiated as an athlete, while the display of her attractive figure was simply a natural by-product of her athletic work as a swimmer. "Esther's is a peculiarly American sex appeal," wrote Wernick, "an athletic, antiseptic, salt-flaked, out-of-doors, fun-loving kind of sex."[48]

This is likely one reason that Williams's pictures were—according to MGM—among the most requested by GIs.[49] Scholars have noted that the most popular pinups were not necessarily the most sultry or suggestive as the women in the pictures weren't viewed merely as "objects of sexual fantasy" but also as "representative women, standing in for wives and sweethearts on the home front."[50] Images that emanated the wholesome beauty soldiers associated with the girls back home—like the iconic pinup of Betty Grable in a white swimsuit and heels smiling coquettishly over her shoulder—were in highest demand. (In fact, Williams's most sought-after picture—the one enshrined as the Esther Williams Trophy—was not a swimsuit picture at all but a glamorous headshot, albeit one that showed plenty of cleavage.) A man dreaming of a Rita Hayworth or Lana Turner was liable to get in trouble, wrote Wernick in his *Life* profile. "But you take Esther Williams, you take nothing but good practical delights, a firm body, a youthful smile . . . a good clean sunny American home, happy chubby children and the invigorating roar of the sea."[51]

As Williams's stardom stretched across two wars, so did her service to the US government as a pinup girl. A World War II veteran told a newspaper decades later that he and his buddy kept a picture of Williams in their locker and greeted Williams every day as they chased German subs all over the North Pacific. "We'd say good morning to her, give her a little peck, then another one at night before we turned in."[52] When North Korea invaded South Korea in 1950, newspapers were again discussing the pinup mills and requests for "pictures of pretty girls in bathing suits" to remind them what they were fighting for—with Williams's still said to be in high demand.

THE NEW FACE OF SWIMMING

Besides GIs, Williams had another massive fan base—the growing number of women and girls practicing synchronized swimming and water ballet. Just as Annette Kellerman had been synonymous with swimming for her generation of the early 1900s, Williams became the same for young women coming of age midcentury. A newspaper in Lancaster, Pennsylvania, wrote that little girls "who aspire to be like Esther Williams, the swimming star," were flocking to synchronized swimming classes.[53] Another wrote that mothers who wanted their daughters to be the "next Esther Williams" were taking them to learn to swim. After *Bathing Beauty* came out, Helen Starr, the choreographer of the Minneapolis Aqua Follies, wrote that the movie not only demonstrated the untapped "entertainment possibilities of aquatics" but also "increased the interest and appreciation of the public as to the all around values and possibilities of swimming as a national sport."[54]

Although Williams was not a synchronized swimmer and all of her formal training had been in speed swimming, to the public watching the popularity of synchronized swimming grow alongside Williams's aquamusicals—with the first national synchronized swimming championship being held two years after *Bathing Beauty*'s release—the two became inextricably linked. "Long seen in Esther Williams movies, synchro swimming is now rated a sport by AAU," wrote one Georgia magazine.[55] Another article about the adoption of synchronized swimming into the AAU featured a picture of a competitive team floating in a formation with Williams perched on a diving board watching from above and a caption that said: "Esther Williams does this stuff in her movies."[56] In 1948, a newspaper announced that the National AAU duet champions would give an exhibition of the types of stunts and routines "introduced to the public in films starring Esther Williams" at the women's pool at Michigan State.[57] There were, however, often "real" synchronized swimmers in the aquachoruses of her movies—women who had come from water ballet groups at school or competitive synchronized swimmers who had turned professional for one of the many aquacade-style shows or to swim on-screen. These women may have introduced Williams to some of the basic stunts that she and members of her water ballets performed, such as the porpoise, backward dolphin "arch," spinning tub, pinwheel, and ballet legs. But even in the spectacularly huge water ballet numbers, Esther never swam in synch but did her "pretty swimming" as a soloist, serving as the focal point of the pattern.

And although these massive Busby Berkeley–inspired water ballets with bedazzled women floating in kaleidoscopic patterns are what often come to mind when people think of Williams's films, the swimming scenes she did underwater sometimes took even greater skill. Prior to her work in movies, Williams hadn't done much underwater swimming, pointed out *Los Angeles Times* film critic Philip Scheuer, "let alone 'danced' an entire ballet by herself" 20 feet below the surface.[58] Yet when she performed her first underwater act in *Ziegfeld Follies*, she was so at ease that the director told her to blow a few bubbles so that audiences would believe she was actually in the water and not just filmed in slow motion flying on invisible wires. Scenes like these required Williams to develop the ability not only to hold her breath for long periods but also to remain submerged in a specific spot or at a specific depth for the cameras without flailing her arms to keep from sinking or bobbing to the surface.

Some of her most deceptively difficult underwater work was performed in an animated dream sequence in *Dangerous When Wet*. In the seven-minute scene, Williams delivers a few gurgly speaking lines and swims through a lively undersea world with the cartoon cat and mouse Tom and Jerry, all the while pantomiming interactions with sea turtles and fish, outswimming a menacing swordfish, and eluding the grip of a handsy French octopus—with all the underwater characters drawn in afterward around Williams's movements. For the scene, she had to learn to do the crawl and backstroke several feet underwater. She made it look effortless, but in her autobiography she described the difficulty and challenged readers to give it a try. When doing the crawl stroke on the surface, you naturally lift your elbows, she explained. However, if you try to do that underwater, the body is propelled toward the surface. To counter the upward momentum and to stay submerged, you must point your toes downward—"an unnatural and ungainly position"—then stroke the arms laterally, which, she pointed out, requires great upper body strength. "Oh yes, don't forget that while you're doing this, you've got dialogue. And don't forget to smile!"[59] Even so, one reviewer had the nerve to write, "All Esther is ever called upon to do is fill a bathing suit attractively, swim and look pretty, dive and look pretty, smile when spoken to and look pretty."[60]

Just as her water ballets encouraged the growth of synchronized swimming, Williams's underwater scenes spurred a midcentury proliferation of underwater roadside attractions like the mermaid show at Weeki Wachee Springs, Florida. In 1947, Newt Perry, a swimmer and underwater stuntman who had trained frogmen in aquatic warfare, sunk a theater in the spring's crystal-clear waters where tourists could watch through large picture windows as girls swam and twirled, ate bananas, and drank Coca-Colas. Perry recruited his performers from a synchronized swimming club called the Aquabelles, comprised of high school students from nearby St. Petersburg, and asked them to adapt the moves they did horizontally on the surface so that they would look good performed vertically underwater. Diana McDonald, one of the original Weeki Wachee Mermaids, recalled that Esther Williams was their biggest source of inspiration. "I was just such a fan of hers it wasn't even funny," said McDonald. "We would remember different things she would do underwater and figure out how two of us could do it, then three of us."[61]

Expanded highway infrastructure and automobile travel in the first half of the century had created a demand for roadside attractions, and the underwater performance idea took off. Aquarena Springs in Texas launched a show similar to Weeki Wachee's, and soon hotels like the Hacienda in Fresno and the Marlin Beach Hotel in Fort Lauderdale were building sublevel cocktail lounges adjacent to their swimming pools, replacing the usual back bar mirrors with large glass windows looking directly into the water. The Marlin invited guests to come "two fathoms down to cocktail, dinner, and entertainment below the briny . . . with water ballets."[62] Posh nightclubs jumped on the bandwagon too with "underwater undressers" like Merma and Divena performing "aqua tease" acts—shedding down to their skivvies while swimming in tanks of water. The *Cleveland Plain Dealer* wrote, "Divena has as many curves as Hollywood's Esther Williams and doesn't hide any of them."[63]

Williams's ease and skill in the vast expanses of Technicolor blue may have made the otherwise alien world of water alluring to those watching her films, but her own work beneath the surface was full of professional hazards. She sustained at least seven broken eardrums over her career from performing high dives and staying deep below the surface for extended periods, and on more than one occasion, held her breath to the edge of hypoxic blackout. The set of *Texas Carnival* nearly became a watery coffin when Esther couldn't find the exit hatch in the underwater tank because the entire interior had been painted black so that her white negligee would show up. MGM directors seemed to see Esther as a literal mermaid, with water so much a part of her nature they never considered the dangers it could

An ad for the Marlin's cocktail lounge, one of several
midcentury attractions offering ballets below the briny.

pose, even as they expected her to perform ever riskier stunts. It was just assumed that if it was wet, Esther could do it—which was pretty much true.[64]

In *Easy to Love*, which was filmed at Florida's Cypress Gardens, Williams not only performed an aquaclown act—entertaining children with her water acrobatics while being chased by mechanical alligators—but was also the centerpiece of a waterskiing extravaganza. For the latter, she wove in and out of shifting patterns made by sixty-eight professional skiers in an intricately choreographed and precisely timed routine—all at high speeds. One would never guess by watching that she was a beginner skier—or pregnant. Busby Berkeley, who directed the film's aquatic scenes, warned Williams that if she fell, the other skiers would chop her to ribbons—that was if the needle-sharp metal bases of the water geysers hidden just under the surface didn't get her first.[65] Even so, Berkeley himself nearly drove Williams into one of the geysers when he swerved perilously close to her in a speedboat to get his shot. Williams put her foot down later when he asked her to dive from a helicopter hovering 70 feet in the air into the center of the speeding "V" of water skiers. She agreed to perform the airlift scene but not the dive. Like Kellerman, Williams took pride in performing her own stunts, and this was one of the only times she used a double.

Despite the difficulty and danger of her water scenes, or the new generation of young women who idolized her, Williams did not receive much love from the critics. *Film Daily*'s opinion that *Bathing Beauty* was "a special treat for the devotees of jive and nonsense" was typical.[66] When critics did throw her films a bone, it was usually just a passing comment about the water ballets like, "Naturally, the numbers are beautiful."[67] As for Williams, take her out of the water, wrote one reviewer, and she was just a mermaid with a "swell figure" who "has never done anything that could be called acting."[68] Or as comedian Fanny Brice (and first wife of Billy Rose) famously said, "Wet she's a star—dry she ain't."[69] *Newsweek* wondered in 1949 if Williams wasn't tired of earning "A's for anatomy, D's for drama."[70]

In fact, she *was* tired. For one thing, she was tired of film critics who, when they weren't ignoring her films, were ignoring the skill and backbreaking labor that went into making them. What was "naturally beautiful" about dangling from helicopters or "whipping down greased slides?" Williams would ask herself.[71] She was also tired of the unimaginative, rehashed, mismatched lovers' plotlines MGM churned out for her, joking that she got déjà vu whenever she read her "new" scripts. But most of all, Williams was just *plain old* tired. As a contract employee, her life and body were in constant service to the studio. She produced an average of 2.5 films a year, with production overlapping and no breaks in between, working an average of 190 hours a month on set and another 20 with MGM's publicity department.[72] Williams had three children with her second husband, Ben Gage, all during her years at the studio. Each time she got pregnant, directors asked what *she* was going to do about it, leaving it on Esther to rally the entire production team to finish the essential scenes before her pregnant belly became too difficult to conceal in a swimsuit. And, of course, it was assumed that her body would bounce right back after each delivery.

After years of asking the studio for more substantive roles, even bringing them scripts she liked only to have them given to other actresses instead, a funny thing happened in the early 1950s: Williams realized that while she may not be a critical success, her *fans* loved her movies—and that was enough. She had reached the top-ten list of MGM's most popular stars—and stayed there. And she was one of only two women among the top ten Hollywood earners. She appeared on more magazine covers than any other actress—an average of fifteen a year.[73] In 1952, the Foreign Press Association of Hollywood awarded her the World Favorite Henrietta Award based on a poll of nine hundred magazines, newspapers, and radio stations.[74] She had such widespread appeal that when the US Navy commissioned MGM to produce *Skirts Ahoy!*, a movie to help encourage recruitment for WAVES, the women's branch of the US Naval Reserves, the government specifically requested Williams to play the lead. (Incidentally, when she saw the sad, shapeless, gray regulation swimsuits female enlistees were required to wear, she convinced the Navy Secretary to make the Cole of California Esther Williams suit—in navy blue of course—the official women's swimwear of the US Navy.)[75]

Williams had, from day one at MGM, assumed her shimmer as America's mermaid was fleeting, and that her next film would be her last, but it turned out that she had tremendous staying power. So she decided to keep making her kind of movies, but to work with the writers to give them "more meaning . . . and less fluff."[76] She understood that just as audiences expected to see Fred Astaire dance, Bing Crosby sing, and Roy Rogers ride, they expected to see Esther Williams swim—but that didn't mean the swimming scenes had to be contrived.[77] "There are lots of stories available about swimmers that have substance and still would be entertaining to the fans," she told the *Los Angeles Times* in 1951.[78] In fact, she was just about to star in one—a biopic about the life of Hollywood's original swimmer, Annette Kellerman, titled *Million Dollar Mermaid*.

MGM pulled out all the stops for *Million Dollar Mermaid*, using a total of seventy-three different sets, including a reproduction of the New York Hippodrome, which had been torn down in 1939, using original blueprints.[79] Writers got the broad strokes of Kellerman's life right, though they did take liberties with the severity of the injuries she sustained when the glass tank she was swimming in shattered during the filming of *Neptune's Daughter*. They also invented a fictional love triangle between Kellerman, her husband, and the owner

One of the iconic water ballet scenes in Million Dollar Mermaid, *directed by Busby Berkeley.*

of the Hippodrome that played out next to her hospital bedside in the movie. The reproductions of Kellerman's Hippodrome shows were directed by Busby Berkeley, whose over-the-top style and directorial genius turned them into true cinematic spectacles that remain the most iconic of all of Williams's films.

In one scene, Berkeley used one hundred swimmers speeding at a "terrific pace" down 40-foot vertical slip-and-slides—the men carrying wind-sock pennants above their heads and the women sailing headfirst down the slides between the men's legs. In the background four hundred smoke pots shoot streaming clouds of red and yellow 50 feet into the air. Then comes Williams, all in red, topped with a tiara of flames, zipping down the slide on her tippy-toes smiling at the camera "as though it's Christmas, her birthday, and her honeymoon rolled into one."[80] Next, swan divers—women and men— come soaring through yellow smoke on swinging trapezes, dozens at a time. Few of the 150 women who auditioned could bring themselves to attempt the trapeze dive, with one who made the cut recalling, "It seemed awfully high."[81] Williams, naturally, had no problem and even performed a somersault off her swing. For the finale of the number, she was hoisted to the rafters while dangling by her hands from a golden ring. "I dropped her from fifty feet into the mass of swimmers below, which exploded into a ferris-wheel effect on the water," Berkeley said later in an interview. "Then they all submerged, and gradually out of the water came Esther on a platform surrounded by beautiful girls . . . an array of five hundred lighted sparklers coming out of the water and forming a background around the whole group."[82]

For another scene, Esther was lifted six stories into the air on a tiny Lucite disk just big enough to stand on as powerful geysers cascaded all around her. She was resplendent in a form-fitting hooded bodysuit covered in fifty thousand gold sequins that Williams likened to chain mail, and a gold crown. Looking down at the water and the ant-sized crew 50 feet below, she leapt from the platform, arching her body and spreading her arms into a beautiful swan dive. But as she plummeted, she had a horrifying realization—moments too late—that the crown, made of inflexible aluminum, would not allow her head to make a clean entry into the water. And unfortunately, she was right. When Williams hit the surface, her head snapped back, shooting lightning bolts of pain through her body and instantly paralyzing her arms. She had broken three vertebrae in her neck and very nearly snapped her spinal cord. Just as she had played Kellerman confined to a hospital bed from her on-the-job swimming injuries, she now found herself in the same situation. Production had to stop for six months as Williams healed inside a neck brace and full-body cast.

Million Dollar Mermaid opened at Radio City Music Hall just before Christmas in 1952 and was an instant box office sensation. The critics were kinder this time, with Margaret Bean of the *Spokesman-Review* writing that Williams "not only reaches the ultimate as an aquatic star but she shows a depth of feeling that gives real warmth to the part she plays."[83] Many expressed that it was the role Williams was born to play. Not only did Williams's professional life as a swimming champion turned swimming superstar mirror that of the woman she portrayed, but Williams had also truly taken on Kellerman's mantle as

*Swimming superstars Esther Williams and Annette Kellerman
together on the set of* Million Dollar Mermaid.

a female aquatic daredevil. "As the girl who defies tradition and convention and shocks a nation," one reviewer wrote, "Miss Williams fills the role to physical and dramatic perfection."[84]

It seemed that Williams's star was at its brightest. *Skirts Ahoy!* came out the same year, followed by *Dangerous When Wet* and *Easy to Love*, prompting *Screenland* to write after the last, "no matter how often you see Esther Williams as a water nymph, she always exudes a fresh sparkle."[85] But Hollywood is a fickle beast, and Williams's next Aquamusical, *Jupiter's Darling*, which started production in 1954, would turn out to be her last. In the film, Williams played a Greek woman promised to a Roman emperor who must swim for her life to escape capture, enabling her to do some rare on-screen speed swimming. In another scene, she breathes life into Grecian statues—played by nearly nude hunky men covered in white makeup—submerged in an underwater statuary garden. When *Jupiter's Darling* came out in early 1955, it was the first Esther Williams film that didn't make a profit. Williams blamed the cost of the film, writing that director George Sidney had been dealing with personal issues at home during production and buried himself in his work, needlessly stretching film shoots late into the evenings, prolonging production and running up costs.[86] Not just that, but he insisted on including a scene that required performing "Hollywood's biggest makeup job"—having three live elephants painted from trunk to toe in bold magentas and purples.[87] But when the film went in the red, it didn't matter how much money all of Williams's other films had made—with her name on the marquee, she was blamed. MGM executives took it as a sign that Williams's fans had abandoned her. *Time* magazine declared her a "has-been."[88]

Suddenly, for the first time in a decade, there was no talk at the studio of Williams's "next" swimming film. Plus, as she wrote in her memoir, she was now in her thirties, and "no one loves a middle-aged mermaid." But bigger factors were at play than one failed film or Williams's age. The motion-picture industry itself was in trouble. Wages remained inflated from the war, making the studios' bloated payrolls costly to maintain; plus the "Big Eight" film companies, including MGM, were reeling from a landmark antitrust Supreme Court decision that forced them to divest their studios from their lucrative theater chains. Home televisions were further nibbling away at the movie business. A review of *Million Dollar Mermaid* three years earlier had opened with, "Metro has concocted a piece of box office glitter that ought to tear everybody from their TV sets."[89] Television had only grown more popular in the intervening years, the number of American homes with televisions skyrocketing from 9 percent to 87 percent between the start and end of the 1950s.[90] And as more middle-class Americans were building backyard pools—spurred by cheaper installation, suburban white flight, and the desegregation of public facilities—these rectangles of glittering turquoise no longer held the mystique or glamour they once had. Williams's Technicolor escapes had soothed wartime audiences, but America was changing and clamoring for new types of entertainment. Movies projecting traditional, consensus-based values were losing their resonance amid the social upheaval of the 1950s and growing counterculture that would define the coming decade.

Williams had several years left on her contract with MGM and would lose almost $3 million in deferred income if she walked. But she could see the writing on the wall and found the idea of "waiting around for the crumbs" to be depressing, so she decided to leave anyway.[91] Williams had worked hard and lived frugally, even as a movie star—still using the luggage she won at a swimming competition as a teenager—but after quitting she learned that she had no financial cushion. Her husband, Ben, who would become her ex-husband in 1959, had frittered—or rather, hemorrhaged—away her wealth, losing tens of thousands at a time in the casinos or on bad investments.[92] Not only had he blown a total of $10 million, but he had taken out loans against her property and failed to pay taxes all those years, and now Williams was in debt to the IRS with a lien against her house. Williams had to keep working, so she acted in two non-swimming films with Universal Studios, launched her own aboveground pool company, and even produced a one-off water show called the "Esther Williams Aqua Spectacle of 1956" at the Empire Pool in Wembley, London, with plans to take the show elsewhere. But for Williams's fans—who were used to seeing her up close on a 40-foot screen surrounded by

Technicolor blue—squinting at a tennis ball–sized version of their star from way up in the stands proved to be a disappointing substitute, and the show flopped.[93]

In 1960, a year after her divorce, Esther made her last big public appearance as a swimmer in the televised special "Esther Williams at Cypress Gardens." She recruited Fernando Lamas, her handsome costar from *Dangerous When Wet*, to perform in the show with her. The two had exchanged steamy flirtations years earlier, and when they reunited at Cypress Gardens, a romance was kindled. Lamas offered her a blunt and unusual proposition: stop being Esther Williams. Leave behind her identity as a glamorous swimming star and become instead Mrs. Fernando Lamas, the doting and dedicated housewife. Surprisingly—or perhaps unsurprisingly given how long she had had to project a certain image of "Esther Williams" to the public—Williams agreed. She became Mrs. Fernando Lamas, writing in her memoir that she spent the next twenty-two years (until Lamas's death in 1982) "tethered" and catering to her third husband's growing demands, including estranging herself from her children.[94] For more than two decades, she completely disappeared from the public, declining countless interviews, and telling one journalist, "I buried Esther Williams."[95] Because of her seclusion, and because she didn't "rot in public"—a phrase Katharine Hepburn used for actors who age in front of the TV cameras—she was instead flash frozen in the public's imagination, forever young, as America's mermaid. And with no more aquamusicals having been made since her last one, the genre she helped create has remained uniquely her own.

The Esther Williams Trophy was decommissioned in 1957 and put on display at the Royal Australian Navy Heritage Centre at Spectacle Island. Williams had long been aware of its existence and the battles for her "honor," receiving updates over the years from sailors about her picture's whereabouts, and often telegramming her congratulations to victors. "Glad to hear my picture is in such good hands," she wrote in one. "Wish I could visit you, but I'm carrying a stowaway at the moment . . . Maybe I'll be in shipshape next time you're in port."[96] Even though the trophy was retired by the Royal Australian Navy only a few years after Williams's Aquamusical career ended, the decision had nothing to do with waning interest in Williams, or her prized likeness—quite the opposite. It was retired out of concern for the safety of naval officers who were staging increasingly risky heists in the effort to win it. "The Esther" had been airlifted off flight decks, heisted off ships via high line, and skulked away by scuba swimmers under cover of night. Chemical alarms had been sounded and smoke bombs detonated to create chaos ahead of a theft attempt. At least one such incident had ended with several men hospitalized.[97] Her trophy had even witnessed history, hitching a ride aboard the HMAS *Nizam* shortly before it became the first Australian ship to enter Tokyo Bay for the surrender of Japan.[98]

Shortly after the Trophy was decommissioned, an American naval officer predicted that its retirement was likely temporary. "Esther" had always returned to her loyal fans, he wrote, so there was no telling where she might turn up next.[99] His words proved to be true—of both Esther the Trophy and Esther the swimming star. When Williams "buried" that side of herself, she couldn't have imagined that it would be resurrected, by popular demand, and given a second life—but that's exactly what happened. When synchronized swimming made its debut as an Olympic sport exactly forty years after *Bathing Beauty*'s release, Williams would come out of seclusion to serve as its television spokesperson. No longer "tethered," she would reunite with her children, and marry again—this time happily and for keeps. She would reap the benefits of the name she built and the swimsuits she helped design, launching the Esther Williams Swimsuit Company. She would be recognized for her role in popularizing the sport of synchronized swimming and a whole new generation would be introduced to her aquamusicals.

This resilience was characteristic of Williams, who modeled female strength both on-screen and in real life. "Of course she was so beautiful . . . but that was an era of beautiful women in films," said her fourth husband and widower, Edward Bell. "What attracted women so much to her was that she was never a victim. She always came out on top, rising up on top of the pylon."[100]

Even her trophy made a comeback. In 1997, the Esther Williams Trophy was heisted right off of Spectacle Island, with the naval battles for her honor resuming among men born long after she made her last film. The trophy remained in active commission until her death in 2013, when the Australian Royal Navy issued the following ship-to-ship communication: "In light of her final request, the Esther Williams trophy is, after a final decommissioning voyage, to be laid to rest as a mark of respect to the lady who gave it life."[101]

CHAPTER 10

SWIMMING SYNCHRONIZED

Is it art? Beauty? Show-business? Or what? . . . It's swimming, isn't it? And the kids are nuts about it.

—SPORTFOLIO, 1948

"**J** ust imagine having the lung power of a long-distance runner, the leg strength of a water polo player in order to get those lifts out of the water, the grace and rhythm of a ballet dancer working to music, a gymnast performing a whole floor exercise underwater holding your breath," Esther Williams told millions of television viewers tuning in from around the world. "And then you add to that, that she must do this all in perfect synchronization with her partner, and that's synchronized swimming."[1]

It was the debut of synchronized swimming as a brand-new Olympic sport at the 1984 Summer Games in Los Angeles. And there was Esther Williams, synchronized swimming personified—at least to many who were watching—front and center with the Los Angeles Olympic Swim Stadium as her backdrop. The ABC network had tapped Williams, now in her early sixties, alongside sportscaster and Olympic gold medalist swimmer Donna de Varona, to serve as an expert commentator for the televised coverage of the inaugural events. The network was touting Williams as the godmother to the sport, the start of it all, and airing clips from her MGM aquamusicals any time they needed a segue into synchronized swimming. Williams had been out of the public eye for more than two decades and no doubt some nostalgic television viewers had tuned in just to see Hollywood's glamorous swimmer in front of the cameras again.

But for those within the world of synchronized swimming who were anxious to demonstrate the athleticism of their sport and to celebrate its hard-won acceptance into the Olympic pantheon, their feelings were more complicated. Williams had helped kick-start the popularity of synchronized swimming in its early years and, in turn, had been embraced by its practitioners—for a while at least. She had been welcomed at early synchronized swimming competitions, with newspapers noting in 1948 that Miss Williams had been invited as a guest of honor at the AAU national synchronized swimming meet in

Des Moines and that she promised to attend if her production schedule permitted. Four years later, she was invited to serve as a judge. And after Williams introduced a new generation to *her* predecessor, Annette Kellerman, through the movie *Million Dollar Mermaid*, Kellerman had been embraced as well, even giving out the awards at the 1954 national synchronized swimming championship.

But that was a long time ago, and synchronized swimming had since moved on and forged its own path. Its practitioners, wanting to be seen not as swimming showgirls but as athletes, had intentionally distanced themselves from their beloved predecessors of the stage and screen and, over the years, increasingly left behind the world of showbiz to align themselves instead with the world of sport. The path had been long and against the current, but they had finally made it and were eager to show the world not what synchronized swimming once was, but what it had become.

Following the success of the first AAU National Synchronized Swimming Championship in 1946—fittingly held in Chicago, where the sport was born, named, and nurtured—the AAU began holding two championships per year, one indoors and one outdoors. With the locations of the championships rotating to different cities across the country, interest in competition quickly spread beyond the Midwest. Because of the coinciding popularity of professional aquacade-style shows, Williams's aquamusicals, and school water pageants, the AAU decided early on to be consistent and use "synchronized swimming" to distinguish the competitive sport from these performance styles. However, the distinction between sport and show would prove to be harder to distill—to those both inside and outside the world of "synchro." This was especially true early on when most of the top teams had emerged from groups founded specifically for entertainment purposes. The Dolphinettes, who won the indoor championship in 1947, were sponsored by the Deauville-McFadden Hotel in Miami Beach (where Aileen Riggin had been a performer when it was called the Deauville Hotel and Casino) and had performed for tourists under the coaching of show producer and Olympic diving champion Pete Desjardins. The St. Clair Synchronettes, who won their first of several national titles in 1948, were founded by Detroit's

Department of Parks and Recreation in the 1930s to put on community water pageants and later evolved into a competitive synchronized swimming club under the coaching of Rose Watson, a former performer in Billy Rose's Aquacades.[2] The Athens Water Follies Club, which would become the reigning champions for most of the 1950s, grew out of the San Francisco Water Follies, a water show group based at the swanky Fairmont San Francisco before the Second World War.

Although the trappings of pageantry and show business would remain for quite some time, the 1950s marked the shift in a new direction and—spurred by new technologies, improved communication, and international collaboration and growth—became a key decade of evolution for the sport. One of the most important early innovations was the introduction of underwater speakers. The Chicago Lake Shore Club, one of the earliest competitve synchro teams, in the 1940s improvised their own underwater sound equipment using a set of speakers they sealed inside coffee cans, connected to the record player on deck, then sunk to the pool floor. They worked surprisingly well, but for most teams, until waterproof speakers became commercially available, there was only silence below the surface. As a result, routines were typically choreographed so that each new action started at the beginning of a phrase of music, enabling swimmers to "catch" the beat when they surfaced before starting the next move.[3] This required using music with a consistent tempo—no symphonic orchestras or classical music.[4] As the use of underwater speakers spread (they made their first appearance at a national competition in 1954), not only did synchronization improve, but with the filler time between moves removed, individual stunts no longer "stuck out like a sore thumb" and routines became tighter and smoother.[5]

Even with underwater sound, however, achieving synchronization still required that swimmers all know when to do what. For those with musical inclinations, that meant (and still does) counting in their heads, but for others, it meant squealing, screaming, or beeping to signal to one another underwater. Dawn Bean, who joined the Athens Club after seeing Billy Rose's Aquacade in San Francisco, had learned to count music from her mother. It was a skill she and her two sisters (who later joined the team) so easily applied to synchronized swimming they didn't realize until attending their first national championship that other groups weren't doing the same. "We heard all these grunts underwater and we were astounded," said Bean. *Sports Illustrated* commented on these underwater vocalizations as well, noting that some teams called them "blubs" and the swimmers designated to make them the "blubbers."[6]

But even the best-laid plans of the musically inclined could be foiled by uncooperative technology. Records were usually played at a standard 78 rpm, but turntables were unpredictable and speeds could be affected by the machine's settings, the voltage used, or even whether or not the motor was warmed up.[7] Sometimes at meets, a team would realize too late that their music was playing faster than usual and they would suddenly have to speed up their swimming. Once, at a performance in Tokyo, the Athens Club had to "improvise a slow-motion Can-Can" when their American record player, set for sixty-cycle AC, was plugged in to the fifty-cycle Japanese current.[8] After a few such incidents, stroboscopes were used at meets to calibrate record speeds and play them at precisely the desired tempo.

A much humbler piece of equipment had an equally large impact on the sport's development: the Laxto nose clip. Although pearl divers had long worn nose pincers carved from bone, and some scientific swimmers in the 1800s crafted similar ones out of vulcanite to wear during their "subaqueous turnings," the options for synchronized swimmers

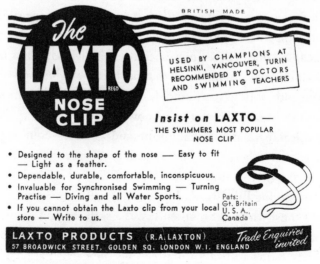

A little piece of equipment that propelled a sport.

in the early years left much to be desired.[9] Those wishing to keep water out of their noses could either tape their nostrils shut with waterproof adhesive or use nose "plugs"—large rubber clamps that stretched across the nose and were held in place with head straps—but the former was only mildly effective and the latter was so unattractive that most synchronized swimmers preferred to let their noses go commando. They would instead exhale strategically when upside down or adapt techniques like curling back the upper lip to seal off the nostrils or applying pressure in the back of the throat to trap air in the nasal passageways. So when the discreet yet effective Laxto was invented by a British swim coach, it was revolutionary. It was made of thin wire coated in rubber and featured a bridge that went under rather than across the nose and stayed in place on its own—at last providing an inconspicuous way to keep water out of one's nose. At just 75¢ apiece, the Laxto quickly became the "prized possession" of every synchronized swimmer.[10]

Able to go underwater with their noses protected, synchronized swimmers were soon doing so many upside-down stunts that speed swimmers started referring to them as "bottoms up" swimmers. "New stunts were being added almost as quickly as competitors could dream them up," wrote Dawn Bean in her book on the history of synchronized swimming.[11] Jean Henning, who swam with the Chicago Lake Shore Club, recalled accidentally inventing a new stunt at practice when she unconsciously moved from a ballet leg directly into a dolphin. "Thus a new stunt, Ballet Leg Dolphin, was born."[12] New publications were popping up to capture and disseminate information about developments in the sport, including books like *Beginning Synchronized Swimming*, published by Betty Spears in 1950, and *Synchronized Swimming* by Fern Yates and Theresa Anderson the following year. All three were physical educators—at Wellesley, Barnard, and an Iowa high school, respectively. The AAU Synchronized Swimming Committee also launched a newsletter, "The Synchronized Swimmer," which was mimeographed and mailed out to members.

Information was also flowing between the United States and its northern neighbor. Canada had continued holding stunts competitions since launching its national championship in the Art of Graceful and Scientific Swimming in 1925. As the popularity of swimming to music spread in the US, the Canadians began adding music to their individual stunt competitions, launching the idea of a "solo" routine. A Montreal newspaper gave Esther Williams part of the credit for spurring interest, writing shortly after: "the average Canadian's knowledge of synchronized swimming took an upcurve" thanks to Williams's underwater solo in *Ziegfeld Follies*.[13] The two countries opened their competitions to one another's swimmers, and Canada's first solo championship in 1948 was won by an American, Beulah Gundling. Since synchro competitions first began in the United States the AAU had only offered team and duet events, but in 1950 the US followed Canada's lead and added solos to its competitions; Canada, at America's influence, added duets and teams the same year.[14]

The AAU debuted the solo event at the 1950 championship, held in Lake Michigan as part of the Chicago Railroad Fair. It had stormed the day before the competition, and the water was choppy, murky, and littered with debris. "I remember seeing a slice of bread floating by," wrote soloist Beulah Gundling. "After one figure I came up with weeds dangling over my tiara and stringing onto my face."[15] Nonetheless, Gundling managed to win first place, her first of several national solo titles. Even though the lake venue had been a disaster—and was the last time a national championship was held in a natural body of water—the addition of the solo category proved to be a boon for the sport. With solo options, swimmers who didn't live near a team or couldn't find a duet partner could still become part of the competitive sport. Moreover, the rules for solos were less restrictive, with no compulsory stunts or strokes, which enabled the swimmer to focus on artistry and showmanship.[16] The solo competition quickly became the most popular event at the national championships, often with double or triple the number of entries as team and duet routines. The concept of synchronized swimming alone, however, would long be a source of confusion and jokes for the media—*Who are they synchronizing with?*—but it was simple. The synchronization was with the music.

With successful collaborations happening across the border and two annual championships being held at home, synchronized swimming leaders at the AAU began to think about greater international expansion. They arranged to present synchronized swimming as a demonstration sport at the 1952 Olympics in Helsinki, with Gundling

St. Clair Synchronettes swimmers Connie Todoroff, Shirley Simpson, Laurine Stocking, and Ellen Richard at the 1952 Helsinki Olympics, where they debuted synchronized swimming as an exhibition sport.

selected as the featured soloist and team and duet routines performed by the St. Clair Synchronettes. Katharine Curtis, who was still working abroad with the Red Cross, traveled to Finland to see the sport she helped establish make its world debut. Curtis called the delegation a "grand group of girls [who] swam like real 'synchro kids'" and reported that their performances were seen at the closing aquatic gala by fifty thousand captivated spectators, including officials from FINA (the international swimming federation) and the International Olympic Committee (IOC), as well as foreign swim teams and coaches.[17] Norma Olsen, the incoming chair of the AAU Synchronized Swimming Committee, took advantage of the warm reception to corner Avery Brundage, the newly appointed president of the IOC, to broach the topic of accepting synchronized swimming as a competitive Olympic event. But Brundage—the same one who had kicked Eleanor Holm off the 1936 Olympic team—told her he didn't want any new Olympic sports that required judges. For many, if it didn't involve a stopwatch or a finish line, it wasn't a real sport.

But even back home, the question of whether synchro was a "real" sport—or whether that was even what its practitioners wanted—had yet to be resolved. As a carryover from the sport's water pageant origins, "themes" were an important part of synchronized swimming, and every routine was supposed to interpret a story or idea, not only through the swimming but also through the music, costumes, and "entrance"—the actions performed on deck before diving in. Some routines even had "backstories" that were read aloud to the audience and judges.

Themes were highly elaborate and creative, as demonstrated by the 1952 AAU National Championship–winning routine, "Four Queens of Wonderland," which was performed by the Athens Club and marked the first time a team from the West Coast won a national title. In the routine, each of the four swimmers represented a different queen from a deck of cards and wore a swimsuit decorated with either a club, heart, diamond, or spade, each of which required three to four

Athens Team swimmers Joan and Lynn Pawson, Dawn Bean, and Sally Phillips in costume for their 1952 national championship "Four Queens" routine.

thousand sequins. They topped their costumes with white wigs meant for would-be Santas that they found in a clearance bin after Christmas and attached to swim caps. For their entry, they built large wooden plaques and painted them to look like playing cards; each swimmer posed in front of the appropriate plaque, standing perfectly still as if she was the queen on her card. Once the music began, the queens came to life, stepping forward one by one before all diving in together and performing stunts and movements in the water meant to depict cutting and shuffling a deck and spreading a hand. "We had what are now outrageous costumes, but that was all part of it," recalled Dawn Bean, who swam as the Queen of Clubs. "It was 'What will I be? What will I wear?' That was synchro in the early days."[18]

The *San Francisco Examiner* wrote that when the Athens Club developed another routine, titled "Sacrificial Dance of the Aztecs," "the girls invaded the research library at the University of California to reproduce authentic costumes and rituals." When they discovered that the Aztecs used obsidian stone rather than steel, they painted their prop knives black.[19] Gundling even worked with a private dance coach to create arm movements in the water that adopted authentic styles of dance from East India for her "Surya" ("the sun") routine. For one international event, Gundling wrote in her memoir that she wanted to create a uniquely American routine for the international crowd. "What do people in other countries think of when America is mentioned?" wrote Gundling. "Cowboys and Indians," of course! She settled on the latter, creating movements in the water to mimic birds, thunder, and lightning for her Native American "Thunderbird" routine.[20] She topped her fringed swimsuit with a wig of long black braids, a headdress, and a few stripes of "war paint" on her face.

With so much effort put into their flamboyant costumes, one newspaper likened synchronized swimmers to "mermaids with sewing machines," and quoted one competitor as saying, "If you can't sew, you might as well not swim."[21] But of course for non-sewing swimmers, plain leotards, gloves, and swim caps could be transformed into just about anything with some imagination, paint, glue, and the endless array of sequins, bugle beads, spangles, tinsel fringe, plastic ruffles, and flowers available for purchase. It seems at times, though, that enthusiastic costume designers forgot they would have to actually swim in them. One swimmer who didn't test her gangster moll costume in the water before a competition learned too late that she had used too much dye when the pool water turned blood-red.[22] Another, who competed on a YWCA team, recalled the difficulty of swimming in clown costumes: "We had imitation bald heads with wool yarn on the side for hair," she said. "When that yarn got wet, it felt like we were swimming with 20 pounds on our head."[23] Props of all types and sizes—from fans to hobbyhorses to bows and arrows—completed the look. But these were typically used only at the start of the routine, and abandoned props floating in the water became such a distraction that competition rules began specifying that any discarded items must be weighted so they would sink. Likewise, removing garments before swimming, like Gundling's detachable tutu or the long, tiered skirt she wore for the deck portion of her Spanish "Espanolerias" routine, had to be done with good effect and not look sloppy.[24]

Themes and costumes may have been fun for swimmers and great for spectator appeal, but to editors of sports pages, swimmers in Santa wigs hardly looked like athletes, and the pageantry was creating serious barriers to gaining recognition as a sport. The *San Francisco Examiner* wrote: "With the music and the colorful costumes a synchronized swimming meet often appears more like a Bimbo revue than a grueling athletic contest."[25] Although it could have been a coup when *Sports Illustrated* sent a reporter to cover the 1954 championships, he left with visions of Billy Rose's Aquacade, writing that synchronized swimmers used "exactly the same kind of contortions which are employed by the chorus mermaids in aquatic shows," but they "costume themselves, if possible, even more gaudily."[26] When the Athens Club was invited, as the reigning national champions, to give a demonstration at the 1956 Olympics in Melbourne, the audience's reaction provided a clear illustration to leaders of the sport of the impression the costuming was giving. Following the marathon 1500-meter race, the synchro swimmers walked out in bedecked suits and feathered headdresses for their "Dance of the Eagles" routine. "The other athletes, watching the spectacle, shook their heads and wondered what the Olympics were coming to," wrote the *San Francisco Examiner*.[27] Calls of "Cock-a-doodle-doo" started mounting from the stands. "We were immediately told to have them remove all the glitter and feathers and appear in plain swimming suits and caps," wrote the group's chaperone Theresa Anderson.

For the next performance they did just that and received "tremendous ovations."[28] As Bean later said, "We had to develop the techniques and the skills to really make the sport look acceptable, and we were not ready for the Olympics. To be a sport, you have to look like a sport."[29]

Some in the synchro community who were looking for a way to rein in the theatrics believed that the sport's rules, which had not had a major overhaul since they were first written, were part of the problem. On the one hand, the rules were too abstract, leaving the scoring of categories like composition and showmanship to the discretion of the judges, and their own personal tastes and biases. But on the other, they were also too restrictive, as they channeled all routines toward the same handful of stunts with high difficulty point values. Teams who didn't load their routines with the hardest stunts didn't stand a chance of winning, but that meant everyone's routines were looking more and more alike—mere demonstrations of the same stunts over and over.

WOMEN'S SENIOR NATIONAL OUTDOOR A.A.U.
SYNCHRONIZED SWIMMING CHAMPIONSHIPS
HOUSTON, TEXAS   10c   JULY 29-30-31, 1955

The program for the 1955 AAU Synchronized Swimming Championships hints at the pageantry that was part of the early competitive sport.

With routines becoming increasingly cookie-cutter, swimmers in turn ramped up the costuming and themes as a way to make themselves stand out. As a result, no one knew what to make of synchronized swimming. "Is it art? Beauty? Show-business? Or what?" asked one magazine. "The AAU swimming promoters shrug their shoulders. It's swimming, isn't it?"[30]

But in 1953, the AAU decided to stop shrugging its shoulders and appointed a committee to study and revise the rules. In their first report, committee chair Ross Bean, Dawn Bean's husband, who was active in the sport's administration, wrote that synchronized swimming needed to decide whether it wanted to be "a pure art" with no rules, or a "pure sport" based on clear, objective parameters for evaluating physical skill—or a compromise in between. The committee aimed for a compromise, drafting rules they hoped would give swimmers some creative flexibility while also ensuring a certain level of technical proficiency. They proposed capping the maximum difficulty score to disincentivize swimmers from bulking up their routines with the hardest stunts, but balanced that with a new requirement that every competitor would have to perform six stunts—individually and not with music—to encourage proper form and execution.[31] Each competitor's individual stunt score would be added to their solo or group routine scores. Moreover, the committee reduced the judging to two basic scoring categories—Execution and Style, each worth a possible ten points—with the hopes that simplifying the scoring would help the sport spread internationally.[32] They proposed applying the rules equally across all events—team, duet, and solo—the last of which had long enjoyed minimal rules and an exemption from the stunt requirement in routines, which some believed enabled soloists to rely on presentation as much as skill.

The new rules were implemented at the AAU convention that year. However, the depth of the divide between the pure art and pure sport folks quickly became apparent as a "hot war" played out on the editorial pages of "The Synchronized Swimmer" newsletter. One argued that moving away from show business "shenanigans" would help get synchro meets onto the sports pages, while another pointed out that there was nothing athletic about having to interpret a theme through costumes and makeup.[33] But for others, it was apparent that the pageantry was part of what they loved most, with one writing to

Beulah Gundling swimming her 1951 AAU national solo championship routine "Surya."

say that not only the costumes but also synchro's application of dance and dramatic action, all came together to "spell ART," and she wanted to keep it that way.³⁴ The latter sentiment was especially true for the soloists. Soon after the new rules passed, solo champion Beulah Gundling left the AAU and formed a new organization—the International Academy of Aquatic Art (IAAA). In lieu of competitions, the IAAA began, in 1955, to hold festivals where "aquatic compositions" were awarded merit levels instead of scores and there were no rules about stunts, costumes, or anything else. Moreover, men and women could freely swim with one another—something that had been disallowed ever since the AAU split them into separate categories. The IAAA was successful in attracting a large number of swimmers and for several years had more registered members than the AAU had registered synchronized swimmers.³⁵ But that was just as well with AAU leaders because, with the most ardent members of the "art" camp gone, they were free to push ahead with what was becoming their ultimate goal—inclusion in the Olympics.

Even though IOC president Avery Brundage had given synchronized swimming the cold shoulder at its first Olympic demonstration in 1952, the exposure in Helsinki had yielded other tangible results. FINA had soon after added synchronized swimming as one of its aquatic sports and formed a committee to draft rules for international competition. In 1955, FINA included synchronized swimming as a competitive event at the second Pan American Games, held in Mexico City. Although only three countries—the US, Canada, and Mexico—sent synchro teams and the Americans won everything, it was the first truly international competition. With rules in place and the first international competition proving to be a success, the next step for the synchro community was spreading the sport and creating a body of international competitors with whom to compete. Before long, delegations of champion swimmers were circling the globe, giving exhibitions and hosting teaching clinics on every continent.

In 1954, the US Department of State sponsored the first of several goodwill tours to the "far east," sending AAU Synchronized Swimming chair Norma Olsen and swimmers from the Athens Club as sports ambassadors to Japan and Korea. In addition to working with local swimmers, they put on aquacade-style shows for US servicemembers stationed in the Pacific. These tours became an annual event, continuing through 1961, and expanded to include Okinawa, the Philippines, Guam, and Hawaii. In 1956, the AAU Synchronized Swimming Committee and the US State Department's International Educational Exchange Service arranged an ambitious sixty-day "around-the-world tour" of twelve countries. Champion divers and synchronized swimmers from several top teams in the US visited England, Italy, Denmark, Sweden, Holland, Switzerland, Egypt, Pakistan, India, Malaysia, and New Zealand, and ended in Australia for ten days of performances at the Melbourne Olympics.[36] The delegation planned to spend a week in Cairo, but shortly after arriving, the Suez Crisis erupted and the swimmers had to be evacuated, along with other American civilians, on a US Navy destroyer headed to Naples, but not before they witnessed a British plane get shot down and crash into the Alexandria harbor.[37] International federations soon began reaching out to North American synchro leaders requesting visits from traveling delegations. At the invitation of the British Amateur Swimming Association, Beulah Gundling and Peg Seller (née Shearer), Canada's first ornamental swimming champion, toured England and Wales, giving demonstrations and clinics. The BBC televised one of the performances, helping bring tremendous attention and large audiences to the events.

In the majority of places these groups visited, the local public had never seen anything like synchronized swimming. Following a performance by the Athens Club in Hong Kong, a local newspaper wrote that the aquatic-minded of the city discovered that "we are a one-horse town" and reported that fifteen hundred spectators "sat through drenching showers to learn with mounting incredulity that there are many things besides swim one can do in the water."[38] Although American-style synchronized swimming was new to other countries at first, some had already been doing related forms of swimming, such as picture floats or stunts, and when touring teams encountered these local practitioners, they would invite their groups to perform or offer them lessons. In Hobart, Tasmania, Gundling was joined by the Royal Life Saving Ballet and was amazed at their "scientific swimming." Their repertoire included a waltz crawl and stunts that were known in synchro circles as the washing tub, spinning top, and canoe. Gundling's husband wrote in his report of the trip, "It was evident that a number of our present day synchronized swimming figures came from this section of the Royal Life handbook."[39]

Japanese swimmers, with their rich aquatic traditions focusing on form and control, were among the earliest and most enthusiastic adopters of synchronized swimming, with fifteen thousand spectators filling the stadium of Tokyo's Meiji Pool for a performance by American swimmers during the first "far east" tour. The AAU and the Japanese Swimming Federation arranged, starting in 1956, an annual Japanese-American synchronized swimming championship in Osaka, with multiple competitors joining from both countries. Even though the American swimmers won the earliest competitions, one wrote in 1958 that the Japanese were making rapid progress. "I caution any reader not to underestimate the Japanese synchronized swimmers. The margin of superiority was small, indeed." She predicted—quite accurately—that the Japanese "will undoubtedly press the United States for top honors when international competition becomes more widespread."[40]

In less than a decade, synchronized swimming had been demonstrated in much of Asia, all over Central and South America, and in every country in Western Europe, including stops at the 1958 Brussels World's Fair and at the Rome Olympics in 1960. A second round-the-world tour had added Syria, Thailand, Singapore, Hong Kong, and Formosa (now Taiwan) to the list. More importantly, the tours were having their intended effect of inspiring swimmers around the world to take up the sport. George Rackham, coach of a British diving school, credited seeing "how polished and technically perfect the United State[s] teams were" with inspiring England's participation as one of nine countries competing in the first European Festival of Synchronized Swimming, held in the Netherlands in 1958.[41] That same year, Norma Olsen wrote that thanks to synchro's "graceful ambassadors" the sport was booming, adding that she had received requests for information from Czechoslovakia, Australia, and South Africa in the past week alone.[42] Synchro had reached the farthest outposts of America as well, Olsen pointed out, citing a letter from a midwestern farmgirl who had been practicing her "Milk Maid" routine in a prairie pond using a windup phonograph for music.[43] The *Saturday Evening Post* wrote in 1955 that there were around twenty thousand active "devotees" of synchronized swimming, while *Sports Illustrated* put the number at twenty-five thousand the following year.[44]

With such progress and enthusiasm at home and abroad, those in the sport naturally felt they were coming close to achieving their Olympic dream. Olsen reported in 1960 that delegates would be making a European tour ahead of the Rome Olympics with the goal of coordinating a plan for synchro's inclusion in the 1964 Olympic Games.[45] But every time the topic was broached, Brundage dismissed synchronized swimming as "aquatic vaudeville" and maintained: "It's not sport. It's show biz."[46] Esther Williams herself interceded but relayed later in a documentary that Brundage told her, "I don't want to hear any more about it. Synchronized swimming is not a sport, it's Esther Williams." Taken aback, Williams responded, "My gosh, you make my name sound like a swear word.'"[47]

In short, male leaders at the IOC—which the *Sunday Times* of London referred to as the "self-appointed guardians of Olympic values"—wanted absolutely nothing to do with synchronized swimming.[48] Javier Ostos, who served two terms as FINA president, later wrote that IOC president Brundage and vice president José de Clark Flores were both "ardent foes of synchronized swimming all their lives, looking upon it as a frivolous attraction that had nothing to do with technique or sport."[49] Brundage may have objected on the basis of synchro's connection to performance, but the fact that it was a "women's sport" was likely part of his hang-up, even if never stated. He was from the old school of male sport gatekeepers who hadn't wanted women in the Olympics in the first place. In his prior role as IOC vice president, Brundage told a newspaper that perhaps the ancient Greeks were right to ban women from even *watching* the Olympic games. As late as 1953, he suggested removing all women's events from the Olympics as a way to cut costs—calling their exclusion "as good a starting point as any."[50]

ON THE BASIS OF SEX

Although synchronized swimming was not officially a women's sport and men had not been formally excluded, their participation had taken a major hit from the get-go when the AAU adopted synchronized swimming in 1940 and separated men and women into their own categories. There seemed to be little interest in starting all-male teams, which left only solos and duets for male competitors—of which there were not very many. Bert Hubbard, who won the duet event with his swimming partner Lee Embrey at the first and last AAU Junior National Men's Championships in 1949 and 1954 ("juniors" was a category for developmental or novice swimmers), made an appeal to the synchro community in his 1953 letter to "The Synchronized Swimmer" for the addition of mixed (male-female) duets, as he believed that would spur renewed interest among men. But the AAU wouldn't budge on allowing men and women to compete in the same categories, and with so few competitors entering the male only events, organizations were reluctant to sponsor men's competitions and the last national-level AAU synchronized swimming championship for men was held in 1955.[51]

Part of the reason for the lack of interest on the part of men was that synchronized swimming had come to be seen as a feminine

*Bert Hubbard in costume for his winning "Viking's Prayer Before Battle"
solo routine at the 1954 AAU Men's Junior National Championships.*

activity. The foundational movements of synchronized swimming
had, of course, originated with men and been practiced by Everard
Digby, Benjamin Franklin, and the swimming professors as a way to
demonstrate their aquatic prowess. But once their "scientific swimming" stunts became the building blocks of group swimming to
music, they became associated not with manly exercises but with water
ballet—with an emphasis on the *ballet.* Digby's "swimming with leg
aloft" had been called different nautical names over the years, like
the "periscope," "submarine," "steamer," "cutter," and "mast," with
illustrations of the move featuring bent-knee, flexed-footed men.
Then Annette Kellerman's book came along and depicted a woman
performing the move with a straight leg and elegantly pointed toes,
and by the 1940s it was being referred to as the "ballet leg." Soon, the
move became "the trademark of feminine Synchronized Swimming,"

wrote Beulah Gundling, and as a result was seen as "too feminine for men."[52]

One man wrote to *Synchro-Info* in 1964 to say he found it "very improper" for boys to participate in synchronized swimming since it is "ballet with water applied." He pointed out that Webster's dictionary defined ballet as a theatrical dance by a group, "especially of women," and called for the sport to be kept for girls only.[53] Even as early as the late 1940s, when national championships were just getting started, an article noted, "the males seem to consider it a sissy sport and sulk in the locker room when the coach calls for water ballet routines."[54] These associations only grew stronger as the aquacades, water shows, and Esther Williams's movies created and solidified an association between synchronized swimming and showgirl entertainment.

The view of synchronized swimming as a "feminine" sport may have pushed men out, but it also served to attract women who might not otherwise have been drawn to competitive sports in the midcentury. Ross Bean wrote in 1953 that synchronized swimming had provided "an outlet for many feminine swimmers more in keeping with their desires for femininity than straight racing."[55] Indeed, compared to synchro, with its choruses of smiling women, regular swimming had started to look almost masculine. A British newspaper wrote, "One of the great assets of the sport is that it teaches girls deportment. They don't, however, develop the big muscles of the champion swimmers because of the variety of activities in their training, including dancing."[56] A swimmer wrote to *Synchro-Info* to say that the pictures the newsletter published of female synchro competitors at meets helped "to convince anxious mothers that the sport does not develop masculine type girls."[57]

While competitive synchronized swimming under the AAU was thriving outside of schools, within the world of education it had continued to flourish instead as a recreational club activity. A survey of 634 colleges and universities in 1953 found that 41 percent—nearly all of the schools that had swimming pools—offered synchronized swimming. Swim clubs remained the women's alternative to competitive swimming, and as Barbara Heller at University of California, Davis, wrote, "the primary objective of a swimming club" is usually "the synchronized swimming production, aquacade, or water show."[58] At Queens College, the Dolphin synchro club was formed, according to an instructor there, after teachers were inundated by "followers of competitive speed swimming."[59] However, just as the female natationists had performed at men's competitive galas a century earlier, women's synchro clubs often provided entertainment at men's swim meets. Coaches didn't mind, as the girls' performances helped pull bigger crowds. "Let's face it," said Norma Olsen in 1948, "Swimming meets of the past didn't draw anyone . . . but with the showmanship and pretty girls in brilliant costumes of synchronized swimming, you've got a talking point."[60]

Another reason the popularity of synchronized swimming soared in schools was that in many places it was one of the few athletic options for women. When Kate Scanlan enrolled at Grinnell College in the early 60s, the school offered no varsity sports for women, so she joined the White Caps synchro club. "We had a ball, but we worked really hard," she said. "Some of it is difficult."[61] For her clubmate Connie Sloop Archea, who had competed on her high school swim team, synchronized swimming was not what she would have chosen if there had been other opportunities, but rather a "consolation prize" for no longer getting to compete as a swimmer. Once, when she was swimming in the pool, the coach for Grinnell's men's varsity team pointed out her good form, telling his swimmers that her freestyle technique was exactly what the stroke should look like. "At the time I took it as a compliment," Archea recalled, "and only later realized the irony of a woman who didn't have the opportunity to swim competitively demonstrating a stroke to those who did."[62]

Of course, some school synchro clubs did want to compete and a number of club-organized, invitational meets were held, such as one at the University of Illinois in 1952 that drew competitors from twelve schools. However, whenever the question of starting interschool synchronized swimming competitions was raised to the American Association for Health, Physical Education and Recreation, which set the standards followed by many schools, they said no. In the 1953 article "Should Synchronized Swimming Be Competitive?," Prudence Fleming of Temple University explained that the women's section of the association had decided two years earlier not to recommend synchronized swimming as a competitive interschool sport because "competitive synchronized swimming eliminates all but the best swimmers," demonstrating a continued emphasis on "sport for all" in women's physical education.[63] She noted that even though teachers and coaches had continued requesting this type of competition for girls, the association stood by its earlier decision. The article cited Norma Olsen at the AAU, who was already pushing for Olympic inclusion and had a different opinion. "Although it is wonderful to compete for the joy and health giving qualities," said Olsen, "it is only through competition that we attain our greatest perfection."

But even with such limited competitive opportunities, some would still begrudge these swimmers any athletic recognition, as demonstrated by what happened to Virginia Shepherd in the late 1950s when she competed with the synchro club at her high school in Ely, Minnesota. The club, known as the "Water Babes," usually put their energy into producing an annual water show, but one year, their coach convinced the school to allow the girls to participate in a statewide synchronized swimming contest. The Water Babes won, and during a team banquet, Shepherd was awarded a varsity letter patch. It depicted a male diver since the school didn't have any varsity letters for women, but Shepherd didn't mind. She was proud to be recognized for what she and her team had accomplished. But shortly after, the school board received a complaint that a girl had been awarded a varsity letter, and Shepherd was called to the coach's office and told she would have to give the letter back. "And I said, 'Give it back?'" she recalled to a reporter years later. "I earned it and I sewed it on to my sweater and you can't have it back."[64]

Shepherd relayed her story to the local media in 2022 as part of its coverage of the fifty-year anniversary of the Title IX landmark legislation passed by Congress expressly to ensure that future students would not face the kind of discrimination she had. Title IX of the Education Amendments of 1972 stated, "No person in the United States shall, on the basis of sex, be excluded from participation in, be denied the benefits of, or be subjected to discrimination under any educational program or activity receiving Federal financial assistance." Although sports were not explicitly mentioned, the ruling ushered in revolutionary and sweeping changes in women's athletics. Even though the new generations of physical educators, particularly those who had begun their careers during the women's movement era of the 1960s, had been pushing for more varsity sports for women, prior to Title IX their hands were often tied. As most women's sports still fell under physical education departments or were classified as clubs, female student athletes had not been privy to the resources of athletic departments and had limited access to facilities like gyms and pools that prioritized varsity teams. But once equal access was written into law in 1972, women in sports no longer had to beg or appeal to the better natures of their male colleagues, and female students were no longer limited to play for play's sake.

Following the passage of Title IX, the Association for Intercollegiate Athletics for Women (AIAW), founded a year prior, stepped in as the governing body for women's college sports, including synchronized swimming, and became the female equivalent of the NCAA. Schools began transitioning their strongest women's honorary sports clubs into intercollegiate teams housed in the athletics departments. Ohio State University, which was among the earliest schools to begin giving women's sports varsity designation, transitioned the recreational Swan Club into the Ohio State varsity synchronized swimming team, which came with a massively increased budget and eight full athletic scholarships, enabling the school to recruit some of the country's top synchro swimmers. When the AIAW held the first Collegiate National Championships in synchronized swimming in 1977 at Michigan State, with fifteen schools represented, Ohio won all events. By 1978, the year by which all schools had to comply with Title IX legislation, nearly thirty colleges and universities offered athletic aid for synchronized swimmers, although Ohio State remained ahead of the pack, winning all but four annual national team titles for the remainder of the century (with the others going to the University of Arizona and Stanford University).[65]

As revolutionary as Title IX was, scholars have argued that its benefits were not equally spread among women of different races and ethnicities, noting that the legislation disproportionately benefited white women in terms of opening new sports to them. Synchronized swimming, and even swimming in general, which had started out as a predominantly white sport, largely remained that way. A report sponsored by the National Association for Girls and Women in Sports titled "Black Women in Sport" looked at studies providing racial breakdowns of different sports at AIAW member schools in 1977 and 1978. The first found that at roughly 220 schools, ninety-two white students and zero Black students participated in synchronized swimming (golf and skiing were other sports with zero participation); a different survey of 205 schools the following year reported that a single Black student and sixty-nine white students participated in the sport.[66] The report noted that Black female students were largely channeled into basketball and track and field sports, though decades of segregation and unequal access to swimming facilities certainly also played a role in their low participation in aquatic sports. Outside the world of AIAW competitive sports—such as community and city synchro programs and noncompetitive college clubs—participation levels among minority groups were slightly better. For example, Howard University, a historically Black institution in Washington, DC, had been home to a recreational synchronized swimming club since the 1960s.

Carla Dunlap, a swimmer with the San Antonio Cygnets who, in 1977, became the first Black woman to win a junior national team championship, added the expense of team dues and pool admission to the list of reasons for lower participation among minorities. "You can go out and run anywhere, but you can't go out and just swim anywhere," said Dunlap. Plus, she said, "There are a lot of sisters who just won't get their hair wet all the time." Pool water—whether chlorinated or salt—followed by the necessary shampooing, is drying and damaging to the hair, explained Dunlap, and can be a barrier to entry for some women. But for Dunlap, who had done both speed swimming and gymnastics, once she tried synchro there was no question she had found her sport. "Synchronized swimming was the best of both worlds," she said, noting that it combined the stunts of gymnastics with the conditioning of swimming. "That creative factor of utilizing the body as a form of art really appealed to me."[67]

Although racial disparities remained, the 1970s had spurred a new consciousness regarding gender equity in sports and led to the transformation of many women's synchro clubs into varsity sports teams. In this new era, and in an ironic twist from earlier days, being a "women's sport" would ultimately help synchronized swimming reach its Olympic goals. But it still wouldn't come easy, and synchronized swimmers, who had been working hard to raise the bar as athletes, would have to fight to earn their place in the world of sports.

RAISING THE BAR

In 1973, the *New York Times* reported that a "renaissance" was happening within synchronized swimming following the decision to eliminate presentation as a scoring criterion and thus rid the sport of its "plumes and flowing trains."[68] The high visibility and long success of the Oakland-based Athens Club—which, as reigning champions throughout the 1950s, went on multiple international tours and even appeared on the *Ed Sullivan Show* with Esther Williams—had sealed California's position as the hub for synchronized swimming and inspired the creation of several new teams that would dominate the sport from the 1960s onward. Leading the pack were the San Francisco Merionettes, the Santa Clara Aquamaids, and the Walnut Creek Aquanuts. As the new front-runners, these teams were also innovating in ways that were transforming the look of the sport.

At the 1964 indoor national championships in Oakland, all anyone could talk about was the Merionettes' routine, "Impresiones del Ballet, Folklórico de México," in which the swimmers had appeared to defy gravity. By using a new technique called the "support scull," which generates upward force by rapidly moving the forearms in and out at a 90-degree angle from the body, they had sustained greater height above the water—while inverted—than anyone had ever seen before.[69] *Sports Illustrated* described the technique as a "wonderous . . . wigwag motion of the hands and forearms, the pitch and vectors of which the swimmer can adjust with great subtlety."[70] Prior to the support scull, a plain vertical twist (360-degree spin with the head down and toes up) executed properly meant the audience would see ankles, maybe a bit of leg. But in their routine, the Merionettes not only performed the more complicated "heron" twist at thigh level, but after the spin, held their bodies at that height for a full 4 seconds before "submerging slowly in precise unison."[71] They won the team event with fifteen points to spare.[72] Soon rules were rewritten to specify greater heights on certain moves.

Moreover, swimmers were no longer simply doing single stunts, as routines were now made up of much longer "hybrids": multiple upside-down stunts mashed together into a single consecutive sequence. At least one prolonged hybrid became de rigueur in every routine, wrote Dawn Bean. Some teams were even starting routines with such long upside-down sequences that swimmers were going full pool lengths before coming up for air.[73] Holding one's breath that long was not only physically difficult but also required mental fortitude, as a swimmer from the San Antonio Cygnets told *Sports Illustrated* writer Roy

Blount in 1971. "You're under there and your blood is pounding, but you know you have to stay under. Sometimes you can't see anybody, and it all closes in on you."[74]

In addition to the long and complex inverted hybrids, a lot more was happening right-side-up. Rather than doing arm strokes while swimming horizontally on their stomachs, synchronized swimmers were traveling upright, having adopted the "eggbeater" kick used by water polo players. The eggbeater's powerful, alternating circular kicks enabled synchro swimmers to move through the water using only their legs, leaving their arms free to do various movements above the surface. In watching the Cygnets—ranked third in the country after the Aquamaids and Merionettes—perform the eggbeater, Blount wrote, "They appear for all the world to be walking smoothly across the bottom of the pool," even though they were in 10-foot-deep water. "Can Don Schollander do that?" Blount asked, referring to the seven-time Olympic gold medaling freestyle champion. "Can Bear Bryant?"[75] But even if swimmers wanted to "walk smoothly" across the pool floor, that was no longer allowed, as penalties were added that same year for touching the bottom.

It took intensive training to achieve these results, and top clubs had an A Team and a B Team, with the former practicing three or four hours every day to vie for national titles. Carla Dunlap, who swam on the Cygnets' A Team, coached by Margaret Swan (and who later became an international bodybuilding champion), joked that the top coaches "really prided themselves in trying to kill you." Their practices included wind sprints of overs and unders, racing against the clock with no break in between until they were dizzy and swimming on "negative oxygen."[76] *Swimming World* writer and speed swimming coach Chris Georges decided he wanted "to make sure all that fancy ballet leg stuff was as hard as they all said," so he joined the Santa Clara Aquamaids for a practice. "I learned my lesson that night," wrote Georges, recalling the grueling "warmup" laps of sprint-loaf kicking, swan kicking ("head-out flutter kick with the arms down at the sides and the fingertips out of the water"), eggbeater with arms raised above the head, and double ballet legs. "I for one," wrote Georges, "will never scoff again at a synchronized swimming workout!"[77]

As synchronized swimming was becoming visibly harder, it was finally getting a bit of respect, with sports journalists like Blount and Georges discussing the physical techniques and athletic training involved. They couldn't help themselves from snickering, though, when it came to the routine titles. Even though themes had been dropped as a scoring criteria, teams were still in the habit of building their choreography around a central idea, which was usually reflected in the routine's title listed in the competition program.[78] Blount, who for the most part had behaved himself in his *Sports Illustrated* coverage, gleefully included gratuitous lists of routines from recent national competitions, including "Blitzkrieg!!—1939" by a duet pair from the Cygnets who "formed a floating swastika with their bodies." Others included "Jazz-A-Ma-Dazz," "Freedom from Behind the Iron Curtain," "Powers from Beelzebub," "Thieves of Alli Baba," and "Resurrection," the last being performed at a meet just before Easter with swimmers forming a cross in the water.[79] In 1973, perhaps spurred by Blount's article, the Walnut Creek Aquanuts started a trend of writing simply "Untitled" on their routine entry form. Shortly after, the title line was dropped from the scoring sheets altogether.[80]

Synchro swimmers were not just becoming more serious competitors, but they were doing so at younger ages. In 1972, a fortuitous merger of two Seattle synchro clubs brought together ten-year-old swimmers Candy Costie and Tracie Ruiz as duet partners. Although they had once been rivals, they worked well together and were said to complement each other in the water like bread and butter. Their coach, Charlotte Jennings Davis, a former national champion with the Santa Clara Aquamaids, sat the girls down and told them that if they continued working hard, they could become national champions. They took Davis's words to heart, waking up at 4 a.m. to train with her before school, followed by an after-school practice and ten-hour days on the weekends. At twelve, they qualified to compete in the national championships, some of the youngest swimmers ever to do so, and in 1977, won first place as the top duet in the National Junior Olympics (an event that had started being offered in 1971).[81] Before long, this dynamic duo would join the first-ever US National Team.

Since its inception, synchronized swimming had—like most sports in the US—been ruled by the AAU, but in 1978, Congress decided to break up the organization's monopoly. It passed the Amateur Sports Act, ruling that sports under AAU jurisdiction must form their own federations. A year later, the United States Synchronized Swimming (USSS) was established, with Judy McGowan, the last AAU Synchronized Swimming Chair, serving as the first USSS president. One of the first priorities of the new governing body was to bring together the best swimmers from across the country and create a national team to send to the increasing number of international meets that were taking place. In the summer of 1979, the USSS held trials and formed a two-squad national team, with Costie and Ruiz among the athletes who made the cut. The two groups would come together for training at designated periods under the coaches of the Santa Clara Aquamaids and the Walnut Creek Aquanauts, both of which had won multiple national championships. Another immediate action of the new governing body was removing the AAU rule that had separated male and female competitors. Under the USSS, men and women could swim in the same routines and compete against one another at all levels of the sport in the United States. However, men would not be allowed by FINA to participate in major international championships or the Olympics until well into the twenty-first century.

THE COLD WAR BATTLE FOR SYNCHRO

Prior to the 1970s, there were no worldwide arenas for swimming and diving competitions other than the Olympics. America's FINA Bureau member, Harold Henning, wanted to change that by establishing global championships for aquatic sports to be held in the years between each Olympiad. The idea caught on, and Belgrade, Yugoslavia, was selected to host the first FINA World Aquatics Championships in 1973. From the beginning, Henning wanted synchronized swimming—a FINA sport—on the program, promoting it as the women's alternative to water polo, but there was resistance from the Soviet Union, where synchronized swimming was not yet a well-developed sport.[82] With the US and the Soviet Union being staunch political and ideological adversaries, sports competitions between the two took on deeper significance, as victories on the playing field were touted as evidence of superior worldviews. So when American swimmer Mark Spitz won seven gold medals and set seven world records at the Munich Olympics in 1972, the Soviet Union immediately demanded that the IOC "minimize the importance of swimming" at the next Olympics by reducing the number of events and spectator capacity.[83] They also wanted synchronized swimming, a sport that America would no doubt dominate, removed from the program at the upcoming inaugural World Aquatics Championships and threatened to withdraw Yugoslavia as the host if it was not eliminated.

Henning, whose wife, Jean, had competed in some of the earliest synchronized swimming competitions, refused to budge on synchro's inclusion. He was backed by FINA president Javier Ostos of Mexico, who would become one of the sport's biggest champions, and it remained on the program.[84] America won all three golds (for solo, duet, and team), Canada claimed the silvers, and Japan went home with three bronze medals. Although demonstrations had been given by synchronized swimmers at every Olympiad from 1952 to 1968, its inclusion at the World Aquatics Championships in Belgrade was critical in providing exposure to synchro as a *competitive* sport rather than an exhibition and catalyzed the movement for Olympic acceptance.

Events to be included in any Olympiad are voted on by the IOC several years in advance, and during Avery Brundage's twenty-year reign as president, the proposal to include synchronized swimming had never even been allowed to come up for a vote. But Brundage retired in 1972 and his successor, Sir Michael Morris (Lord Killanin) of Ireland, did not harbor the deep-seated determination to keep synchro out of sportdom—even calling it an "elegant sport."[85] With Brundage out of the way, FINA put forward a proposal to the IOC congress to include synchro on the program at the 1980 Olympics in Moscow. It did not pass, in part because of Soviet opposition and also because the IOC was looking to downsize, not to add events.[86] Ostos was determined, though, and immediately set his sights on getting the sport into the 1984 games, which Los Angeles was bidding to host. He met with delegates from the Los Angeles committee, convincing them to lobby the IOC to include these events if they secured the bid, which they agreed to. It was an easy sell to the LA committee as they could play up the California connections to the sport in their marketing. Plus, the committee planned to make the LA games the most widely televised to date and believed synchro, with its music and underwater footage, would make for great TV viewing.[87]

One of the strict criteria the IOC had set for considering synchronized swimming's inclusion was that several countries on at least three continents must be competing and demonstrating "evidence of an enthusiastic and understanding public."[88] When fifteen countries, including Egypt, Australia, New Zealand, Japan, Mexico, and multiple European nations, sent synchronized swimming competitors to the 1978 FINA World Aquatics Championships in Berlin, it was clear that they had achieved that milestone. The United States won gold for the team category, while Canada came in first for solo and duet, making it the first international competition the United States did not completely dominate, which showed that there had been a real competition. Although the Soviet Union had yet to compete in the synchro events at any FINA championship, it sent a Russian synchro coach, Valentina Sharova, to observe the competition in Berlin. Dawn Bean, who was there serving as a competition judge, asked Sharova through her interpreter when the Soviets would start entering synchro competitions. "When we can beat you," she was told.[89] The Soviet Union may not have been ready for synchronized swimming just yet, but it was preparing for the day it would. Moreover, it was fostering ambitions for its own "women's sport"—and one in which it knew it would dominate.

On the eve of the 1980 Summer Games in Moscow, members of the IOC and delegates from sports federations around the world gathered at the Bolshoi Theater for the IOC annual session. The surroundings were elegant, but the mood was tense. The Olympiad starting in only a few days would be the smallest in decades. Sixty-five countries had withdrawn their participation in the Olympics as part of an American-led boycott of the games launched in protest to the Soviet invasion of Afghanistan. But there was still business to attend to—such as planning for the 1984 Olympics, confirmed to be held in Los Angeles—and many of the countries boycotting the games, including the US, sent delegates to the session.

Among the items on the IOC's agenda was the proposed inclusion of two new sports—both for women only—at the 1984 Olympiad: rhythmic gymnastics and synchronized swimming. Although originated by political adversaries—the Soviet Union and the United States, respectively—the two sports otherwise shared similar trajectories. Like synchronized swimming, rhythmic gymnastics grew out of traditions dating to the 1800s and became a competitive sport in the 1940s. Both spread globally over the following decades as their practitioners nurtured dreams of Olympic acceptance. And perhaps most significantly, the superpowers likely to dominate in each sport were locked in a geopolitical cold war, with neither willing to give the other an edge. Now the fate of both of these "women's sports" was to be decided by the IOC's seventy-seven voting members—all of whom were men.

Rhythmic gymnastics came up for a vote first. It had its naysayers, particularly on the basis that it would be difficult to score objectively, but it received a passing majority. Next up was synchronized swimming. FINA president Robert Helmick made his case, arguing that synchronized swimmers were always fighting against the "masculine concept" that synchro is not a real sport. "We have shown," said Helmick, "that it requires as much training as water polo. It requires athletic strength and skill to attain good results."[90] Similar concerns were raised about scoring, but others called for consistency, arguing that if rhythmic gymnastics was accepted, synchronized swimming should be too. It was voted in—at long last—but only for the duet event. Each qualifying country would be allowed to send two synchro competitors and an alternate ("a pair and a spare"). It was not a grand slam, as it left out the team and solo events, but it was still a massive win for the sport. After all these years, synchronized swimming would finally be in the Olympics. Ostos later wrote that the fact that it and rhythmic gymnastics "rose to the rank of Olympic sports together" was one of the biggest factors that helped synchronized swimming's acceptance, and that had there not been a strong push by several countries for rhythmic gymnastics, synchro might not have made it onto the program.[91]

In 1983, FINA—still hoping to expand the sport's Olympic footprint—proposed adding a solo event at the '84 games, pointing out that it wouldn't require sending any additional athletes if the soloist was selected from the three athletes already on the roster. The idea was voted down because of Soviet and Eastern bloc "dissension," but, in a twist of irony, solos ultimately made it onto the program only two months before the Olympics because of the Soviet Union's last-minute withdrawal from the 1984 Games in LA (supposedly in retaliation for the US-led boycott of the Moscow Olympics four years earlier, though many believed they stayed home because of fears of athletes defecting) and the need to fill the vacated television airtime.[92] Avery Brundage, who died three years after his retirement, did not live to see the day that "aquatic vaudeville" was accepted into the Olympics. As Joy Cushman, who had several conversations with Brundage during her time as AAU Synchro chair in the 1960s, pointed out, only half kidding: "He said it would be over his dead body, and it was!"[93] Or as Esther Williams later wrote, "Finally, the grouch died, and a new Olympic sport was born."[94]

THE NEW OLYMPIC GLAMOUR SPORT

On the US national team, Tracie Ruiz and Candy Costie had continued to swim, and win, together, so when duets—*their* event—was admitted into the Olympics, they found themselves sudden Olympic hopefuls. They won the Pan Pacific Championships, the National Sports Festival, and the Senior National Championships (together as a duet and Ruiz as a soloist)—for four consecutive years.[95] As students at the University of Arizona on full athletic scholarships, they competed in collegiate nationals and won those too. As *Sports Illustrated* put it, "they were winning everything in sight."[96]

Even though they were ahead of the pack in the United States, Costie and Ruiz weren't leaving anything to chance and decided to take a leave of absence from college, returning to Seattle to train full-time with Charlotte Davis, their original coach, who had turned them into champions. Under Davis, they trained for eight hours a day working on endurance swimming, perfecting their routines, doing weight and flexibility training, and drilling figures—short sequences of maneuvers that had their foundation in scientific, ornamental, and stunt swimming but had grown exponentially more difficult over the years. Figures were used to evaluate a swimmer's technical skill and counted for a full fifty percent of the overall score, with the routine making up the other half. Canada, with its long history of ornamental swimming competitions, was known for its excellence in figures execution; two years earlier, they had earned the gold in duet at the World Aquatics Championships in Guayaquil, Ecuador, because of their high figures score, even though Ruiz and Costie had scored higher on their routine. So now the Olympic hopefuls were spending countless hours drilling figures to ensure that didn't happen again. When the Olympic trials were held in Indianapolis in April 1984, Costie and Ruiz earned the coveted honor of becoming the first American synchronized swimmers selected to represent their country at the Olympics. Sarah Josephson was selected as their alternate.

While Ruiz and Costie were eating, sleeping, and breathing synchronized swimming, much of the rest of America was suddenly waking up to the fact that the sport even existed. Articles about synchro were suddenly appearing in major publications and even in-flight magazines, with the *New York Times* announcing synchronized swimming and rhythmic gymnastics as the new "glamour events" of the Olympics.[97] Coverage of the sport was a mixed bag—with discussions of its difficulty woven in with references to its show-business past and the remaining trappings of performance, like makeup and smiles. "Synchronized swimmers may look like cupcakes," wrote *Sports Illustrated*, "but they're tough cookies."[98] Synchro was often compared to figure skating, ballet, or gymnastics, but as the article pointed out, athletes of those other sports weren't holding their breath while performing their most difficult maneuvers. Another magazine wrote that in their costumes, Ruiz and Costie could be mistaken for contestants in the Miss America pageant, but cautioned readers not to be fooled: "Hidden under the glamorous trappings of their sport—the waterproof makeup, the glittering bathing suits and the sequined hair of synchronized swimming—are a couple of Olympic athletes. *Tough* Olympic athletes."[99]

The subject of hair gelling was particularly irresistible to reporters. Earlier synchronized swimmers had, like Esther Williams, used Vaseline on their hair to keep it in place during competitions, but in the late 1970s, they moved instead to using unflavored gelatin, which was far less messy, and not only shellacked the hair in place but gave it a dazzling shine. *Sports Illustrated* relayed the steps: stir several packets of gelatin in a cup of hot water until it becomes a thick goo, then comb it through the hair. Next, put the hair in a high ponytail, run it through a "donut" (a hair accessory that makes a bun look bigger), secure it all with a hairnet and bobby pins, then give the entire thing a good coating of gelatin. "Voila. Ballet-dancer look," wrote the author. "All set? Uh-uh." Next up was attaching the headpiece, "a sparkling creation" designed to match the suit, followed by makeup. "Waterproof, of course. . . . Now for the hard part. Put a smile on your face and keep it there."[100]

References to Billy Rose, Busby Berkeley, and Esther Williams were constant, with some writers even expressing sympathy at the incessant comparisons. "It is the rare synchronized swimming story that doesn't mention dear ol' Esther," wrote *Swimming World*, "and it is a rare synchro athlete that doesn't suffer from the showbiz stereotype of Esther backstroking effortlessly across the big screen."[101] After all those years of trying to gain acceptance as a sport, said Bean, "the only thing that was in everyone's mind was Esther Williams' movies."[102] Charlotte Davis said in an interview ahead of the Olympics that the very future of synchro was riding on whether the swimmers were perceived as athletes. "They've got to do a good job selling it as a sport," said Davis, "not as an aquatic . . . Esther Williams-like show."[103] But developing their own identity separate from the aquamusical star wasn't easy, especially since Esther Williams, who had been cocooned away with Fernando Lamas for more than two decades before his passing in 1982, was suddenly everywhere now that the ABC network had picked her as their color commentator. And every time synchronized swimming was mentioned on television, it seemed to always show a clip of Williams hurtling down a waterslide or hanging from a trapeze, rather than footage of actual synchro athletes.

But for ABC and the LA Olympic Committee, there couldn't have been a more natural choice than the glamorous Los Angeles native, while Williams herself was delighted to be asked, writing later that she was "proud to be an inspiration, a godmother to the sport."[104] And even if some were conflicted about having Williams touted as the face of the sport's competitive side, it was a thrill for many of the athletes to meet her. Ruiz told a reporter that Williams's movies had inspired her growing up. "There is that certain spark you get from watching them," she said.[105] The network paired Williams with Donna de Varona, a star in her own right as an Olympic gold medalist who set eighteen different world records and was voted by the Associated Press and United Press International as the most outstanding woman athlete in the world. She had gone on to become a groundbreaking sportscaster and worked to ensure that Title IX was interpreted to include protections for women's sports.

The effects of that historic legislation had since reverberated throughout women's sports, and for the first time in history, the 1984 Olympic Games included a 26-mile marathon race—long held as the "crown jewel" of the Olympics and a "symbol of masculine prowess"—for women.[106] Even though only 20 percent of the athletes at the games were women, it was far more than in any previous Olympiad, prompting the *New York Times* to declare the XXIII Olympiad "The Women's Olympics."[107] And among these women athletes were synchronized swimmers—eighteen duet pairs and seventeen soloists—from twenty-two countries, all eager to demonstrate their sport to the world. "All of us wanted to go out there and show we aren't just water ballerinas," said Canadian competitor Carolyn Waldo. "We were athletes, and we were to be taken seriously."[108]

The day of the opening ceremony, July 28, the usual smog hanging over Los Angeles cleared and "Mother Nature smiled on Southern California," wrote Dawn Bean, who served as the Olympic competition director for synchronized swimming.[109] Tracie Ruiz recalled the magic of walking through the tunnel into the Memorial Coliseum with the American team—522 athletes in total—and emerging into the packed stands and hearing the sound of nearly one hundred thousand spectators cheering when the team was announced. "At that moment, it's just like, wow, we made it," said Ruiz. "This is the start, you know, this is the start of it all."[110]

Synchronized swimming, which would begin a week later, had been the second of all the Olympic events to sell out, according to the *New York Times*, with 15,500 tickets sold for both the preliminaries and for the finals. The former would narrow the entries down to eight duets and eight solos to compete in the finals. The synchro competition itself would be comprised of two parts: the figures execution and the routine (for duets the figures scores of the two swimmers were averaged). For the figures portion, each competitor was required to perform six figures, which were selected from six possible groups and announced shortly before the Olympics. On the day of the figures competition, the first event of the finals, Esther Williams told television viewers there would be "no frills today, just skill alone." They had to be performed slowly and to very exacting standards, with one newspaper reporting that each figure took an average of a minute and a half.[111] All the drilling the Americans had done paid off when Ruiz earned the highest figures score and Costie came in fifth, for an average score of 96.584. The Canadian duet swimmers, Sharon Hambrook and Kelly Kryczka, were a close second with 96.034, leaving open the possibility for an upset during the routine portion. The Japanese duet swimmers—Saeko Kimura and Miwako Motoyoshi—came in third at 90.99, making them strong contenders for bronze if they performed well in the routines. Several newspapers commented on the technical and unflashy nature of the figures competition, with one writing, "there were no sequined suits and hats, no bright make-up, no Michael Jackson hits, just plain black suits, goggles, swim caps and concentration."[112]

If viewers wanted sparkle and rhythm, they got it the next day with the event everyone was waiting for—the routines. Of the top contenders, the Japanese were up first, sporting white swimsuits with plunging V-necks and orange flames roaring up the sides; the pair excelled in connected moves, creating interesting configurations with their legs above the surface. Up next were the Canadians in red and white chevron suits. To the sound of trumpet calls they front flipped from the deck straight into the pool, then kept the energy up with tunes like "Sabre Dance" and ending with back-to-back lifts to "Rock Around the Clock." They received a standing ovation and a score of 98.2 points.

Costie and Ruiz, the last to swim, would have to score 97.7 to capture the gold. To Coach Davis, for whom the Olympics had not been an option during her championship days, being on deck at the first Olympic synchronized swimming competition and watching the women she had helped get there was a thrilling dream come true—but also nerve-racking. "We were the ones to beat," said Davis. "We were the target."[113] But the twenty-one-year-old Americans had been swimming in tandem for a decade. "We were ready. We were exhilarated,"

Ruiz said later. "This was our chance."[114] The two exuded confidence as they walked in on deck in their sparkly red, white, and blue suits. To a musical mélange of piano, harp, and conga drum, they dove in and—as spectators watched in awe—did not surface for a solid fifty seconds, traveling down the pool while performing one complex upside-down hybrid after another, including a lift where Costie propelled Ruiz's entire body out of the water, giving the appearance that she was doing a headstand on the surface. "Ordinary mortals would be blacking out, or at least regretting their life's sins," wrote the *Los Angeles Examiner*. "But Candy and Tracie, presumably still smiling five feet under, kept waggling their legs in the air with synchronized glee."[115] Their routine included a clip of Michael Jackson's "Wanna Be Startin' Somethin'," with a bit of breakdance-inspired choreography, and a debut move called "thread the needle," in which their touching feet appeared to create the eye of a needle that they threaded their other legs through. Their routine concluded with "I'm a Yankee Doodle Dandy," which "set the audience of flag waving Americans overboard in their enthusiasm," reported Bean.[116] With a score of 99

Candy Costie and Tracie Ruiz, the first American synchronized swimming Olympic champions.

points, Ruiz and Costie handily won the duet competition, with Canada coming in second and Japan third. "How do I feel?" exclaimed Costie to the *Los Angeles Times*. "It feels absolutely incredible!"[117]

All that was left was the solo routine, and few doubted that it would go to Ruiz, who had not been defeated in an international solo competition in four years. The *Los Angeles Times* even wrote that when the solo event was added at the eleventh hour, it was as if the IOC announced "they were mailing Ruiz a gold medal."[118] Ruiz did indeed win the gold, but it certainly wasn't handed (or mailed) to her. Her routine, which featured an entire minute underwater without surfacing, was described as "difficult, innovative, and charismatic."[119] Canada, this time represented by soloist Carolyn Waldo, again came in second, and Motoyoshi of Japan came in third. The final medal count for the first Olympic synchronized swimming events was two golds for the US, two silvers for Canada, and two bronzes for Japan. These same three countries would earn all the Olympic medals in synchronized swimming for the rest of the century.

The *Los Angeles Examiner* wrote: "For millions of viewers, a star is born. I'm not talking about any individual athlete, but a whole sport—synchronized swimming."[120] The synchro community, having achieved its goal of Olympic inclusion, took a moment to take it all in. "The anticipation, the Games themselves, and now the memories of those wonderful weeks," wrote Bean, "are something that can never be forgotten, nor ever duplicated in our lifetime."[121] However, there was still much work to be done. Now that synchro was safely in the Olympics, the next battle was to get the team competition—the true heart of the sport and its "showcase" event—accepted.

THE TEAM DREAM

Shortly after the IOC's 1980 vote to accept synchronized swimming details of the deliberations trickled out, and leaders in the sport took steps to address the various reasons team routines had not been accepted. The variable sizes of teams—which up to that point could include as few as four or as many as eight swimmers—had caused some IOC members to question whether judging differently sized teams against one another would create disadvantages for some. It was a fair question since synchronizing fewer people is easier, yet at the same time larger groups can create more interesting patterns and powerful lifts. In response to the concerns, FINA promptly changed the rules, requiring teams to have exactly eight members—no more, no less—at all major international competitions. In a similar vein, FINA also set specific time lengths for routines, rather than allowing a range. Going forward, team routines would be five minutes, duets four minutes, and solos three and a half, each with a fifteen-second grace period in case the music ran slightly over or under.

Following the 1984 Olympics, which exposed television audiences all over the world to synchronized swimming, the sport experienced immediate international growth. The World Aquatics Championships two years later saw record participation, with entries for twenty-four solos, twenty duets, and fifteen teams—including, for the first time, entries from Russia and China.[122] Former national competitors and coaches of winning teams were in demand to give clinics in countries with developing programs, and several major international workshops and seminars were held for judges and coaches around the world.[123] It seemed with IOC concerns addressed and greater interest in the sport than ever, the team event would be a shoo-in, but when FINA brought its inclusion for the 1988 games in Seoul to the IOC for a vote, it was defeated. Javier Ostos reported to the community that the rejection had been based primarily on the large number of athletes that would have to be added for the team event but added that part of the issue was that synchro was still "regarded more as a spectacle than as a sport."[124]

And the media was playing a big role in perpetuating this view. Coverage of the sport had been largely positive surrounding the 1984 Olympic debut but grew increasingly negative ahead of the 1988 Olympics, when synchro was again included as a duet and solo event. Some have pinpointed the turning point to a now famous *Saturday Night Live* skit that aired two months after the 1984 summer games.[125] The skit featured actors Martin Short and Harry Shearer as two brothers who want to become the first male Olympic synchronized swimmers. Shearer tells his wife he's leaving his accounting firm to pursue their dream, and Short admits to the cameraman that he can't swim but he's working on it. In the water scenes he wears an orange life vest and prominent nose clip even though they never leave the shallow water for their splashing around. The five-minute "mockumentary" included scenes directly copied from an up-close-and-personal feature on Ruiz and Costie that showed the swimmers lifting weights, practicing in a dance studio, and gelling their hair for a swim; it even included some of the same music that was used in their routine.

Even though the sketch was clearly making fun of them, synchronized swimmers took it in good-natured stride. Davis said years later that she was "sort of flattered" and thought it piqued people's interest in the sport. "I mean, it was a funny skit if you watch it," she said.[126] In fact, Betty Watanabe, who became the executive director of United States Synchronized Swimming in 1985, even tried to get Short and Shearer to attend the 1991 Olympic Festival, or better yet, get in the pool, as a way to bring publicity to the sport.[127] The skit quickly became a cult classic and still makes it onto every *Saturday Night Live* top-ten best skits list, but as *Sports Illustrated* later wrote, "Tracie Ruiz and Candy Costie won Olympic gold for the U.S. in Los Angeles that summer; Harry Shearer and Martin Short foundered in the shallow end that fall, and America has been as confused as hell about synchronized swimming ever since."[128]

As the new go-to pop culture reference to showcase any time synchronized swimming was in the news, it was even aired following the closing ceremony of the 1992 Olympics in Barcelona. When NBC flashed a picture of twins Karen and Sarah Josephson, the American Olympians who had just won a gold medal for their duet, the network followed it not with footage of their swim, but with a clip of the *SNL* skit instead.[129] Harry Forbes wrote a letter of complaint to NBC Sports that was published in *Synchro* magazine, calling the move a "real slap in the face" to the Olympic champions. He questioned why "snide remarks" are the norm for a sport that is comparable to figure skating and gymnastics, yet more difficult because of the aquatic medium.[130]

When synchro first splashed onto the Olympic scene, sportswriters had treated it with benign bemusement or ignored it altogether. But once synchronized swimmers were on the medal stands being recognized along with the athletes of sports with finish lines, the trolls came out. An interview with Harry Shearer in 1991 revealed a level of mean-spiritedness and "outrage" that had been behind his beloved comedy skit. He told the *Los Angeles Times* that while watching the synchronized swimming competition during the '84 Olympics, "I got absolutely teed off at the idea that these women wearing lipstick in the swimming pool were getting the same gold medals as other people were getting for what I considered real athletic achievement."[131] He asked, if this was worth a gold medal, why not "marathon waiting at the supermarket" or "championship oil changing"? He had popped a cassette into his VCR to record their swims and began hatching the idea of a skit mocking the sport that would hopefully make sure it never saw a second Olympiad. But of course it did, and shortly after the *Los Angeles Times* interview with Shearer, the paper published a response from the Josephson sisters, who were training as hopefuls for the 1992 Olympics at the time. They gave Shearer high marks for humor but said he clearly had no idea about the sport's physical requirements. "Lose the life jacket, venture into the deep end and try floating upside down underwater for 30 seconds while keeping your legs in a vertical position above water," they challenged him. "Then, we'll talk."[132]

Synchronized swimming was an easy target—low-hanging fruit for (predominantly male) sportswriters and media personalities, like one from the *Monterey Sunday Herald* who wrote that he kept waiting to see swimmers with bananas on their caps or an aerial shot of them floating in the shape of Olympic rings or spelling out MGM. "Give me real swimmers racing to the wall," he said. "That's a sport. It's got a stopwatch."[133] The *Seattle Post-Intelligencer* ran a letter from a reader named Sherry Weinberg written in response to the "sexist drivel" from one of its journalists about synchronized swimming: "The problem here is that it is still OK in our society to define what is a sport and who is an athlete entirely from a male perspective." She pointed out that testosterone makes men develop greater physical strength, but women excel in balance, flexibility, "kinesthetic awareness," and fine motor control, adding, "there is no inherent reason why athletes who excel in basketball, long jump or wrestling should be considered 'more athletic' than athletes who excel in swimming, synchronized swimming or race-walking."[134]

Synchronized swimmers had ditched their themes and flashy costumes, and the US had continued to bring home medals (two silvers for duet and solo in 1988, with Canada defeating America in both). Yet because of the negativity, synchronized swimming remained under threat of cancellation and was a regular candidate for the chopping block every time the subject of Olympic overcrowding came up. In 1990, Charlotte Davis attended the first Television Workshop for Aquatic Sports, and wrote in a report afterward that in order for the sport "to grow, and at the very least, survive," the synchro community needed to take a "hard look" at the broadcasters' suggestions, which included shortening the time on deck and simplifying the rules.[135] Some suggestions, however, put aesthetics above athletic performance, like covering the lines on the bottom of the pool, as they were said to be distracting to audiences during the underwater footage. The lines, however, help synchro swimmers maintain spatial awareness while they are upside down, without goggles, and trying to stay in pattern. Another suggestion was to get rid of nose clips—an absolutely essential piece of equipment—because, as the TV experts argued, they "distort the swimmer's face and look bad on close-ups." In fact, the following year, Executive Director Watanabe was advised by both an NBC Sports director *and* IOC president Juan Samaranch to do something about the unattractive nose clips, the former saying, "you have some of the most attractive female athletes, and that clip takes away from the beauty."[136] As a result, the *Los Angeles Times* reported, Watanabe had launched a project to create an effective one that goes *inside* the nose, an idea that has been revisited over the years but never widely took off.[137]

The tension between aesthetics and athletics was nothing new, of course: "It would never do to come to the surface red faced," a synchronized swimmer told a reporter in 1955. Instead, she said, they must "come up smiling as if to say, 'This is so easy and so much fun.'"[138] That idea had lingered even as synchro had grown so much more difficult, perhaps because, as Karen Josephson said, "it is not attractive to see someone gasp for air and look like they are not going to make it."[139] But those pleasant expressions were having the effect of masking the tremendous efforts the athletes were putting in, and another idea Davis relayed in her report was to stop " 'pretending' to look like everything is easy with constant smiles. Why not show the public that it is tiring and grueling?"[140]

That was an idea Watanabe could get behind, and when it was pointed out that all audiences could see were the "ballet-like movements" above the water and not the rigorous action below the surface, she decided to fix that by inviting sports photographer Ken Levine to take some underwater shots that would capture the athleticism. But by the time Levine got into position to shoot the ongoing action, he needed to surface for air. He then got an oxygen tank but found that he still couldn't keep up with the swimmers as they traveled all over the pool. He told the *Los Angeles Times* the experience made him "a convert of the sport."[141]

The national team issued a media challenge, welcoming any journalist to come and try synchro out for themselves. Soon *Miami Herald* humor columnist Dave Barry was writing, "There's an old saying in journalism: 'Be careful what you make fun of, because you could find yourself upside down attempting a Vertical Split while your lungs rapidly fill with water.'" Barry, along with *Herald* colleague and sportswriter Dan Le Batard, had taken the bait and joined the country's top synchronized swimmers at the pool at Emory University. Le Batard wrote, "What these girls do is beyond me . . . At one point they formed a human forklift locking their bodies together parallel to the surface somehow lifting Dave all the way out of the water." Even the "girly" ballet leg made them sink so fast they "left dents" in the pool floor, wrote Barry, and caused the lifeguards to inch a bit closer to the deep end. "After about 45 straight minutes of alternately eggbeatering and sinking," Barry went on, "I came to the surface and using what little air I had left in my lungs shouted: "THIS IS THE HARDEST SPORT IN THE WORLD!"[142]

These sorts of testimonials from synchro "converts" were helping to counter some of the negative stereotypes. Meanwhile, the sport had another big thing going for it: the IOC was looking to boost female participation in the Olympics, and they particularly wanted more "women's events" and not just women doing "men's" sports.[143] Moreover, even if sportswriters didn't love synchro, the spectators did, and synchronized swimming had continued to be a sellout event in Seoul and Barcelona. Perhaps synchro leaders felt possibility in the air because, according to the *Washington Post*, they offered the IOC a trade: take duets and solos in exchange for a new team event—with the hope that duets would be restored next time around.[144] With these factors working together, plus the continued lobbying of FINA and synchro federations around the world, the IOC voted to add the team competition as the sole synchro event for the 1996 Olympics in Atlanta.

With the team dream finally realized, it was time to put together America's "Dream Team." In October 1995, United States Synchronized Swimming held national trials in Indianapolis and selected ten swimmers (a team of eight plus two alternates) to train for the games in Atlanta the following year. This elite cadre came from the country's top clubs and had been swimming with and against one another for the better part of their lives, each one carrying multiple championship titles. "We knew we had the horses," said Charlotte Davis, who was now the national team director. The challenge was to harness that individual talent, she said, and make them jell as one. "When you have that many stars, you have to figure out a way to make them all shine, or nobody shines."[145] That's where legendary coaches Chris Carver and Gail Emery of the Santa Clara Aquamaids and Walnut Creek Aquanuts, respectively, came in. Carver had coached the national team to the gold at every elite international competition since 1991 and Emery had been coaching America's Olympic champions since 1982.

Training had become even more intense and rigorous in the dozen years since synchro's Olympic debut, and in addition to spending six to eight hours a day in the pool, the Dream Team's cross-training included running, plyometrics, intensive flexibility, and gymnastics for the aerial lifts and throws. Some of the team added personal ballet training or rock climbing in what free time they had left.[146] They knew other countries were working hard to catch up; the Associated Press reported that Japan's team was training sixty hours a week and that the Russians had incorporated not only gymnastics but also water polo and—somewhat inexplicably—football and basketball into their training.[147] So in addition to working the team harder, the American coaches added performance-enhancing mental training. "When you get to the top, a big part of it's in your head," said Becky Dyroen-Lancer, captain of the 1996 Olympic team and nine-time grand slam winner (a sweep of golds in solo, duet, team, and figures). They practiced visualizing the crowds, the volunteers, and imagined the ground under their feet at the stadium, she said. Then they visualized performing the routine and performing it *perfectly*.[148]

But training that hard for months on end, and shoulder-to-shoulder with the same nine people all day, every day, can wear down anyone. So a few weeks before the Olympics, Dyroen-Lancer huddled the team together and pulled out something she had been saving for when the going got toughest: a bottle she had filled with water from the Georgia Tech Aquatic Center—where they would soon be competing in the XXVIth Olympiad. She ceremoniously poured the water into the team's practice pool, saying later that it was a moment that "really charged everybody up."[149]

The hardest ticket to get in Atlanta in the summer of 1996 was to the synchronized swimming events, which were reportedly being scalped at $500 a pop.[150] Nearly fifteen thousand live spectators would watch from the stands, while the millions viewing the events from home would see the sport at its finest, as both underwater and aerial footage would be used to capture the work happening under the surface and give a bird's-eye view of the beauty of the group patterns performed by the eight best teams in the world (as determined by Olympic qualifiers): those of the United States, Canada, Japan, Russia, France, China, Italy, and Mexico. For the synchro community, the mood was particularly celebratory. Not only had the sport survived threats of being cut, but it had a bigger presence than ever, and audiences would finally get to see the precision and power of eight swimmers moving as one. Serendipitously, it was exactly fifty years

The 1996 American Dream Team was all smiles following their winning technical routine swim at the Olympic Summer Games in Atlanta.

since the first national synchronized swimming championship had been held, *and*, on top of all that, the Olympics were back in America, where it had all started.

In addition to the debut of the team event, there were other spectator-friendly changes. The slow-moving figures competition had been eliminated and replaced with a short (two-minute-and-fifty-second) "technical" routine, which required swimmers to perform certain elements in a designated order and would account for 35 percent of a team's score. The five-minute free routine, the star event, made up the remainder of the score. As one article stated ahead of the technical routine, "expectations rested on Team USA which was undefeated in the last quadrennium," but they weren't fazed by the pressure, thanks to all their mental preparation. "We've been planning and training. It really worked this morning and we did everything the way we did it in practice," said swimmer Jill Savery after their technical swim, which gave the Americans a .442 lead over Canada and a .537 lead over Japan heading into the free routine.[151]

On the day of the free event, the three front-runners were the last to swim. In their free routine themed around the four seasons, Japan was said to exhibit "traditional artistic flair" while Canada swam with "great precision and energy" to variations on their national anthem.[152] The American team was up last with a routine Chris Carver described as "very aerobically complex" and difficult due to its intricate upside maneuvers.[153] In purple suits and headpieces with swirls of sparkles, the eight swimmers dove into the water to the sounds of instruments tuning up. They performed to a medley called "Fantasia on an Orchestra," which made a progression through the sections of an orchestra—string, woodwind, percussion, and horn—while the swimmers' movements represented those of the instruments, including eight pairs of inverted legs playing one another like bows and strings. When the group huddled under the water, catapulted two of their members through the air in simultaneous back layout somersaults, and then immediately lifted a third so high and so steady it was as if she was standing on the surface, the crowd roared. The *Atlanta Daily Journal* wrote, "There wasn't a bad note in the performance."[154] Perfection is a "highly subjective concept," added the *Ventura County Star*, yet "you simply know it when you see it."[155] And the judges saw it. All but one of the ten gave them a perfect score, but with every routine's highest and lowest scores tossed out, that left the US Dream Team with a row of perfect tens: the sport's first perfect score in Olympic history. With their technical and free routines combined, America scored 99.720, earning the gold medal for the debut Olympic team event. Canada went home with the silver and Japan the bronze.

Emily Porter LeSueur, of the US team, told a reporter, "I think of all the days we got to the pool at six in the morning, and got home at seven at night. The feeling is exhilarating." Indeed, their "dedication and sacrifice paid off," noted the reporter, adding that the team swam "together, as one. In perfect rhythm."[156] Canadian Cari Read was not disappointed with second, saying, "If you walk away and only look at the color of the medal, the night is a hollow experience."[157] Indeed the successes that night could not be measured in fractions of points or Olympic bling. The victory belonged to the athletes, as well as to the sport itself, which had come so far since a committee sat around Katharine Curtis's kitchen table, drafting the rules that would turn spectacle into sport and merge athletics with artistry.

After the 1996 Olympics, the entire US national team—several of whom were married or engaged, and all of whom had spent years of their lives in serious training—retired from competition. As one journalist asked: "After achieving perfection, what else is there?"[158] America had dominated the sport since its inception, but the 1996 Olympics would prove to be a turning point. Those coming up behind America's Dream Team were strong but did not have the same level of competitive experience. Moreover, the rest of the world was improving, and the Russians, who missed the bronze by only a narrow margin, had been doing their homework. Back in 1982, Tracie Ruiz and Candy Costie, along with the top swimmers from West Germany and Canada, had been invited to the first Soviet Women's Day Competition in Moscow. Costie told *Sports Illustrated* at the time that the Soviet coaches asked lots of questions and "were hanging off the diving boards videotaping every move that we made."[159] Several more Soviet Women's Day meets had been held over the years, attended by some of the world's best synchronized swimmers, and several American coaches had traveled to Moscow to help build up the synchro program there.

In fact, once the American synchro community had started

sharing its knowledge and expertise all over the world—enabling Olympic competition to become a reality—they had never stopped. But as a result of their efforts to share and grow the sport they so loved, the gap was closing. Chris Carver, who had been among those who led international clinics, told a journalist ahead of the 1996 Olympics that the US had long been "the leader and state of the art," but other countries were now adding their own creativity and ideas to the sport. Even though helping other countries had meant giving away her "secrets," Carver had no regrets. "I feel this way—you can only better the sport if you share," she said. "If you're wise you keep working harder to stay ahead."[160]

The United States did work hard, but at the 2000 Olympics in Sydney, Russia catapulted to the top, winning the gold in both the team and duet event (the duet returned to the Olympic program that year), while the American team walked away empty-handed for the first time in history. It was clear that synchronized swimming was no longer just an American sport—it had taken on a life of its own. It was the dawn of a new era, and these emerging front-runners would be the ones to lead the sport into the twenty-first century. They, along with the rising wave of athletes all over the world, would continue to innovate and change synchro's ever-evolving look—but through it all, some constants would remain. For these dynamic dancers of the water, and their fans, there would always be—as one sportswriter put it—"The spectacle. . . . The music. The artistry. The precision. The athleticism."[161]

FASTER, HIGHER, STRONGER— TOGETHER

It's not just people in the water trying to be pretty. These people are athletes, they're animals, and they're extremely dynamic. The athleticism surpasses SO many expectations.[1]

—BILL MAY, 2022

The Olympic motto, "faster, higher, stronger," perfectly encapsulates the ways synchronized swimming—renamed artistic swimming by the international swimming federation, FINA, in 2017—has evolved during the twenty-first century. In 1996, *Inside Sports* named it one of the five toughest events at the Olympics, and the athleticism and difficulty have only escalated in the decades since.[2] National team–level athletes now train for thirteen to fourteen hours a day and must have not only a host of technical skills but also tremendous lung capacity, physical strength, flexibility, and endurance.

Official figures or elements, once called things like "kip," "monkey roll," and "marching on water," now have names like "thrust fishtail helicopter spinning 180" and "rocket split bent knee twirl hybrid." If they sound hard, it's because they are. Moreover, they are done higher in the water than ever. A grading scale for judges shows the tremendous heights that swimmers today must achieve to earn top points: an inverted thrust, in which one propels the body vertically out of the water while upside down, requires reaching heights nearly to the armpits; for boosts executed right side up, the hips and even the crotch of the swimsuit should be visible above the water—with all of that power coming purely from whatever momentum the swimmer can generate by sculling or kicking hard enough to create resistance against the water. Moreover, they are often done while *moving.* According to the rules, artistic swimmers should not remain in one spot but be traveling constantly, making multiple laps up and down the pool, and covering all sides and corners while weaving in and out of patterns.

Teams are swimming in ever tighter formations as well. In the 1980s, the typical distance between swimmers was 2 or 3 feet, according to Holly Vargo-Brown, head coach of Ohio State's synchronized swimming program, but that distance has since contracted to about 8

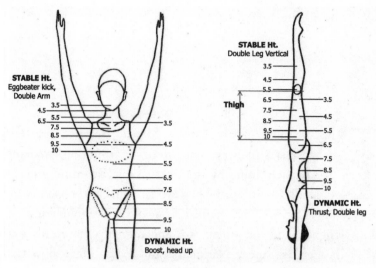

STABLE Ht.
Eggbeater kick,
Double Arm
3.5
4.5
5.5
6.5
7.5
8.5
9.5
10

3.5

4.5

5.5

6.5

7.5

8.5

9.5
10

DYNAMIC Ht.
Boost, head up

STABLE Ht.
Double Leg Vertical
3.5
4.5
5.5
6.5
7.5
8.5
9.5
10

Thigh

3.5

4.5

5.5

6.5

7.5

8.5

9.5

10

DYNAMIC Ht.
Thrust, Double leg

The height scoring scale from World Aquatics shows the varying points swimmers are awarded according to how high they can propel themselves above the surface of the water.

inches.[3] Swimming so close together is not only harder but also riskier. "You're battling each other in the pool," said Mariya Koroleva, who represented the US in the duet event at the 2012 and 2016 Olympics, "and that's where the danger is."[4] The *New York Times* reported in 2016 on the high prevalence of concussions and brain injuries among synchronized swimmers, writing that even though things may appear calm on the surface, underwater it's a "combat zone." Multiply that by eight pairs of legs kicking hard enough to eject human bodies as high as ten to twelve feet out of the water—sometimes in close proximity to teammates' faces who are performing an inverted hybrid or are submerged deeper to prepare to lift a teammate. After all, as a trauma physician told the *Times* reporter, "a kick in the head is a kick in the head, whether it happens in the pool or not."

Besides the kicking, the throws have gotten so high that if "flyers" come down wrong or land on teammates, the impact can lead to serious injury. Bill Moreau, director of sports medicine for the US Olympic Committee, estimated that about half of the synchronized swimmers under his watch had had concussions.[5] In 2013, three out of eight members of the national team heading to the Pan American Games were concussed.[6] Unlike in football, where concussions are well documented and regular pauses enable athletes to be examined immediately after sustaining a blow, artistic swimmers—who are trained to keep going no matter what—could be in the middle of a four-minute routine when they get hit. Moreover, they might not recognize some signs of concussion, such as blurred vision, dizziness, and disorientation, which are similar to the effects that can come with spinning around upside-down underwater on little oxygen.[7]

Another danger of artistic swimming is the risk of hypoxic blackout. Often the first question synchronized swimmers are asked is how long they can hold their breath. The answer is "a long time" (a reporter once timed Tracie Ruiz at 2 minutes and 25 seconds), but that is actually not the point. In routines, breath holding is done in spurts.[8] "If the routine is three minutes, we go 17 seconds underwater, then 15 seconds above, then 17 seconds under again," said Jaime Czarkowski, a member of the US national team. "It's a lot of up

The Santa Clara Aquamaids—with Krystal Li as the base and Elizabeth Zakharov as the flyer—demonstrate how high swimmers can be catapulted into the air.

and down."⁹ Teams have moved away from extremely long periods of immersion (like when Ruiz and Costie stayed under for almost a full minute at the start of their duet at the 1984 Olympics), but even so, the athletes still spend half or more of the entire routine underwater. When swimmers surface, gasp for air, then submerge again, it sometimes mirrors hyperventilation—fast, shallow breathing—that artificially lowers the carbon dioxide levels in the body. As carbon dioxide buildup is what triggers the need to breathe, lowering it can enable a swimmer to stay under longer, but at the risk of the body not receiving the all-important trigger that air is needed immediately to keep the brain functioning. When that happens, the person loses consciousness.

At the 2022 World Aquatics Championships in Budapest, US national team member and former Olympian Anita Alvarez fainted at the end of her solo routine. Pictures of her limp body sinking to the floor of the deep end, and of US national team coach Andrea Fuentes diving in and pulling her to safety, went viral. Fuentes, who holds four Olympic medals from her years as a competitor on the Spanish national team, realized before the lifeguards that something was wrong when she didn't see Alvarez pop up the instant the music stopped, telling a reporter that at the end of a routine "the first thing you want to do is breathe."¹⁰ Alvarez was pulled out unconscious but made a full recovery and later told the *Los Angeles Times* that she wondered whether the incident would make people finally recognize how difficult the sport is.¹¹

While artistic swimming gets far more respect from the media than it used to, most people still have no idea how hard it is. Selina Shah, the team physician for United States Artistic Swimming, puts it this way:

> They are doing cardio movements like a sprinter doing a 100-meter dash or a football player running across a football field to make a touchdown or soccer player running across a soccer field. It is similar work, but you don't see it. You don't hear them grunting like you sometimes do the tennis players at Wimbledon. All of that work is hidden by the grace and beauty of their movements.¹²

The *New York Times* pointed out that in addition to creating "improbable aquatic configurations and executing shockingly complex leg movements while upside down and not breathing," artistic swimmers "have to do each move at the same time and make it seem fun and not hard at all, even when they are heaving, hypoxic and about to pass out."[13] And indeed, making it seem "not hard at all" is practically written into the sport's official rules, which state that swimmers must maintain "an illusion of ease" throughout routines and make their movements "appear effortless and powerful without splash or struggle." And when they finally get the brief chance to snatch a gasp of oxygen, their breathing must be quiet, not "sputtering" or "explosive or wheezing."[14]

This same idea of ease was explored by George Browne in his kinesiology study of Annette Kellerman's underwater movements. Browne wrote that achieving grace in a performance like hers required projecting an "economy of effort" and "the impression of enjoyment, charm, and grace" even though the swimmer may actually be exerting tremendous force or "acting under physical pain or mental anguish."[15] It seems it was an illusion even a century ago with ornamental swimmers.

Swimmers on the Davis AquaStarz set up for a basket toss to propel their "flyer" through the air.

But whereas in the past, giving an appearance of charm and ease might have been about hiding exertion, particularly in the days when women were not supposed to sweat or raise their heart rates in public, now the requirement is about projecting mastery in the aquatic element. The 2023 artistic swimming rules continue by noting that the athletes must demonstrate "total command" and in their "richness of movement" give the impression of "owning the water."[16] The only problem with all of this, Browne wrote presciently in 1917, was that the spectator must "have sufficient experience with the technique of the art to be able . . . to judge of the *difficulties overcome* if he would judge fairly."[17] Most people can at least appreciate the winded feeling that comes from sprinting or the difficulty of maneuvering gracefully on ice skates, but only a tiny minority of the viewing public has ever even dabbled in synchronized swimming or has any concept of the "difficulties overcome" to make such tremendous feats appear effortless.

The escalating difficulty of the sport is perhaps inevitable as part of the constant drive within athletics to push the limits and demonstrate elevated human performance and capability. In sports where there is no "stopwatch, scale, or measuring tape" for setting and breaking records, wrote sport historian Kevin Wamsley, the only way to show evolution in human ability is "to deliver more excitement in the form of risk, and more complicated patterns of movement—more twists, more somersaults."[18] Although Wamsley was writing specifically about gymnastics, the same holds true for artistic swimming. The addition in 2013 of a difficulty score as one of the three major scoring categories has also been a major factor. The difficulty category was added as a way to reward teams that were innovating and taking bigger risks, but the greater emphasis on earning difficulty points has also served to further propel the sport's evolution in the direction of extreme athleticism. Stephan Miermont, a choreographer who has worked with Olympic teams in multiple countries, has seen these changes unfold in the way routines have been written over the years. In the 1990s, the focus was on creating something beautiful and "on theme" with the music, he said. Think America's gold-winning 1996 "Fantasia on an Orchestra" routine. Then around 2010, speed became the driving factor.

"Everybody was like . . . move, move, move, move," said Miermont. "And I think Russia brought that to the sport because they showed us how much faster we could move."[19] Indeed, Russia's national team, which has proven to be unbeatable since it catapulted to the top at the 2000 Olympics, has raised the bar exponentially on the sport's difficulty.

While America may have initiated the race, it is no longer the one setting the pace. The US team has not taken home an Olympic gold medal since earning a perfect score at the debut Olympic team event at the 1996 games in Atlanta, while Russia has swept the gold in both the duet and team events at every Olympiad of the twenty-first century. Japan and Canada remained on the medal stand in 2000, but that would be the last time for the latter. The United States did come back for a silver in 2004, but then it continued to fall behind and has not made it past the qualifiers to send a full team of eight swimmers to the Olympics since Beijing in 2008. China has risen to consistent second place standing while third has been contested in recent Olympiads between Japan and Ukraine.

Getting a spot at the Olympics is not easy, even for top contenders. There are very few spots available for the team event—eight in Beijing 2008 and London 2012, and upped to ten spots in Tokyo 2020 and Paris 2024. On top of that, in 2004 the international swimming federation FINA (now called World Aquatics) switched to a continental qualifiers system that guarantees a spot for each of the five designated continents, as determined by regional championships. However, the Olympic host country automatically gets the spot for its continent. That leaves the rest of the world to compete for the remaining handful of spaces at the Olympic qualifiers. The system was implemented with the worthwhile goal of ensuring continental balance, but it also, at times, has meant that the teams competing at the Olympics are not necessarily the ones that would have emerged on top if there had been a global competition. For example, in 2015 Canada won the Pan American Games, the Olympic qualifying event for the Americas. That would have normally earned Canada a place at the 2016 Olympics in Rio, but since Brazil was the host country it went to their team instead, even though they came in fourth at the Pan American Games. That left Canada to contend for one of the three available spots remaining at the Olympic qualifiers, which they missed when they came in fourth and—as a result—did not get to compete at the Olympics. The United States, on the other hand, didn't even try to qualify. After failing to earn a spot in the team event at the London Olympics in 2012, sending only a duet to the summer games that year, the US continued to fall behind in international rankings. By the time the qualifiers for Rio 2016 came around, leaders at United States Synchronized Swimming (USSS) felt that the chances of earning a spot were so low that preparing and sending a team was not a good use of limited resources. There are far more spots for duets (24 that year), so they pinned their hopes instead on duet pair Anita Alvarez and Mariya Koroleva, who did qualify and compete in Rio, where they came in fifth.

Funding plays a key role in all of this. In the US, Olympic sports receive limited support from the nongovernmental United States Olympic and Paralympic Committee (which was known as the US Olympic Committee until 2019). The Committee, which gets its funding from corporate sponsors and TV broadcast rights, doles out dollars according to past performance. Dubbed "money for medals," the system gives the most to sports winning the largest number of medals and reduces funding for those that come home empty-handed. With only two medal events per Olympiad, artistic swimming is already at a disadvantage compared with sports with multiple medal events like swimming or gymnastics (which had thirty-seven and fourteen medal opportunities, respectively, in Tokyo 2020). After the American synchronized swimmers failed to bring home a medal from the 2008 or 2012 Olympiads, the US Olympic Committee's funding for the sport dropped to its lowest point in seventeen years.[20]

The Voice of America reported in 2009 that America was one of only three countries in which Olympic athletes receive no government funding.[21] Meanwhile, in some countries, like China, national sports teams receive financial support from their governments, not only enabling them to invest in top coaches and training but also, in many cases, to provide salaries to athletes. This kind of support allows elite artistic swimmers in these countries to train full-time without the stress of being a financial burden on family or having to take out loans and to remain longer in the sport. Government cash awards to Olympic medalists reach six figures in many countries. In Russia, where national team athletes receive prizes like cars and apartments from corporate sponsors, artistic swimmers often compete in multiple Olympiads. Svetlana Romashina, the most decorated athlete in the sport, has competed in four—Beijing, London, Rio, and Tokyo—and holds seven gold Olympic medals. Having seasoned competitors on the team makes a huge difference. So does the length of time athletes train together. In some of the top competitor countries like Russia and China, kids who show promise often move to synchronized swimming schools, sometimes away from their families, to train under professional coaches with other top aspirants. By the time they're old enough to be on the national team, these swimmers have already been training and competing together for years, which makes a big difference in a sport built around the concept of synchronization.

Even though synchronized swimming originated in the United States, which dominated the international arena for decades, the seat of power has firmly shifted to Russia, leaving the US and many other countries struggling to keep up. But as Dawn Bean wrote in her history of synchronized swimming, America can take "maternal pride" in seeing how truly global it has become and how much the countries the US helped in the past have improved—and raised the bar for the entire sport in the process.[22]

So where do men fit into all of this? Ever since the Beckwith Frogs and swimming professors were usurped by their sisters and the water queens, women have reigned in synchronized swimming. Even though the first competition under Katharine Curtis in 1939 was between two co-ed teams, for most of synchronized swimming's history, it has been a "women's sport." After United States Synchronized Swimming (USSS) took over as the national governing body for synchro in 1979, men were allowed to compete alongside women within the United States. But since they continued to be excluded internationally, there were limited prospects for male competitors and no Olympic male role models to inspire boys to take up the sport, so synchronized swimming continued to draw few male swimmers . . . few, that is, but not none.

In upstate New York in the early 1990s, ten-year-old Bill May had the option of sitting on deck and watching his sister's synchronized swimming class or joining in. He chose the latter and quickly discovered not only that he had a natural knack for synchro, but that the sport combined three of his greatest loves: gymnastics, the water, and performing.[23] Within a few years, May had advanced so much that he had outgrown any local coaching options, so in 1995 at the age of sixteen, he moved to California to train under coach Chris Carver with the country's top team, the Santa Clara Aquamaids. May began swimming duets with teammate Kristina Lum, and the two were propelled to the spotlight in 1998 when they won the duet competition at the US national championships—the first "mixed" (male and female) duet to do so. After competing at the international Goodwill Games, one of the few international events he was eligible to participate in, May became a cause célèbre for men's inclusion in synchronized swimming and was voted USA Synchronized Swimming Athlete of the Year in 1998 and 1999.

But that was the limit to how far May could go. A *Sports Illustrated* reporter who profiled May during the 2000 US Olympic squad trials described the bittersweet moment when May sat in the stands and cheered with tears in his eyes for his teammates as they received their Olympic uniforms and folded flags—the same teammates he had trained with seven days a week for ten-hour days.[24] Even though

Bill May and Kristina Lum performing their winning
"mixed-duet" at the 1998 Goodwill Games.

he had known this moment would come eventually, it didn't take the sting out of the fact that his talent was irrelevant. Ahead of what would turn out to be a tide-changing Olympiad for the sport, and the beginning of Russian dominance, national team coach Carver was asked if May would have earned a spot if he had he been allowed to try out. "He not only would have made the team," she responded, "he would have been among the very top of the competitors on the U.S. team."[25]

American leaders in the sport began rallying to get mixed duets added to the Olympic program, with plans to bring the idea for a vote at the 2001 FINA congress. Although USSS president Judy McGowan had gotten several countries on board, Russia remained opposed. Not only had the Russians just unseated the United States as the top team in the world in Sydney, but they didn't have any Bill Mays of their own and, as ESPN wrote, weren't about to risk their newly earned spot at the top "for the sake of gender equity."[26]

FINA advised McGowan to let it go, warning that adding men could endanger the sport's place in the Olympics. The IOC was still trying to increase the proportion of female competitors and synchronized swimming's status as a women's sport had helped to keep it on the Olympic roster. "Title IX put a great emphasis on women's sports at that time," said Carver years later. "When we got to the Olympics, I think people were very much afraid that our unique status as a women's sport had helped us get there."[27] The fight to make synchronized swimming an Olympic sport had been so uphill, and its hard-won status felt so tenuous, that even those who wanted to see men included were hesitant to push too hard. Ultimately, McGowan did not bring it for a vote, feeling her job was to protect the sport, and, as ESPN pointed out, there weren't "throngs of boys fighting for equality" in synchronized swimming.[28] Only one other man, Benoit Beaufils of France, who had also trained under Carver, was competing at the level of May.

But Olympic priorities change, along with spectator preferences, and a decade later, the IOC began calling for more mixed-gender events. FINA seized the opportunity, adding mixed duets at the 2015 Aquatic World Championships in Kazan, Russia. It was a dream come true for May, Beaufils, and the small but growing number of male competitors around the world. May and his former partner Kristina (Lum) Underwood—both in their late thirties—came out of retirement to train together for the free routine, while May paired with Christina Jones, a 2008 Olympic competitor in Beijing, for the technical routine. All three were working as aquatic performers in Cirque de Soleil's Vegas water shows, which not only had kept them in great shape but also facilitated training together. Benoit Beaufils also came out of retirement to compete, representing France with his duet partner and Olympic bronze medalist Virginie Dedieu.

Even though Russia was hosting the event and entered a mixed duet pair—Darina Valitova and Aleksandr Maltsev—many in Russia remained against men's inclusion. The BBC quoted Russian sports minister Vitaly Mutko as saying that synchro should be "a purely feminine sport," while the captain of the Russian Olympic synchro team, Angelika Timanina, told the reporter: "We're used to classical synchronised swimming, feminine synchronised swimming."[29] Perhaps that is why Maltsev told the BBC that mixed duets should play up the traditional power/grace divide between men and women. "In a mixed duet the man should personify strength, power," he said. "The woman, on the contrary, beauty and grace."[30]

Many of the mixed duets opted to play on gender dynamics, treating it more like pairs figure skating than the "matchy-matchy" style of female synchro duets. This approach can also help with the practical problem of differing body compositions, explained Bill May. "A guy fires his muscles differently than a woman, their strength is different, their buoyancy is different, and, a lot of times, flexibility is different," he said. "Trying to make all of that complement each other is very difficult."[31] He and Lum, from their earliest days as duet partners, opted for gender dynamism, prompting *Sports Illustrated* in 1999 to describe one of their routines as ranging from "playful to explosive to wanton," adding that there was something elemental and "impossibly sexy" about "all that skin and muscle and water."[32]

At the 2015 debut mixed duet competition at the World Championships in Kazan, May and Jones won the gold for their technical mixed duet, while he and Lum won the silver for their free routine. The Russians won in reverse—gold for free and silver for tech. Many hoped that the introduction of the mixed duet in Kazan was just a first step and that it would soon become part of the Olympic program, but it was not added for either the 2016 or the 2020 games. Having hit a glass ceiling, May went back to Cirque de Soleil for several years before leaving to become a coach for his former team, the Aquamaids. But he told the BBC that even if it didn't happen until he was eighty-five, if the Olympics ever opened to men, he would be there to compete.

So with all these changes, whatever happened to swimming pretty? Alongside the increasing strength demonstrated in synchro routines, the aesthetic has changed as well, and new presentation styles aim to project power as much as or more than beauty. In Tokyo, Russian duet pair Svetlana Romashina and Svetlana Kolesnichenko swam to music called "Spiders." In flesh-colored suits adorned with giant black arachnids and webs, they imitated spiders on deck before diving in. They wore dark eye makeup and slicked-back hair. The only thing about them that might have brought to mind Esther Williams was their shared aquatic medium. Plastered-on smiles are no longer the norm in the sport, but a new kind of fixation on the athletes' facial expressions has emerged. As the sport has become one of the most difficult in the Olympic pantheon and its exertion harder to mask, the Internet has filled with roundups of synchro "fish face" pictures—unflattering close-ups of swimmers caught grimacing or mid-gasp for air.

All this leaves some viewers a little nostalgic for the sport's earlier forms. Loretta Barrious Larsen and Ellen Richard Zaccardelli—both national champions and gold medalists (in team and duet, respectively) at the 1955 Pan American Games, the first international synchronized swimming competition—find the routines today to be more athletic than when they were competing, but the style of swimming less enjoyable to watch. Zaccardelli described it as "choppy and fast and splashy," adding that "you only see the girls once in a while when they bob up their heads out the water for a few strokes. . . . Everything's very stiff and precise, which is good, but I miss some of the beauty of the other kind of swimming."[33] Larson noted that routines are so action packed that there is a movement on every beat of the music. "Ours was more flowing," she said, "more Esther Williams-ish, if you wanna say."[34]

A number of professional aquatic performance groups have formed in response to this nostalgia, both meeting and fueling the demand for the synchro styles of yesteryear. Many employ former competitive synchronized swimmers yet offer a retro-glam look that is in sharp contrast to the gelled hair, nose clips, and "fish faces" of the sports arena. These groups typically opt for midcentury-inspired bathing suits, rubber swim caps with chin straps, often strolling on deck with parasols and sometimes even swimming in high heels. The most well known is the Los Angeles–based Aqualillies, who perform at high-end events and product launches, and have appeared on television shows like *The Marvelous Mrs. Maisel, Glee,* and *Jane the Virgin.* The organization's co-director, Mary Ramsey, competed in the junior Olympics and collegiate synchro, but when she first saw the Aqualillies perform in 2009, she was immediately drawn to their aesthetic, saying she had never seen synchro done "so professionally, so polished . . . so glamorous."[35] Ramsey became a performer and later joined the business side of the organization, helping manage their troupes in Miami, New York, Las Vegas, Europe, Canada, Australia, and a more recent addition: a male troupe called the Aquawillies.

The popularity of the Aqualillies and groups like them is part of a larger pop-culture resurgence in synchronized swimming, which has become a go-to way to insert camp glamour, comic relief, or a cultural touchstone to bygone eras into film and music projects. For the Coen brothers' movie *Hail, Caesar!* the Aqualillies performed a spectacular water ballet scene featuring Scarlett Johansson as a midcentury swimming star à la Esther Williams. Synchronized swimmers have performed in music videos for Beyoncé, Justin Bieber, Nicki Minaj, Sébastien Tellier, Katy Perry, Ariana Grande, Maroon 5, and others—not to mention commercials for everything from cell phones and makeup to home insurance and Disney resorts. The demand for synchro entertainment and the preference for the aquamusical aesthetic show that, in Mary Ramsey's words, "The desire for these kinds of beautiful Busby Berkeley style water show spectaculars never left."[36] Whereas many in the sports world no longer identify with Esther Williams or her style of swimming, for the Aqualillies, she is the Queen Mother and greatest inspiration. When Williams passed away in 2013, her husband Edward Bell invited the Aqualillies to perform at her memorial service, saying that Esther considered the group a continuation of her swimming legacy. They continue to put on a public performance every August on Williams's birthday in her memory.

The Aqualillies combine the athleticism of competitive synchronized swimming with the glamour of an Esther Williams aquamusical.

For 1996 Olympic gold medalist Becky Dyroen-Lancer, who choreographed the synchronized swimming scene in the 1999 movie *Austin Powers: The Spy Who Shagged Me*, the pop-culture appeal of synchronized swimming is not just a matter of nostalgia but also an attraction to its unique blend of athleticism and glamour. "We're not just models," she said. "Synchronized swimmers are beautiful, athletic women, so I think that has some chops." She added that not all sports lend themselves to entertainment, whereas synchronized swimmers "love to perform" and can do so many interesting things in the water.[37] Similarly, Ramsey said Los Angeles audiences are so accustomed to seeing beautiful women walking around modeling in swimsuits that they are often surprised when the Aqualillies actually get in the water. "Beautiful girls are a dime a dozen," she said, "but girls that are actually talented with a skill like that . . . I don't think you find that every day."[38]

In fact, it was partly the recognition that audiences love to be entertained that led to the sport's name change in 2017, according to

Cornel Mărculescu, who was FINA executive director at the time. "Today, sport should be a show," said Mărculescu. "If sport today doesn't provide this interest for television, if they don't create a show, they lose . . . viewers around the world."[39] According to Mărculescu, International Olympic Committee president Thomas Bach thought a different name for the sport would hold more audience appeal than "synchronized swimming," and urged FINA to change it. But the sport didn't want that, and when Mărculescu tasked the FINA Technical Synchronized Swimming Committee with proposing an alternative name to be voted on by the organization, they pushed back, said Virginia Jasontek, the honorary secretary to the committee. "But then he came back to us a second time and said, 'I really need you to come up with another name,'" recalled Jasontek. The committee "fought hard" for a year and a half, she said, but eventually decided that if the goal was to grow the sport and keep it relevant, it was better to lose its long-established brand than the good graces of FINA and the IOC.[40] After debating a few names, they ultimately landed on artistic swimming, hoping it would align the sport with artistic gymnastics, an Olympics powerhouse.

When the name change was brought for a vote at the 2017 FINA general congress, it passed quickly, which Judy McGowan, president of United States Synchronized Swimming at the time of the change, believed was by design. Normally, she explained, important issues specific to a single aquatic discipline are first raised for discussion or a straw vote within that sport's own technical congress.[41] That way you have people who understand the sport voting on the issues that affect it, and not, for example, high divers voting on water polo rules. But the name change proposal was sent directly to the general congress, a body of delegates from across aquatic disciplines representing 176 countries—many of which did not have synchronized swimming programs. One of the few synchro delegates who was present, Lori Eaton, said the vote took place so quickly that there was no chance for deliberation and that most people around her didn't even understand what had happened.[42] Likely, delegates from other sports assumed that if the proposed new name came from the sport's own Technical Committee, that must have been what its practitioners wanted.

But it wasn't, as demonstrated by the fact that 11,044 people signed a petition launched shortly after the announcement asking FINA and the IOC to reverse their decision. Kris Harley-Jesson, who created the petition, wrote that besides not conveying the extreme athleticism of the sport, the name change "pays absolutely no respect to Synchronized swimmers, past and present."[43] To her, the way the change happened, and the fact that neither FINA nor the IOC responded to the outcry, came down to "elitist men" at these "old boys' clubs" making unilateral decisions without consulting those with the most skin in the game—the athletes.[44] Her sentiments were echoed by those who signed the petition, with many expressing the feeling that the new name would undo the sport's tremendous advances. One signer wrote: "Artistic Swimming doesn't just take us a step back, it sends us careening backwards down an entire flight of stairs to the birth of our sport. We have come too far and worked too hard to have someone make a decision that could wipe us out in a heartbeat."[45]

At first United States Synchronized Swimming—which oversees all levels of the sport domestically—said it would not adopt the new name, but that became increasingly difficult as other countries began falling in line and rebranding their national federations. In 2020, under CEO Adam Andrasko, the US federation did the same, changing its name to USA Artistic Swimming. Andrasko pointed out the difficulty, particularly for a "judged sport," of bucking global trends, arguing that it was important to show "alignment and solidarity with the international federation." But taking a positive spin, he added that the new name also posed an opportunity to show "how much more powerful and athletic" the sport had become.[46]

Ahead of Tokyo 2020, where the new name made its Olympic debut, Bill May acknowledged that the change was difficult but added, "I think in the long run, it's going to prove to be a good thing." He pointed out that several synchro events, including mixed duets and the acrobatic routine (previously called the highlight routine), which focuses on the spectacular aerial throws, often stray from strict synchronization. He connected the name change to other developments in the sport such as the push to include these events at the Olympic level and the growing movement for gender equity. "I think the name change is really going to help drive these new events and further the evolution of the sport," said May.[47] His remarks were prescient. In November 2022, World Aquatics announced that the acrobatic routine would be added to the team event program for international championships and the Olympics. This new event, which must include at least seven acrobatic moves from different categories including airborne, balance, and platform (the latter two each involve creating a human base or platform for other swimmers to stand on or be launched from), ramps up the thrill factor for spectators and goes to show that the world of sport has not forgotten that people love spectacle.

News of an even more momentous change came the following month when the IOC announced it had agreed to accept male competitors for the 2024 Olympics in Paris—allowing up to two male swimmers on each team of eight. After four decades of synchronized/artistic swimming being a women-only sport at the international and Olympic levels, it was a historic reversal. "Aquatics sports are universal and men have proven themselves to be excellent artistic swimmers," said World Aquatics president Husain Al-Musallam following the announcement. "I look forward to seeing this new dimension of artistic swimming being shared with the world in Paris."[48] Giorgio Minisini, an Italian artistic swimmer who won gold for his mixed duet at the 2022 World Aquatics Championships with his partner Lucrezia Ruggiero, was elated: "For 20 years, I have been swimming knowing that one thing was sure in my life: artistic swimming at the Olympics was a female sport . . . Now, everything is different. I feel like I could fly."[49]

USA Artistic Swimming head coach Andrea Fuentes celebrated the decision and noted the new possibilities having diverse body types on the team could bring: "You can make the most impactful acrobatics to have ever happened in our sport, no? So it changes everything."[50] Bill May, who had remained a leading voice in the movement for male inclusion, came out of retirement a second time after the announcement. At the age of forty-four, he began training as a member of the US Senior National Team with the hopes of an American comeback and of finally realizing his Olympic dream in Paris. The US had been working hard to reclaim a spot at the top, and only a few months later won second place in the new acrobatic routine at the World Aquatics Championships in Fukuoka, Japan, making Bill May the first American man to win an international championship team medal.[51] Then

The 2023 US Senior National Artistic Swimming Team: Audrey Kwon, Dani Ramierz, Ruby Remati, Calista Liu, Anita Alvarez, Nikki Dzurko, Bill May, Natalia Vega, Keana Hunter, Jaime Czarkowski, Megumi Field, and Jacklyn Luu.

in February 2024 at the qualifiers for the Paris Summer Games, the US made an even more historic comeback, earning a team spot at the Olympics for the first time since 2008—and May was among the athletes who made it happen.

Men's Olympic inclusion didn't come in the form many expected it to—as mixed pairs—but it is a truer version of the co-ed sport that Katharine Curtis originally envisioned, with men and women swimming together on the same teams. Curtis, who wrote all the way back in 1941 that she hoped the separation of men and women was only temporary, would have no doubt been thrilled had she lived to see the change.[52] In a way, the addition of men is a signal that the sport has fully arrived—and not because it needed men to legitimize it. Synchro is no longer propped up on the wobbly crutch of being a "women's sport," nor is it subject to the shifting attitudes toward whatever that means. "Whereas saving the sport all those years ago relied heavily on keeping it all female," wrote ESPN, "the world now is a place that is leaning toward obliterating strict notions of gender completely."[53] In fact, the IOC announced in 2023 that the Paris 2024 summer games would mark the first Olympiad in history to achieve full gender parity, with 5,250 male competitors and 5,250 female competitors.[54] In this new world, it is fitting that artistic swimming's specialness is no longer built on exclusivity but instead on the power, dynamism, beauty, and awe of what humans can do in the water—together.

So is synchronized—or artistic, scientific, or whatever you want to call it—swimming a sport or is it entertainment? Should its focus be on athleticism or aesthetics? Perhaps what all of this rich history shows is that it can be—and is—both. To repeat the apt words penned by a sportswriter in 1948: "It's swimming, isn't it? And the kids are nuts about it."[35]

ACKNOWLEDGMENTS

Writing a book is far more challenging and involves far more people than I ever imagined, and I'd like to take this space to thank those individuals who helped, in a variety of ways, to bring this project to fruition. I am fortunate to work at Georgetown University, where I have benefited from both institutional support and the personal support of my colleagues at the Center for Contemporary Arab Studies. I owe a great deal to Georgetown's director of scholarly publications, Carole Sargent, a wellspring of publishing and writing knowledge who has been an amazing mentor to me. Carole not only was instrumental in helping me draft my proposal but also was one of the first people I discussed my book concept with, and the seriousness and enthusiasm with which she greeted what was just a delicate, unformed seed of an idea at the time played a large role in my decision to pursue it. I am also deeply indebted to Joseph Sassoon, who has been a constant cheerleader and sage sounding board since I began this project. Both he and the wonderful Dana Al Dairani saw to it that I had the space and resources necessary to write the book on deadline while also continuing my full-time job. I will be forever grateful to you both for your kindness and friendship. Special thanks go to Rochelle Davis and Fida Adely as well, for their encouragement and support through the many stages of research and writing. I am especially grateful to Sopanit (Dede) Angsusingha, my brilliant and indefatigable research assistant. No task was too large or too small for Dede, and this book would not have come together nearly as well without her exceptional organizational skills and research prowess. Thank you, Dede! The interlibrary loan specialists at Georgetown deserve recognition as well, particularly Dana Aronowitz, Jess Fenander, and Amanda Rudd, who tracked down countless sources and articles that were critical to my research. I doff my hat to your detective skills!

Researching this book was incredibly rewarding, in large part because of the people I got to know in the process who generously shared their own research, expert knowledge, and personal experiences with me. Chief among them are Lea Bean, chair of the history committee for USA Artistic Swimming, along with her mother, Dawn Pawson Bean, who was not only a monumental pillar within the world of synchronized swimming but also the sport's foremost historian. The Beans warmly welcomed me as a newcomer to the field, answered questions, connected me with individuals I would not have otherwise found, and—with remarkable generosity of spirit—shared dozens of digitized magazines and other archival materials that greatly informed my research. I treasure both my signed copy of Dawn's book, *Synchronized Swimming: An American History* (now dog-eared from much love and research consultation!) and my memories of sitting with her and Lea and hearing firsthand about the sport's early years. Others deserving thanks include Bert Hubbard and Donna Dorn of the International Academy of Aquatic Art for their enthusiastic support—and to Bert especially for photocopying and mailing materials to me. Dave Day and Margaret Roberts, both experts on Victorian natationists, lent me rare swimming books from their collection, facilitated my research in England, and showed me warm hospitality while I was there. Cathy Goodwin graciously invited me to a reenactment of the Modern Mermaids synchronized swimming performance and, along with Jordan Whitney-Wei, provided helpful information on the life of Katharine Curtis. Thank you to Keith Myerscough, Fred Dahlinger, and Edward O'Donnell, who shared their research on ornamental swimmers, water circuses, and the *General Slocum* disaster, respectively. Tony Staley at the Amateur Athletic Union, Peter Shrake at Circus World Museum, and several staff members at the Royal Lifesaving Society were kind enough to make scans and send hard copies of research materials. The archives at the International Swimming Hall of Fame were an invaluable resource, and I owe thanks to several folks who helped me there over the years, including Marion Washburn, Ivonne Schmid, Laurie Marchwinski, and Todd Eller, with particular thanks going to Bruce Wigo for freely sharing his connections and rich knowledge of swimming history. I am grateful to many at USA Artistic Swimming (formerly USA Synchronized Swimming), particularly Adam Andrasko and Judy McGowan, for responding to numerous queries, and to my teammates Linda Thomson and Vittoria De Maurizi for lending me their collections of historical materials. To all the remarkable individuals who graciously shared their own personal memories and experiences with me, thank you! It's been a true pleasure, and even the stories that regrettably couldn't be included due to space limitations were nonetheless vital in helping to contextualize and breathe life into the historical narrative.

As the research began taking shape as a manuscript, I was supremely fortunate to have in my orbit of friends several talented writers and editors who were willing to give of their time and expertise to read drafts at various stages of the writing. I am particularly indebted to Ellen Ficklen, Morgan Flaherty, Helen Jackson, Laurie Lesser, and Laurie McClellen, each of whom provided insightful feedback and suggestions that greatly improved upon the text. It has been a privilege and pleasure to work with Liveright senior editor Gina Iaquinta, whose early and continued enthusiasm for the project has been contagious and sustaining. I am deeply grateful for her shared vision and keen editorial eye, which were critical in shaping the book. I'd like to thank a few other key individuals on the W. W. Norton team, including editorial assistant Maria Connors, who kept things running smoothly; production manager Anna Oler; project editor Susan Sanfrey; copyeditor Rebecca Rider; and art director Sara Wood, who also designed the beautiful cover. And finally, to my wonderful agent, Esmond Harmsworth, thank you for being such a wise and valued partner throughout this journey!

I'd be remiss if I did not also recognize a handful of individuals who influenced my life in ways that proved catalyzing. They include my teachers at the Johns Hopkins MA in Writing program, particularly Tim Wendel and Sue Eisenfeld, who shaped and prepared me as writer, and my former boss, Kate Archambault, without whom this book would have never even become a glint in my eye. Kate not only discovered the synchronized swimming class that became my first foray into the sport, but practically pushed me out the office door and to the pool, setting in motion a series of life-changing events (thank you, Kate!). I am grateful to my teammates on the DC Synchromasters for warmly receiving me more than a dozen years ago and for being the beautiful swimmers and people that you each are. I found my home away from home in the water with you!

I have saved the biggest thanks to the end—for my family, whose unfailing support made this book possible. The love and encouragement of my parents, Gerry and Bob, have not only made me who I am today but also spurred me on at every stage of the book writing endeavor. At the eleventh hour, when the going got tough, they put on their reading glasses and helped me through the final push. Thanks to my brother Jim for reading chapters, texting encouragement, and helping prepare the images for the book. And finally, I want to thank Khair, my best friend, husband, and partner in this crazy life, who has supported me in countless ways large and small—from the meals delivered to my desk and the hours spent taking pictures at archives to being the anchor that kept me moored whenever I doubted I was up to the task. This book belongs to each of you.

NOTES

PROLOGUE

1. Digby Diehl and Esther Williams, *The Million Dollar Mermaid: An Autobiography* (New York: Simon and Schuster, 1999), 41.
2. Jeff MacGregor, "Out of Sync," *Sports Illustrated*, August 23, 1999, 70.

CHAPTER 1: SCIENCE

1. This and all English quotations from Everard Digby's *L'Art de Nager* are taken from the English translation of Thévenot's French translation of Digby's book: *The Art of Swimming Illustrated by Proper Figures with Advice for Bathing* [. . .] (London: Dan Brown et al., 1699; Ann Arbor: Text Creation Partnership, 2022). This quote is from p. 46.
2. He was called this, by most accounts, because he preferred water to beer, but with his proclivity for swimming being well known, that could have contributed to the nickname.
3. Benjamin Franklin and Frank Woodworth Pine, *The Autobiography of Benjamin Franklin* [. . .] (Garden City, NY: Garden City Publishing Company, 1927), 94–95.
4. Franklin and Pine, *Autobiography of Benjamin Franklin*, 94–95.
5. Thévenot, *Art of Swimming*, 3.
6. K. M. Coleman, "Launching into History: Aquatic Displays in the Early Empire," *Journal of Roman Studies* 83 (1993): 48–74.
7. Oscar Broneer, "Review: Gli Spettacoli in Acqua Nel Teatro Tardo-Antico. By Gustavo Traversari," *American Journal of Archaeology* 65, no. 4 (October 1961): 412.
8. Coleman, "Launching into History"; Alexandra G. Retzleff, "John Chrysostom's Sex Aquarium: Aquatic Metaphors for Theater in Homily 7 on Matthew," *Journal of Early Christian Studies* 11, no. 2 (2003): 198.
9. Lena Lencek and Gideon Bosker, *The Beach: The History of Paradise on Earth* (New York: Penguin Books, 1999), 28–29.
10. Nicholas Orme, Early British Swimming: 55 BC–AD 1719 (University of Exeter, 1983).
11. Michael West, "Spenser, Everard Digby, and the Renaissance Art of Swimming," *Renaissance Quarterly* 26, no. 1 (Spring 1973): 13.
12. Thévenot, *Art of Swimming*, v.
13. Thévenot, *Art of Swimming*, 35.
14. Thévenot, *Art of Swimming*, 46.
15. Captain Stevens, *Captain Stevens' System of Swimming* (London: Biggs and Son, 1845), 9.
16. Henry Peacham, *The Compleat Gentleman Fashioning Him Absolute in the Most*

Necessary & Commendable Qualities Concerning Minde or Bodie [. . .] (London: John Legat for Francis Constable, 1622; Ann Arbor: Text Creation Partnership, 2022), 180.

17. "The Art of Swimming," *Sharpe's London Magazine of Entertainment and Instruction for General Reading*, July 1861, 43; Martin Cobbett, *The All-England Series: Swimming* (London: George Bell and Sons, 1890), 8.

18. "From Benjamin Franklin to O[liver] N[eave, before 1769]," in *Experiments and Observations on Electricity* [. . .], 4th ed., by Benjamin Franklin (London: 1769), 463–68.

19. Benjamin Franklin, *The Works of Benjamin Franklin Including the Private as well as the Official and Scientific Correspondence*, Vol. 5 (New York: Knickerbocker Press, 1904), 6.

20. Scott Cleary, "The Ethos Aquatic: Benjamin Franklin and the Art of Swimming," *Early American Literature* 46, no. 1 (2011): 51–67.

21. Ralph Thomas, *Swimming: With Lists of Books Published in English, German, French and Other European Languages* [. . .] (London: Sampson Low, Marston and Company, 1904).

22. Cleary, "Ethos Aquatic."

23. *Witches Apprehended, Examined and Executed, for Notable Villanies by Them Committed Both by Land and Water* [. . .] (London: Printed at London for Edward Marchant, 1613; Ann Arbor: Text Creation Partnership, 2022).

24. Francis Hutchinson, *An Historical Essay Concerning Witchcraft: With Observations Upon Matters of Fact* [. . .] (R. Knaplock, 1720), 174.

25. Hutchinson, *Historical Essay Concerning Witchcraft*, 174.

26. "A Witch Trial at Mount Holly," *Pennsylvania Gazette*, October 22, 1730, Franklin Papers, Founders Online, National Archives.

27. Cleary, "Ethos Aquatic," 59.

28. Sarah B. Pomeroy, *Benjamin Franklin, Swimmer: An Illustrated History* (Philadelphia: American Philosophical Society Press, 2021).

29. Miss Powers, "Why Do Not Women Swim? A Voice from Many Waters" (Ladies' National Association for the Diffusion of Sanitary Knowledge, 1859), 7. Pamphlet from the Wellcome Collection: https://wellcomecollection.org/works/dyvxwksu.

30. Sir George Head, *A Home Tour Through the Manufacturing Districts of England, in the Summer of 1835* (London: John Murray, 1836), 46.

31. "Bathing at Ramsgate," *The Times*, August 25, 1846.

32. Elizabeth Gaskell, *The Life of Charlotte Bronte*, Vol. 1 (London: Smith, Elder, and Company, 1904; Project Gutenberg, 2005).

33. Derek Forbes, "Water Drama," in *Performance and Politics in Popular Drama: Aspects of Popular Entertainment in Theatre, Film, and Television 1800–1976*, eds. David Bradby, Louis James, and Bernard Sharratt (Cambridge: Cambridge University Press, 1980), 101.

34. Forbes, "Water Drama," 98.

35. Charles Sprawson, *Haunts of the Black Masseur: The Swimmer as Hero*, 1st ed. (Minneapolis: University of Minnesota Press, 2000), 32.

36. Thomas, *Swimming*, 45.

37. "Sargeant" Leahy, *The Art of Swimming in the Eaton Style* (London, Macmillan & Co., 1875), 13.

38. "Manly Exercises," *Boys Own Magazine*, September 1, 1862, 356.

39. "British Swimming Society," *The Times*, September 6, 1843; "Swimming," *Bell's Life in London and Sporting Chronicle*, July 18, 1874.

40. Dave Day and Margaret Roberts, *Swimming Communities in Victorian England* (Cham, Switzerland: Palgrave Macmillan, 2019), 38; Charles Newman, *Swimmers and Swimming or The Swimmer's Album* (London: The Pictorial Press, 1898), 22.

41. Thomas, *Swimming*, 129.

42. "Swimming," *Bell's Life in London and Sporting Chronicle*, June 16, 1877, 3.
43. "A Practical Swimmer," "Swimming and Swimmers," *London Society: An Illustrated Magazine*, Vol. 10 (London: William Clowes and Sons, 1866), 49; "Professor Beckwith's Swimming Galas," *The Era*, September 3, 1876.
44. Newman, *Swimmers and Swimming*, 14.
45. "A Practical Swimmer," 49.
46. "Professor Beckwith's Swimming Entertainments," *The Era*, October 11, 1874.
47. Violet Greville, "The Victims of Vanity," *National Review* 21 (March 1893): 76.
48. Miss Powers, "Why Do Not Women Swim?," 12.
49. Miss Martineau, "Miss Martineau on Swimming for Ladies," *Wells Journal*, September 24, 1859.
50. "Opening of The Swimming Bath for Ladies," *English Woman's Journal*, Nineteenth-Century Serials Edition, August 1858, 415.
51. "Opening of The Swimming Bath," 413.
52. Mater-Familias, "To the Editor of the English Woman's Journal," *English Woman's Journal* 25 (March 1, 1860): 68.
53. Dave Day, " 'What Girl Will Now Remain Ignorant Of Swimming?' Agnes Beckwith, Aquatic Entertainer and Victorian Role Model," *Women's History Review* 21, no. 3 (July 1, 2012): 419–46; "Another Long Swimming Feat," *Northern Echo*, September 6, 1875.
54. "Extraordinary: Swimming Feat by a Girl," *North and South Shields Gazette and Daily Telegraph*, September 2, 1875.
55. "A Lady Swimmer in the Thames," *Sheffield Daily Telegraph*, September 2, 1875.
56. "The Force of Example," *New York Times*, September 27, 1875.
57. "Miss Beckwith's Swim to Greenwich," *The Star*, September 4, 1875.
58. "Professor Beckwith's Swimming Galas," *The Era*, September 3, 1876.
59. George Gipe, "Naiad Agnes Plunged Women into Spectator Sports 100 Years Ago," *Sports Illustrated*, March 31, 1975.
60. Day and Roberts, *Swimming Communities in Victorian England*, 83.
61. "Facilities for Learning to Swim," *The Penny Illustrated Paper and Illustrated Times* [hereafter shortened to *Penny Illustrated*], September 11, 1875.
62. Agnes Beckwith, "Crossing the Channel," *Bell's Life in London and Sporting Chronicle*, Nineteenth Century UK Periodicals, August 10, 1878.
63. "Swimming," *The Graphic*, no. 302, September 11, 1875.
64. *Sporting Gazette*, September 11, 1875.
65. "Followers of Captain Webb," *Penny Illustrated*, July 8, 1876.
66. Day and Roberts, *Swimming Communities in Victorian England*.
67. Archibald Sinclair, *Swimming* (London: George Routledge and Sons, 1909), 9.

CHAPTER 2: STAGE
1. "Miss Beckwith's Swim," *Birmingham Daily Mail*, July 2, 1880; "Miss Agnes Beckwith's Thirty Hours' Swim," *Bell's Life in London and Sporting Chronicle*, May 8, 1880.
2. "Lady Swimmers," *Penny Illustrated*, November 8, 1884; "Another Lesson to Ladies," *Penny Illustrated*, September 10, 1887.
3. Francis Buckland, *Curiosities of Natural History* (London: Richard Bentley, 1868), 101–6.
4. "The London Music Halls: The Canterbury," *The Era*, October 8, 1887.
5. Framley Steelcroft, "Some Peculiar Entertainments," *Strand Magazine* 11 (1896).
6. Keith Myerscough, "Nymphs, Naiads and Natation," *International Journal of the History of Sport* 29, no. 13 (October 2012).
7. "Entertainments at the Baths," *Gloucestershire Chronicle*, October 21, 1893.
8. Lewis Carroll, *Private Journals of Charles Lutwidge Dodgson*, Vol. 8 (Luton: Lewis

Carroll Society, 1997–2000), 347–82, quoted in Lindsay Smith, *Lewis Carroll: Photography on the Move* (London: Reaktion Books, 2015), 203.

9. "At Home in the Water: Champion Swimmers Beating the Fishes in Their Own Element," *New York Times*, June 9, 1883.

10. "How the Girls Swim," *National Republican*, July 20, 1883.

11. "The Lady Swimmer: Miss Agnes Beckwith," *Hearth and Home*, August 6, 1891, 383.

12. "Champion Swimmers: Willie and Agnes Beckwith Give a Fancy Exhibition," *St. Louis Post-Dispatch*, March 28, 1887.

13. Dave Day, " 'What Girl Will Now Remain?,' " 430.

14. "Houdini, Tarzan and the Perfect Man: The White Male Body and the Challenge of Modernity in America (Review)," *Journal of Social History* 36, no. 3 (2003): 21.

15. Day, " 'What Girl Will Now Remain?' "

16. "Champion Swimmers."

17. "Champion Swimmers."

18. E. K. Reader and L. M. Reader, "Types of Women Athletes: Miss Agnes Beckwith," *Sandow's Magazine of Physical Culture* (London, Ontario: University of Western Ontario, March 1902), 191.

19. "Swimming," *The Graphic*, September 21, 1878.

20. "Champion Swimmers."

21. "In Grand Combination P.T. Barnum and Co's Greatest Show on Earth and the Great London Circus and Adam Forepaugh's New and Great Show Circus, Menagerie and Hippodrome," 1887.

22. Dave Day, "From Lambeth to Niagara: Imitation and Innovation Among Female Natationists," *Sport in History* 35, no. 3 (July 3, 2015): 364–90.

23. Day, "From Lambeth to Niagara."

24. "The New Sensation—The Female Minstrels and the Can-Canners," *Wilmington Morning Star*, April 8, 1875.

25. "Opinions of the Press on Sallie Swift, the Original and Champion Lady Club-Swinger," *New York Clipper*, May 8, 1875.

26. Armond Fields, *Women Vaudeville Stars: Eighty Biographical Profiles* (Jefferson, NC: McFarland and Company, 2006).

27. Fields, *Women Vaudeville Stars*.

28. Robert W. Snyder, *The Voice of the City: Vaudeville and Popular Culture in New York*, 2nd ed. (Chicago: Ivan R. Dee, 2000), 17.

29. Fields, *Women Vaudeville Stars*.

30. Michael Bennett Leavitt, *Fifty Years in the Theatrical Management* (New York: Broadway Pub. Co, 1912); "The Oxford."

31. "A New Wonder!" *New York Clipper*, October 23, 1875.

32. "A New Wonder!"

33. "City Summary," *New York Clipper*, November 20, 1875.

34. "Unqualified Success. Lurline the Water Queen and Watson the Man Fish," *New York Clipper*, November 20, 1875.

35. "Unqualified Success."

36. "Unqualified Success."

37. "Olympic Theatre," *Brooklyn Daily Eagle*, December 1, 1875.

38. "Lurline, the Water Queen at the Olympic Theatre," *New York Daily Herald*, November 8, 1875.

39. "City Summary," *New York Clipper*, October 14, 1876.

40. Aquarius, "Swimming: Lurline at the Oxford," *Sporting Life*, January 5, 1882.

41. "Three Minutes and Four Seconds Under Water. Lurline the Water Queen," *New York Clipper*, July 22, 1876.
42. W. B. Tegetmeier, "Swimming: Existence in the Water—'Lurline,'" *The Field*, February 11, 1882.
43. Tegetmeier, "Swimming: Existence in the Water."
44. "Unqualified Success."
45. Chas Weightman, *The Art of Swimming* (New York: Robert M. De Witt, 1873), 71.
46. "The Oxford," *Lloyd's Weekly Newspaper*, January 1, 1882.
47. "Olympic Theatre."
48. "New York Aquarium," *Times Union*, February 16, 1877.
49. "Notice!," *New York Clipper*, April 29, 1876.
50. "Miss Lurline," *Barcelona Daily [Diario de Barcelona]*, July 13, 1877.
51. "Aquatic Notes," *Bell's Life in London*, December 31, 1881.
52. "Comparative Popularity," *Berrow's Worcester Journal*, April 8, 1882.
53. "Celebrities Photographed," *Chicago Tribune*, February 6, 1876.
54. Aquarius, "Swimming: Lurline at the Oxford."
55. Hunter Barron, "Swimming: Existence in the Water—'Lurline,'" *The Field*, February 18, 1882.
56. Lennox Browne and Emil Behnke, *Voice, Song, and Speech: A Practical Guide for Singers and Speakers*, 4th ed. (New York: G. P. Putnam's Sons, n.d.), 118.
57. Barron, "Swimming: Existence in the Water."
58. "Notes," *Cincinnati Enquirer*, September 30, 1890.
59. "The Theaters," *Minneapolis Journal*, December 5, 1896.
60. "Clark-St. Dime Museum," *Chicago Tribune*, May 16, 1897.
61. "The Water Queen's Story," *Mexico Weekly Ledger*, March 31, 1881. The unnamed performer may be LaSelle the Water Queen because the article says she performs in the tank with Captain Beach, and LaSelle performed all over the country with Beach.
62. "The Mozart Specialties," *Santa Cruz Surf*, August 7, 1884.
63. "The Water Queen's Story."
64. "A Circus Fish Story," *Chicago Weekly Post*, May 2, 1872.
65. "The Water Queen's Story."
66. "Notes."
67. Brooks McNamara, "'A Congress of Wonders': The Rise and Fall of the Dime Museum," *Emerson Society Quarterly* 20, no. 3 (1974): 224.
68. "Music and Drama," *Public Opinion*, October 1886.
69. "Music and Drama."
70. "Sandow Horsewhipped by Lurline," *Evening Express*, July 3, 1893.
71. "New York Letter," *Albany Daily Democrat*, July 20, 1893.
72. "Lurline Dies in London. At One Point Worth $50,000," *Wilkes-Barre Times Leader, Evening News*, October 13, 1898.
73. "Gossip of Stageland," *Times-Tribune*, May 10, 1898.
74. "Theatrical News," *Buffalo Courier*, May 15, 1898.
75. Don Stacey, "Water Spectacles in the Circus," *King Pole*, September 2006, 17.
76. Stacey, "Water Spectacles in the Circus," 20.
77. Myerscough, "Nymphs, Naiads and Natation," 1917.
78. Fred Dahlinger Jr., "Paris on the Prairie: An 1894 Nouveau Cirque in Chicago," *Bandwagon* 56, no. 2 (April 2012).
79. "The Earl's-Court Exhibitions," *The Standard*, May 22, 1893.
80. *Bath Chronicle*, no. 7791 (Thursday, December 31, 1908): 3.
81. "World's Fair at Islington," *The Era*, January 21, 1899.

82. "Swimming for Women: Some Practical Hints. Miss Agnes Beckwith Interviewed," *Daily News*, November 27, 1903.
83. "Swimming: An Interesting and Seasonable Topic for Perusal in These Broiling Days," *Inter Ocean*, July 21, 1883.
84. Reader and Reader, "Types of Women Athletes: Miss Agnes Beckwith," 192.
85. "The Water Queen's Story."
86. "Swimming: Interesting and Seasonable Topic."
87. "Swimming: Interesting and Seasonable Topic."

CHAPTER 3: STARDOM

1. Annette Kellermann, *Physical Beauty: How to Keep It* (New York: George H. Doran Company, 1918), 248.
2. Annette Kellerman, *How to Swim*, 1st ed. (New York: George H. Doran Company, 1918), 52.
3. "Are Women's Figures Becoming More Masculine?" *St. Louis Post-Dispatch*, December 5, 1909.
4. Emily Gibson and Barbara Firth, *The Original Million Dollar Mermaid: The Annette Kellerman Story*, 1st ed. (Crows Nest, NSW, Australia: Allen and Unwin, 2005), 88.
5. Kellermann, *Physical Beauty*, 166.
6. "Diving Venus Shapes Corsetless Course: Proves to Audience There Is Nothing Under Bathing Suit But Her," *Fort Worth Star-Telegram*, November 28, 1909.
7. Kellerman, *How to Swim*, 14.
8. Kellerman, *How to Swim*, 14.
9. Gibson and Firth, *Original Million Dollar Mermaid*.
10. Kellerman, *How to Swim*, 20.
11. Gibson and Firth, *Original Million Dollar Mermaid*, 28.
12. Kellerman, *How to Swim*, 22 and 48.
13. Kellerman, *How to Swim*, 13; Gibson and Firth, *Original Million Dollar Mermaid*, 33.
14. Gibson and Firth, *Original Million Dollar Mermaid*, 29.
15. Ishbel Johns, "Boston Arrest a Mistake, Says Annette," *Boston Globe*, October 11, 1953.
16. Mary Gould Lytle, "Women Swimmers and Water Athletes," *Evening Herald*, August 11, 1906.
17. "'One and All' Notes," *Cornishman*, February 28, 1907.
18. "Lady Swimmers: Who Is the Champion? Miss Kellerman Challenged," *Manchester Evening News*, March 24, 1906.
19. "Great Lady Swimmer," *Evening Bulletin*, June 1, 1907.
20. "Famous Swimmer Coming," *Boston Evening Transcript*, April 19, 1907.
21. "The Biggest Day of the Year at White City Next Friday," *Chicago Tribune*, July 28, 1907.
22. "The Biggest Day of the Year."
23. "The Biggest Day of the Year"; F. C. McCarahan, "Late Chicago News," *The Billboard*, June 29, 1907.
24. "Out of Town: Lottie Mayer," *Variety*, April 1910, 19.
25. "White City's Fame Grows," *Herald News*, June 16, 1907.
26. "Bathing Suit Must Be Cut," *Boston Post*, November 7, 1908.
27. Johns, "Boston Arrest a Mistake."
28. One of the few historians who discuss this discrepancy, Stephen Wilk, believes that Kellerman fabricated the story to deflect attention from a potentially more damning scandal in which she was named as the cause of marital strife in a divorce suit. See *Lost Wonderland the Brief and Brilliant Life of Boston's Million Dollar Amusement Park* by Stephen Wilk (Amherst: Bright Leaf, 2020).

29. Charles Samuels and Louise Samuels, *Once Upon a Stage: The Merry World of Vaudeville* (New York: Dodd, Mead and Company, 1974), 39.

30. Kellerman, *How to Swim*.

31. "Annette Kellerman. 'Diablo,' Dancing and Aquatic," *Variety*, November 1908, 12.

32. "Fifth Avenue," *Variety*, December 1908.

33. "Colonial," *Variety*, January 30, 1909, 15.

34. "Miss Annette Kellerman the Diver at the Hipp," *Times Recorder*, November 11, 1909.

35. Mae Tinee, "She Interviews the 'Divess' and Sees 'The' Union Suit," *Chicago Tribune*, December 18, 1910.

36. Ana Kokkinos and Michael Cordell, dirs. *The Original Mermaid*, documentary (Hilton Cordell and Associates, 2002).

37. "Annette Kellerman: 'On the Beach at Boulogne,'" *Variety*, January 1909, 13.

38. "Kellerman: Nymph Will Disport Herself in Water and Air at Orpheum," *Los Angeles Times*, March 20, 1921.

39. Samuels and Samuels, *Once Upon a Stage*, 40.

40. "Advocates Swimming on the Curriculum of Public Schools," *The Province*, June 12, 1909; Arthur L. Price, "Water Nymph's Tights Cling and Cling," *San Francisco Call*, July 25, 1910.

41. "What Is Offered This Week in the Popular Priced Theatres," *Bangor Daily News*, November 18, 1909.

42. "What Is Offered This Week"; "Fifth Avenue," *Variety*, December 1908.

43. "Advocates Swimming on the Curriculum."

44. Dudley Sargent, "Are Athletics Making Girls Masculine?" *Ladies' Home Journal*, March 1912, 11.

45. "Are Women's Figures Becoming More Masculine?"

46. Gibson and Firth, *Original Million Dollar Mermaid*, 4.

47. "Modern Woman Getting Nearer the Perfect Figure: Dr. Dudley A. Sargent of Harvard Denies That She Is Getting Masculine, But She Is Getting More Sensible," *New York Times*, December 4, 1910.

48. "Modern Woman Getting Nearer the Perfect Figure."

49. Dudley Sargent, "Modern Dance as Athletic Exercises," *New York Times*, January 3, 1909.

50. Kellerman, *How to Swim*, 43–44.

51. Kellermann, *Physical Beauty*, 50–51.

52. J. B., "Annette Kellermann," *The Soil: A Magazine of Art*, March 1917, 113.

53. Kellerman, *How to Swim*, 45.

54. "Diving Venus Shapes Corsetless Course."

55. "Miss Kellerman Praises Swimming," *Boston Herald*, November 7, 1908, 10, quoted in Mark Allan Herlihy, "Leisure, Space, and Collective Memory in the 'Athens of America': A History of Boston's Revere Beach" (PhD diss., Brown University, 2000), 145.

56. Kellerman, *How to Swim*, 39.

57. Marilyn Morgan, "Drowning in Culture: Gender, Swimming and Stereotypes," *Consuming Cultures* (blog), March 25, 2017.

58. "You Can Thank Her for This," *Daily News*, February 23, 1964.

59. "New York Fashions," *Harper's Bazar* 29, no. 24: 503. The magazine title was spelled "Bazar" until the end of the 1920s when it was changed to "Bazaar."

60. Annette Kellerman, "Prudery as an Obstacle to Swimming," *Physical Culture* 22, no. 1 (August 1909): 122.

61. Kellerman, "Prudery as an Obstacle to Swimming," 122.

62. "Annette Kellerman Has Unique Costume," *Pittsburgh Press*, September 19, 1909.

63. "Gimbels Advertisement," *New York Times*, June 7, 1911.

64. Kellerman, *How to Swim*, 31.

65. Walter H. Bernard, "Annette Kellerman as Neptune's Daughter," *Motion Picture Magazine*, June 1914, 57–62.

66. "Mermaid Tops Orpheum Bill: Kellerman in Pictures Big Mason Feature," *Los Angeles Times (1886–1922)*, June 7, 1914.

67. "Annette Kellerman at Savoy in 'Neptune's Daughter,'" *Fall River Daily Evening News*, June 19, 1915.

68. Percy Hammond, "Annette Kellerman in Pretty Pictures," *Chicago Tribune*, May 19, 1914.

69. "Annette Kellerman at Savoy."

70. "Silver Loving Cup Is Presented to Fox at Premier," *Motion Picture News*, November 4, 1916, 2820.

71. "Million Dollar Picture Beautiful Represents Highest Development in Art of Illustrated Music," *San Francisco Chronicle*, December 31, 1916.

72. "Through Our Own Opera Glasses," *Baltimore Sun*, May 6, 1917.

73. "Through Our Own Opera Glasses."

74. Hammond, "Annette Kellerman in Pretty Pictures."

75. "Kellerman Form Causes Woman to Beat Husband," *Toledo Blade*, January 10, 1917, quoted in *Blue Vaudeville: Sex, Morals and the Mass Marketing of Amusement, 1895–1915*, Andrew L. Erdman (Jefferson, NC: McFarland and Company, 2007), 98.

76. "Public Likes," *The Moving Picture World*, August 21, 1920.

77. "Public Likes."

78. *Journal of Commerce*, quoted in "Annette Kellerman in 'A Daughter of the Gods' at the Victoria Theater," *Evening News*, February 18, 1918.

79. "A Million Staked on One Woman's Nerve," *Post-Crescent*, March 7, 1917.

80. Kellerman, *How to Swim*, 34.

81. "Mermaid Ballet in Fox Spectacle," *Motography*, July 8, 1916, 91.

82. Kellerman, *How to Swim*, 118.

83. "Mermaid Ballet in Fox Spectacle."

84. "Movies," *Daily Standard*, October 6, 1917.

85. "Movies."

86. "Mermaid Ballet in Fox Spectacle."

87. "'A Daughter of the Gods,' Gigantic Feature, Makes New Movie History," *Oakland Tribune*, February 7, 1917.

88. "Million Dollar Picture Beautiful."

89. George H. Browne, "The Psychology of Grace," *Mind and Body*, September 1917, 210.

90. Browne, "Psychology of Grace," 199.

91. Philip K. Scheuer, "Annette Kellerman's All for Esther Now," *Los Angeles Times*, March 23, 1952.

92. Kellerman, *How to Swim*, 212.

93. Kellerman, *How to Swim*, 212.

94. Norman Clarke, *The Mighty Hippodrome* (New York: A. S. Barnes and Company, 1968), 23.

95. "What News on the Rialto?," *New York Times*, 1916, sec. Fashion Society Drama Music.

96. Milton Epstein, "The New York Hippodrome: Spectacle on Sixth Avenue from 'A Yankee Circus on Mars' to 'Better Times,' a Complete Chronology of Performances, 1905–1939 (Volumes I and II)" (PhD diss., New York University, 1993).

97. "Aquatic Act at the 'Hip,'" *New York Dramatic Mirror*, February 3, 1917.

98. "Diving Act at Hippodrome: Annette Kellermann Replaces Pavlowa in 'The Big Show,'" *New York Times*, January 23, 1917.
99. "Diving Act at Hippodrome."
100. Browne, "Psychology of Grace," 201.
101. "Hippodrome's Sensational Success," *Montclair Times*, March 10, 1917.
102. "Hippodrome's Sensational Success."
103. "The Diving Venus," *BBC Radio 4* (A Falling Tree Production for BBC Radio 4, January 14, 2017).
104. Helen Bagg, "Fifty-Two Vacation Weeks a Year," *Green Book Magazine*, October 1920, 86–87.

CHAPTER 4: SAFETY

1. "Band Played Amid Flames," *New York Times*, June 16, 1904.
2. "Band Played Amid Flames."
3. Edward T. O'Donnell, *Ship Ablaze: The Tragedy of the Steamboat General Slocum*, ill. ed. (New York: Crown, 2004), 115, 118.
4. "Band Played Amid Flames."
5. O'Donnell, *Ship Ablaze*.
6. "Nurse Swims to Rescue," *Baltimore Sun*, June 16, 1904.
7. "Honor by Congress: Girl Heroine of the Slocum Is Given Medal," *Evening Star*, March 18, 1909.
8. "Terrible Disaster at New York: Excursion Steamer in Flames," *Daily Telegraph*, June 16, 1904.
9. "Report of the United States Commission of Investigation Upon the Disaster to the Steamer 'General Slocum'" (Washington, DC: Government Printing Office, October 8, 1904), 25.
10. "Report of the Disaster to the 'General Slocum,'" 6.
11. Alwyn Knight, "The Commodore: Thar She Blows," *The Red Cross Courier*, March 1939, 10.
12. "Is Important to Everyone: Slocum Disaster in New York Arouses Thinking People," *Appleton Post*, June 30, 1904. Quoting an editorial in the *Chicago Tribune*.
13. George H. Corsan, *The Diving and Swimming Book* (New York: A. S. Barnes and Company, 1926), 86.
14. "Women and Children Eager to Be Swimmers," *Standard Union*, July 6, 1904.
15. "Chicago Women Who Swim," *Inter Ocean*, May 10, 1896.
16. "Second Annual Report of the United States Volunteer Life Saving Corps of Rhode Island Department" (Providence, RI: E. L. Freeman and Sons, Printers, January 1907), 58.
17. "Should Learn to Swim," *Democrat and Chronicle*, July 7, 1895.
18. "You Can Thank Her for This," *Daily News*, February 23, 1964.
19. "Every Woman Should Swim," *New-York Daily Tribune*, June 25, 1904, 5.
20. "Women and Children Eager to Be Swimmers."
21. "New York: A Daily Resume of Gotham Gossip," *Pittsburgh Press*, June 29, 1904.
22. Commodore W. E. Longfellow, "The Growth of the Life Saving Idea in America," n.p., accessed from the International Swimming Hall of Fame (ISHOF) Archives: Longfellow Files; "Skit Portrays Red Cross Work," *Tampa Times*, February 25, 1946.
23. "Life-Savers Teach Children to Swim," *Standard Union*, August 18, 1904.
24. Evening Star, "Cutting Down on Potomac River's Summer Death Toll," August 8, 1915.
25. "To Save the Drowning—Press Floating Rib," *New York Tribune*, August 17, 1919.

26. Oscar W. Hoar, *Biographical Sketch of Commodore Wilbert E. Longfellow*, A Publication of the Commodore Longfellow Society (Punta Gorda, FL: The Renshaw Press, n.d.).

27. Hoar, *Biographical Sketch of Longfellow*.

28. Archibald Sinclair, *Swimming and Life Saving* (London: Health and Strength Library, 1906), 24.

29. Commodore W. E. Longfellow, "Women Life-Savers: Their Feats of Skill and Daring Win Recognition by the Red Cross," *Ladies' Home Journal*, June 1920, 45.

30. "First Annual Report of the United States Volunteer Life Saving Corps of Rhode Island Department of State" (Providence, RI: E. L. Freeman and Sons, Printers, January 1906), 10.

31. "Women Are Not Safe in the Water in Clinging Skirts Declares Girl Champion of Women's Life Saving League," *Evening Sun*, August 2, 1913.

32. "Commodore W. E. Longfellow—He Saves Lives and Limbs," *Des Moines Register*, March 23, 1940.

33. "You Can Thank Her for This," 10.

34. "Brooklyn Girl Swims Hell Gate's Rapids," *Brooklyn Daily Eagle*, September 6, 1909.

35. "You Can Thank Her for This," 10.

36. Marguerite Mooers Marshall, "Women Here Form League for Life-Saving, Urge Girls to Learn to Swim," *Evening World*, July 12, 1911.

37. "Girl Life-Savers Are Preparing for Heroic Work During This Summer," *St. Louis Star and Times*, May 4, 1913.

38. G. Elliot Flint, "Modern Woman Is Making Rapid Progress in the Water as Well as on Land," *New-York Daily Tribune*, November 12, 1911.

39. Flint, "Modern Woman Is Making Rapid Progress."

40. "No Corsets, No Frills for Would-Be Mermaids," *New-York Tribune*, July 4, 1913.

41. Janet Barry, "Swimming Tank Is the Garden Where Girls Can Grow Beauty," *Evening Telegram*, January 30, 1912.

42. National Women's Lifesaving League, "An Exhibition in Swimming, Diving, Life-Saving" (exhibition program), Manhattan Beach Bathing Company, July 19, 1914, accessed from the ISHOF Archives: Adeline Trapp Files.

43. "Kid M'Coy's Rainbow Bath Suit Outshines Girl Life Savers, Who Drag Ducks and Fruit from Sea," *New York Herald*, August 15, 1915.

44. Lisa Bier, *Fighting the Current: The Rise of American Women's Swimming, 1870–1926* (Jefferson, NC: McFarland and Company, 2011).

45. "Mermaids of Minneapolis," *Star Tribune*, September 14, 1913.

46. "Brave Suffragists Save 'Anti' from Sea," *New York Times*, July 18, 1915.

47. "Girls Show Speed and Prowess in the Water," *New York Tribune*, July 18, 1915.

48. "Brave Suffragists Save 'Anti' from Sea."

49. Flint, "Modern Woman Is Making Rapid Progress."

50. "Seek to Prevent Ocean Disasters," *Times Union*, October 9, 1912.

51. "Seek to Prevent Ocean Disasters."

52. "Wilbert E. Longfellow: The Hobby That Became a Life Work," International Swimming Hall of Fame 2014 Yearbook, 2014, 93–95.

53. "Moving Picture Lecture on Life Saving," *Courier-News*, November 28, 1913.

54. "Burdened by Home Work," *Richmond Times-Dispatch*, May 10, 1913.

55. Edith Leora Dennis, "The Genesis and Development of the American Red Cross Water Safety Service" (PhD diss., New York University, 1943), 9.

56. Dennis, "Genesis and Development of the American Red Cross," 45.

57. Dennis, "Genesis and Development of the American Red Cross," 26.

58. Knight, "The Commodore," 11.
59. Longfellow, "Women Life-Savers," 45.
60. Longfellow, "The Growth of the Life Saving Idea."
61. "Inez Seymour Milton," *Baltimore Sun*, October 4, 1914.
62. "Lifesaving Corps Elects Star Mermen," *Los Angeles Evening Express*, April 10, 1916.
63. "Girl Life Guards Save Many Lives," *Central New Jersey Home News*, August 17, 1915.
64. Dennis, "Genesis and Development of the American Red Cross," 106.
65. "Society Women Are Anxious to Qualify as Life Savers," *Tampa Tribune*, May 17, 1918.
66. "Woman Life Guard Is Put on Job," *Belleville Daily Advocate*, June 29, 1917.
67. "Woman Life Guard Busy. Asbury Park Men Try to 'Take Turns' at Being Rescued," *New York Times*, July 29, 1917.
68. Longfellow, "Women Life-Savers," 45.
69. "Women's Life-Saving Corps: Red Cross Plans That Will Lessen Materially Dangers of Boating and Swimming," *Red Cross Bulletin*, May 17, 1920, 6.
70. "Women's Life-Saving Corps," 5.
71. Longfellow, "Women Life-Savers," 130.
72. B. Dean Brink, "Recreational Method of Teaching Swimming," in *Games and Recreational Methods for Clubs, Camps and Scouts*, ed. Charles F. Smith (Dodd, Mead and Company, 1924), 188.
73. "Foreword," in *Water Pageants, Games and Stunts*, by Olive McCormick (New York: A. S. Barnes and Company, 1933), v.
74. Commodore W. E. Longfellow, "Swimming Instruction Through Water Plays and Pageants," *American City* 35 (July 1926): 56–59.
75. Hoar, *Biographical Sketch of Longfellow*.
76. Commodore W. E. Longfellow, "Water Plays and Pageants Help Swimming Grow," *Mind and Body* 31, no. 333 (December 1924): 322–25.
77. Commodore Wilbert E. Longfellow, "Let's Dramatize Aquatics," *Red Cross Courier*, September 1937, 6–9.
78. "'Along the River Bank' Water Pageant Canada 1938," *Winnipeg Tribune*, April 23, 1938.
79. "Aquatic Carnival Tuesday; All Out," *Herald Examiner*, 1927, Chicago Historical Society: Katharine Whitney Curtis Papers.
80. A. L. Fisher, "The Mermaid's Water Revue," *Sportswoman*, September 1927.
81. Jeff Wiltse, *Contested Waters: A Social History of Swimming Pools in America* (Chapel Hill: University of North Carolina Press, 2010).
82. "Water Pageant by Girl Swimmers at 137 St. Y," *New York Age*, March 31, 1928.
83. "Water Pageant at Banneker Pool," *Washington Tribune*, August 17, 1940.
84. "Local Businesses to Close for Labor Day Celebration," *Herald-Sun*, September 2, 1945.
85. "Camps in Richmond Area Getting Ready," *Richmond Times-Dispatch*, May 2, 1948.
86. "Neptune's Cure for Piracy: A Water Pageant," February 1931, accessed from the ISHOF Archives: Beulah Gundling Files.
87. Commodore W. E. Longfellow, "Swimming in Peace and War: A Water Ballet," n.d., accessed from the ISHOF Archives: American Red Cross Files.
88. Longfellow, "Let's Dramatize Aquatics."
89. Allene De Lura Good, "Water Pageants and Their Use in Educational Programs" (Master's thesis, University of Texas, 1937), 10–11.
90. Hoar, *Biographical Sketch of Longfellow*.
91. Knight, "The Commodore," 9.
92. Wilbert Edmund Longfellow, foreword to McCormick, *Water Pageants, Games and Stunts*, v.

CHAPTER 5: SIDESHOW

1. Punch Wheeler, "Carnival News. Rice & Dore Water Carnival Opens at Portland, Ore., April 4–11," *The Billboard*, April 18, 1914.
2. "Water Carnival Aids Baseball," *Great Falls Tribune*, May 22, 1914.
3. "Adelade De Young With Rice & Dore—Water Carnival Coming," *Ogden Standard*, July 12, 1913.
4. "Water Carnival Coming," *Canton Press*, August 27, 1915.
5. "Skidroad to Have Many Features," *Vancouver Sun*, August 28, 1913.
6. "Big New Water Show at the River Front," *Daily Gate City*, August 13, 1915.
7. "The Barnum Show Affords a Holiday of Real Delights," *York Daily*, May 7, 1895.
8. "Tustin Is a High Diver," *Rock Island Argus*, September 20, 1895.
9. "Coming Amusements: The Water Carnival at the Circus Bills at the Park," *Indianapolis News*, May 25, 1895.
10. "The Secret of Neptune's Daughter," *New York Times*, December 2, 1906.
11. "The Secret of Neptune's Daughter."
12. Wendell Phillips Dodge, "Under the Water with Submarine Actors," *Theatre Magazine*, 1909, 140.
13. "Opportunity to See Some Hyppodrome Attractions," *Warren Times Mirror*, June 15, 1911.
14. "Opportunity to See Some Hyppodrome Attractions."
15. "Girl Swimmers Scarce," *Variety*, July 1911, 22.
16. "J. Frank Hatch Shows," *The Billboard*, May 6, 1911, 6.
17. "Carnival Opens Next Week," *The Dispatch*, August 9, 1912; "Skidroad to Have Many Features."
18. "Water Carnival Aids Baseball."
19. "Over 15,000 People Pass Through Gates of Alabama State Fair," *Age-Herald*, October 7, 1914; "Water Show Opens Monday," and " 'Disappearing Water Ballet' Is Headliner of New Vaudeville Program," *Herald and Review*, September 22, 1912.
20. "Midway Rush Deprives Performers of Supper," *Courier-Journal*, September 17, 1914.
21. "Miscellaneous," *The Billboard*, September 2, 1911, 58.
22. "Danbury Fair Opens in Glory," *Hartford Courant*, October 4, 1911.
23. "Girls Are Expert in Swimming Art," *Los Angeles Evening Express*, March 17, 1911.
24. "Easier to Dive in Montana Than It Is at Seashore," *Billings Gazette*, June 11, 1914.
25. National Women's Lifesaving League, "An Exhibition in Swimming, Diving, Life-Saving" (exhibition program), Manhattan Beach Bathing Company, July 19, 1914. Accessed from the International Swimming Hall of Fame (ISHOF): Adeline Trapp Files.
26. "How the Girls Swim," *National Republican*, July 20, 1883.
27. Annette Kellerman, *How to Swim*, 1st ed. (George H. Doran Company, 1918), 254.
28. Maud Gray Jamieson, "Country Girl Made Good! Life and Loves of Maud Gray Jamieson" (unpublished memoir, n.d.), family archive of John Jamieson.
29. "Pretty Girls Dive for Prize on Stage," *Salt Lake Telegram*, June 12, 1912.
30. "Letter to Miss Lucile Anderson from John F. Conroy, Empress Theatre," June 20, 1912, accessed from the ISHOF Archives: Lucile Anderson Collection.
31. "The Biggest Sensation of 1913," *Altoona Times*, January 13, 1913.
32. "A Gift of Frank and Nancy Faulkner," 119, Lucile Anderson Collection, ishof.org, accessed January 7, 2023.
33. "St. Louis, MO. Lottie Mayer Swims Twenty-Six Miles in Record Time," *The Billboard*, June 25, 1910.
34. "Carnival News: A Message from the Ferari Shows," *The Billboard*, September 14, 1912.

35. Jamieson, "Country Girl Made Good!"
36. "Elks' Razzle Dazzle," *The Billboard*, May 6, 1922.
37. See *The Billboard*, March 23, 1918, 75; October 27, 1917, 2; October 11, 1919, 67.
38. See *The Billboard*, May 4, 1912, 64.
39. "Cora Beckwith Wants Diving Girls," *The Billboard*, July 28, 1917, 13.
40. "The Perfect Woman: Miss Annette Kellerman," *The Sketch*, August 21, 1912.
41. "Inez Wood and Her Water Nymphs," 123, Lucile Anderson Collection, ishof.org, accessed January 7, 2023.
42. "John F. Conroy and His Diving Girls Are Coming Attraction at Colonial," *Akron Beacon Journal*, November 23, 1912.
43. "Tampering with Trifles," *Houston Post*, April 26, 1913.
44. "Film and Bathing Girls in Person Will Be Sure Fire. Comedy Hits on High," *Film Daily*, April 13, 1919.
45. "Queen of the Sea—Fox Special," *Motion Picture News*, September 14, 1918, 1758.
46. Jamieson, "Country Girl Made Good!"
47. "Diving Venus' Act Scored; Pastor Displeased With It," *Oakland Tribune*, September 14, 1914.
48. See *The Billboard*, August 14, 1920, 61; April 28, 1917, 2.
49. H. E. Wilkinson, *Memories of an Iowa Farm Boy* (Ames, Iowa: Iowa State University Press, 1994), 122.
50. Wilkinson, *Memories of Iowa Farm Boy*, 124.
51. Janet M. Davis, *The Circus Age: Culture and Society Under the American Big Top*, 3rd ed. (Chapel Hill: University of North Carolina Press, 2002).
52. "Water Carnival Brings High Diver," *Richmond Palladium*, September 2, 1914.
53. Chas McDonald, "The Panama-Pacific International Exposition Ready for the Tickets," *The Billboard*, February 20, 1915, 14.
54. "The Water Circus," *Jackson Daily News*, September 18, 1914.
55. McDonald, "Panama-Pacific International Exposition," 14.
56. "Exposition's First Day Is a Record Breaker," *Los Angeles Times*, February 21, 1915.
57. Jamieson, "Country Girl Made Good!"
58. McDonald, "Panama-Pacific International Exposition," 56.
59. "Diving Girls on Zone at Fair Are Envied by Visitors," *San Francisco Examiner*, July 18, 1915.
60. "Striking Achievement of Y.W.C.A.," *Los Angeles Times*, September 26, 1915.
61. "Joy Zone Entertainers Crowding Fair Hospital," *San Francisco Examiner*, April 7, 1915.
62. "Exposition's 'Zone,'" *Variety*, March 1915.
63. "Water Lions and Diving Nymphs at Pantages," *Edmonton Bulletin*, November 14, 1916.
64. Jamieson, "Country Girl Made Good!"
65. "Shows Unloading for Fair Here This Week," *News and Record*, October 7, 1917.
66. "Submarine Girls at Carnival," *Sioux City Journal*, August 18, 1918.
67. "Big Crowds at the Lambs' Carnival," *Morning Call*, May 4, 1917.
68. Herb Dotten, "In This Corner: Pardon, Park," *The Billboard*, June 23, 1956.
69. George L. Hotchkiss, "Is There Safety in Danger?," *Illustrated World*, April 1923, 233.
70. "Girl Is Killed on Stage," *Prescott Daily News*, October 27, 1913.
71. "Boston Girl Takes Dizzy 125-Foot Plunge into 6 Feet of Water," *Boston Post*, March 6, 1921.
72. "How the Comic Artist Won His Blind Bride," *San Francisco Examiner*, February 7, 1926.
73. "Lamonaca's Band Remains at Park," *San Francisco Call*, April 20, 1913.
74. "Bull Escapes, to Terrorize Crowd on Closing Day," undated newspaper, Nova Scotia, accessed from the ISHOF Archives: Lucile Anderson Collection.

75. "Easier to Dive in Montana Than It Is at Seashore."

76. A. L. Wooldridge, "The Lists Are Full," *Picture-Play Magazine*, October 1925, 83–85, 103.

77. Hotchkiss, "Is There Safety in Danger?," 233.

78. "Rice's Submarine Girl Acts," *The Billboard*, April 21, 1917, 32.

79. "Diving Venus at Lakeside Park," n.d. Auburn, NY, accessed from the ISHOF Archives: Lucile Anderson Collection.

80. "World at Home Shows," *The Billboard*, July 28, 1923.

81. Greta Paige, "'Tiser Social Editor Goes Backstage in Follies Show," *Elmira Advertiser*, August 21, 1954.

82. Dotten, "In This Corner."

83. "How a Girl Beat Leander at the Hero Game," *Literary Digest* (August 21, 1926): 67.

84. A. L. Wooldridge, "Girls Who Risk Their Lives," *Picture-Play Magazine*, March 1925, 111.

85. "Audience at Carnival Greatly Pleased at Ancestors' Antics," *Evening Herald*, April 26, 1917.

86. "Suffragists at Tea with Circus Women," *New York Times*, April 8, 1912.

87. "Suffragists at Tea with Circus Women."

88. Josephine DeMott Robinson, *The Circus Lady* (New York: Arno Press, 1926), 277.

89. Punch Wheeler, "Story of the Great Water Circus," *The Billboard*, December 18, 1920.

CHAPTER 6: SPORT

1. Michael K. Bohn, *Heroes and Ballyhoo: How the Golden Age of the 1920s Transformed American Sports* (Washington, DC: Potomac Books, 2009).

2. "How a Girl Beat Leander at the Hero Game," *Literary Digest* 90 (August 21, 1926): 52.

3. "The American Girl," *Washington Post*, August 8, 1926.

4. Glenna Collett, "Sports for Women," *Woman's Home Companion*, September 1924.

5. Nancy Theriot, "Towards a New Sporting Ideal: The Women's Division of the National Amateur Athletic Federation," *Frontiers: A Journal of Women Studies* 3, no. 1 (1978): 1–7.

6. Alice Bertha Foster, "Basket Ball for Girls," *American Physical Education Review*, September 1897, 152–53.

7. Brad Austin, *Democratic Sports: Men's and Women's College Athletics During the Great Depression* (Fayetteville, AR: University of Arkansas Press, 2015), 108.

8. "Hot Shot for 'Jim' Sullivan," *New York Times*, July 19, 1913.

9. "No Women Athletes for American Team: Olympic Committee Adopts Plan to Raise Funds for the Berlin Games," *New York Times*, March 31, 1914.

10. Lisa Bier, *Fighting the Current: The Rise of American Women's Swimming, 1870–1926* (Jefferson, NC: McFarland and Company, 2011).

11. "Mermaids Win Fight in A.A.U.," *The Times* (Munster, IN), November 21, 1916.

12. "Women Swimmers and A.A.U.: Advocates of Water Sports for Sex in Favor of Supervision by Women," *New York Times*, November 22, 1914.

13. Bier, *Fighting the Current*, 94.

14. Meg Keller-Marvin, "Aileen Riggin Soule: A Wonderful Life in Her Own Words," *ISHOF News* (blog), August 19, 2019.

15. Tim Dahlberg, Mary Ederle Ward, and Brenda Greene, *America's Girl: The Incredible Story of How Swimmer Gertrude Ederle Changed the Nation*, 1st ed. (New York: St. Martin's Press, 2009), 69.

16. Aileen Riggin, "No Fish Ever Died of Pneumonia," *American Magazine*, August 1931, 57, 143.

17. Mary Henson Leigh, "The Evolution of Women's Participation in the Summer Olympic Games, 1900–1948" (PhD diss., The Ohio State University, 1974), 306.

18. Aileen Riggin, "Woman's Place," *Collier's*, May 14, 1932, 11.

19. Margaret Costa and Carmen E. Rivera, eds., *An Olympian's Oral History: Aileen Riggin, 1920–1924 Olympic Games, Diving* (Los Angeles: LA84 Foundation, 1999), 19.

20. Betty Grimes, "We're Going to Win the Swimming Events," *Akron Evening Times*, August 29, 1920.

21. David Barney, "American Genesis: The Archeology of Women's Swimming at the 1920 Olympic Games," *Journal of Olympic History* 18, no. 2 (July 2010): 37.

22. Grimes, "We're Going to Win."

23. Grimes, "We're Going to Win."

24. Costa and Rivera, *An Olympian's Oral History*, 23.

25. Keller-Marvin, "Aileen Riggin Soule."

26. Ernest A. Bland, ed., *Olympic Story: The Definitive Story of the Olympic Games from Their Revival in 1896* (London: Rockliff, 1948); Leigh, "Evolution of Women's Participation," 307.

27. Paula Dee Welch, "The Emergence of American Women in the Summer Olympic Games 1900–1972" (EdD diss., University of North Carolina at Greensboro, 1975), 26.

28. Mark Dyreson, "Icons of Liberty or Objects of Desire? American Women Olympians and the Politics of Consumption," *Journal of Contemporary History* 38, no. 3 (2003): 435–60.

29. "How Weak Is the Weaker Sex?," *Woman Citizenship*, September 1925, 15.

30. Frederick Henry Sykes, "The Social Basis of the New Education for Women" (Speech given at the Alumni Association of Teachers College, Columbia University, New York, February 24, 1917).

31. "Editorials: Greeks, Girls, and 1944," *The Nation* 118, no. 3060 (February 27, 1924): 222.

32. Leigh, "Evolution of Women's Participation," 151.

33. "Man's Athletic Crown in Danger," *Literary Digest*, July 28, 1923, 56.

34. "Man's Athletic Crown in Danger," 56.

35. "How Weak Is the Weaker Sex?," 15.

36. Helen Lenskyj, *Out of Bounds: Women, Sport and Sexuality* (Toronto: Women's Press, 1987), 12.

37. Pierre de Coubertin, "Les Femmes aux Jeux Olympiques," *La Revue Olympique*, July 1912; Leigh, "Evolution of Women's Participation," 76.

38. Luther Halsey Gulick, "Athletics from the Biologic Viewpoint," *American Physical Education Review* 9 (September 1906): 158–59.

39. Frederick Rand Rogers, "Olympics for Girls?," *School and Society* 30, no. 763 (August 10, 1929): 190–94.

40. "Cycling," *Star Tribune*, July 20, 1895.

41. "Off the Blackboard," *Indianapolis Times*, January 25, 1929.

42. Paul Gallico, "Women in Sports Should Look Beautiful," *Reader's Digest*, August 1936, 12.

43. Gallico, "Women in Sports," 12.

44. Paul Gallico, *Farewell to Sport* (New York: Alfred A. Knopf, 1940), 234–36.

45. Gallico, *Farewell to Sport*, 235.

46. Dick Hyland, "Are Women Champions," *Good Housekeeping* (May 1934): 38, quoted in Leigh, "Evolution of Women's Participation," 349.

47. Betty G. Hartman, "On Intercollegiate Competition for Women," *Synchro News*, May 1958, 6.

48. Claire Parker, "Swimming: The 'Ideal' Sport for Nineteenth-Century British Women," *International Journal of the History of Sport* 27, no. 4 (March 1, 2010): 675–89.
49. Gallico, "Women in Sports," 14.
50. "Water Nymph Won Beauty by Her Swimming," *Washington Herald*, November 19, 1922.
51. Jeane Hofmann, "Ann Curtis, Helser Will Resume 'Feud,'" *San Francisco Examiner*, August 19, 1945.
52. "New Zealand's Challenge to America's Girl Swimmers," *Palm Beach Post*, March 25, 1923, 11.
53. Paul Gallico, *The Golden People* (New York: Doubleday, 1965), 56.
54. Gallico, *Farewell to Sport*, 246.
55. David B. Welky, "Viking Girls, Mermaids, and Little Brown Men: U.S. Journalism and the 1932 Olympics," *Journal of Sport History* 24, no. 1 (1997): 24–49.
56. Welky, "Viking Girls, Mermaids, and Little Brown Men."
57. "Five Lovely Daughters," *Washington Times*, September 14, 1932.
58. "Crabbe Annexes Swim Thriller by Inches," *Los Angeles Times*, August 11, 1932.
59. Gallico, *Farewell to Sport*, 246–47.
60. Gallico, *Golden People*, 57.
61. Gallico, *Farewell to Sport*, 246–47.
62. Marilyn Morgan, "Aesthetic Athletics: Advertising and Eroticizing Women Swimmers," in *Consuming Modernity*, edited by Cheryl Krasnick Warsh and Dan Malleck (Vancouver: UBC Press, 2013), 136–60.
63. Tom Reichert, *The Erotic History of Advertising* (Amherst, NY: Prometheus Books, 2003).
64. Rochelle Jones, "Twenties Weren't So Roarin': Olympic Champs Recall Old Days," *Fort Lauderdale News*, December 15, 1968.
65. I am grateful to Bruce Wigo of the International Swimming Hall of Fame for first alerting me to the connection between women's swimming and the Florida real estate expansion of the 1920s.
66. Jane Watts Fisher, *Fabulous Hoosier: A Story of American Achievement* (New York: R.M. McBride and Co, 1947), 149.
67. Angela J. Latham, *Posing a Threat: Flappers, Chorus Girls, and Other Brazen Performers of the American 1920s* (Hanover, NH: University Press of New England, 2000).
68. Truman B. Handy, "The Mid-Day Frolic," *Motion Picture Classic*, June 1920, 19.
69. Handy, "Mid-Day Frolic," 20.
70. Rob King, *The Fun Factory: The Keystone Film Company and the Emergence of Mass Culture* (Berkeley: University of California Press, 2008), 238.
71. "The World-Wide Hubbub About Bathing Clothes," *Buffalo Courier*, June 11, 1922.
72. Latham, *Posing a Threat*, 72.
73. Latham, *Posing a Threat*, 65.
74. Jeff Wiltse, *Contested Waters: A Social History of Swimming Pools in America* (Chapel Hill: University of North Carolina Press, 2010).
75. "The Stockingless Vogue," *The Delineator*, June 1923.
76. Alicia Hart, "Spend Extra Minutes on Make-Up," *Oklahoma News*, August 25, 1932.
77. Marian Hale, "What to Wear at the Beach This Summer—Marian Hale Tells," *Arizona Republic*, June 24, 1922.
78. "The Well Dressed Woman," *Lexington Herald*, July 27, 1924.
79. Hale, "What to Wear at the Beach."
80. Keller-Marvin, "Aileen Riggin Soule."
81. Keller-Marvin, "Aileen Riggin Soule."

82. "Olympic Mermaids Have Lots of 'It,'" *Chillicothe Constitution-Tribune*, July 26, 1932.

83. "Olympic Champion Is Filmdom Find—And Is She Happy!," *Alton Evening Telegraph*, September 7, 1932.

84. Costa and Rivera, *An Olympian's Oral History*, 45.

85. Buck Dawson, *Mermaids on Parade: America's Love Affair with Its First Women Swimmers* (Huntington, NY: Kroshka Books, 1999), 246.

86. Dawson, *Mermaids on Parade*, 246.

87. Dawson, *Mermaids on Parade*, 246.

88. B. F. Keith's New York Hippodrome Program, May 23, 1926, ISHOF Archives: Annette Kellerman files.

89. Costa and Rivera, *An Olympian's Oral History*, 46.

90. Keller-Marvin, "Aileen Riggin Soule."

91. Austin, *Democratic Sports*; Ellen Gerber, "Chronicle of Participation," in *The American Woman in Sport* (Reading, MA: Addison-Wesley, 1974), 3–176.

92. Agnes R. Wayman, *Education Through Physical Education: Its Organization and Administration for Girls and Women*, 2nd ed. (Philadelphia: Lea and Febiger, 1928), 29.

93. Wayman, *Education Through Physical Education*, 19.

94. Gerber, "Chronicle of Participation."

95. Keller-Marvin, "Aileen Riggin Soule."

96. Blanche M. Trilling, "The Playtime of a Million Girls or an Olympic Victory—Which?," *Nation's Schools*, August 1929, 51.

97. Trilling, "The Playtime of a Million Girls," 53.

98. Trilling, "The Playtime of a Million Girls."

99. Gerber, "Chronicle of Participation."

100. Laura Robicheaux, "An Analysis of the Attitudes Toward Women's Athletics in the U.S. in the Early Twentieth Century," *Canadian Journal of History of Sport and Physical Education*, no. 6 (May 1975): 17.

101. Harry Alexander Scott, *Competitive Sport in Schools and Colleges* (New York: Harper and Brothers, 1951).

102. Austin, *Democratic Sports*, 139.

103. Susan K. Cahn, *Coming on Strong: Gender and Sexuality in Twentieth-Century Women's Sports*, 1st ed. (Cambridge, MA: Harvard University Press, 1998), 70.

104. Gerber, "Chronicle of Participation," 56.

105. Austin, *Democratic Sports*, 106.

106. Deborah Lynn Cottrell, "Women's Minds, Women's Bodies; The Influence of the Sargent School for Physical Education" (PhD diss., The University of Texas at Austin, 1993), 65.

107. Scott, *Competitive Sport in Schools and Colleges*, 455.

108. L. de B. Handley, *Swimming for Women: Preliminary and Advanced Instruction in Competitive Swimming, Fancy Diving and Lifesaving* (New York: American Sports Publishing Co., 1924), 7.

109. Georgia Bradshaw Herald, "A Study of the Physical Education Program for College Women in America" (MA thesis, University of Southern California, 1929), 66.

CHAPTER 7: SYNCHING UP

1. Jean M. Henning, "How It Began," *Synchro*, August 1985, 19–21.

2. "Normal Coeds Are Modern Mermaids in Fair Swimming Act," *Chicago Normalite*, October 1, 1934, Chicago Historical Society: Katharine Whitney Curtis Papers.

3. I am grateful to Cathy Goodwin for sharing her research on the choreography and details of the Modern Mermaids' routines.

4. A Century of Progress Publicity Division, "For Immediate Release: Water Carnival," July 2, 1934, University Library Department of Special Collections, University of Illinois at Chicago.

5. Dawn Pawson Bean, *Synchronized Swimming: An American History* (Jefferson, NC: McFarland and Company, 2005), 11.

6. "Century of Progress Swimming and Athletic Celebrities Visit in A. Ross Hoyt Home in City," *The Monitor*, January 3, 1935.

7. Bean, *Synchronized Swimming*, 10.

8. "Fair Maidens in Rare Form," *Greenwood Commonwealth*, September 7, 1934.

9. "World's Fair Notes," *Chicago Tribune*, August 27, 1934; "World's Fair Notes," *Chicago Tribune*, June 21, 1934; "Bathing Girls Play in Fair Spray," *The Times* (Munster, IN), July 3, 1934.

10. Bean, *Synchronized Swimming*, 10.

11. C. W. Farrier, "A Century of Progress International Exposition," Letter of Recommendation, July 31, 1934, Chicago Historical Society: Katharine Whitney Curtis Papers.

12. "Young Girl Swims Across the Lake; Breaks Record," Unknown clipping, 1912, Chicago Historical Society: Katharine Whitney Curtis Papers.

13. "A Page of Sports for Women Readers," *Wisconsin State Journal*, December 3, 1916.

14. Jordan Whitney-Wei, *Katharine Whitney Curtis: Mother of Synchronized Swimming* (Jefferson, NC: McFarland and Company, 2020).

15. Deborah Lynn Cottrell, "Women's Minds, Women's Bodies: The Influence of the Sargent School for Physical Education" (PhD diss., The University of Texas at Austin, 1993), 39.

16. Mabel Lee, "The Case for and Against Intercollegiate Athletics for Women and the Situation As It Stands Today," *American Physical Education Review* 29 (January 1924): 17.

17. Agnes R. Wayman, "Competition," *American Physical Education Review* 34 (October 1929): 469.

18. Ethel Perrin, "Athletics for Women and Girls," *Playground* 17 (March 1924): 660.

19. Juliette Gordon Low, *How Girls Can Help Their Country: Handbook for Girl Scouts* (Savannah, GA: Press of M.S. & D.A. Byck Co., 1917), 49.

20. Ina Gittings, "Why Cramp Competition," *Journal of Health and Physical Education* 2, no. 1 (1931): 54.

21. S. E. Bilik, "Why Women Athletes Lack Charm," *Plain Talk: It Speaks for Itself*, February 1929, 176.

22. "A Page of Sports for Women Readers."

23. Cottrell, "Women's Minds, Women's Bodies," 62.

24. Cottrell, "Women's Minds, Women's Bodies," 60.

25. Betty G. Hartman, "On Intercollegiate Competition for Women," *Synchro News*, May 1958, 60.

26. Whitney-Wei, *Katharine Whitney Curtis*.

27. Agnes R. Wayman, *Education Through Physical Education: Its Organization and Administration for Girls and Women*, 2nd ed. (Philadelphia: Lea and Febiger, 1928), 263.

28. Robert Pruter, "Girls Interscholastic Swimming in the Chicago Public Schools, 1917–1934," *Illinois H.S.toric* (blog), Illinois High School Association, n.d.

29. Buck Dawson, Gene Kerr, and Paul Gallico, *Mermaids on Parade: America's Love Affair with Its First Women Swimmers* (Huntington, NY: Kroshka Books, 1999), 157.

30. Katharine Curtis, *Rhythmic Swimming: A Sourcebook of Synchronized Swimming and Water Pageantry*, rev. ed. (Minneapolis: Burgess Publishing Co., 1942), v.

31. Katharine W. Curtis, "Competitive Synchronized Swimming," *Journal of Health and Physical Education* 12, no. 1 (January 1941): 18–20, 59–60.

32. Keta Steebs, "Washington Island's Kay Curtis Becoming a Legend in Her Time," *Door County Advocate*, June 14, 1977.

33. Curtis, *Rhythmic Swimming*, v.

34. Steebs, "Washington Island's Kay Curtis."

35. Katharine Curtis, *A Source Book of Water Pageantry* (Chicago: The College Press, 1936), 4.

36. Marian Louise Stoerker, "The Origin and Development of Synchronized Swimming in the United States" (Master's thesis, University of Wisconsin, 1956), 12.

37. Stoerker, "Origin and Development of Synchronized Swimming," 12.

38. "Melrose Woman Pioneered Water Ballet," *Melrose Evening News*, July 22, 1971, box 827, Smith College Archives: Gertrude Goss papers (CA-MS-00152).

39. Dorothy W. Woodruff, "Smith College Office of Publicity," April 25, no year, box 827, Smith College Archives: Gertrude Goss papers (CA-MS-00152).

40. Katharine Curtis, "A Plea for More Interest in Stunt and Fancy Swimming," *Official Aquatic Guide, 1928–1929*, n.d., 49, quoted in Bean, *Synchronized Swimming*, 6.

41. Gertrude Goss, *Stunts and Synchronized Swimming* (Boston: Spaulding-Moss Co, 1957).

42. Bean, *Synchronized Swimming*, 9.

43. George Hebden Corsan, *The Diving and Swimming Book* (New Haven, CT: A. S. Barnes, 1924), 77.

44. Helen Anna Magrane, "Survey of the Program of Swimming Activities for Women in Colleges and Universities of the United States" (Master's thesis, University of Washington, 1932), 66–67.

45. Wayman, *Education Through Physical Education*, 220.

46. Wayman, *Education Through Physical Education*, 268.

47. Magrane, "Survey of the Program of Swimming Activities," 64.

48. "The Lady Swimmer: Miss Agnes Beckwith," *Hearth and Home*, August 6, 1891.

49. Louis de B. Handley, *Swimming and Watermanship* (Macmillan, 1922), 78.

50. Gertrude Goss, "The Water Show: Fun for Swimmer and Audience," *Beach & Pool*, November 1950, 8–9.

51. Stoerker, "Origin and Development of Synchronized Swimming"; Thomas Kirk Cureton, *Warfare Aquatics: Course Syllabus and Activities Manual*, 1st ed. (Champaign, IL: Stipes Publishing Co., 1943).

52. "Aquabelle Routines Designed with Buttons," *Star Tribune*, July 11, 1948.

53. "Hertford Swimming Club," *Hertfordshire Mercury*, August 10, 1878.

54. "English Channel Swim: Experiences of Jabez Wolffe in His Eighth Attempt," *Omaha Daily Bee*, August 21, 1909.

55. Steebs, "Washington Island's Kay Curtis."

56. Goss, "The Water Show," 8.

57. Gertrude Goss, "Swim to Music—It's Fun," in *The Official NSWA Aquatics Guide*, 1947.

58. "College Girls Swim to Music to Save Nerves for Exams," *Brooklyn Daily Eagle*, February 2, 1930.

59. Magrane, "Survey of the Program of Swimming Activities."

60. Evelyn K. Dillon, "Swim to Music," *Journal of the American Association for Health, Physical Education, and Recreation* 23, no. 1 (January 1, 1952): 17–18.

61. Steebs, "Washington Island's Kay Curtis."

62. Nury Vandellos, "Army Tour Expert Invented Swim Show," *Overseas Weekly*, March 13, 1955, Chicago Historical Society: Katharine Whitney Curtis Papers.

63. "Melrose Woman Pioneered Water Ballet."

64. Goss, "Swim to Music," 35.
65. Vandellos, "Army Tour Expert Invented Swim Show."
66. Vandellos, "Army Tour Expert Invented Swim Show."
67. Curtis, "Competitive Synchronized Swimming," 67.
68. Stoerker, "Origin and Development of Synchronized Swimming," 22.
69. Stoerker, "Origin and Development of Synchronized Swimming," 17.
70. William Arnold Krauss, "An Aquatic Program for the Senior High School" (Master's thesis, University of Southern California, 1947), 14–15.
71. Curtis, "Competitive Synchronized Swimming," 18.
72. "Watson Plans Coed Aquacade," *Daily Tar Heel*, May 17, 1941.
73. Helen M. Starr, "Water Ballet," *Official Aquatic Guide, 1945–1947*, Official Sports Library for Women, 20.
74. Curtis, *Rhythmic Swimming*, 92.
75. "Smith Girls Waltz in Water," *Springfield Sunday Republican*, April 11, 1948, box 827, Smith College Archives: Gertrude Goss papers (CA-MS-00152).
76. "Century of Progress Swimming."
77. Curtis, "Competitive Synchronized Swimming," 18.
78. "Century of Progress Swimming."
79. Tony Thomas and Jim Terry, *The Busby Berkeley Book* (Greenwich, CT: New York Graphic Society, 1973).
80. Florence Fisher Parry, "On with the Show: Wherein a Billion Dollar Super Super SUPER Comes to the Stanley," *Pittsburgh Press*, October 14, 1933.
81. Thomas and Terry, *Busby Berkeley Book*, 71.
82. Lillian A. C. Burke, "Aquatic Pageant Procedures," *Journal of Health and Physical Education* 18, no. 6 (June 1, 1947): 372–73.
83. Allene De Lura Good, "Water Pageants and Their Use in Educational Programs" (Master's thesis, University of Texas, 1937), 51.
84. Martha J. Vaught, "Lights On!," *Health and Physical Education* 22, no. 2 (February 1940): 92.
85. Goss, "The Water Show."
86. Martha M. Patterson, "A Survey of the Lighting, Make-up, Costumes, and Accompaniment Currently Used in Watershows by a Selected Sample of Midwestern Colleges" (MA thesis, Michigan State University, 1955), 36.
87. Goss, "The Water Show."
88. Vaught, "Lights On!"
89. Sue Gerard, *Just Leave the Dishes* (Columbia, MO: Whip Poor Will Books, 2002), 114.
90. Holley J. Smith, "Make Pools Pay with Pageantry," *Beach & Pool*, October 1939, 28.
91. Joan Carlson and Josephine Neff, "Black Light Your Water Ballet," *Journal of the American Association for Health, Physical Education, and Recreation* 25, no. 3 (March 1, 1954): 19–20.
92. Carlson and Neff, "Black Light Your Water Ballet."
93. Patterson, "Survey of the Lighting."
94. Smith, "Make Pools Pay with Pageantry," 28.
95. Oscar W. Hoar, *Biographical Sketch of Commodore Wilbert E. Longfellow*, A Publication of the Commodore Longfellow Society (Punta Gorda, FL: The Renshaw Press, n.d.).
96. Cureton, *Warfare Aquatics*, 3.
97. Cureton, *Warfare Aquatics*, 39.
98. Bean, *Synchronized Swimming*, 19.
99. Curtis, "Competitive Synchronized Swimming," 18.

100. Frank J. Havlicek, "Letter to Buck Dawson, Executive Director, Swimming Hall of Fame in Nomination of Katherine Curtis for Induction," December 19, 1967, ISHOF Archive: Katharine Curtis Files.
101. Curtis, *Rhythmic Swimming*, 1.
102. Curtis, *Rhythmic Swimming*, 2.
103. Henning, "How It Began," 20.
104. Curtis, "Competitive Synchronized Swimming."
105. Stoerker, "The Origin and Development of Synchronized Swimming," 36.
106. Curtis, *Rhythmic Swimming*, 3.
107. Bud Harvey, "Rippling Rhythm," *Sportfolio: The Illustrated Digest of All Sports*, May 1948, 71.
108. Lucy Hawkins, "Follow Your Heart's Desire," *The Wisconsin Alumnus*, University of Wisconsin, February 1941.
109. David Clarke Leach, "Synchronized Swimming," *Amateur Athlete*, June 1940, 7.
110. Vandellos, "Army Tour Expert Invented Swim Show."
111. Hawkins, "Follow Your Heart's Desire," 101.
112. Bean, *Synchronized Swimming*, 20.
113. Whitney-Wei, *Katharine Whitney Curtis*, 65.
114. Steebs, "Washington Island's Kay Curtis."
115. Marilyn Eastridge, "The Development of a Progression of Synchronized Swimming Skills to Accompany the American Red Cross Beginner Swimming Progression," The University of North Carolina at Greensboro, 1965.
116. Joni Evans Zuber, "The Tritons Chicago Teachers College," *The Synchronized Swimmer*, March 1952, 9.
117. Curtis, *Rhythmic Swimming*, 2; Curtis, "Competitive Synchronized Swimming," 18.

CHAPTER 8: SPECTACLE

1. Stephen Nelson, *"Only a Paper Moon": The Theatre of Billy Rose* (Ann Arbor, MI: UMI Research Press, 1987); "Billy Rose's Aquacade New York World's Fair 1939 Program," 1939.
2. Nelson, *"Only a Paper Moon,"* 103.
3. Richard Reinhardt, *Treasure Island: San Francisco's Exposition Years* (San Francisco: Scrimshaw Press, 1973), 106.
4. Arthur Pollock, "Playthings: Amusement Activities Shift for the Nonce to the World's Fair, Where Shakespeare and Billy Rose, Two Titans, Entertain," *Brooklyn Daily Eagle*, May 14, 1939.
5. "Billy Rose's Aquacade Golden Gate International Exposition 1940 Program," 1940.
6. Nelson, *"Only a Paper Moon,"* 74.
7. Ben Hecht, *Charlie: The Improbable Life and Times of Charles MacArthur* (New York: Harper, 1957), 149.
8. Harriet Wright and Brie Austin, *I'd Do It Again!: A Memoir* (iUniverse, Inc., 2005), 30.
9. Pollock, "Playthings"; Henry W. Clune, "Seen and Heard by Henry W. Clune," *Ithaca Journal*, July 17, 1937.
10. Ruth Hopkins, "Showmen Take Over Divers, Too," *Baltimore Sun*, August 6, 1939.
11. Pollock, "Playthings."
12. Hopkins, "Showmen Take Over Divers, Too."
13. Kara Elizabeth Fagan, "The Spectacle of Female Athleticism in Classic Hollywood, 1935–1955" (PhD diss., The University of Iowa, 2016), 98.
14. Burns Mantle, "Now the 'Aquacade' Christens the Fair with a Great Splash," *Daily News*, May 5, 1939.

15. "New York's World of Tomorrow Revisited," *Calgary Herald*, February 16, 1963.

16. "Unveilings at New York's World Fair Include Most of the Midway Beauties," *Hutchinson News*, June 16, 1939.

17. Maurice Zolotow, *Billy Rose of Broadway*, unpublished manuscript, 1945, 373, New York Public Library: Billy Rose Theater Collection, quoted in Nelson, *"Only a Paper Moon,"* 49.

18. Nelson, *"Only a Paper Moon,"* 66.

19. Advertisement for Cleveland Aquacade, 1937, New York Public Library: Billy Rose Theatre Collection, quoted in Nelson, *"Only a Paper Moon,"* 66.

20. Billy Rose, *Wine, Women and Words* (New York: Simon and Schuster, 1948), 25.

21. Hugh Abercrombie Anderson, *Out Without My Rubbers: The Memoirs of John Murray Anderson* (New York: Library Publishers, 1954), 179.

22. Hopkins, "Showmen Take Over Divers, Too."

23. Hopkins, "Showmen Take Over Divers, Too."

24. "Birth of an Aquabelle," *Tampa Bay Times*, April 21, 1940.

25. Helen M. Starr, "Water Ballet," *Official Aquatic Guide, 1945–1947*, Official Sports Library for Women, 22.

26. Starr, "Water Ballet," 22.

27. Wright and Austin, *I'd Do It Again!*, 27.

28. Anderson, *Out Without My Rubbers*, 177.

29. Hopkins, "Showmen Take Over Divers, Too."

30. Hopkins, "Showmen Take Over Divers, Too."

31. Wright and Austin, *I'd Do It Again!*, 27.

32. Elmore Bacon, "News," quoted in *Meet Me on Lake Erie, Dearie!: Cleveland's Great Lakes Exposition, 1936–1937*, by John Vacha (Kent, OH: Kent State University Press, 2011), 178.

33. "The Aquacade Is a Water Ballet," *Greenville News*, June 18, 1939.

34. Julian Lee Rayford, "Billy Rose: The Bantamweight Colossus," *Theatre Arts*, n.d.; Nelson, *"Only a Paper Moon,"* 109.

35. W. Ward Marsh, *Plain Dealer*, and Bacon, "News," quoted in Vacha, *Meet Me on Lake Erie, Dearie!*, 177–78.

36. "Ramblings," *Republican and Herald*, March 22, 1940.

37. "The Once Over: 'Only a Hippodrome Mother,'" *Boston Globe*, May 20, 1939.

38. "Pretty Girls Set Records at National Swimming Meet," *Life*, August 14, 1939, 59.

39. Digby Diehl and Esther Williams, *The Million Dollar Mermaid: An Autobiography* (New York: Simon and Schuster, 1999).

40. Kyle Crichton, "Big Splash," *Collier's*, September 26, 1942, 96; Diehl and Williams, *Million Dollar Mermaid*, 41.

41. "Billy Rose's Aquacade New York World's Fair 1940 Program," 1940, 9.

42. "Billy Rose Aquacade 1940 Affidavit," *San Francisco Examiner*, May 24, 1940.

43. Diehl and Williams, *Million Dollar Mermaid*, 45.

44. Diehl and Williams, *Million Dollar Mermaid*, 47.

45. Diehl and Williams, *Million Dollar Mermaid*, 47.

46. Diehl and Williams, *Million Dollar Mermaid*, 53.

47. Diehl and Williams, *Million Dollar Mermaid*, 44.

48. "Look, a Bathing Beauty Who Swims!," *New York Times*, March 28, 1943.

49. Reinhardt, *Treasure Island*, 110.

50. Paul Carvalho, dir., *The Mermaid's Club* (documentary) (Montreal: Perception Films Inc., Productions Colin Neale, Les), aired August 12, 2022.

51. John Wesley Noble, "Prettiest Things Afloat," *Saturday Evening Post*, July 2, 1955, 54.

52. Gertrude Goss, "The Water Show: Fun for Swimmer and Audience," *Beach & Pool*, November 1950, 8–9.
53. Holley J. Smith, "Make Pools Pay with Pageantry," *Beach & Pool*, October 1939, 27.
54. Helen Schwartz, "Recent Developments in High School Girls' Physical Education Programs," *Journal of Health and Physical Education* 13, no. 9 (November 1942): 321.
55. "Watson Plans Coed Aquacade," *Daily Tar Heel*, May 17, 1941.
56. "Waterbabies," *American Magazine*, November 1940, 93.
57. Maxine Umbra, letter to Billy Rose, March 27, 1939. New York World's Fair 1939 and 1940 Incorporated records, New York Public Library. I learned of this source through Yasmine Marie Jahanmir, "'We Rule the Waves': Athletic Labor, Femininity, and National Collective in Billy Rose's Aquacade," *Drama Review* 61, no. 3 (Fall 2017): 112–31.
58. "Water Follies Open Tonight," *Boston Globe*, April 8, 1937.
59. Gill Wood, "Lavish Water Show Opens Tomorrow," *Vermont Sunday News*, July 1, 1951.
60. Robert Considine, "On the Line with Considine," *Washington Post*, August 12, 1939.
61. Considine, "On the Line."
62. Hopkins, "Showmen Take Over Divers, Too."
63. LeRoy Ashby, *With Amusement for All: A History of American Popular Culture Since 1830* (Lexington, KY: University Press of Kentucky, 2012).
64. "Fun and Gee Whiz Stuff Seen in 'Aqua Parade,'" *Cincinnati Enquirer*, April 1, 1949; "Buster Crabbe Presents: Aqua Parade of 1948 Official Souvenir Program," International Swimming Hall of Fame (ISHOF): Water Show files.
65. John A. Baule, "Ahhhquatennial: Fifty Fabulous Years," *Hennepin History Magazine*, Summer 1989, 23–27.
66. Ken Fleming, "Aqua Follies Has Girls, Girls—And Water," *Seattle Post-Intelligencer*, July 30, 1959.
67. "Fabulous Follies: Aqua Follies Presents the Greatest War Show in the World," *Star Tribune*, July 12, 1959.
68. "Tin Roses Have Shapely Stems," *Star Tribune*, July 19, 1951.
69. "Detroit Riverama Festival Presents Aqua Follies of 1955," official publication, ISHOF Archives: Water Show files.
70. "1948 Minneapolis Aqua Follies program," ISHOF Archives: Water Show files.
71. "City Gets Preview of Queens Tonight," *Star Tribune*, July 17, 1947.
72. "Johnny Weissmuller Watercade of 1950 Program," ISHOF Archives: Water Show files; "Fun and Gee Whiz Stuff"; "Buster Crabbe Again Presents First-Class Combination Show," *Montreal Daily Star*, June 8, 1949.
73. Louis Sheaffer, "Everything's Ship-Shape at Elliott Murphy's Aquashow," *Brooklyn Daily Eagle*, June 25, 1952.
74. Jeanette McFadden, in-person interview with author, October 1, 2016.
75. McFadden, interview with author.
76. Laura Soles, video interview with author, February 14, 2021.
77. Robert E. Kerper Jr., *Splash! Aquatic Shows from A to Z: Their Art, Planning and Production Plus Aquatic History and Trivia*, 1st ed. (Philadelphia: Robert E. Kerper, 2002), 19.
78. "Thirty City Girls in Aqua Follies," *Star Tribune*, June 27, 1943.
79. "Newsreel and Aqua Follies Advertisement," *Minneapolis Star*, August 6, 1943; "Firemen Bought War Bonds," *Star Tribune*, July 31, 1943.
80. "AC Apprehensive of Army's Move," *The Billboard*, July 3, 1943.
81. Dawn Pawson Bean, *Synchronized Swimming: An American History* (Jefferson, NC: McFarland and Company, 2005), 23.

82. Kerper Jr., *Splash! Aquatic Shows from A to Z*, 21.

83. "Aquacade of Stars Opens Pool Sunday," Dibble Data: National Library of Medicine Collections.

84. Curley Grieve, "Sports Parade: SF's Joanne Millin, 18, Sensation as Headliner in Seattle Aqua Follies," *San Francisco Examiner*, July 28, 1955.

85. "Exhibit Shows Swimming Has Special Wartime Role," *Evening Star*, June 25, 1942.

86. "Exhibit Shows Swimming Has Special Wartime Role."

87. "Swimming in Wartime," June 24, 1942, ISHOF Archives: Longfellow Files.

88. "Exhibit Shows Swimming Has Special Wartime Role."

89. "Water Carnival at Country Club Pool Tonight," *Corpus Christi Caller-Times*, July 9, 1944.

90. "Fort to Stage 2nd Aquacade Next Sunday," *News-Pilot*, July 6, 1944.

91. "First Camp Aquacade Will Be Given Tonight in Area 2 Pool," *Camp Lejeune Globe*, February 14, 1945, 15, North Carolina Digital Collections.

92. Camp Lejeune Aquacade Program, March 7–8, 1945, North Carolina Digital Collections.

93. "Additional Swimmers Needed for Aquacade," in *Katharine Whitney Curtis: Mother of Synchronized Swimming* by Jordan Whitney-Wei (Jefferson, NC: McFarland and Company, 2020), 88.

94. Katharine Curtis, "Newsletter," June 24, 1945, in Whitney-Wei, *Katharine Whitney Curtis*, 90.

95. Whitney-Wei, *Katharine Whitney Curtis*.

96. Katharine Curtis, letter to ATW, June 10, 1945, in Whitney-Wei, *Katharine Whitney Curtis*, 88.

97. Swensen, letter to ARC, June 25, 1945, in Whitney-Wei, *Katharine Whitney Curtis*, 93.

98. Katharine Curtis, "Newsletter," June 24, 1945, in Whitney-Wei, *Katharine Whitney Curtis*, 91.

99. Commodore Wilbert E. Longfellow, "Let's Dramatize Aquatics," *Red Cross Courier*, September 1937, 6.

100. Bud Harvey, "Rippling Rhythm," *Sportfolio: The Illustrated Digest of All Sports*, May 1948, 62.

CHAPTER 9: SILVER SCREEN

1. Captain Paul E. Trejo, "Esther Lives On," *Tin Can Sailor*, March 2000, 1–5.

2. Sources conflict regarding whether the events triggering the start of the Trophy happened in 1942 or 1943. According to the Royal Australian Navy, it started in 1943. "Esther Williams Trophy," Royal Australian Navy: Serving Australia with Pride, accessed July 22, 2022, https://www.navy.gov.au/customs-and-traditions/esther-williams-trophy.

3. "Esther Williams Trophy."

4. "Esther Williams Trophy"; W. B. Hayler, "The Esther Williams Saga," *Our Navy*, October 1960, 14–16, 53.

5. Hayler, "Esther Williams Saga."

6. "Esther Williams Trophy."

7. Sidney Carroll, "Good, Clean, Wholesome SEX," *Pageant*, December 1953, 42.

8. "I Buried Esther Williams," *Australian Women's Weekly*, November 9, 1977, 19.

9. Laura Jacobs, "The Glittering Rise and Fall of Sonja Henie, Ice Skating's Original Queen," *Vanity Fair*, February 11, 2014.

10. Digby Diehl and Esther Williams, *The Million Dollar Mermaid: An Autobiography* (New York: Simon and Schuster, 1999), 57.

11. Diehl and Williams, *Million Dollar Mermaid*, 58.
12. Diehl and Williams, *Million Dollar Mermaid*, 61–62.
13. William Poster, "Hollywood Caterers to the Middle Class: An Appraisal of Metro-Goldwyn Mayer," *The American Mercury*, August 1951, 82–91.
14. Diehl and Williams, *Million Dollar Mermaid*, 73.
15. "'Bathing Beauty': Its Aquaballet Is the First Color Water Pageant to Reach the Screen," *Life*, April 17, 1944, 79.
16. "Ladies of the Screen Become Pin-Up Girls," *Tampa Tribune*, May 30, 1943.
17. Diehl and Williams, *Million Dollar Mermaid*, 99.
18. Diehl and Williams, *Million Dollar Mermaid*, 110.
19. Diehl and Williams, *Million Dollar Mermaid*, 110.
20. Diehl and Williams, *Million Dollar Mermaid*, 113.
21. Diehl and Williams, *Million Dollar Mermaid*, 111.
22. *Life*, April 17, 1944, cover.
23. "Many Selling Slants Can Be Built Around 'Bathing Beauty' Story-Title," *Showman's Trade Review*, July 8, 1944, 20; "Bathing Beauty: MGM—Water Carnival Plus," *Motion Picture Herald*, May 27, 1944, 33.
24. Diehl and Williams, *Million Dollar Mermaid*, 116.
25. Diehl and Williams, *Million Dollar Mermaid*, 117.
26. "Esther Williams Life Story," *Modern Screen*, May 1946, 104.
27. "Esther Williams Life Story," 104.
28. Diehl and Williams, *Million Dollar Mermaid*, 123.
29. "The New Pictures, June 4, 1945," *Time*, June 4, 1945.
30. Ben Gage, "Esther's Like That," *Modern Screen*, January 1947.
31. Robert Wernick, "The Mermaid Tycoon," *Life*, April 16, 1951, 14.
32. Diehl and Williams, *Million Dollar Mermaid*, 163.
33. Carroll, "Good, Clean, Wholesome SEX," 48.
34. Carroll, "Good, Clean, Wholesome SEX," 48.
35. Carroll, "Good, Clean, Wholesome SEX," 50.
36. Laura Michelle Thomas, "Local and Global Mermaids : The Politics of 'Pretty Swimming'" (Master's thesis, University of British Columbia, 2001).
37. Kirsten Pullen, *Like a Natural Woman: Spectacular Female Performance in Classical Hollywood* (New Brunswick, NJ: Rutgers University Press, 2014); Kara Elizabeth Fagan, "The Spectacle of Female Athleticism in Classic Hollywood, 1935–1955" (PhD diss., The University of Iowa, 2016).
38. Diehl and Williams, *Million Dollar Mermaid*, 153.
39. Diehl and Williams, *Million Dollar Mermaid*, 119.
40. Helen Rose, *Just Make Them Beautiful: The Many Worlds of a Designing Woman* (Santa Monica, CA: Dennis Landman Publishers, 1976), 73.
41. "Splish-Splash: The Esther Williams Interview," Cladrite Radio, May 27, 2011.
42. "Look, a Bathing Beauty Who Swims!," *New York Times*, March 28, 1943.
43. Unnamed author, article torn out of unknown magazine, n.d., 53, accessed from the International Swimming Hall of Fame (ISHOF) Archives: Esther Williams file.
44. Diehl and Williams, *Million Dollar Mermaid*, 195.
45. Wernick, "The Mermaid Tycoon," 144.
46. Carroll, "Good, Clean, Wholesome SEX," 51.
47. Kyle Crichton, "Big Splash," *Collier's*, September 26, 1942, 13.
48. Wernick, "The Mermaid Tycoon," 144.
49. "Korea Is Latest on Pin-up Circuit," *Press Democrat*, August 8, 1950.
50. Robert B. Westbrook, "'I Want a Girl, Just Like the Girl That Married Harry James':

American Women and the Problem of Political Obligation in World War II," *American Quarterly* 42, no. 4 (1990): 596.

51. Wernick, "The Mermaid Tycoon," 144.
52. Dennis McCarthy, "Vet Sends Greetings to Favorite Pinup Esther Williams," *Los Angeles Daily News* (blog), August 10, 2008.
53. "YWCA Offers Instructions in Synchronized Swimming," *Intelligencer Journal*, March 21, 1950.
54. Helen M. Starr, "Water Ballet," *Official Aquatic Guide, 1945–1947*, Official Sports Library for Women, 19.
55. "Here's a Hard-Hitting Reply," *Macon Telegraph*, September 2, 1956.
56. Bud Harvey, "Rippling Rhythm," *Sportfolio: The Illustrated Digest of All Sports*, May 1948, 71.
57. "Women Swimmers to Give Demonstration," *Lansing State Journal*, January 30, 1948.
58. Philip K. Scheuer, "Water Ballet: Esther Williams Is Moviedom's Most Glamorous Mermaid," n.d., ISHOF Archives: Beulah Gundling files.
59. Diehl and Williams, *Million Dollar Mermaid*, 229–30.
60. Cited in Fagan, "The Spectacle of Female Athleticism," 122.
61. Diane Wyatt McDonald, in-person interview with author, August 19, 2015.
62. "Two Fathoms Down Advertisement," *Fort Lauderdale News*, January 24, 1954.
63. "Divena Is Lauded by Writers," *Sedalia Democrat*, August 24, 1951.
64. Diehl and Williams, *Million Dollar Mermaid*.
65. Diehl and Williams, *Million Dollar Mermaid*.
66. "Reviews of New Films: Bathing Beauty," *Film Daily*, May 31, 1944.
67. Jane Wilkie, "Wet She Is—Dry She Ain't!," *Modern Screen*, September 1953, 60.
68. "Reviews of New Films: Bathing Beauty."
69. Wilkie, "Wet She Is—Dry She Ain't!," 60.
70. "M-G-Mythology," *Newsweek*, June 13, 1949, 82.
71. Wilkie, "Wet She Is—Dry She Ain't!," 60.
72. Wernick, "The Mermaid Tycoon."
73. Wernick, "The Mermaid Tycoon."
74. Elisa Leonelli, "The Henrietta Mystery Solved," Golden Globes, August 26, 2015.
75. Diehl and Williams, *Million Dollar Mermaid*.
76. Wilkie, "Wet She Is—Dry She Ain't!," 62.
77. Wilkie, "Wet She Is—Dry She Ain't!," 62.
78. John L. Scott, "Esther Williams Happy to Float on Commercial Success Wave," *Los Angeles Times*, February 25, 1951.
79. "'Million Dollar Mermaid' Uses 73 Major Sets," *Los Angeles Times*, December 29, 1952.
80. Pullen, *Like a Natural Woman*, 84.
81. "A Mermaid Finds Tour Hard Work," *Des Moines Tribune*, December 2, 1952.
82. Tony Thomas and Jim Terry, *The Busby Berkeley Book* (Greenwich, CT: New York Graphic Society, 1973), 169.
83. "Motion Pictures: Esther Williams Praised for Work in New Picture," *Spokesman-Review*, December 21, 1952.
84. "Extravagant 'Million Dollar Mermaid' Is Famed Annette Kellerman's Story on Screen," *Brooklyn Daily Eagle*, December 21, 1952.
85. "Constant Nymph," *Screenland*, January 1954, 17.
86. Diehl and Williams, *Million Dollar Mermaid*.
87. "Here Come the Painted Pachyderms," *Los Angeles Times*, September 12, 1954.
88. Diehl and Williams, *Million Dollar Mermaid*, 265.
89. "Motion Pictures."

90. "History of Air Conditioning | Department of Energy," accessed July 27, 2022.

91. "I Buried Esther Williams."

92. Diehl and Williams, *Million Dollar Mermaid*, 281.

93. Diehl and Williams, *Million Dollar Mermaid*.

94. Williams wrote in her memoir that she agreed to stop being Esther Williams and become Esther Lamas in 1961, even though she and Lamas did not actually marry until 1969. She wrote that she was "tethered" for twenty-two years, until Lamas's death in 1982.

95. "I Buried Esther Williams."

96. Vernon Scott, "Photo Sparks Naval 'Battle' of Thefts," *Courier-Journal*, August 1, 1953.

97. Blake Stilwell, "Allied Navies in the Pacific Fought for a Photo of This Actress for 70 Years," Military.com, March 17, 2022; "Esther Williams Trophy."

98. Hayler, "The Esther Williams Saga."

99. Hayler, "Esther Williams Saga."

100. Edward Bell, phone interview with author, May 25, 2022.

101. "Esther Williams Trophy."

CHAPTER 10: SWIMMING SYNCHRONIZED

1. Imasportsphile III, "Olympics—1984 Los Angeles—ABC Profile—Synchronized Swimming and Esther Williams," (YouTube post), April 22, 2016.

2. "For Europe: Charm from Detroit," *Detroit Free Press*, August 3, 1952.

3. Lillian A. C. Burke, "Aquatic Pageant Procedures," *Journal of Health and Physical Education* 18, no. 6 (June 1, 1947): 414.

4. Evelyn K. Dillon, "Swim to Music," *Journal of the American Association for Health, Physical Education, and Recreation* 23, no. 1 (January 1, 1952): 17–18.

5. Ella Peckham, "The Idea File," *Synchro Info*, October 1964, 16.

6. Roy Blount, "And Now for the Resurrection," *Sports Illustrated*, April 12, 1971, 100.

7. Ross C. Bean, "Regulation of Music Speed: Stroboscopic Timing," *Synchro Info*, December 1963, 5–6.

8. John Wesley Noble, "Prettiest Things Afloat," *Saturday Evening Post*, July 2, 1955, 55.

9. Robert Henry Wallace Dunlop, *"Plate-Swimming" with Notes on the Science of Natation* (New York: G. Routledge and Sons, 1877), 83.

10. "The Laxto Nose Clip," *Synchro News*, February 1958, 29–30.

11. Dawn Pawson Bean, *Synchronized Swimming: An American History* (Jefferson, NC: McFarland and Company, 2005), 39.

12. Jean M. Henning, "How It Began," *Synchro*, August 1985, 19.

13. "Women in Sport with Jane Tiel," *The Gazette*, June 11, 1949.

14. Laura Michelle Thomas, "Local and Global Mermaids: The Politics of 'Pretty Swimming'" (Master's thesis, University of British Columbia, 2001).

15. Beulah Gundling, *Dancing in the Water*, 1st ed. (Marion, IA: Linn Litho, 1976), 44–45.

16. "Rule Changes Through the Years," *Synchro Info*, February 1972, 10–12.

17. Katharine Curtis, "Synchronized in Helsinki (Extracts from a Letter from Kay Curtis)," *Synchronized Swimmer*, November 1952, 5.

18. Paul Carvalho, dir. *The Mermaid's Club* (documentary), Montreal: Perception Films Inc., Productions Colin Neale, Les, aired August 12, 2022.

19. Rick Setlowe, "The Water Follies," *San Francisco Examiner*, August 21, 1960, 6.

20. Gundling, *Dancing in the Water*, 63–64.

21. Setlowe, "The Water Follies," 6.

22. Noble, "Prettiest Things Afloat," 55.

23. "In the Swim Again," *New York Times*, July 19, 1973.

24. "Proceedings of Synchronized Swimming Symposium at Michigan State College," *Synchronized Swimmer*, March 1955, 6.
25. Setlowe, "The Water Follies," 5.
26. *Sports Illustrated* staff, "Soundtrack: The Pool Players," *Sports Illustrated Vault | SI.Com*, August 30, 1954.
27. Setlowe, "The Water Follies," 4.
28. "Drive for International Recognition," *Synchro Info*, February 1972, 22–23.
29. Carvalho, *The Mermaid's Club*.
30. Bud Harvey, "Rippling Rhythm," *Sportfolio: The Illustrated Digest of All Sports*, May 1948, 71.
31. Ross Bean, "On Synchronized Swimming Rule Changes," *The Synchronized Swimmer*, October 1953, 1.
32. "Synchronized Swimming Rule Revision to Combine Solo, Duet and Team Competition as Passed at the Convention in Washington, D.C. at the Willard Hotel November 26–29, 1953," *Synchronized Swimmer*, January 1954, 2.
33. Ross Bean, "The Question Right, Left and Center," *The Synchronized Swimmer*, October 1954, 14.
34. Jane Houghten, "Synchronized Swimming—Art or Sport?," *Synchronized Swimmer*, November 1954, 20.
35. Bean, *Synchronized Swimming*, 54.
36. Bean, *Synchronized Swimming*, 62.
37. Bean, *Synchronized Swimming*, 62.
38. Quoted in Noble, "Prettiest Things Afloat," 52.
39. Henry Gundling, "Synchronized Swimming Introduced to Australia," *Synchronized Swimmer*, March 1955, 3.
40. Marge Dineen, "AAU-Sponsored Tour," *Synchro News*, October 1958, 141.
41. George Rackham, *Synchronized Swimming* (London: Faber and Faber, 1968), 23.
42. Norma J. Olsen, "AAU-Sponsored World Tours Face a Challenge," *Synchro News*, February 1958, 24.
43. Pat Paterson, "Memorabilia," *Synchro*, October 1985.
44. Noble, "Prettiest Things Afloat"; Lee Griggs, "Swimming Plus," *Sports Illustrated Vault | SI.Com*, June 6, 1955.
45. Norma J. Olsen, "Highlights of Swimming Tour in Japan and Korea," *Synchronized Swimmer*, August 1954.
46. Bean, *Synchronized Swimming*, 197.
47. Carvalho, *The Mermaid's Club*.
48. Rob Hughes, "Saviour of the Olympics?," *Sunday Times*, December 2, 1984.
49. Javier Ostos, "The Past, Present, and Future of Synchronized Swimming," *Synchro*, October 1984, 19.
50. Arthur Daley, "Sports of The Times: More Deadly Than the Male," *New York Times*, February 8, 1953.
51. Bean, *Synchronized Swimming*, 51.
52. Beulah Gundling, "Viva La Ballet Leg!" *The Aquatic Artist*, Third Quarter (1972): 15.
53. James S. Harris, "Keeping Tradition in Synchronized Swimming," *Synchro-Info*, August 1964, 4.
54. Harvey, "Rippling Rhythm," 60.
55. Ross C. Bean, "On Synchronized Swimming Rule Changes," *Synchronized Swimmer*, October 1953, 1.
56. Les Wilson, "Excerpt from the Sun Day article," *Synchro*, February 1982, 15.
57. Lillian DeSha, "The Mailbox," *Synchro-Info*, August 1970, 3.

58. Barbara J. Heller, "Aquatics Briefs: So You're in Charge of an Aquacade!" *Journal of Health, Physical Education, Recreation* 42, no. 1 (January 1, 1971): 87–88.

59. Doris Layson Bullock, "How Many College and University Swim Clubs Are There?," *Synchro News*, January 1958, 9.

60. Griggs, "Swimming Plus."

61. "Fit for Life," *Grinnell Magazine*, Spring 2017.

62. "Fit for Life."

63. Prudence Fleming, "Should Synchronized Swimming Be Competitive?," *Official Aquatics, Winter Sports, and Outing Activities Guide*, July 1953, 61.

64. Hannah Flood, "Ely Woman Cherishes Varsity Letter Earned before Title IX," FOX 9 KMSP, Minneapolis-St. Paul, June 23, 2022.

65. Allison Leigh Housman Logan, "The Ohio State University Synchronized Swimming Program, 1928–1995: 'The People. The Tradition. The Excellence.' " (PhD diss., The Ohio State University, 2012).

66. Tina Sloan Green et al., "Black Women in Sport," American Alliance for Health, Physical Education, Recreation and Dance (Reston, VA: National Association for Girls and Women in Sport, 1981), 49–55.

67. Carla Dunlap, phone interview with author, May 26, 2023.

68. "In the Swim Again," *New York Times*, July 19, 1973; "Rule Changes Through the Years."

69. Bean, *Synchronized Swimming*, 83.

70. Blount, "And Now for the Resurrection," 99.

71. Bean, *Synchronized Swimming*, 92.

72. Dawn Bean, "My Impressions," *Synchro-Info*, April 1964, 6.

73. Bean, *Synchronized Swimming*, 113.

74. Blount, "And Now for the Resurrection," 104.

75. Blount, "And Now for the Resurrection," 98.

76. Dunlap, interview with author.

77. Chris Georges, "A Male's Point of View," *Synchro*, June 1980, 34.

78. Bean, *Synchronized Swimming*, 108–9.

79. Blount, "And Now for the Resurrection," 99.

80. Bean, *Synchronized Swimming*, 109.

81. "Through the Pages of Synchro with Candy and Tracie," *Synchro*, February 1984, 9–17.

82. Bruce Wigo, "Remembering the 1st World Championships—Belgrade '73," *Swimming World*, May 2020, 33.

83. Bruce Wigo, "Remembering the 1st World Championships," 32.

84. Jean M. Henning, "How It Began: Synchronized Swimming," *Swimming and Water Polo, Diving and Synchronized Swimming: Magazine of FINA*, 1987, ISHOF.

85. "The World Aquatic Games," *Synchro-Info*, November 1978, 10.

86. Dawn Bean, "Hope for the Olympics?," *Synchro-Info*, December 1977.

87. Kenneth Reich, "Olympic Water Polo, Diving Proposal OKd," *Los Angeles Times*, October 8, 1977.

88. Ostos, "The Past, Present, and Future of Synchronized Swimming," 20.

89. Dawn Bean, "Thoughts on the World Games," *Synchro-Info*, November 1978, 11.

90. Pedro Palacios, Edgar Mont-Roig, and Juan Manuel Surroca, *President Samaranch: 21 Years in the Presidency of the IOC That Changed Sport Throughout the World*, Samaranch Foundation, n.d., 71.

91. Ostos, "The Past, Present, and Future of Synchronized Swimming," 20.

92. "The 1984 Olympic Games," *Synchro*, August 1984, 10; Mark Dyreson, "Global Television and the Transformation of the Olympics: The 1984 Los Angeles Games," *International Journal of the History of Sport* 32, no. 1 (January 2, 2015): 172–84.

93. Joy Cushman, phone interview with author, August 13, 2021.
94. Diehl and Williams, *The Million Dollar Mermaid*, 395.
95. Bean, *Synchronized Swimming*.
96. Demmie Stathoplos, "That Syncing Feeling," *Sports Illustrated*, August 2, 1982, 27.
97. George Vecsey, "The Women's Olympics: Sports of the Times," *New York Times*, August 4, 1984.
98. Stathoplos, "That Syncing Feeling," 28.
99. Mark Merfeld, "Making Ends Meet," *Swimming World*, October, 1985, 25.
100. Stathoplos, "That Syncing Feeling," 28.
101. Merfeld, "Making Ends Meet," 28.
102. Carvalho, *The Mermaid's Club*.
103. Merfeld, "Making Ends Meet," 28.
104. Diehl and Williams, *Million Dollar Mermaid*, 396.
105. Elizabeth Mehren, "This Isn't Like Being in Movies," *Los Angeles Times*, August 13, 1984.
106. Dyreson, "Global Television and the Transformation of the Olympics," 178; Vecsey, "The Women's Olympics."
107. Vecsey, "The Women's Olympics."
108. Carvalho, *The Mermaid's Club*.
109. Dawn Bean, "The XXIIIRD Olympiad," *Synchro*, October 1984, 11.
110. Tracie Ruiz-Conforto, phone interview with author, September 20, 2022.
111. Bean, "The XXIIIRD Olympiad."
112. David Gritten, *Los Angeles Examiner*, quoted in Bean, "The XXIIIRD Olympiad," 12.
113. Charlotte Davis, phone interview with author, September 20, 2022.
114. Carvalho, *The Mermaid's Club*.
115. David Gritten, *Los Angeles Examiner*, quoted in Bean, "The XXIIIRD Olympiad," 12.
116. Bean, "The XXIIIRD Olympiad," 14.
117. Bean, *Synchronized Swimming*, 135.
118. John Weyler, "For Ruiz, Boycott Has Added Something to Games: Another Gold," *Los Angeles Times*, August 13, 1984.
119. John Weyler, "Ruiz Gets Set to Go It Alone," *Los Angeles Times*, August 11, 1984.
120. David Gritten, *Los Angeles Examiner*, quoted in Bean, "The XXIIIRD Olympiad," 12.
121. Bean, "The XXIIIRD Olympiad," 11.
122. Bean, *Synchronized Swimming*, 137.
123. Bean, *Synchronized Swimming*, 139.
124. Javier Ostos, "Solo, Duet . . . Team?" *International Swim & Water Polo*, Winter 1984, 30, quoted in Bean, *Synchronized Swimming*, 136.
125. Dawn Bean, "Synchro History—As I Know It," *Synchro*, December 1992, 50.
126. Davis, interview with author.
127. "Synchronized Swimming Survives a Joker," *Los Angeles Times*, July 15, 1991.
128. Jeff MacGregor, "Out of Sync," *Sports Illustrated*, August 23, 1999, 70.
129. Due to a judge inputting a score incorrectly, Canadian soloist Sylvie Frechette was announced as the solo winner, but when the error came to light, it was re-awarded to American Kristen Babb-Sprague. Canada appealed and ultimately both were awarded gold, with no one receiving silver.
130. Harry Forbes, quoted in "Olympic Media Images," *Synchro*, December 1992, 22.
131. "Synchronized Swimming Survives a Joker."
132. Theresa Munoz, "Hey, Harry Shearer, It's No Laughing Matter," *Los Angeles Times*, July 15, 1991.

133. Mike Littwin, *Monterey Sunday Herald*, quoted in "Olympic Media Images," *Synchro*, December 1992.
134. Sherry Weinberg, *Seattle Post-Intelligencer*, quoted in "Olympic Media Images," 21.
135. Charlotte Davis, "Report from the First Television Workshop for Aquatic Sports," *Synchro*, August 1990, 7.
136. Mary Ann Hudson, "They've Finally Hit It Right on the Nose," *Los Angeles Times*, April 2, 1992.
137. Hudson, "They've Finally Hit It Right on the Nose."
138. Curley Grieve, "Sports Parade: SF's Joanne Millin, 18, Sensation as Headliner in Seattle Aqua Follies," *San Francisco Examiner*, July 28, 1955.
139. Munoz, "Hey, Harry Shearer."
140. Davis, "Report from the First Television Workshop."
141. Mary Ann Hudson, "Fans Still Not Getting the Picture," *Los Angeles Times*, April 3, 1992.
142. Dave Barry and Dan Le Batard, "Hey, Dan, Let's Go Synchro," *Miami Herald*, July 30, 1996.
143. Dawn Bean, "An Olympic Plan," *Synchro*, December 1992, 23.
144. "Teams Make Olympic Debut," *Washington Post*, 1996.
145. Davis, interview with author.
146. Carter Gaddis, "Can This Really Be a Sport?," *Tampa Tribune*, June 21, 1996.
147. "Synchronized Swimmers Rule," *Elko Daily Free Press*, August 3, 1996.
148. Becky Dyroen-Lancer, phone interview with author, July 18, 2021.
149. Molly Blue, "The World Is Catching Up to U.S.," *Ledger-Enquirer*, January 28, 1996.
150. Bean, *Synchronized Swimming*; Gaddis, "Can This Really Be a Sport?"
151. Laura LaMarca, "The Perfect Olympic Moment," *Synchro Swimming USA*, Summer/Fall 1996, 14.
152. LaMarca, "The Perfect Olympic Moment," 14.
153. David Casstevens, "Mocking Doesn't Dull Synchronized's Gold," *Arizona Republic*, August 3, 1996.
154. Jill Vejnoska, "Americans Swim a Symphony of Pure Perfection," *Atlanta Journal*, August 3, 1996.
155. McManis, "Synchronized Swimmers Perform Perfectly."
156. Casstevens, "Mocking Doesn't Dull Synchronized's Gold."
157. Vejnoska, "Americans Swim a Symphony of Pure Perfection."
158. McManis, "Synchronized Swimmers Perform Perfectly."
159. Stathoplos, "That Syncing Feeling," 28.
160. Blue, "The World Is Catching Up to U.S."
161. Casstevens, "Mocking Doesn't Dull Synchronized's Gold."

EPILOGUE: FASTER, HIGHER, STRONGER—TOGETHER
1. Aimee Berg, "One-on-One with the O.G. of Artistic Swimming, Bill May," World Aquatics, June 20, 2022.
2. Jill Vejnoska, "Sudden Popularity Is Buoyant," *Atlanta Constitution*, July 10, 1996.
3. Ken Belson, "Synchronized Swimmers Find Danger Lurking Below Surface: Concussions," *New York Times*, July 19, 2016.
4. Belson, "Synchronized Swimmers Find Danger."
5. Belson, "Synchronized Swimmers Find Danger."
6. Gillian R. Brassil, "Beauty, Athleticism and Danger in the Pool," *New York Times*, August 2, 2021.
7. Brassil, "Beauty, Athleticism and Danger in the Pool."

8. Demmie Stathoplos, "Ready to Dazzle Again," *Sports Illustrated*, August 8, 1988.

9. David Wharton, "'This Is Crazy If You Think About It, No?' Inside the World of Artistic Swimming," *Los Angeles Times* (Online), November 10, 2022.

10. ABC News, "US Swimmer Rescued by Coach from Bottom of Pool After Fainting in World Championship," ABC News, June 23, 2022.

11. Wharton, "'This Is Crazy If You Think About It, No?"

12. Selina Shah, phone interview with author, July 13, 2021.

13. Sarah Lyall, "It's a Bird! No, It's a Crocodile! Synchronized Swimming Themes Can Be Mystifying," *New York Times*, August 16, 2016.

14. "Artistic Swimming Manual for Judges, Technical Controllers, Referees and Coaches 2022–2025," World Aquatics, April 24, 2023.

15. George H. Browne, "The Psychology of Grace," *Mind and Body*, September 1917, 208.

16. "Artistic Swimming Manual."

17. Browne, "The Psychology of Grace," 208.

18. Kevin B. Wamsley, "Womanizing Olympic Athletes: Policy and Practice During the Avery Brundage Era," in *Onward to the Olympics: Historical Perspectives on the Olympic Games*, eds. Gerald P. Schaus and Stephen R. Wenn (Waterloo, Canada: Wilfrid Laurier University Press, 2007), 280.

19. Stephan Miermont, phone interview with author, July 26, 2022.

20. David Ingold and Eben Novy-Williams, "Money for Medals: Inside the Performance-Driven Funding of U.S. Olympic Teams," Bloomberg.com, August 5, 2016.

21. VOA, "Olympic Funding Often Reflects Country's Values," VOA News, October 27, 2009.

22. Dawn Pawson Bean, *Synchronized Swimming: An American History* (Jefferson, NC: McFarland and Company, 2005), 170.

23. Jeff MacGregor, "Out of Sync," *Sports Illustrated*, August 23, 1999, 71.

24. MacGregor, "Out of Sync," 70.

25. "Male Synchro Swimmer Barred from Olympics," ABC News, August 30, 2000.

26. Taffy Brodesser-Akner, "Water's Edge: The Story of Bill May, the Greatest Male Synchronized Swimmer Who Ever Lived, and His Improbable Quest for Olympic Gold," *ESPN the Magazine*, March 30, 2016.

27. Vicki Valosik, "Where Did 'Synchronized Swimming' Go?," *The Atlantic* (blog), August 7, 2021.

28. Brodesser-Akner, "Water's Edge."

29. William Kremer, "Why Can't Men Be Olympic Synchronised Swimmers?," *BBC World Service*, July 21, 2015.

30. Kremer, "Why Can't Men Be Olympic Synchronised Swimmers?"

31. Berg, "One-on-One with the O.G. of Artistic Swimming."

32. MacGregor, "Out of Sync," 72.

33. Ellen Richard Zaccardelli, phone interview with author, June 24, 2022.

34. Loretta Barrious Larsen, phone interview with author, June 17, 2022.

35. Mary Ramsey, phone interview with author, July 20, 2015.

36. Ramsey, phone interview.

37. Becky Dyroen-Lancer, phone interview with author, July 18, 2021.

38. Ramsey, phone interview.

39. Valosik, "Where Did 'Synchronized Swimming' Go?"

40. Virginia Jasontek, phone interview with author, July 28, 2021.

41. Judy McGowan, phone interview with author, July 7, 2021.

42. Lori Eaton, phone interview with author, July 14, 2021.

43. "Our Sport Is Called 'Synchronized Swimming!,'" Change.org, July 23, 2017.

44. Kris Harley-Jesson, phone interview with author, July 2, 2021.
45. "Our Sport Is Called 'Synchronized Swimming!'"
46. Adam Andrasko, phone interview with author, July 9, 2021.
47. Bill May, phone interview with author, July 30, 2021.
48. SwimSwam, "Men Eligible to Compete in Artistic Swimming at Olympics for First Time in Paris," SwimSwam, December 22, 2022.
49. Christina Marmet, "Men Allowed to Compete in Olympic Artistic Swimming Events for First Time in 2024," *Inside Synchro* (blog), December 22, 2022.
50. Nick Zaccardi, "Something New for Artistic Swimming: Men," *NBC Sports* (blog), November 23, 2022.
51. Dan D'Addona, "Reflecting on Historic World Championships for Artistic Swimming, Bill May and USA," *Swimming World News* (blog), July 23, 2023.
52. Katharine W. Curtis, "Competitive Synchronized Swimming," *Journal of Health and Physical Education* 12, no. 1 (January 1941): 18–20, 59–60.
53. Brodesser-Akner, "Water's Edge."
54. Guillaume Depasse, "Paris 2024: The First Games to Achieve Full Gender Parity," Olympics.com, March 8, 2023.
55. Bud Harvey, "Rippling Rhythm," *Sportfolio: The Illustrated Digest of All Sports*, May 1948, 71.

ILLUSTRATION CREDITS

Frontispiece
Photo by Bruce Mozert taken in Silver Springs, Florida, circa 1950. State Archives of Florida, Florida Memory.

Page 13
Boston Public Library, Rare Books Department.

Page 17
The Art of Swimming: Illustrated by Forty Proper Copper-plate Cuts . . . With Advice for Bathing. By Monsìeur Thevenot. Done out of French, 3rd edition, by Melchisédec Thévenot (London, 1789).

Page 19
Captain Stevens' System of Swimming: The Only Rules for a Quick Initiation into the Same, 2nd ed. (London: Biggs and Son, 1845).

Page 21
"Witches apprehended . . . ," 1613. Wellcome Collection. Attribution 4.0 International (CC BY 4.0).

Page 24
"Mermaids at Brighton" by William Heath, 1829. The Miriam and Ira D. Wallach Division of Art, Prints and Photographs: Print Collection, the New York Public Library, https://digitalcollections.nypl.org/items/6105553f-115f-57dd-e040-e00a18062da5.

Page 27
Swimming and Life-Saving by Capt. W. D. Andrews, G.C.V. (Toronto: William Briggs, 1889).

Page 29
The Diving and Swimming Book by George Corsan (New York: A.S. Barnes & Company, 1924).

Page 40
British Library, London, UK© British Library Board. All Rights Reserved/Bridgeman Images.

Page 42
British Library, London, UK© British Library Board. All Rights Reserved/Bridgeman Images.

Page 48
Learn How to Swim: Pointers About Swimming and Aquatics, by Clara Beckwith (Baltimore: W. U. Day Printing Co., 1893). General Collections of the Library of Congress, Washington, DC.

Page 49
Swimmers and Swimming or The Swimmer's Album by Charles Newman (London: Pictorial Press, 1898).

Page 55
The great New York Aquarium, the only extensive aquarium ever established on the continent of North America: grand public opening on Wednesday, October 11, 1876. Digital Collections, Beinecke Rare Book and Manuscript Library, Yale University.

Page 56
University of Rhode Island, University Archives and Special Collections.

Page 59
The *Times-Picayune* (New Orleans, LA), March 8, 1885.

Page 63
A rendering of the Nouveau Cirque's water basin in cross section by Louis Poyet (1846–1913) published in *La Nature*, March 20, 1886.

Page 73
George Grantham Bain Collection, Prints & Photographs Division of the Library of Congress, Washington, DC.

Page 81
Dudley A. Sargent, "Are Athletics Making Girls Masculine?" *The Ladies' Home Journal*, March 1912 (via HathiTrust).

Page 85
How to Swim by Annette Kellerman (George H. Doran Company, 1918).

Page 90
Courtesy of the David S. Shields Theatrical Photographs Collection.

Page 91
Motion Picture Classic, May 1916. Courtesy of the Media History Digital Library.

Page 94
How to Swim by Annette Kellerman (George H. Doran Company, 1918).

Page 97
F. H. Tucker, Prints & Photographs Division of the Library of Congress, Washington, DC.

Page 105
The San Francisco Call (San Francisco, CA), June 16, 1904. Chronicling America: Historic American Newspapers. Library of Congress, Washington, DC.

Page 111
Detroit Publishing Company photograph collection, Prints & Photographs Division of the Library of Congress, Washington, DC.

Page 114
George Grantham Bain Collection, Prints & Photographs Division of the Library of Congress, Washington, DC.

Page 119
From the article "Women Life-Savers: Their Feats of Skill and Daring Win Recognition" by Commodore W.E. Longfellow, published in *The Ladies Home Journal* June 1920, page 45.

Page 120
Courtesy of The American National Red Cross. All rights reserved in all countries.

Page 123
From the *Red Cross Courier*, Vol. 18, March 1939, p. 10. Courtesy of The American National Red Cross. All rights reserved in all countries.

Page 127
Pageants, Games and Stunts by Olive McCormick (New York: A.S. Barnes & Co., 1933).

Page 136
Prints & Photographs Division of the Library of Congress, Washington, DC.

Page 143
International Swimming Hall of Fame.

Page 148
Movie still from *The Spieler* (Ralph Block Productions, 1928).

Page 151
San Francisco History Center, San Francisco Public Library.

Page 155
International Swimming Hall of Fame.

Page 164
George Grantham Bain Collection, Prints & Photographs Division of the Library of Congress, Washington, DC.

Page 169
Wittemann Collection, Prints & Photographs Division of the Library of Congress, Washington, DC.

Page 180
The Saturday Evening Post, June 27, 1925.

Page 182
National Photo Company Collection, Prints & Photographs Division of the Library of Congress, Washington, DC.

Page 186
State Archives of Florida, Florida Memory.

Page 195
Courtesy of Jordan Whitney-Wei.

Page 196
Courtesy of Jordan Whitney-Wei.

Page 203
Illustrations by Virginia Dix Sterling in *Stunts and Synchronized Swimming* by Gertrude Goss (Spaulding-Moss Co., 1957). Courtesy of Smith College Special Collections.

Page 204
The Aquatic Art Book of Water Shows, compiled and edited by Beulah Gundling, 1964.

Page 206

Illustrations by Virginia Dix Sterling in *Stunts and Synchronized Swimming* by Gertrude Goss (Spaulding-Moss Co., 1957). Courtesy of Smith College Special Collections.

Page 213

From "Lights on!" by Martha J. Vaught, *The Journal of Health and Physical Education*, February 1940.

Page 215

"A Tale of the Toys," Dolphin-Seal Club, Historical Print Photograph Collection, UA 104.7.208, Martha Blakeney Hodges Special Collections and University Archives, The University of North Carolina at Greensboro.

Page 233

Donald G. Larson Collection on International Expositions and Fairs, Special Collections Research Center, Fresno State Library, California State University, Fresno.

Page 239

San Francisco History Center, San Francisco Public Library.

Page 245

Seattle Municipal Archives, Record Series number (5801-02).

Page 250

University of North Texas Libraries Government Documents Department.

Page 259

Sea Power Centre—Australia.

Page 264

Yank, The Army Weekly, October 1945.

Page 267

The Film Daily, July 24, 1944.

Page 268

International Swimming Hall of Fame.

Page 278

Fort Lauderdale News (Fort Lauderdale, FL), January 24, 1954 (via newspapers.com).

Page 281

MGM Lobby Card.

Page 283

International Swimming Hall of Fame.

Page 294

Advertisement from the "1955 Amateur Athletic Union Synchronized Swimming Handbook."

Page 297

Courtesy of Lea Bean.

Page 298

Amateur Athletic Union. Courtesy of Lea Bean.

Page 301

Texas Swimming & Diving Hall of Fame.

INDEX

Page references in *italics* refer to illustrations.

Aquabelles, *See also* Southern California Aquabelles
performers in Billy Rose's Aquacade, 225, 232–35, *233*
performers in the Aqua Follies, 243–44
name of synchronized swimming club in St. Petersburg, Fla., 277
Aquacade, *See* Billy Rose's Aquacade
Aqua Dears (performers in the Aqua Follies), 243–44
Aquadorables (performers in Elliott Murphy's Aquashow), 244
Aqua dramas, 25, 137
Aqua Follies (Minneapolis, Minn.), 233, 243–45, 247, 252, 275
Aqua Follies (Seattle, Wash.), *245*
Aqualillies, 354, 355, *355*
Aquamaids, *See* Santa Clara Aquamaids
Aquamusicals, 1, 258, 264–71, 284, 354–55
Aquaquettes (performers in Buster Crabbe's Aqua Parade), 244
Aquarena Springs (Tex.), 277
Aquariums, 25–26; *See also* Royal Aquarium (Westminster, England)
"Aqua tease" acts, 277
Aquatennial (Minneapolis, Minn.), 243, 248
"Aquatic entertainments," 29
Aquatic warfare, 217–18, 250–51, 277
Aquatic World Championships (FINA/World Aquatics), 318–19, 351, 352
Archea, Connie Sloop, 309
Aristotle, 138
Arte Natandi, De (Digby), 12–13, *13*
Artistic swimming, 3, 7–8, 95, 341, 343–44, 346, 348, 355–59

"Art of Graceful and Scientific Swimming" (championship meet), 202–3, 295
Art of Swimming, Made Safe, Easy, Pleasant and Healthful, The (Franklin), 20
Art of Swimming, The (Digby), 12
ASA (Amateur Swimming Association), 35–36
Associated Press, 324, 333
Association for Intercollegiate Athletics for Women (AIAW), 312
Association of Directors of Physical Education for Women in Colleges and Universities, 189
Astaire, Fred, 271
Athens Water Follies Club (Oakland, Calif.), 293–94, *298*, 298–300, 305, 314
At Home in the Water (Corsan), 122, 203
Atlanta, *See* Olympic Games: 1996 Atlanta
Atlantic City, N.J., 124, 156, 181–82, 248
Attitudes toward women's swimming, 22, 29–33, 166, 176–78
Austin Powers: The Spy Who Shagged Me (film), 355
Australia, 71, 167 304, 306, 319
Australian crawl (swimming stroke), 167

Bach, Thomas, 356
Back layout (swimming position), 5
Backstroke, 173, 176, 203
Bailey, James, 136–37
Ballet, 80, 93–94, 97, 262, 291, 308–9, 322, 332, 333
Ballet leg (swimming movement), 5, 8, 94, 203, 217, 276, 295, 315, 332
Ballet Leg Dolphin stunt, 295

Ballet swimming, *See* Water ballet
Ballyhoo, 144, 148–49, 153
Baltimore Sun, 228–29, 232, 242
Baltimore YMCA, 117
Barcelona, 56; *See also* Olympic Games: 1992 Barcelona
Barnard College, 188, 200, 295
Barnum, Phineas T., 47, 50, 135–37, 242
Barnum and Bailey's Water Carnival, 135–37, *136*
Barnum & Bailey Circus, 149, 158
Barnum's American Museum, 50, 58
Barron, Hunter, 57
Barry, Dave, 332
Basketball, 82, 165, 175, 187, 196–97, 313, 330, 333
Bath, England, 18
Bath and Washhouses Act (1846), 26
Bath Club (London), 73
Bathing 23-26, 31, 54, 180; *See also* Mineral spas
Bathing attire, *See* Swimming attire
Bathing beauty, 180–83, 186, 243; *See also* Mack Sennett's Bathing Beauties; *Bathing Beauty* (film)
Bathing Beauty (film), 264, *267*, 268, 275, 279
Bathing machines, 23–24, 79
Bauer, Sybil, 173
Bean, Dawn Pawson, *298*
in Athens Club, 293–95, 298–99, 301
as competition judge, 319
early interest, 239
on hybrid stunts, 314
and 1984 Olympics, 324, 326–27
on US "maternal pride," 349
on Esther Williams, 323
Bean, Ross, 302, 309
Beating the water (swimming movement), 17

"Dagger Dance," 220
Dali, Salvador, 230
Dangerous When Wet (film),
269, 276, 284, 286
Danube River, 73
Dardanelles, 25
Dark Ages, European, 12
Dartmouth College, 211
Daughter of the Gods, A
(film), 89–92, *90, 91,*
94, 97
Davis, Charlotte, 321, 323,
325, 331, 333
Davis AquaStarz, *345*
Dawson, Buck, 186
Dean, Bobbie, 153
Deauville-McFadden Hotel,
185–86, 292
De Coubertin, Pierre, 174
Dedieu, Virginie, 352
Delaney, Jack, 187
DeMott, Josephine, 158–59
Denmark, 304
Denning, Florence, 105,
106
Denver, Colo., 153
Desjardins, Pete, 227, 292
Detroit, Mich., 244
Detroit Board of Education,
197
Detroit Department of
Parks and Recreation,
292–93
De Varona, Donna, 291,
323–24
Dibble General Hospital,
249
Diehl, Charlie, 243
Digby, Everard, 9, 12–14,
16–21, 27–29, 95–96,
201, 217, 308
Dime museums, 58–62, 79
Disappearing acts, 98, 135,
137-40, 152, 158; *See
also* Neptune's Daugh-
ter shows
Distance swimming, *See*
Endurance swimming
Diving, 144–59; *See also*
Diving girls
acrobatic diving, 141-42,
147
and Annette Kellerman,
75, 80, 88–89, 91, 98
as demonstration of

women's capabilities
91–92, 158–59
fancy diving, 141, 152,
167, 171–72
high diving, 88, 89, 91,
98, 137, 145, 155–57
at Olympic games, 166–
67, 171–72
safety of, 153–57,
282–83
Diving bells, 137–39, 154
Diving girls, 140-47; *See also*
Jantzen; Diving
as athletes and stunt-
women, 141–44, 155–8
and appearance, 86, 140,
143, 146
and respectability,
147–53
and striking out on their
own, 157–59
Diving Girl, The (film), 147
Diving horses, 134, 140, 156
Divinhood, 154
Dodgson, Charles (Lewis
Carroll), 44
Dolphin (swimming stunt),
194, 203, 219, 276,
295
"Dolphine, the Water
Queen," 138
Dolphinettes (at the
Deauville-McFadden
Hotel), 292
Dolphin-Seals (at University
of North Carolina,
Greensboro), *215*
Dolphin Synchro Club (at
Queens College), 309
Dore, Harry, 135, 139
Dream Team, *See* US
national teams
Drowning
as metaphor for sin, 16
prevention of, 46–47
rates, 7, 106, 116, 117,
128
shallow-water, 59–60; *See
also* Hypoxic blackout
Duet event 296, 297, 302,
307, 316, 320, 321,
357; See also Mixed
duets; Olympic Games
for specific years
Dunlap, Carla, 313, 315

Dunn, Velma, 247
Durante, Jimmy, 270
Dyroen-Lancer, Becky,
333–34, 355

Eardrums, burst, 153, 278
Eastland (ship), 118–19
East River, N.Y., 103, 112,
265
Easy to Love (film), 270,
273, 279, 284
Eaton, Lori, 356
Ederle, Gertrude, 163–64,
164, 167, 172, 185–
87, 190, 227
Ed Sullivan Show, 314
Eggbeater kick, 315
Egypt, 304, 319
Ellington, Duke, 247
Elliott Murphy's Aquashow,
244, 247
El Mirador Hotel, 248
Elyot, Thomas, 16
Embrey, Lee, 307
Emerson, Art, 257
Emery, Gail, 333
Emory University, 332
Emperors (Roman), 14
Empress Theater, 142
Endurance swimming
Alton, Ill. to St. Louis,
Mo., (Mississippi
River) 144
English Channel, 33, 34,
72–73, 163–65, 187,
206, 270
Lake Mendota, 196
River Thames, 33–34,
39, 72
Royal Aquarium (West-
minster, England),
39–41, 205
Yarra River, 71
Yorkville to Clason Point
(East River), 112
Endurance walking, 45
England, 11, 16, 18, 21, 26,
33, 41, 44, 57, 62–63,
74, 109, 167, 172,
205, 304–6
English Circus and German
Water Carnival, 64, 135
English Woman's Journal, 32
Epstein, Charlotte, 114,
166–67